The imperfect peasant economy

The Loire Country, 1800–1914

The imperfect peasant economy

The Loire Country, 1800–1914

Gregor Dallas

Department of History, Smith College

Cambridge University Press

Cambridge
London   New York   New Rochelle
Melbourne   Sydney

Published by the Press Syndicate of the University of Cambridge
The Pitt Building, Trumpington Street, Cambridge CB2 1RP
32 East 57th Street, New York, NY 10022, USA
296 Beaconsfield Parade, Middle Park, Melbourne 3206, Australia

First published 1982

Printed in the United States of America

Library of Congress Cataloging in Publication Data
Dallas, Gregor.
The imperfect peasant economy.
Bibliography: p.
Includes index.
1. Loire Valley (France) – Economic con-
ditions.   2. Loire Valley (France) – Rural
conditions.   3. Peasantry – France – Loire
Valley – History.   I. Title.
HC277.L64D34   330.944′5   81–21558
ISBN 0 521 24060 3   AACR2

pour Micheline
tibi semper idem

La liberté est application, effort perpétuel, contrôle rigoureux de soi, sacrifice éventuel . . . elle est invitation à vivre courageusement et, à l'occasion, héroïquement.

Georges Lefebvre, *Quatre-vingt-neuf*

Contents

Figures and tables

Tables

Preface

Rural France has its commentators, its sociologists, its historians. The purpose of this book is not simply to add new details to an already respectable body of literature – though there is value to that – but to explain, theoretically and through the use of historical documents, how and why a certain rural form of household economy managed to maintain itself in France right through the nineteenth century. The imperfect peasant economy depicted in the following pages is one in which the principal motive for production and consumption of goods is not to take maximum advantage of the market, in the way most economists would define that advantage, but to achieve a balance between effort and need that will assure the preservation of the family smallholder.

Man is a conservative animal. The smallholder system in France was a system that worked, and had worked for centuries. It had already demonstrated its tremendous adaptive capacities during the crisis years of the late Middle Ages as well as during the difficult years of the seventeenth century. This book traces the means by which family smallholders again adapted themselves to the novel situation that arose in the century of the railway.

In addition to analyzing this process of self-preservation, we shall look at how such a real economy of smallholders – an imperfect peasant economy, described here with the help of historical documents – can be contrasted with the more abstract models of peasant economies that anthropologists and sociologists have drawn up in recent years. This was not by any stretch of the imagination a subsistence economy – the market did play a critical role in household decision making – and rural families did at times employ outside labor. But the imperfect peasant economy did establish a set of priorities that has deluded many market economists, and those of a like mind, into thinking that France was something of an anomaly, that its population showed signs of irrationality and backwardness. From the perspective of the household we not only see the most essential factors at work in France's rural economy but we have a refreshing new view of French urban and industrial growth in the nineteenth century. Economic development becomes less mechanical and more subject to the family-oriented values of the local population. Thus, Nantes' industrial advantage over Orléans had a great deal to do with the contrasting patterns of interdependence that one finds between the two cities and their hinterlands.

xii

Of course, we cannot limit ourselves to economics. The rural household was more than just a provider of goods and services. Chapter 7 outlines its more biological functions. I have also endeavored to show how attitudes that helped shape the economy of the two regions studied here influenced other areas of social life. For instance, the regional contrast in religion and politics is linked, I believe, to the different local levels of economic intensity of production and to the corresponding differences in the breadth of choice and opportunity that they presented to the population. In this sense, the drive for a balance between effort and need can be viewed as a process involving the full range of social action – mental as well as material.

Such a large task has required the assistance of others. More people have helped and encouraged me in the preparation of this book – from the initial ideas, through the research and data gathering, to the final draft – than I can acknowledge by name or even hope to repay.

Because so much of the book is based on materials collected *sur le terrain* in France, my debt to French archivists and librarians is enormous. The staff of the Bibliothèque Nationale and the Archives Nationales gave a great deal of assistance in searching out some of the more intractable sources on nineteenth-century agriculture and proved to me how ill-founded these institutions' reputation of "facelessness" is. The director and staff of the Archives du Loiret helped me track down alternatives to the materials destroyed in the fire of 1940, and the staff of the Archives de la Loire-Atlantique were cheerfully patient with the herculean task of making so many hefty documents available to me. I am especially grateful to Mlle. M. Illaire, conservateur-adjoint, for her assistance in the location of many yet unclassified documents. The Services du Cadastre at Orléans and at Nantes extended me their hospitality during the many months that I labored on the *matrices cadastrales*. And my visits to several of the village archives of Loiret and Loire-Atlantique provided me not only with documents but also with pleasant memories for which I am most grateful.

I have accumulated many debts in preparing the statistics published here. The greatest of these is to Rudolph Bell of the Department of History, Rutgers University, who calmed my first fears of the computer and introduced me to many of the quantitative techniques employed in this book. The transcription of data from microfilm to standard forms was an enormous task that I could never have completed without the assistance of M. and Mme. A. Derreumeux and Alexandra Mamentov. Figures 2.1 and 3.1 were drawn by Maureen Dunphy. Figures 2.2, 2.3, 4.1, and 4.2 are reproduced with the permission of the Bibliothèque Nationale. The remaining illustrations have been drawn by Charlotte Carlson. Although all computer programs and calculations were done by myself, I owe a great deal to the technical and professional assistance I received from the personnel at the Rutgers computer center.

The members of my dissertation committee were helpful, and the work has benefited from their critical reading. Traian Stoianovich and Mary Hartman gave me much useful advice at various stages of the project. The help that I have had from Michael Curtis has gone well beyond what his duties as an "outside reader" called for; my debt to him is very great. And I have been singularly fortunate in having Peter Stearns as a director; his detailed running commentaries and editorial suggestions have made this a better book.

This book has gone through several drafts. None of them would have been presentable without the diligent typing, often over the midnight oil, of Eleanor White, Barbara Bunting, and Isabelle Reymond.

Finally, I thank Walter Lippincott and the two anonymous readers of Cambridge University Press for giving me much food for thought in the preparation of this last draft.

None of these people can be faulted for any errors that may appear in the statistics or in the text; for that I accept full responsibility.

G.D.

Princeton, New Jersey
May 1982

Part I
Introduction

1   Aims and scope

Why should an Englishman, trained in America, be interested in French peasants? Initial reasons are rarely the most important, but they do provide the catalyst. When I began this study in the early 1970s, my intention was to describe and analyze a rural society's reaction and contribution to the early forms of "industrialism" as they appeared in France. To many in a Britain that was at that time preparing, squeamishly, for membership in an expanded European community, France seemed an exception to the generally accepted rules of modern economic order. Indeed, France presented a formidable paradox. Its economy looked decidedly prosperous beside Britain's, yet how many English-speaking economic and social historians continued to explain that France was a late starter? that it was bound to traditional modes of production? that its population included a disproportionately large number of artisans and, more remarkably, of peasants? In the early 1970s, British newspaper readers were told a great deal about the inefficiencies of France's small-scale, labor-intensive production units. I remember one excited BBC reporter pointing out that the trip across the Channel to Brittany involved more than those choppy fourscore nautical miles; it was a journey into the preindustrial age. How could France survive and, apparently, survive so well?

To answer that question it seemed perfectly logical to return to the early stages of "industrialism" to see just how the French course of action differed from the prescribed economic model. That would take one back, according to the consensus today, to the mid-nineteenth century: France, under Napoleon III, "industrialized."[1] But, in order to study development, it was necessary to go beyond the limits of the Second Empire – I felt that the study would have to span at least a century, or three generations, to have any meaning at all. So I found myself going back to the Napoleonic Wars and moving forward to the First World War.

From the start my principal concern was with the peasantry. Here was the exception that needed explaining. Of course, the peasantry had hardly been ignored by historians. France possesses a rich literature – a large proportion written by the indomitable Gallican *thésards* – on peasant folklore, farming techniques, and other social customs. These works are more than simple rural histories; they have established methods that have become models for historical research both within and outside France (Georges Lefebvre, Marc Bloch, and Lucien Febvre are household names for social historians today). But precious little of this impressive output of rural histories was devoted to the peasantry of the nineteenth century. Historians of that period onward, being eager to show change in the human condition, have tended to concentrate on the cities – their trade and their government – and, until recently, have almost entirely ignored the rustic beyond those city gates. Yet a glance at the official French census tables will tell us that, until 1931, the majority of Frenchmen lived in the countryside. Though the last 15 years have seen this gap in our knowledge partially filled, most of the more recent rural studies either stop short at the mid-nineteenth century[2] or concentrate on such isolated districts that it is difficult, if not impossible, to generalize from them what the *average* reactions to the evolving nineteenth-century economy might have been.[3] We should remember that the mass of the "rural population" recorded by the census did not live in the mountain districts, isolated plateaus, or the Mediterranean backcountry. They lived in the low-lying coastal plains, along the fertile river valleys, and around the major urban centers.

My decision to limit myself to two regions was again made at the outset of the work. French rural histories might exaggerate the countryman's isolation, but they do not exaggerate his attachment to the land. France was, and remains, a country fashioned after its regions. French rural history is, of necessity, French local history. This is not to deny the presence of a national myth, of a national sense of belonging (which can be traced back at least as far as the *Chanson de Roland*). But it is impossible to understand the character of *French* peasant society without a knowledge of and, even more, a feeling for the regions. De Gaulle's famous quip about the difficulty of governing a country with 328 types of cheese was founded on that basic truth.

To avoid an overly parochial history, this had to be a comparative work. The advantages were obvious: comparison allows one to attain a depth of research impossible in national studies while it opens one to a level of generalization higher than anything derived from a simple regional study. The dangers were equally evident. A comparison of two entirely different regions can lead only to a series of drawn-out platitudes; this has occurred too often in the comparative works of some sociologists who masquerade their cultural ignorance behind a technical language that communicates nothing and, in truth, means even less.

I deliberately picked one of the least-isolated areas of France, the Loire Country, and focused on the regions closest to two of its largest towns, Orléans and Nantes. We shall see how these two regions at once complemented and differed from one another. Both cities are on the same river; one has a river port, the other a seaport. Both regions lie on the same latitude and have similar climates, but one is situated on the calcareous Paris Basin, the other in the granitic Massif Armoricain. Further, Nantes was to become one of France's major industrial cities, Orléans was not.

Major industrial cities? One problem troubled me more than most. What does one mean by "industrialism"? I soon realized that I was attempting to answer a loaded question. Each small town and village I visited, every conversation I had with the residents, pointed to a culture that was not merely unaware of how its locality "reacted and contributed" to an "industrial way of life" but to a culture where such abstract notions of historical process were entirely irrelevant. Moreover, the experience was repeated in the regional capitals, Orléans and Nantes. To be sure, there was ample concern about the numbers who annually left the fields for city jobs (especially among the young), the mechanization of agriculture, and the organization of cooperatives and unions to combat agriculture's problems. All this could have been fitted into currently acceptable notions of an "industrializing" society. But that is not what the members of this society were telling me.

These were, of course, personal impressions. They had not and, indeed, could not be subjected to the rigors of statistical analysis. But by what rite were such impressions to be superseded by abstract historical theory? I would be wary of calling this an alien culture. The quality of life appeared as satisfactory as any I knew in Britain and superior to some sectors I had found in America. They would appear no less prosperous. Their language was different, but I could hardly describe myself as having been out of place.

I thus saw my work developing, willy-nilly, into a critique of the widespread, albeit loosely defined, theories of "industrialization." My position grew along three main lines of thought. In the first place, I found myself reacting to the teleological element implicit in the very term "industrialization." There was no preordained purpose to the manner in which this rural society had evolved – much, I learned, was the product of mere chance. Second, I started to take a more critical look at the linear, hierarchical schemas that dominate our literature on social structures. A linear view of society complements a linear view of time, but neither adequately corresponded to the reality I was describing. Finally, I realized that this was not to be a study of the gradual assimilation of these rural communities into a larger, more complex society, but rather a study of how they managed to maintain their own particular forms of cultural identity.[4]

The second issue – that of social structure – loomed above all the others. The term "peasantry" needed to be defined and some sort of delimitation on who were peasants and who were not had to be set. The most immediate problem to be resolved was whether one should regard the peasantry as a social class. My conclusion was, essentially, that one should not; the notion of a peasant class was, to borrow Teodor Shanin's phrase, so decidedly awkward that it ceased to be analytically useful.[5] For example, within the Marxist tradition, where class has been defined by its relationship to the means of production and, in particular, by the amount of property it owns, one is forced to consider the peasantry, which simultaneously consists of owners and workers of the land, as both entrepreneurs and laborers – an ambiguity that would hardly clarify the complexities of a group that was, in fact, internally differentiated by many contradictory and changing forms of property ownership. Marx, we know, had no special love for peasants or at least felt that they had no important historical role to play and, hence, were not worthy of any extensive amount of attention.[6] Marxists today, under the conviction that peasants could not engage collectively in class struggle and that their way of life tended toward division rather than unity, have apparently rejected the notion of a peasant class and now speak rather in terms of peasant systems. This has been presented either in a "historical" context (a stage preceding capitalism in which private property is underdeveloped and the worker is still a proprietor) or as a "subsumed" system within the more general capitalist system. In the latter case, the peasantry has been defined by the form of its exploitation by the "nonproducers" – through rent rather than wage labor. This, it has been argued, leads to a differentiation within the peasantry and hinders their final assimilation into the larger system. Although their historical schema is rigid and this broad definition of "rent" is about as impractical a notion as a "peasant class," the Marxists have brought to notice two important issues, namely, the possibility of considering peasantry as a complete social system and the central role of property within that system. This last point had not, I felt at the beginning of my own work, received the attention it merited.[7]

Was Weber a better alternative? There is little doubt that his definition of class is much more flexible than that of the Marxists and, as a result, is easier to accommodate into a study on peasants. A class, says Weber, consists of people who have life chances in the market of ideal as well as material goods and services. A predetermined set of opportunities is the principal ingredient of class structure – an attractive proposition by virtue of its acknowledgment of free choice and the psychological implications that this conveys. What is more, the social and economic orders in the Weberian sense are not identical, though they are obviously related: Whereas the economic historian concentrates on the complexity of market mechanism, or the framework of choice, the social historian will (or should) concern himself with the actual choices societies have made. (These are two entirely different approaches. The market might define a given range of opportunities, but it cannot effectively explain final choices: To assume that the same kind of choice will always be made is to assume extraordinary naiveté among the market's participants.) Weber does return to the market and the market rationale to establish the premise of class development, and it is here that the student of peasant society will encounter his first difficulties. For Weber, "The market and its processes 'knows no personal distinctions': 'functional' interests dominate it. It knows nothing of 'honor.' "[8] In a similar vein, Karl Polanyi explains that the market system corresponds to the ascendancy of formal economics, "a situation of choice that arises out of an insufficiency of means."[9] As we shall see, the formal logic of the market was not the only, nor even the primary, logic of the two peasant societies compared here.[10]

As a sequel to Weber's insistence on life chances in the market, I should also mention those – Ralf Dahrendorff springs immediately to mind[11] – who have defined class in terms of power structure (Weber described "power" as "the chance of a man or a number of men to realize their own will in a communal action . . .").[12] This might work well in the study of a society as politically articulate as, say, postwar West Germany, but it makes little practical sense when applied to the nineteenth-century French peasantry. It would find itself translated into such amorphous terms as the "ruled," a sort of âme damnée, establishing itself as a coherent, recognizable force only during years of severe stress but otherwise sinking into an apparent acquiescence of the powers that be.

In the place of a specific class, I finally defined the peasantry in terms of a pattern of interplaying social and economic sectors. I have emphasized the existence not of a peasant class but of a peasant society, a peasant economy; that is, a complete social group that includes distinctions of property holding, market involvement, and the ability to exercise power.

This has determined the shape of the book. My analysis of the social whole takes two different approaches. First, I concentrate on the forms of social and economic exchange found in our two regions. This helps to establish the crucial relationship between the society and its region and, more particularly, to define the outer spatial limits of that society. Second, I attempt to assess the manner in which the individual was associated with the group. Here we are especially concerned with changes in the lived experience over time, in its historical as well as individual, developmental sense. The two approaches, combined, provide a means of determining the kind of opportunities that French society saw before it and the kind of opportunity it actually took.

Accordingly, I have divided this study into three parts. Part I provides the essential background for the rest of the work: I have first outlined the main contrasts and similarities between the major regions concerned, stressing the geographic facts (Chapter 2), and have then presented a conceptual framework for the analysis of their societies (Chapter 3). Part II begins this actual analysis by concentrating on exchange and the problems of social structure as defined in physical space: What were the potential relationships between the urban and rural communities (Chapter 4)? What social channels existed to make these relationships possible (Chapter 5)? How did rural society – given the varied land resources that it had at its disposal – actually take advantage of such relationships (Chapter 6)? Part III then looks at the same societies from the angle of time and the lived experience of time. This part is divided into a study of rural demography (Chapter 7) and the implications this has for the organization of rural properties (Chapter 8). Finally, Chapter 9 concentrates on the problem of agricultural crisis and indicates how the essential pattern of rural society retained the character that we define earlier in the study as "peasant."

Let me point out that the study of a non–English-speaking society does create some language problems. The word *métayer,* for instance, is not accurately translated by the word "sharecropper"; nor does "day-laborer" adequately convey the meaning of *journalier.* In such cases, I decided to use the original French term rather than an inadequate and possibly misleading translation. Also, recent rural history is a relatively new field involving novel and sometimes complicated ideas. I have made an effort to avoid the excessive use of jargon out of the conviction that a phrase is preferable to a neologism (I belong to that ancient school of stylistics that maintains that new ideas are more important than new words.) Readers dismayed at the use of some mathematics in the following pages may be assured that few of the techniques employed fall outside the limits of a first-year course in statistics. Again, I have kept the jargon to a minimum, confining most of it to the tables and endnotes.

My hope is that this work will be compared with the rural histories on earlier periods and will also help explain the presence of an "anachronism" that seems to be here to stay for a while longer. It should at least provide a basis for a different, less unilinear view of European society over the last century and a half – a period that has until now been almost entirely, if not entirely, seen in terms of "class" and "industrialization." An alternative approach is not merely possible. It is sorely needed.

2 The Loire Country: the land and its settlement

Water, earth, fire, and air were, for the old philosophers, the basic elements that made up the physical universe and, inasmuch as man was a physical being, the rudiments of human existence. If this had been correct, the huge area of central France that we refer to as the "Loire Country"[1] should have been the cradle of mankind. It possessed, in abundance, all four elements: its waters were fed from north and south by myriad streams and rivers, a fertile soil produced a rich vegetation, there was the warmth of its sun, and an almost continual westerly breeeze brought rain from the nearby Atlantic coast.

The Loire Country, we know, played a more modest historical role – man's first settlements were elsewhere. Nonetheless, the area was far from insignificant. For France itself, this area was crucial. It contributed, in the first place, to the unification of the nation by supplying a critical link between the northeastern portion of the country and the west and south. The lack of any natural barrier between the Loire and the Seine greatly facilitated the trend toward centralized government; together, the two rivers drain 38 percent of France's land surface[2] – no small fact when one considers that the main means of transport was, through most of the past, by water. But the Loire Country also contains some of the most persistent limits in French history. In its eastern parts, the river itself represents a border between "northern" and "southern" styles of land settlement, and there is an equally important distinction to be made between the whole eastern region and the West.

These uniformities and contrasts in the physical and human geography of the Loire Country are so fundamental to the present study that it is best to recognize them from the very beginning.

1. Physical geography

To start, there is an event to be kept in mind – though one that occurred so long ago that only a geologist would be interested in its actual timing.[3] This was the redirection of the river Loire to a western opening in the Atlantic Ocean. Until that had happened, practically all of the waters of the ancient highlands in France's center (the Massif Central) flowed directly northward because of the virtual permanent existence of a sea that covered at times part, at times the whole of present-day northern France. It was the muck and sediment left by this primeval sea that gave

9

rise to the low-lying plains of Belgium, the Netherlands, all of southeastern England and, in France, the Paris Basin – that vast region stretching from the border of the old rocks of Brittany to the Ardennes and from the Massif Central to the English Channel. To these marine deposits were added the rocks, pebbles, and silt that the torrents of water from the Massif Central loaded onto the southern half of the Basin. On meeting with the sea, some very curious patterns took shape. Sometimes the fluvial deposits prevailed over the marine and sometimes the reverse occurred, so that the whole of the southern Basin was scattered with small, varied subregions.

It is important to remember just two of these: the Sologne and the Beauce. In the Sologne, the rivers clearly won the battle over the sea. In this subregion, enclosed roughly by four lines drawn between the present towns of Orléans, Tours, Bourges, and Sancerre,[4] massive deposits of cold, water-logged sands and clays collected in layers that were sometimes 60 meters thick. When the sea finally withdrew, this particular spot of France was left with great stretches of impermeable, acidic soils, peppered with stagnating ponds. Not so for the Beauce. Here, immediately to the north of the Sologne, between Chartres, Etampes, Orléans, and Vendôme, the sea got the upper hand, leaving behind a thick carpet of seaborne remains, which were to provide the bedrock to a highly permeable, limestone plateau. Though this was certainly the most important characteristic of the Beauce, the river forces were not entirely left out. Before the sea finally withdrew, they succeeded in spreading out a layer, albeit a very thin one, of sand, silt, and clay: a loam that, once above sea level, was capable of holding a certain quantity of rainwater, but never enough to form streams or ponds. The Beauce therefore became an essentially dry region in contrast to its water-laden southern neighbor.

The revolution that eventually thrust the river system westward resulted from the folding of the central and eastern portions of the Paris Basin and the subsequent depression of the west: Maine, the Touraine, and Anjou sunk so low that their lands, formerly dry, were invaded by a new sea, the *mer de Faluns,* or "Sea of Shell Marls," after the chalky deposits it left behind. It was a decisive event. A glance at the map (Figure 2.1) indicates its dramatic effect on the drainage patterns in central France. By the time the river reaches Orléans, its new bearing is well defined. In a little over 100 kilometers, the river has turned 90 degrees from its original direction. By the same token, the Cher and the Creuse make their own brusque turns to the west. An interesting exception is the Vienne, whose course is east–west, instead of south–north, as if it were going to join up with the Charente and flow straight into the ocean from there. But at the last minute, it literally takes a right-angle bend in order

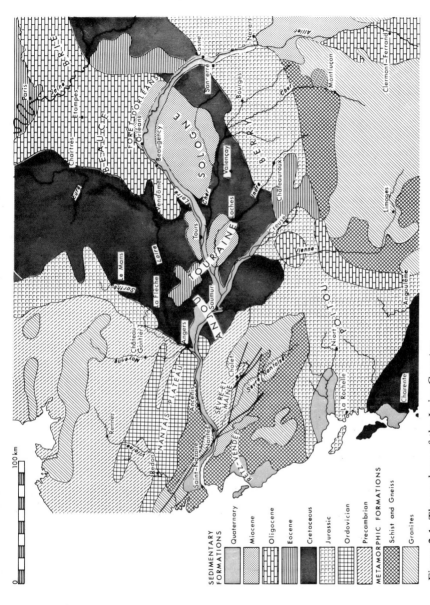

Figure 2.1. The geology of the Loire Country.

to flow north until, on being joined by the Creuse, it starts to follow the trend of the rest of the Loire basin. Thus, a large area of central France stood with its face forcibly turned to the ocean and its eyes focused on one specific point: Nantes.

The Nantais is, in geological terms at least, completely separate from the Paris Basin. It forms, rather, a part of the southern mantle of the Massif Armoricain, a huge area built of a tangle of schists, gneisses, and other dark granitic rocks, which makes up the major portion of France's "West."

The transition between the Paris Basin and the Massif is remarkably sudden. A traveler following the Loire westward is bound to notice it as he passes a point south of Angers. A prewar geographer put it this way:

The valley narrows: the Authon [a minor tributary] and the Loire approach one another and, near the confluence, in the middle of an island, the church of Saint Maurille, Ponts-de-Cé, becomes visible, mounted on the summit of a black rock. This is the true frontier separating the Paris Basin from the Massif Armoricain.[5]

Charles Tilly recognized this abrupt contrast in his justly famous sociology of the Vendée War.[6] On the northern side of the river, anyone taking the train from Paris to Nantes will see the change. After covering well over 200 kilometers of the Paris Basin, the train arrives at Angers. From there, the rail makes a rightward curve, crossing the river Maine by means of a rather impressive viaduct. A panorama is opened. Below is a flat expanse of land, often flooded, surrounding the river; in front is a formidable wall of black rock, stretching from north to south. The rail soon enters this mass, gouging out a passage that gives a very good idea of the hardness of the base in the new area. On the approach, one cannot help but think of the ancient *mer de Faluns* beating against its foot.

The portion of the Massif Armoricain that the Loire crosses is in many respects representative of the whole geographic region. It is flat: The highest point in the whole of the department of Loire-Inférieure,[7] for instance, is only 115 meters above sea level.[8] Its most common rocks are sandstone, crystalline, and slate. The slate weathers down into a sticky, very heavy clay, which, because of its impermeability, encourages the spread of clusters of trees and shrubbery – something men learned to develop into hedgerows that were to surround practically every field in the region. This kind of wooded country is so distinctive that it has earned itself a special name, the *bocages,* and covers most of the interior parts of the Massif as well as some of the neighboring Paris Basin.

But two important factors force us to separate this particular area from the rest of the Massif and include it within the Loire Country. There is, first, the weather. Snow hardly ever falls here, and even if it does, it sticks to the ground only on extremely rare occasions. The summers are also much warmer than in the northern parts of the Massif so that a wider variety of crops can be cultivated. Thus maize (only introduced in the seventeenth century) is more abundant and the vine, unknown in Normandy and Brittany proper, can be easily harvested here. The second factor is the presence of the Loire itself. Together with its tributaries, the river started anew its old game with the sea – a combat we have noted once took place at the borders of the Massif Central and the Paris Basin. Distinct subregions were once again created. During the same geological revolution that pushed the Loire westward, the Massif Armoricain started to "pitch": its northern extremities rose while its south, including the whole area in which we are interested, slowly sank.

Only three subregions interest us: the Pays de Retz, Sèvre-et-Maine, and a plateau to the north of the Loire.[9] Of these, the Pays de Retz certainly presents the most puzzles. Through its deranged, jumbled terrain passes a wide granitic band – running rather like a break-water northwest–southeast – where the campaign between river and sea has been concentrated. The result is an odd melange of water-logged clays and hard granite stone that have gathered together during the continual flood and ebb of the sea level over recent geological time. For instance, the Lac de Grand Lieu, the largest lake in metropolitan France, is an example of how a rise in sea level since the last ice age caused a bottleneck in the flow of waters to the sea. The pattern extends as far south as the Vendée, another region that geographically extends almost to the mouth of the Gironde. It is because of the affinity of the Pays de Retz with the Vendée that we decided to name the region surrounding the Lac de Grand Lieu Retz–Vendée.

In contrast to Retz–Vendée, Sèvre-et-Maine, which takes up the whole of Loire-Inférieure southeast of Nantes, has many more surface crystalline rocks to betray the presence of the Massif. But most distinctive is the web of natural waterways formed by the confluence of a series of streams and rivers, which have created some extremely fertile soils. Furthermore, being an inland region, it is protected from the violent oceanic storms that frequently hit Retz–Vendée, at the same time being near enough to the coast to reap the benefits of a maritime climate.

For the third region, we have to cross the Loire to reach a flat, wooded area that stretches all the way to Châteaubriant. In the Nantais Plateau – I can think of no better name – one finds most of the classic features of the Massif Armoricain. Clays provide a heavy topsoil for scattered copses and woods whose floors are covered with either brambles or ferns. And the weather, though not cold, is sufficiently different north of the Loire to prevent the growth of such a rich variety of plants as can be found on the south side.

Considering the whole of the middle and lower course of the Loire in the context of its physical geography, we are struck most by the variety of the territories it crosses. One evidently cannot regard the Loire Country as a single, uniform region. The marked contrast between the geology of the Massif Armoricain and the Paris Basin precludes this. There are also the many subregions to be taken into account. Indeed, from the examples we cited, the river Loire seems to be one of the most consistent boundaries between one subregion and another; between the fertile plains of the Beauce and the heathlands of the Sologne, between the Nantais Plateau and Sèvre-et-Maine. But, all this being said, two common factors have been noted: the weather and the westward-flowing river. Let us emphasize the second. No historical work on the area can afford to ignore that one dramatic event that turned all the natural drainage toward the Atlantic Ocean. When man finally arrived (a few million years later), it was this revolutionized river system that helped him superimpose his own distinct patterns on the landscape. The human geography of the area is, in this sense, a logical sequel to the physical.

2. Human geography: trade and the towns

Trade routes make the most conspicuous patterns in human geography. In the case of France, two major trends have made indelible marks. The first is a south–northward trend, with its origin in the Mediterranean Basin. From here, the ancient Phoenicians pioneered a sea route that, to the present day, has carried ships past Spain to northwest Europe, thereby giving the first impetus to the development of the ports of Brittany and, later, of the Gulf of Gascony. There was also the land route, established in prehistoric times, that took advantage of the Rhone Valley and the narrow watershed lying between it and the Seine. The second trend, from east to west, must have relied heavily, from the very start, on the presence of the Loire if only because there is no other major river system in France, with the dubious exception of the north–westward-flowing Gironde, which has such a clearly defined westerly course. The earliest trade routes along the Loire probably began with the Roman occupation.[10]

The two trends, once established, were clearly going to generate important crossroads in the Loire Country. Although the Rhone–Seine axis passed a little way – and only a little way – to the east of the area,[11] the most important road from Paris to Spain, the *Grande Route d'Espagne,* cut right through its center, encountering Orléans, Tours, and Poitiers before passing on to Bordeaux and the Spanish border. The Loire, on the other hand, apart from providing its essential link between Paris and the Atlantic, was a main artery for traffic from the east of the country, especially from the eastern Masssal Central and the Alpine region. Nantes, for instance, was, for a long time, considered Switzerland's major direct outlet to the Atlantic.

It is therefore no surprise to learn that there has been a long urban tradition in the area.[12] Before the nineteenth century, industry, to be sure, was largely local and controlled by artisan associations. But in trade we witness some early developments that are reminiscent of the commercial associations formed in the Rhineland and coastal stretches of medieval Germany, even though in the Loire Country they were all on a much smaller scale.[13] However, the Loire's virtual monopoly of trade routes to the west became critical only after France began to take an interest in America and, especially, the West Indies. It was then that the crossroads established between the south–northward and east–westward trends began to have a major effect on the Loire Country.[14]

Orléans and Nantes were pinpoints of activity, as is evident from their populations. Orléans, according to Georges Lefebvre, counted 36,850 inhabitants in 1791, with another 14,489 in its suburbs.[15] Nantes, as early as 1700, had a population of over 40,000 and by the first census (1801) was recording 74,000.[16] Tours, a commercial port in its own right, which had a population of 21,500 in 1789, was the only town in the Loire Country that came close to these figures. Otherwise, the towns were all of average size for the period.[17]

It is not hard to see why Orléans and Nantes should have become so important. Orléans was situated at the Loire's closest point to Paris, Normandy, Artois, and the manufacturing centers of Flanders and the Lowland countries. A waterway to these important regions had been assured by the cutting of the Canal de Briare (1605–42) and the Canal d'Orléans (1679–92). The town was also at the command of practically all traffic sailing up and down the river to its west as well as to the south. In short, Orléans was simply the most practical spot on the Loire to build a commercial warehouse. Nantes was in an equally strategic position. It was almost exactly at this point that the fluvial part of the Loire Valley came to an end and the tides of the Atlantic began to be felt. Tidal waters had caused a sudden deepening of the riverbed here to such an extent that ocean-going ships could be brought right up to the town's quays.[18] In addition, the town stood at the confluence of two important tributaries of the lower Loire, the Erdre and the Sèvre-Nantaise. Well protected from the Atlantic storms (and also the foreign invader), Nantes made an ideal setting for the Loire's maritime port.

Both towns were very much a part of the rapid economic expansion that took place in France throughout the eighteenth century. The last 30 or 40 years of the Old Regime are usually considered the most prosperous period in the history of Orléans. The number of sugar refineries grew and its vinegar plants, some of which dated back to the fourteenth century, were operating at full capacity.[19] Nantes, in the meantime, found a new and extremely lucrative occupation: the slave trade. France, it has been

estimated, controlled about one-quarter of this miserable business between 1723 and 1740, with Nantes taking the lion's share. After the Trea-
ty of Paris (1763), though the value of the slave trade probably did not
decline a great deal, sugar once again became king.[20]

The bequest of the seventeenth and eighteenth centuries to the Loire
Country was, then, trade; trade at a scale that had never before been
practiced. Its beneficiaries, however, were not evenly spread: Nantes and
Orléans clearly came to dominate the area by virtue of their fortunate
position on crossroads established more than a thousand years earlier.
Each town obviously benefited from the other's successes. Yet, as early
as the 1700s, differences between their economies began to emerge that
were going to make a brutal contrast one century later. Orléans in 1789,
as Lefebvre is at pains to remind us, remained attached to its artisan
modes of production. Manufacture, here, was poorly equipped and very
dispersed. For the average Orléanais in the eighteenth century, there was
no need for it to be otherwise; after all, they were prosperous enough.
Nantes, on the other hand, was much more heavily industrial. It had to
be. As an ocean port as well as a river port, Nantes' prosperity was not,
like Orléans', just a question of putting up and maintaining warehouses;
Nantes' trade required ships, and to get them, it had to build them. The
old naval dockyards proved insufficient and, in the course of the century, two more were opened in the commune of Nantes alone, in addition
to those that sprang up a little way downstream at Haute-Indre, Basse-
Indre, Couëron, Le Pellerin and, further on, at Paimboeuf.

Even in the eighteenth century, shipbuilding was a large-scale enterprise. Its presence gave the town an important head start over Orléans (as
well as all the other towns of the Loire Country), which in the nineteenth
century was to prove decisive, not only for the few living within the urban limits of the two towns, but also for the multitude that inhabited the
surrounding countryside.

3. Human geography: the countryside

The territories that encircled Orléans and Nantes were in several ways
typical of the Loire Country's rural geography. Their locations brought
to the fore two issues that, to a greater or lesser degree, influenced all
rural life in the area: a sharply diversified physical environment and the
presence of a complicated network of trade routes, always in the end
leading to a major market center. These two geographical facts, now
outlined, are the keys to understanding the rural contrasts that developed
in the nineteenth century.

What kind of comparisons should one anticipate?

General outlines

Roger Dion makes it quite clear that the main contrasts in the Loire Country's agriculture are between the North and the South.[21] Paul Bois is equally convinced of a Center–West difference.[22] In fact, both opinions are well grounded. In the first place, the Loire Country can be considered as a zone of transition between the regular strip-field system (Marc Bloch's *champs ouverts et allongés*), which dominated most of north-western Europe, and the irregular "square" fields *(champs irréguliers)* found in southern Europe.[23] From Orléans to Tours, the Loire marks, with few exceptions, a boundary between the two types of agriculture. Northward, vast open plains extend, where cereals have for centuries been the main crops. Southward, livestock rearing has been relatively more widespread because the land is less fertile. This is also true of the *bocage* country of the West. But here, choice spots of land were set off from the rest for continuous cultivation,[24] and by the end of the eigh-teenth century, owing to the density of population, most of this section of the Loire Country was enclosed.

Soil conditions were obviously a major factor in the geographical distribution of these three agrarian "regimes."[25] Even so, the early establishment of a market economy in the Loire Country must be one of the principal reasons why there were so many *human* subregions within the area. In the Loire Country, we find some classic examples of how, in the coincidence of a certain soil type with a commercial outlet, men of the land were able to gather into communities and, further, into subregions, or *pays,* each one of which embraced a whole culture, an entire living entity. Gâtinais, Hurepoix, Beauce, the Sologne, Perche, the Gâtine Tourangelle, the Mauges, the Pays de Retz all belonged to the same general area; but the presence of markets had allowed each to take ad-vantage of its own particular resources with the result that, within some very short distances, sharp variations in the rural economy and society can be noted.

The Orléanais and the Nantais

Both the general characteristics of the three agrarian regimes and the im-portance of these local differences are glaringly obvious when attention is focused on the countrysides around Orléans and Nantes. As the largest markets in the Loire Country, the two towns tended to heighten the con-trasts.

Unfortunately, we have had to adhere to administrative units rather than rural regions in selecting the areas for detailed study because that is the way most data are presented. France, at the turn of the nineteenth century, was divided into arrondissements, cantons, and communes. In its zeal to create a single national identity, the government at that time drew boundaries that cut right across the old provinces, dissecting all the natural regions that made up the rural geography of our area. The Beauce, for instance, was henceforth a part of no less than three departments, Loir-et-Cher, Eure-et-Loir, and Loiret. Three departments (Loiret, Loir-et-Cher, and Cher) were likewise responsible for the administration of the Sologne. This is certainly one of the most tantalizing practical research problems for anyone undertaking a recent rural history of France. However, it also has one big advantage: it guarantees a very good cross section of the types of agriculture to be found in a single administrative area.

The regions chosen represent the largest workable units possible for the kind of study we wish to pursue. It would be too much work to take the whole of the departments of Loire-Inférieure (capital, Nantes) and Loiret (capital, Orléans); a project of this scale would require the examination of statistics and documents of well over 500 communes. The arrondissements of Orléans and Nantes are more practicable. The arrondissement of Orléans, in the nineteenth century, covered 240,000 hectares and counted 105 communes. Because the arrondissement of Nantes is significantly smaller (177,000 hectares), we have added the neighboring arrondissement of Ancenis, giving a total area of 225,000 hectares, including 93 communes. We will call these regions, surrounding Orléans and Nantes, the Orléanais and the Nantais, respectively.[26]

Rural society and economy in the Orléanais can be understood only within the context of its four geographic subregions (see Figure 2.2):

1. The Beauce, consisting of 32 communes (33 with the creation of Le Bardon in 1856) situated in the northwest of the region
2. The Sologne, with 12 communes in the south
3. The Forêt d'Orléans, with 26 communes in the northeast, and
4. The Loire Valley, with 35 communes running through the center.

Between the Beauce and the Sologne there lay, within a matter of a few kilometers, the whole difference between the two separate agrarian regimes, the regular strip field system of the North and the irregular "square" fields of the South. The cultivation of wheat was by far the major occupation of the people of the Beauce at the end of the eighteenth century. The population was grouped into villages, some of which had become important local marketing centers, such as Artenay and Patay. The Sologne, on the other hand, was largely an area of heath, shrubbery, stagnant waters, and wide, open expanses of waste – "méchant et pauvre pays."[27] Throughout the seventeenth and eighteenth centuries the region had been haunted by poor health and disease, giving it one of the highest rates of mortality in the whole of France.[28] Poor lands; a sparse, un-

Figure 2.2. The Orléanais in the mid-nineteenth century. (By permission of the Bibl. nat. Paris.)

healthy population: it was hardly the formula for a tight-knit, disciplined society as found in the Beauce. Roger Dion, following in the footsteps of Marc Bloch, spoke of the individualism of the area. Perhaps "isolationism" is more to the point.

The infertile sands and clays of the Sologne do not end at the Loire Valley. Between Orléans and Gien, they extend to the right bank of the river, covering the limestone that makes up the bedrock of the Forêt d'Orléans, the largest forest in France. In the eighteenth century, this subregion had some important similarities with the Sologne. Settlements were small and isolated, and cultivation played only a secondary role. However, the woods furnished work for a large, and perhaps major, proportion of the inhabitants – something that would have been impossible in the shrublands of the Sologne. Furthermore, the forest was dominated by one vast property: the domain of the Dukes d'Orléans, an appanage of the French royal family since the fourteenth century.[29] Strict surveillance of the domain by appointed guards curtailed the freedom of the inhabitants to exploit local resources to a degree that woud not have been found in the Sologne.[30]

The Loire Valley itself, because of its fertile alluvial soil, presents a fourth, absolutely distinctive, subregion. Cultivation was at such a highly intensive level that not even the Beauce approached it. Market gardening, fruit farming, and, most important, viticulture forced the inhabitants into dense clusters of villages and even towns, which spread along both banks of the river. All the major towns of the Orléanais were to be found within this subregion: on the left bank, Jargeau, Olivet, and Cléry-Saint-André; and on the right bank (in addition to Orléans), Châteauneuf, Meung, and Beaugency. The population of the Loire Valley was the most urbanized, the most exposed to collective life, in the whole Orléanais.

The Nantais should also be divided into geographic subregions (see Figure 2.3):

1. The Nantais Plateau, consisting of 25 communes situated in the north
2. Retz–Vendée, with 27 communes in the southwest (28 with the creation of La Planche in 1855)
3. Sèvre-et-Maine, with 18 communes in the southeast (21 with the creation of La Regrippière and Le Landreau in 1863 and Les Sorinières in 1865), and
4. The Loire Valley, with 23 communes running through the center (25 with the creation of Barbechat in 1857 and Le Fresne in 1868).

Bocages dominated the northern and southern extremes of the region. These were merely extensions of the wooded country found in eastern or "Upper" Brittany, western Maine and Anjou, and most of the depart-

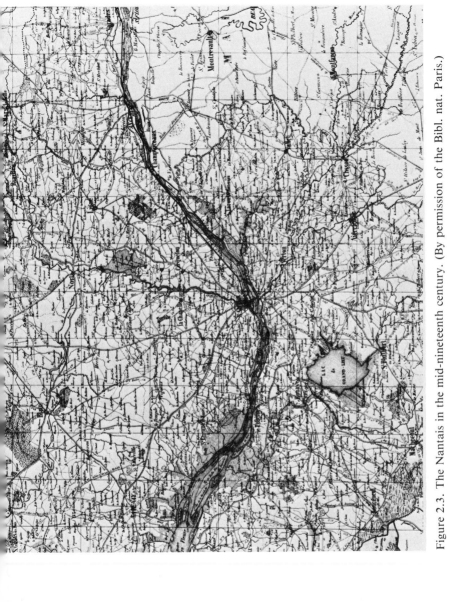

Figure 2.3. The Nantais in the mid-nineteenth century. (By permission of the Bibl. nat. Paris.)

ment of Vendée. We have already mentioned the infertility of the
Plateau's soils and the natural preference for raising stock. It was probably the combination of these two facts that forced the inhabitants to
enclose their arable land; stray animals would have been disastrous for
cultivation that was marginal at best. But the system apparently proved
to be such a success on the Nantais Plateau that wide areas were already
coming under the plow by the opening of the nineteenth century.

Retz–Vendée, the other subregion where extensive areas of *bocages*
were to be found, was less well-off because of its marshes. As in the
Sologne, stagnant waters brought little benefit to the inhabitants. At
Machecoul,

The waters from several large brooks and small streams . . . cover, with little
depth, a large area of ground. The badly maintained ditches are not able to provide an outlet [for the water] – the land and air, so to speak, absorb it. Nevertheless, this does result in puddles that are evaporated through the heat: those of
the ditches stagnate, rot; fishes and insects putrefy. From this originates those
stinking vapors that bring to the animals, immersed in such an atmosphere, the
sources of an infinity of serious diseases, and, too often, the scourge's germ,
whose effects destroy the hope of the cultivator, attacks the public well-being and
causes universal desolation.[31]

Evidently, not even the presence of Nantes was sufficient to pull the area
out of this cheerless condition.

In sharp contrast, Sèvre-et-Maine and the Loire Valley had easily the
best natural resources of the Nantais to respond to the urban market.
Their network of streams and rivers, spreading a rich alluvium over some
very wide areas, opened the way to a highly intensive, specialized
agriculture. Sèvre-et-Maine, for instance, was considered, even at the
outset of the nineteenth century, to be an important wine-producing
region. In the Loire Valley, as in the Orléanais, there were orchards,
vineyards, and vegetable plots. However, market gardening was probably more extensive here, especially in the cantons closest to Nantes, and
industrial crops – quite unknown in the Orléanais – were widespread.
Once more, the intensity of agriculture obliged the inhabitants to live in
villages and small towns rather than in scattered settlements. The most
important of these towns were Clisson in Sèvre-et-Maine and Ancenis,
Oudon, Rezè, and Indre in the Loire Valley.

To sum up, the Nantais had a significantly larger area dedicated to intensive agriculture than the Orléanais. Sèvre-et-Maine together with the Valley represented over one-third of the region's surface. In addition, even
the poor soils of the Plateau appear to have been made productive by
1800. In the Orléanais, intensive agriculture was largely confined to the
Loire Valley, though the fertile plains of the Beauce were certainly ex-

ploited to the brink of their capacity. This regional distinction was going to prove decisive in the course of the nineteenth century.

It has to be pointed out that neither the situation in the Nantais nor that in the Orléanais could have ever arisen without the long urban tradition of the Loire Country. The continual presence of traders and their commercial allies allowed a number of communities to make maximum use of their own local resources, but given the tremendous variation in physical geography, this could only result in important regional differences. From its mouth up to the sand-butted banks at Orléans, the river Loire spanned a series of settlements that had never, in modern times, been isolated; practically all development here was the product of association with the urban centers.

Nevertheless, though the town provided an opportunity for regional specialization, they could hardly be considered the sole cause of events in the countryside. Throughout the nineteenth century, the Loire Country was to remain predominantly rural. In 1901 over 70 percent of the population of the Loire Country lived in communes that had agglomerated settlements of less than 2,000 inhabitants while the average for the whole of France was only 59 percent. In Loire-Inférieure and the Loiret, the proportions were 64 and 68 percent, respectively.[32]

This resilience of the rural population in the face of France's growing urban and industrial sectors is, in my opinion, the result of the peculiar workings of a peasant economy – an informal economic system, which can be demonstrated to operate in the rural sector's landholding patterns, its demography, and especially its relationship with the urban centers. But before we do this, a more precise definition of the term "peasant economy" is required.

3 "The theory of peasant economy"

It would be impossible to sum up all major studies on peasant society that have been filling library shelves over the last 20 or 30 years. It would hardly even be desirable. I would like to concentrate instead on a theoretical model that has grown out of several of these studies, the most important by far being the work of the Russian economist Alexander Chayanov. I shall begin by discussing an ideal rural system (i.e., a "peasant economy" in the most perfect state) before noting what major imperfections one might anticipate in the reality of the Loire Country 100 years ago.

Theory and history have never been the happiest of bedfellows. The very static character of so many contemporary social and economic theories arising from a popular orientation toward questions of structure rules that kind of intimacy out immediately. Thus, kinship networks are basic to most anthropological analyses, role relationships form the groundwork of sociology, and an economist invariably turns his skills around some sort of market mechanism. Although there is room for movement in each of these systems, there is also a hard element of control, in terms of both time and space, in all of them. There has to be. There is simply no way (*pace* Goldmann and others of that ilk) that changing phenomena can be included unless they are to be subsumed under the generally motionless scheme: one is either describing a particular kind of structure or one is not. At the heart of the whole problem is the fact that a theorist is imprisoned by his first unavoidable assumptions, he has no body upon which to build his theory; if he does make them, he leaves himself no space to move beyond them. History, on the other hand, is about change in human behavior.

This ghastly dilemma comes out particularly clearly in economics, which has traditionally confined its logic to only one kind of animal, Aristotle's much pampered "economic man," whose orderly responses to prices, wage rates, and market conditions provide the underpinning to most advanced theories in the field.[1] Should or, rather, can rural historians support the same kind of assumptions? In the case of a peasantry, such as the one under study here, the size of the landholding, the limitations of family labor, or a combination of the two often confined cultivators to a number of alternatives that fell well short of the realm of choice required for economically rational action. Our answer, therefore, would probably have to be "No." Even, for instance, if it could be proved that per capita agrarian income rose during the nineteenth century, could we be sure that Jacques Bonhomme knew this? Even if he did, could we turn to modern economic theory in judgment of his consequent actions? If his presumptions were not the same as those of men living in a contemporary market environment, one is forced to concede that his responses also in all likelihood, differed. Economic historians have made, over the last decades, enormous efforts to establish the general levels of price, rent, wage, profit, and capital accumulation in various regions throughout Europe in bygone centuries. When the direct data are not available, they have been obliged to base their estimates on shadow pricing techniques and the like. But, despite the rapid progress made in social history, these efforts have still to be matched by similar ones that would link the market's participants to such abstract categories of market development. What was the meaning of these market forces to the lives of those who formed them? Even more to the point, what was their importance?[2]

The debate itself is an old one. Years ago, Marcel Mauss criticized the indiscriminate application of current economic theories to the past. "The economic way of thinking," he proposed, "is a recent way of thinking."[3] As an anthropologist, he chose to demonstrate this in tribal communities. In his celebrated "Essai sur le Don," he contended that the notion of value in primitive tribes could be understood much better in a religious and moral context than in terms of the market.[4] Then Karl Polanyi picked up the gauntlet; this time with a later kind of society in mind. Only in the last two centuries, he claimed, has Western man so organized his livelihood that it would fall into line with a system of price-making markets. The employment of contemporary economic theory (which makes the market its sole frame of reference) for studies of periods earlier than this date, therefore, involves an artificial identification of the economy with a market form – what Polanyi called the "economic fallacy."[5] Peasant economy is just one of the more recent types of community to come under this sort of critical approach.[6] The point that I should like to emphasize in this study is that contemporary theories are of questionable value in the analysis not only of such human organizations as the Yoruba tribesmen or the Malay fishermen but also of two major urban centers in the nascent industrial state of nineteenth-century France.

On a more general note, the main issue is this: almost as soon as one starts to turn back the pages of history, the analytical tools that have developed from and transformed the contemporary world are found to be blunted and their utility anachronistic. In such instances, our presentist theories have to be either thoroughly revised or rejected outright.

For the rationalist, there are some gratifying ways out of the problem. The great teleologies of the nineteenth century provide an excellent example of this. "Truth," a very noble word in those days, was determined by the extent to which it reflected movement and change. The "behaviorist" dilemma, which we just mentioned, was solved, in appearance at least (and impressively so), by regarding that movement as necessarily constructive. Thus, the Hegelian system was directed toward the gradual ascendance, through a logical sequence of stages, of a single, absolute idea. The certainty and degree of inevitability in this whole system continues to command tremendous popular appeal: it gives an account of the transitory nature of ideas and theory while, at the same time, claiming to have uncovered a formula to historical transition itself. From this point of view, the most plausible way of going about the analysis of peasant society would be first to establish, in general terms, the basic rationale behind the historical process and then to work out exactly how our particular case, the peasantry, fits into it. On the practical side, this would mean proving that peasant society either belonged to a distinct phase in the ongoing historical project or that it could be subsumed under some wider stage of development that did provide a link in the same rational momentum.

We might recall that Marx, in his famous "inversion" of the Hegelian system, had formulated five economic, as opposed to ideological or philosophical, stages in the rational evolution of human society: primitive tribalism, the ancient communal and state system based on slavery, feudalism, capitalism, and, finally, socialism.[7] Should peasant society be added as a sixth stage, presumably between feudalism and capitalism? or should it be considered as a specific aspect of feudal or capitalist society? or does the peasantry, recognized by the rural sociologist Henri Mendras to make up, today, the majority of mankind, present us with an anomaly that has nothing to do with such a logical course of development?

If we adopt this last position, we have at once two vast methodological problems to tackle. First, by opening ourselves to the possibility that there is no rational process in human development, we are essentially admitting that, far from being necessary, the transition from one social structure to another is arbitrary and that there is, between structures, no logical connection that could be applied to humanity as a whole. Specifically, this would be in direct conflict with the idea that peasantry is a "phase in the evolution of human society."[8] Second, such an opinion would run against the basic sentiment of most historians since the days of Herodotus; that is, that there is a purpose in all human development and that the object of a historian is to find out what this purpose is.

The position I take in this study is that we should look at peasant society as one specific means of providing for human needs – one that cannot be adequately described by contemporary theories on market societies but that has, nonetheless stuck to some of the most advanced regions of our Western civilization right up to the present age. Peasantry is not a necessary step in social development. But, viewed in its own terms, the peasantry reveal patterns of behavior that follow their own distinctive rationality. As we shall see, these are patterns that may occur within the constraints of several different types of environment. And, most important of all, they are patterns that are not necessarily inconsistent with the operation of market forces.

1. The theory of peasant economy

The most basic, distinctive quality of a peasant society, I would argue, is its own special understanding of what is meant by the optimum, or best possible, way of life. This is a specific kind of idealism that can be, and has been, demonstrated to operate through a peasant society's patterns of sociability and even in its moral and religious traditions.[9] But it is in economics – the way the society organizes its material livelihood – that this sense of the optimum finds its most concrete expression. This is one of the chief discoveries of Alexander Chayanov, who established, with the backing of more than a decade's work on the property surveys of Russia's provinces, that, although peasants at an individual level were intent upon maximizing their income, the degree to which they actually put their labor into productive use was based on a unique concept of profitability that had nothing to do with the market farmer's quest for highest *net* profit. The contemporary economists' idea of maximization therefore was seen to have little bearing on the initiatives of producers on the peasant farm. Chayanov went further. Beyond the individualistic, microeconomic notion, he presented the rudiments of a national, or macroeconomic, theory of peasant society by recognizing that, as long as this specific type of rural population remained a significant part of the total supply and demand functions, the entire economy was bound to be affected in some way.[10]

In imitation of Chayanov, I would like to define the term "peasantry" at these two economic levels. Indeed, I have made this one of the guiding principles in organizing this study. Part II, Space, insofar as it deals with patterns of exchange between different economic sectors, is largely confined to a macroeconomic analysis; and Part III, Time, which deals with the individual experience of time as well as historical developments, includes the main body of my microanalysis. For the sake of clarity, let me begin with an outline of the latter.

At a microeconomic level, we should concentrate on the decision-making strategies that at once determine and are themselves determined by the way the units of production and consumption are organized in a peasant society.[11] In Chayanov's theory, both production and consumption units are synonymous with the peasant family, which, by his definition, employs no outside labor. Peasant economic strategies are consequently centered around the establishment of an equilibrium between the satisfaction of the family's needs and the drudgery or self-exploitation of its own labor. The uniqueness of the peasantry lies in the mechanism of this "labor-consumer balance."[12] Because the units of production and consumption are embodied in one entity, the family, it is impossible, Chayanov claimed, to divide the economic realities of the system further than (a) the family's gross income, (b) the sums spent from this on capital renewal, (c) the family's budget, and (d) the savings not invested in the family's own farm. It is only after production and consumption are separated that, with the employment of outside labor, the total costs of production, so indispensable in the reckoning of net profit, can be objectively calculated. Until that happens, the labor product of the peasant family is *undifferentiable*, and the amount of labor exerted depends on the family's subjective evaluation of its needs against the effort required to fulfill them rather than, as in the case of a strict market agriculture, the maximization of net profit. The chief ambition of the peasantry thus comes close to that of Balzac's rustics: *donner le moins possible pour le plus possible.*[13]

Chayanov's own theory was especially pertinent to countrysides of low population density. Here the quantity of cultivatable land would appear unlimited and the main distinction between the ideal system of market farming and the ideal system of peasant farming is to be felt more in terms of a varying size of the farming units rather than in a contrast of actual labor intensity per acre of land. In Russia, where these conditions prevailed, Chayanov demonstrated that the area of peasant landholding was tied directly to the family life cycle: it expanded as the number of family members increased. Because extensive farming (such as the cultivation of grains) normally requires less labor per unit of output than intensive farming (industrial crops, horticulture, etc.), one would expect a peasantry desiring satisfaction by means of the lowest possible effort to adopt the former. The market farmer, in attempting economies of scale, would also prefer an extensive type of culture. The only difference between the two systems would presumably be that the farmer's exploitation would be both larger and more stable. Given this situation in Russia, it is small wonder that Chayanov chose to bring out the distinctions between market and peasant economies by concentrating on the area of exploitations.

Obviously, these conditions did not apply to nineteenth-century

France, so Chayanov's ideas are not directly applicable here. Instead, we have to reformulate the theory to accommodate the type of rural economy that existed in France 100 years ago. I shall argue, in the remainder of this chapter, that Chayanov's distinctions between ideal market and ideal peasant economies are even more pronounced and are infinitely more varied when attention is turned to a situation, such as was found in France, where the levels of population were sufficiently high to create recognizable limitations on the quantity of cultivatable land available. Under these conditions, the peasant family, constantly striving to meet its needs through a singly defined unit of labor, at once begins to intensify production. First, the family can no longer expand and contract its farm at will. The area of land inherited or purchased by a young family is much less likely to be extended with the increasing size of the family than was the case in Chayanov's Russia. In all probability, a constant acreage will prevail over the family cycle or, at the very least, any increase in territory will be achieved through the acquisition of distant, isolated plots rather than by the purchase of land adjoining the original farm. The scattering of peasant properties in this fashion has been noted as particularly characteristic of the densely populated Mediterranean littoral.[14] Furthermore, a larger total number of families obviously means that the initial area cultivated by each family is that much smaller than in sparsely populated regions. The density of this population can, however, reach extremely high levels. Because there are no wages, or no means of calculating in money the costs of production, the peasant family will continue to intensify cultivation until it has satisfied its personal demands, defined largely by habits of consumption established over several generations.

It is, then, demographic pressures acting on customary patterns of consumption rather than the logic of the market that primarily determines the intensity of cultivation in a peasant society. It is precisely on this point that the behavioral assumptions of the classical market economists become problematic and it is why their categories of price, rent, wage, profit, and capital accumulation are, by themselves, insufficient to describe a rural economy such as that of France in the nineteenth century. The market obviously plays an important role,[15] but only insofar as it provides a partial means of satisfying the personal demands of the family. It is not an independent factor molding the structure of economy. In the "unfavorable" market situation of rapidly declining prices for agricultural products, the peasantry will continue to intensify cultivation, pay high land prices and rents, and even borrow at exorbitant rates of interest until the internal equilibrium between the displeasure of their efforts and the satisfaction of their demands has been met. Conversely, high agricultural prices will induce further intensification only when personal demands remain unfulfilled and the marginal product of their labor is deemed, subjectively, worthwhile. However, because high agricultural prices usually owe their origin to shortages within the rural communities themselves, thus keeping the peasantry close to or even below levels of subsistence, it is likely that the returns to labor will be high. A close association between patterns of cultivation and low prices is much less likely because the price decline is often initiated by the advance of new, outside supplies, which have little to do with the old communities. This was, for example, manifestly the case in France and many other western European countries after the 1870s, when there was a rapid increase in grain imports from North America and the Ukraine.[16] Therefore, in a peasant economy, the optimum level of intensification, being *relative* to the *internal needs* of the family, is in all probability going to be significantly higher than a market farmer's optimum, which, because it is defined at the point of diminishing marginal *net profit,* is *absolute* and can be pushed no further than the market will permit.

Even so, it would be an obvious fallacy to claim that there are no absolute limits to intensification in the peasant society. Though difficult, if not impossible, to specify in quantitative terms, such limits can be abstractly defined at a point beyond which the satisfaction of needs cannot be achieved through the singular efforts of the family. The excessive fragmentation of peasant properties can lead to the creation of such diminutive plots that, no matter what crops are cultivated, no matter how many hours of labor are exerted, the product always falls short of demand. Alternatively, physical factors, such as the weather or soil exhaustion, might make former levels of farming intensity inoperable. In either case, if the internal family equilibrium cannot be maintained, the society will suffer a crisis more severe than any sustained under market agriculture because the critical point is reached so much later. A peasant agricultural crisis ushers in a period of massive population movement – if not expressed by violent increases in mortality, then by a sudden rise in rural emigration – and wholesale reorganization of farming practices. This means the eradication or, at least, severe modifications of the peasant economy.

Whatever the final outcome, the social effects of such a crisis must be total; an exhausted agriculture and the subsequent widening of the gap between product and needs creates a decline in manufacture through a stagnant demand and a consequent drop in any such service requirements as are tied to that manufacture. So the very activities that could provide some alternative to cultivators in distress are themselves restrained by the same original cause. Here, then, lies the leaven of a new order: either starvation and disease reduce population densities significantly enough to create the novelty of a higher per capita income or the major sectors of production are themselves transformed sufficiently and early enough to permit the population to maintain its numbers. Both cases imply periods of considerable social upheaval.

The fate of this rural economy is, then, clearly tied to events in the nonagricultural sector – a principle that seems to have been recognized by most historians who have written on the subject, especially those who have concentrated on long-term rural developments.[17] The main tenor of their argument has been similar to my own: the growth of manufacture, commerce, and systems of market delivery allows agricultural specialization (and, thus, intensification) and also initiates improvements in agricultural technology. By this means, agriculture can break loose from its original optimal limits. Some convincing historical evidence has been found to back up the idea. Both the rural malaise of the Carolingian age and the depression of the fourteenth and early fifteenth centuries were relieved by periods of relative prosperity that coincided with a spurt in the growth of commerce and urbanization; in the first case, in northern Italy and along the Rhineland Corridor and, in the second, on the westward-facing shores of the Atlantic Ocean.

This is in no way to suggest that agriculture should be looked upon as the obedient spouse of the city's economy. Our own comments suggest a rather lively relationship. If, at a microeconomic level, we can speak of each unit of agricultural production in terms of an attempt at the maximization of satisfaction against the efforts to produce it, then, given the material restraints imposed by an increasingly dense population, there must exist the desire to find an alternative means of self-exploitation, so long, of course, as the alternative provides sufficient fulfillment to account for the exertions expended in both its adoption and continuation (a "crisis" succeeds when this is not the case). In such a fashion might a rural economy take up a more intensive form of cultivation or turn toward part-time artisanal activities – the "putting-out" industries. The countryside, therefore, supplies the urban centers with a quantity of different products that vary not so much with the condition of the market as with its own demographic situation. This is why it is so important to realize that a proliferation of intensive cultures or even cottage industries need not necessarily imply change in the underlying rationale of the rural economy because it is this economy, itself, that provides the major stimulus for such developments.

How seriously is this picture modified when, instead of focusing on the operation of individual units of agricultural production, we take a total view of the whole peasant economy? In other words, what sort of effect does a macroeconomic approach have on our argument? Can we still speak of an underlying rural stimulus for change?

Macroeconomics is less concerned with the actual process of producing than with the exchange of commodities already produced and particularly with the resultant interactions between an economy's main sectors. The topic lends itself to analogies with a physical plant: we are familiar enough with "distribution flows," "bottlenecks," and "conveyor belts." There is no denying the explanatory power of these images. But our conception of national or regional economies is so suffused with them that they have become by and of themselves a determinant of economic theory. For instance, unless we have in mind some Parkinsonian horror, the movement of a commodity through a physical plant has a starting point and a destination. There is therefore a temptation, when studying an economy, to look for a starting point in one sector and a destination in another; one might even try to identify "mediating" sectors between the two. It could work if we were only interested in a single commodity or even a type of commodity but not in the case of a whole economy. Though some self-centered groups might say otherwise, there is no beginning, there is no end. That is why it can only be misleading to speak of a "mediator" class in the context of an economic whole: all men are mediators. (In Chapter 5, I suggest the term "connector" to emphasize the contrast between this concept and the more narrowly defined "mediator" of anthropological literature.)

How, then, are we to conceive this whole? In the case of a peasant economy, it is extremely difficult to work out which sectors should be included and which should not. The limits are not at all clear. The logical solution is to consider all those sectors that are indispensable for an economy's survival. In a peasant economy, we have seen that this must involve an urban element: in order to maximize its gains, a peasantry has to be able to resort to alternative means of self-exploitation; this is feasible only in the presence of an urban market. One can be even more specific. The particular form of maximization that we noted in discussing the peasant farm is based on a definite range of alternatives. Although a peasantry cannot objectively distinguish cost (input) from profit (output), it can find an outlet for its labor product beyond the immediate confines of the village community.[18] Anthropologists have, in fact, been arguing this for years. "Peasants," wrote A. L. Kroeber in a much-quoted flurry of the pen, "constitute part-societies with part-cultures that live in relation to market towns."[19] He was implying, really, a degree of economic choice. An urban market and its communications network assure a rural economy a wide scope of possibilities for production. One may even argue that this urban market *defines* at any given moment the outer limit of all production possibilities. But our logic can go no further. We cannot, for instance, say that in a peasant economy the main *initiative* for rural change comes from the town. That must reside in the countryside itself if we are to recognize our own premises, that is, a peasantry's ignorance, by nature of its subjective labor–consumer balance, of the commercial optimum imposed by market forces. The main initiative comes under the hammer of a rural demography, driving the countryside to levels of production unacceptable in an objective commercial agriculture.

It therefore seems correct to assume that at a macroeconomic level a peasant economy describes an entire society, urban as well as rural, in which the town, because of its market, provides the potential for development while the country supplies its own impetus.[20]

This does not mean that the relationship between town and country is entirely mutual. As Edward Fox has vigorously argued, the development of commercial specialization allows a town, or at least important economic and social sectors of a town, to pursue a life detached from the surrounding countryside. A near-independent economy is established. In Fox's own words,

The principal business of the [commercial] towns would be the exchange of goods in quantity with other commercial towns. It is this that distinguished them from the self-sufficient agricultural market towns and committed them to the interdependence of a large linear (circular) economic system.[21]

The general effect of Fox's analysis is to place the geographic layout of a given territory under two lights. The first picks out only the commercial summits, giving a wide and rather dazzling picture of an international community that operates through lines of multilateral exchange. Fox's own examples are the urban communities of the Aegean littoral of the ancient world, the Rhineland Corridor of the Middle Ages, and the northwestern European coastlands during the early modern period. A second light would be more diffuse, displaying whole areas rather than particular points. It is in this light that a peasant economy is to be analyzed. Towns stand in brighter contrast than the adjacent rural districts, but this time because they are the nodal points of exchange for the entire area: they become absorbed into the general pattern of urban–rural interdependence just described. On these grounds, Fox has asserted that the critical distinction between economies of a given territory "lie not between town and country, but between commerce and trade."[22] A town built on long-distance commerce is not expected to have much of a rapport with its hinterland, whereas the life of an agricultural market town is founded upon the existence of an active rural surrounding. Therefore, although a peasant economy must include nonagricultural sectors, it need not include all sectors within a given territory. There may be two separate economies present as, we shall see, was the case of the Nantais.

However, the presence of a large town, even if a major part of its primary products are bought from distant sources, must have implications for the rural economy. The diagram (Figure 3.1) indicates what some of these may be. In the center are the urban market and com-

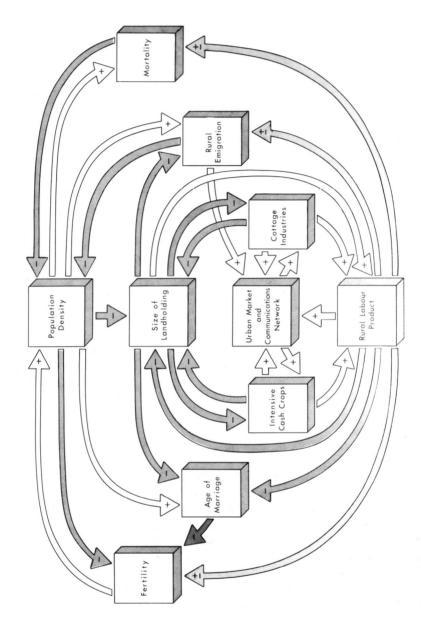

Figure 3.1. Factors in the peasant economy.

munications network, which, together, should be taken to define the potential limits of a rural economy at any particular moment of time, because of the range of production opportunities they offer.

By considering this urban market as potential rather than existing, we hit upon a rather crucial point. Although the linkages between the leading sector of a town and the countryside may be weak, there is no reason to assume that the entire urban population is geared to the same insular pursuit. There may be groups actively oriented toward trade with the hinterland or, at least, the interest for this may be there – to what extent depends on the size and demands of the town but also on what the countryside can offer. If such minority groups do proliferate, the designation of "town types" becomes difficult. This is increasingly the case as the countryside itself directs its own energies to the openings offered by the markets and jobs of the large town. An influx of rural migrants as well as goods will create sectors that have little in keeping with the original character of the town but that, nevertheless, form an integral part of it. The dominating aspect of one, single urban occupation is thus dampened by a realization in the countryside of the advantages the town can offer. Contemporary examples of this are most obvious in many Third World cities, where rural penetration has been so extreme that the term "peasant town" seems more appropriate than either "commercial," "market," or "industrial town." Curiously, there has been little written on this subject with regard to Europe.[23]

As to the country's own internal reactions to the large urban center, we might, first, emphasize an interplay between two broadly defined factors, land and the population. The special character of their relationship gives us one of the best indications of the limits of intensive farming in the peasant economy. There has to be a market to develop the land's resources to any degree. But, as I already argued, in the case of a peasant economy, it is not the market that dictates the intensity of exploitation; that remains tied to the prevailing demographic situation in the countryside: specifically, the spread of small properties, as a result of an increasingly dense population, obliges the owners to adopt an intensive agriculture. Yet this is obviously not a simple case of cause and effect. The average size of exploitation influences future rates of demographic growth (as indicated in Figure 3.1 by its effect on the age of marriage and fertility) and the extent to which intensive cultivation is actually feasible implies how small that average can be. So we come back to the town as a sort of *agent provocateur,* a sector that, by providing an outlet for a variety of farmed goods, makes the temptation to choose an intensive agriculture as a source of livelihood quite irresistible.

The motivation here is what we have already described as the pressure to satisfy subjective household needs. The goal of each household is to have enough productive land to bring satisfaction; security is when the farm acreage exceeds that minimum. So when a market effectively lowers the required minimum by accepting specialized agricultural products, it improves the chances of a satisfactory and secure livelihood *in the eyes of the cultivators themselves*. However, this hope is short-lived if their main reaction is to attempt to improve the working capacity of the household by increasing the number of its members – a dismal reminder of Malthus's old vicious formula:

When from a prospect of increasing plenty in any country, the weight that represses population is in some degree removed; it is highly probable that the motion will be continued beyond the operation of the cause that first impelled it.[24]

A population pushed once again to its limits creates an irreconcilable difference between the determination of each cultivator to expand his acreage, in order to assure an adequate gross income, and the overall tendency of property sizes to diminish. Of course, this is partially offset by further intensified use of the land. But that too has its limits, fixed as much by the soil's productivity as by the market. There are the cottage industries to provide another means of intensifying the efforts for support. In this case, however, the market and, probably more important, plain human exhaustion mark a boundary to the volume of goods that can be supplied. Whatever the method, then, it appears unlikely that intensification alone could relieve a peasant household system from an almost inevitable limitation in production.

What really makes population, in my opinion, such a dynamic factor is that it is demographic pressure, again, that is going to force an outlet from the dilemma. A high mortality is obviously the least desirable route of escape, even though by striking at the physically and economically most vulnerable, it might strengthen the surviving population.[25] But a peasant community's awareness that such a distasteful outcome is possible can initiate action that will contribute to a more positive form of relief. This could be either individually or collectively inspired. Thus, emigration and the use of birth control are both largely, though not entirely, the result of individual decisions. Neither can take place unless their advantages are consciously realized by the persons concerned; and it takes the threat of overpopulation to arouse that consciousness. Alternatively, there is the possibility of a collective response. It is to be expected that a peasant community, although immensely competitive by tradition, is, under pressure, going to appreciate that there are some benefits to be gained from a pooling of its resources. In this fashion, farming techniques can be refined by the sharing of otherwise prohibitively expensive machinery, just as final distribution can be improved by the collection of the farms' products into a single, common stock. The significance of this sort of cooperation is that it opens the door to a concentration of production without sweeping away the essential elements of family enterprise.

2. Imperfections in the peasant economy

So far we have considered the peasant economy only in an ideal situation, enabling a fairly simple division of the analysis into micro- and macroeconomic levels. At the microeconomic level, we have argued that the peasant family household, acting as both a producing and a consuming unit, drives under demographic pressure toward a much higher optimum in terms of work intensity (or man-hour input) than would be considered possible in classical market theory. At the macroeconomic level, we have argued that the peasant economy comprises several sectors, urban as well as rural, which because of their interdependent character are all exposed by a greater or lesser extent to the same tendency of highly intensive production. For a social historian, this model is of interest, first, because of the likelihood it presents of extreme social dislocation once this intensive optimum has been exceeded and, second, because it points to several internal remedies that can be adopted by a society willing to take up the challenge of "crisis" by altering its own demographic patterns, which were the original cause of the problem.

But in accepting these appealing aspects of the model, we must also recognize its drawbacks. In the case of the nineteenth-century French rural economy, some of its assumptions are amiss. Most of these imperfections will be dealt with in subsequent chapters; but one assumption is so obviously at odds with the French situation that it bears mention here – that is, that the peasant family is self-contained, that it employs no outside labor.

This brings us to a very tricky topic. The exact character and social position of the French agricultural laborer is hard to define. Full-time wage earners, of course, are a fairly clear-cut case. This group, because of its direct dependence on its employers, conformed to the classic idea of a rural proletariat; bounden, poor, and landless. As dependent labor, their rate of income was solely determined by outside sources. Their income, therefore, has to be viewed as objective and, as such, can have little to do with a subjective labor-consumer balance as previously described. It follows, then, that they should not be considered as part of a peasant economy, at least at the microeconomic level. Instead, they can be fitted rather neatly into the classical economic framework.

The difficulty of definition arises with the part-time wage earner, who might own land or at least have direct access to land that can be exploited *to his own personal advantage*. His wages are earned from work done for only a few days of the week and often for several different employers. Evidence, which will be presented in later chapters, suggests that even this type of work was confined to certain periods of the year (in both our regions at any rate). Furthermore, in several instances, one family might do labor for another on the basis of a mutual agreement that the second would return the same or similar labor services to the first family. This kind of society is clearly not going to be easily divided into owner–employers and the employed.

Can it then be described as a peasant economy? With certain qualifications, yes. There is no reason why a part-time wage should not be considered in the same way as the income derived from the part-time cottage industries. Both can be viewed as a means of intensifying the economy without seriously altering the mechanics of the labor–consumer balance.

Historians have already begun to accept the existence of a peasant economy in France. Emmanuel Le Roy Ladurie has argued that, in the eighteenth century, this kind of economy was characteristic of those regions where the land was directly in the hands of the peasantry.[26] This probably comprised more than half of France at the time. However, the rest of the countryside, being in the hands of large landowners, was, according to Le Roy Ladurie, part of a completely different type of economy, one that based its income on fiscal privileges, seigneurial dues, and rent. Like wages, we should view these revenues as objective earnings because their source is totally beyond the confines of a family unit, even though their value is determined as much by law and privilege as by market forces (thus creating additional difficulties for anyone attempting the classic economic approach). Le Roy Ladurie's position is that these two economies, the peasant and the domanial, coexisted in France before the Revolution with little sign of one encroaching upon the other. In this sense, the main qualification to be made in using this idea of peasant economy is based on physical whereabouts: the model is confined to areas where the land is in the direct possession of peasant families. Consequently, the peasant economy can be viewed as the definition of one pole of a dichotomized society.

But what of the small *fermiers* and *métayers* who rented and exploited large areas of the domain? or the full-time wage earners who lived within the peasants' territory? In the nineteenth century, the picture becomes increasingly complex.

There is obviously a question of degree involved here. We have to have a sense of just how far we can move away from an ideal situation before the analytical schema has to be rejected. This is not to say that "imperfections" in the real world are to be viewed entirely negatively, from the theoretical angle; the whole point of this chapter has been to pose questions, rather than to limit answers. The task is less one of defining an all-embracing, universal system than of finding the most suitable logic for describing an imperfect reality.

In the following chapters we shall be focusing on the rural population of two small regions spanning the river Loire. How can we best describe the imperfect peasant economies of these two regions?

Part II
Space

4 Relative space: town and country

The census enumerators of 1851 recorded a population of 155,100 and 405,010 for the Orléanais and the Nantais, respectively. Within the city limits of Orléans, there lived 47,493 inhabitants, whereas Nantes could proudly boast of 96,362. Beyond these two huddled centers, the population spread across the countryside in a pattern that is already somewhat familiar to us. In the Orléanais, the Loire Valley, with an average of 82 inhabitants/km², easily prevailed in terms of demographic density over the other subregions. At the same time, a very clear distinction could be seen between the relatively dense subregions of the Beauce and the Forêt d'Orléans (both averaging 32 inhabitants/km²) on the right bank of the Loire, and the infertile Sologne (with a meagre 18 inhabitants/km²) on the left. The Nantais was very much more thickly populated; the entire region, even with its city excluded, had almost twice as many inhabitants per square kilometer as the Orléanais. The Loire Valley and the crowded hillsides of Sèvre-et-Maine both had, on average, more than 100 persons per square kilometer, and even in the *bocage* country of the Nantais Plateau there were 55 inhabitants/km²; in that of Retz–Vendée, there were 74.

The contrasts between and within our two regions had been just as important during the Revolutionary epoch and were to be no less remarkable at the advent of World War I (see Table 4.1). So, whereas the Loire Valley was at all times the most populated part of the Orléanais, the Sologne was always the most deserted. In the Nantais, the Loire Valley and Sèvre-et-Maine consistently prevailed over the other two subregions. Furthermore, the Nantais, in general, was always more densely populated than the Orléanais.

These simple figures thus attest to a continuity in the basic pattern of human settlement in our two regions through the nineteenth century. The main characteristics of that pattern are what we will be concentrating on in the next three chapters: first, in terms of the relationship between the crowded urban centers and the more scattered populations of their hinterlands, second, in terms of a sampling of social groups actively encouraging association among these populations, and third, from the point of view of the regions as a whole – all of this is in the attempt to establish the main spatial divisions of society in the Orléanais and the Nantais.

I must point out here that I am not attempting to impose a form of

43

Table 4.1. *Average number of inhabitants per square kilometer by subregion, 1801, 1851, 1911*

Subregion	1801	1851	1911
Beauce	27.7 (7.9)	32.1 (6.4)	28.7 (6.2)
Sologne	12.6 (3.6)	17.7 (3.5)	24.7 (5.3)
Forêt	23.3 (6.5)	32.5 (6.4)	28.9 (6.1)
Valley	72.8 (23.7)	82.4 (18.8)	74.6 (18.4)
Orléanais	35.5 (41.7)	42.6 (35.2)	40.5 (36.1)
Plateau	46.4 (16.5)	54.5 (13.6)	50.0 (13.5)
Retz–Vendée	33.3 (12.9)	74.2 (20.2)	60.3 (17.8)
Sèvre-et-Maine	55.6 (10.6)	105.1 (14.0)	96.7 (13.9)
Valley	87.7 (18.3)	116.2 (17.0)	117.9 (18.7)
Nantais	51.0 (58.3)	80.9 (64.8)	73.6 (63.7)

Note: The figures in parentheses are percentages of the total population of the Orléanais and the Nantais combined. The communes of Nantes, Chantenay, and Doulon (Nantais) and Orléans have been excluded.
Sources: INSEE, Direction régionale de Nantes, *Populations par commune de 1801 à 1962* (Nantes, 1966); INSEE, Direction régionale d'Orléans, *Populations par commune de 1851 à 1962* (Orléans, 1966); *Annuaire du Loiret* (occasionally *Almanach*) (Orléans, An XI–1912).

geographical determinism on this study. In fact, the following pages will show how great the variation can be between populations with distinct attitudes and opportunities, even though placed in similar physical environments. Nonetheless, where one lives does imply what one is – and this could be the result of a haphazard grouping of activities unrelated to the physical environment itself. The point is that an analysis of the spatial divisions in each region should uncover the range of social facts that constitute the "imperfect peasant economy." What are its limits? What are its main sectors? These are the chief macroeconomic problems posed in the last chapter.

Let me emphasize that when I speak of continuity in these three chapters I do not mean timelessness.[1] Space can create an illusion of permanence – not an especially human trait. We all know of Macbeth's fatal conviction that Birnham wood could never march on Dunsinane hill. In no way can one isolate the human dimension of space from time; but we can address ourselves to the prevailing attitudes of a society toward space. In particular, we can focus on the manner in which one group perceived its neighbor, the type of exchange that passed between them, and the way this narrowed or broadened each group's view of its own potential for survival. We are, after all, interested in how a certain kind of society managed to perpetuate itself. Hence, *relative* space.

In this chapter we shall be looking at the main population centers and at the kind of opportunities for economic exchange they offered to themselves and to those next door. This will require consideration of the industrial activities in these centers, their market, and the communications system.

1. Riverside cities

In the mid-nineteenth century, one of the most effective ways of covering physical space was by steamboat. A traveler from Orléans to Nantes could choose one of several companies, the best known probably being Henri de Rochejaquelin's *Inexplosibles,* so formidably named because he guaranteed no burst boilers, a very real hazard in the earlier days of steam navigation. The craft were comfortable – Eugène Hatin, one of the 100,000 passengers who took the trip in 1843, described them as "mobile epicures."[2] They were also fast. A boat, leaving Orléans at 11:30 A.M., could be in Tours that same evening and, the following night, would dock at Nantes.[3] But, more extraordinary for the times was the slight draft of these vessels. The problem of building a fast, mechanically powered boat that could also be piloted over the Loire's perpetually changing sandbed had been challenging the imagination of engineers since the early 1820s. By the mid-1830s, the dockyards at Indret were launching steamboats with drafts of 18, 13, and 10 inches.[4] One such boat, piled with coal, weighed anchor at Orléans early in November 1837 and, in spite of the reportedly low waters, set sail for Nevers the following week; it displaced only six inches of water. As a journalist remarked at the time, "If it succeeds in getting there, the navigation problem of the Loire is resolved once and forever."[5]

That had been the whole point of the effort. It was a matter of tremendously grave concern during this age of technological innovation that the Loire should be proven not only a viable corridor for commercial and popular travel but also – a reflection, perhaps, of the current wave of material optimism – that it could be improved. The Loire had, for centuries, provided riches to its towns and an open market to the countryside, and there was absolutely no alternative way in which the continued welfare of the area could be conceived. Most specifically, technology had to be employed, not to change, but to preserve the roles of these two key centers of the Loire Country, Orléans and Nantes. Orléans should retain its historical character as a collecting point on the crossroads of southern and western traffic; Nantes should remain the major seaport that it always had been, sending and receiving goods to and from every corner of the world.

Nantes

For Eugène Hatin, on his arrival by boat at the Quai de la Fosse amid a "forest of masts," it must have seemed that wealth was still Nantes' ancient privilege. The city as he described it was "very well built, very well planned; several districts, including the Ile Feydeau, the Quartier Graslin, and Place Royale, can be compared with the best districts of the capital. The Quai de la Fosse, with its fine avenues and its handsome mansions, festooned with infinitely rich balconies, are especially admired by strangers." And he had no doubts about where all this richness came from: "it is to maritime commerce that this town owes all her splendor. Her ships part . . . with wines, spirits, honey, sugar, cloths and other materials of wool and silk."[6] Nor was this an isolated impression. Over 30 years later, the commercial activity of Nantes still stimulated the quill:

The port . . . offers at the moment the most animated spectacle. The quays are fringed with vessels and covered with merchandise continually being moved by a crowd of wagons and hundreds of dock hands to the town's warehouses and stores. It is a general congestion. On the docks, on the public roadway, even on the promenades, carriage and pedestrian traffic is being permanently held up. The warehouse has become insufficient to contain all the arriving goods, and the Chamber of Commerce has had to rent a number of stores in the districts neighboring the river.[7]

Although, at the surface, commerce appeared to flourish, Nantes' actual position as a major seaport was being seriously undermined. Nantes, France's first maritime city at the beginning of the eighteenth century, now found itself tottering behind practically every other main port of the nation. Table 4.2 gives a rough idea of just how low in relative terms the city had sunk. By 1875 Nantes had fallen to the ninth rank, a lower position than either of the inland river ports of Rouen and Paris.[8] It was trading in only 3.9 percent of all the commodities exchanged in France by way of boat and contributed less than 2 percent in the customs' proceeds. This was not at all a good record in the eyes of the policymakers at Nantes and had been, in fact, one of the major reasons why in the early 1850s the city had encouraged the development of Saint Nazaire, formerly a fishing village 70 kilometers downstream of Nantes, as an ocean port. But even with Saint Nazaire included into a sort of "Greater Nantes,"[9] the total tonnage of the two ports combined was only fifth in rank, or well under a third of the merchant tonnage that passed through Marseille's docks and less than two-thirds of the tonnage exchanged in either of Nantes' two major competitors for the Atlantic trade, Bordeaux and Le Havre. And the situation does not appear to have made much headway by 1913, when Nantes, in spite of lavish expenditures on a maritime canal and the improvement of the riverbed,[10] ranked tenth, with 109,000 metric tons, in order of warehouse storage. Nantes and

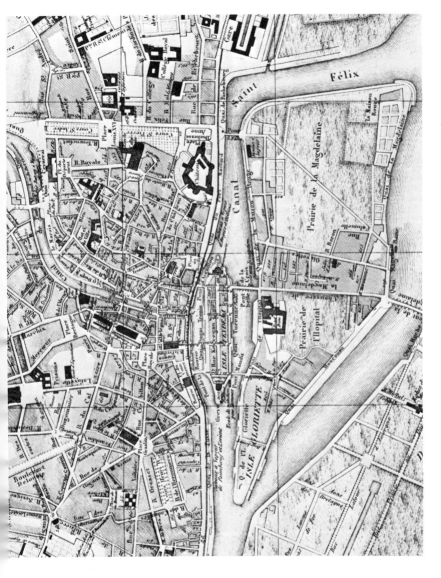

Figure 4.1. Nantes in the mid-nineteenth century. (By permission of Bibl. nat. Paris.)

Table 4.2. *Total metric tonnage of combined imports and exports in the major ports of France, 1833 and 1875 (in 000 metric tons)*

Port	1833	1875
Marseille	1,021	2,181
Bordeaux	501	1,131
Le Havre	687	1,019
Dunkirk		883
Rouen	324	496
Dieppe		423
Paris		328
Saint Nazaire		*325*
Nantes	*273*	*304*
Boulogne		291
Calais		205
Bayonne		90
Nice		41

Sources: For 1833, A. Guépin and E. Bonamy, *Nantes au XIXe siècle* (Nantes, 1835), p. 341; for 1875, Statistique générale de la France, *Annuaire Statistique* (Paris, 1878).

Saint Nazaire, combined, ranked only sixth, behind Marseille, Le Havre, Rouen, Bordeaux, and Toulon.[11]

For many a citizen of Nantes, the town's maritime business was not what it should have been. Their main grievance was governmental preference – the favors and prejudice that the administrators in Paris showed for Nantes' cutthroat rivals. Thus, the members of the city council of Nantes probably expressed a fairly widespread sentiment when they stated on 15 January 1853 that "past governments had granted everything to Le Havre: docks and rail. Their niggardliness toward us had always been extreme, and the struggle between Le Havre and us could never be equal."[12] Le Havre was the prized *bête noire*. "Nantes, more so than Le Havre, conducts a business that is rightfully her own," the council declared. "Today Le Havre's purely artificial prosperity tends to decrease in favor of Rennes, Dunkirk and, principally, Nantes."[13]

This was an idle hope. At that very moment, Le Havre was hoarding the profits earned from earlier trade concessions; concessions that gave it a permanent advantage over Nantes. The new transatlantic steamers were a case in point. In 1845, Nantes, although complaining that the preference "that belongs to her by right has been lively disputed by rival ports," fully admitted the unlikelihood of ever being conceded a line to the United States. But Nantes did expect, at the very least, to be granted the Brazil line.[14] Yet no sooner had this been confirmed – by laws of 1846 and 1847, than the frightful discovery was made that Le Havre, Bordeaux, and Marseille were acting *in concert* to deprive Nantes of even that meagre concession.[15] As a matter of fact, Nantes did manage to keep the line open, but not without continual attempts by Le Havre to have it closed.[16]

Le Havre, situated at the mouth of the Seine (a meandering river, which was extremely difficult to navigate by sail but which could be very effectively exploited by steam), obviously did have the favor of the capital. However, that definitely did not explain everything. In 1835, Ange Guépin and Eugène Bonamy, two medical doctors with a remarkable taste for writing, suggested that Nantes' decline was the result of a tendency of European trade to orient itself around the Mediterranean, "as before the discovery of the compass."[17] Although this hardly accounts for Bordeaux' or Le Havre's vitality, it might explain Marseille's marked hegemony. One can also argue that Nantes' previous strength had been legislated away in one very direct sense. On 4 February 1794, slavery was outlawed in all of France and its dependencies. Although Napoleon, by decree of 1802, reestablished the actual institution of slavery, the western ports of France do not appear to have ever again practiced the trade. For example, no mention of this can be found in the minutes of the parliamentary commission set up in 1840 to investigate the possible effects of abolition.[18]

But the most important cause for Nantes' lag was the fact that the major part of its commerce consisted of primary products. Nantes exported mules, dairy products, and grains to the French colonies; honey, potatoes, and other vegetables to North Africa; and wines, in quantities that varied with the harvest, to the European countries, especially Holland, Belgium, and Great Britain. The city imported sugar from the colonies; furs, cotton, phosphates, and guano from the Americas; and salted meat together with a whole host of agricultural products from the other European countries.[19] In a century when the secondary, or industrial, sector was contributing most of the country's economic growth, it is not surprising that Nantes, with its attention largely focused on trade in these primary products, began to fall rapidly behind.

From this rather dismal state of affairs, Nantes could take two courses of improvement: it could build up its secondary sector to be on an equal footing with the other French ports, or it could so develop its primary sector that the question of the city's commercial backwardness and poverty would never even arise – Eugène Hatin was probably not alone in noticing that the city was "surrounded by immense grasslands and fertile hillsides."[20]

At first inspection, Nantes does not appear to have had much of a taste for large-scale industry. In 1847, the average number of workers per establishment, taking every industry into account, was under 20. The median number was less than 10. Even when these figures are broken down by industry, nothing colossal is evident (see Table 4.3). Furthermore, most of the median estimates are doubtlessly too high. These statistics are based on a certain amount of grouped data; the original source, by combining several establishments, gives only 66 categories of industry, the largest being that of the cabinetmakers, which includes 225 establishments of 2,000 workers, or an average of 8.9 workers per establishment – a statistic that has obviously affected our calculation of the overall median.

Twenty years after this survey was made, the small size of Nantes' industrial establishments continued to be emphasized. A parliamentary inquiry of 1873 remarked that the generally good sanitary conditions found in the city were due to "the small number of large industries."[21] An even later regional report might have supplied the reason when it noted that "the talent of the worker at Nantes is particularly appreciated" and went on to cite the success of shipbuilding, a key industry, as being largely the result of the high-quality workmanship of the artisan metallurgists.[22] Artisanry is constantly being underscored as a central element in the city's industrial organization.[23] In the 1880s, Nantes became the "ville mère," or capital town, of a national association of *compagnons,* embracing, among other cities, Le Mans, Tours, Bordeaux, and Lyon.[24] Retailing was also generally done in small stores and boutiques. Thus, in spite of the competition of two large retail chains set up in the early days of the Third Republic[25] and the prolonged commercial crisis of the 1890s,[26] the average number of workers employed by the retail outlets at Nantes in 1912 was between 2 and 15.[27]

But all this should not conceal the existence of some significantly large establishments concentrated in three vital limbs of Nantes' industrial anatomy: naval and machine construction, the sugar refineries, and the preserved food industries. Table 4.3 indicates a higher average employment in these industries. To start with, by 1847, shipbuilding was no fledgling enterprise at Nantes; its origins can be traced back at least as far as the seventeenth century (see Chapter 2, Section 2). One result was that dockyards were scattered along both banks of the Loire, and this, together with the fact that much of the work was contracted out to small establishments, such as the metallurgists, explains why the figures recorded in Table 4.3 are somewhat lower than one might expect. Yet, the industry's total output was prodigious. In the 1830s, Nantes was launching an average of about 25 ships a year, all between 150 and 700 metric tons;[28] in the early 1890s, it was launching almost twice that number of ships *per annum.*[29]

During those 60-odd years, an enormous complex of naval yards, forges, and machine manufacture had developed at Indret, on the left bank of the Loire, just a little downstream of Nantes. The entire layout,

Table 4.3. *Breakdown of workers by industry in Nantes, ca. 1847*

Industry	Total establishments	Number of workers		
		Total	Mean	Median
Construction				
Naval	16	595	37.2	32.0
Machine	17	1,266	74.5	60.0
Building	3	22	7.3	4.0
Metalwork	32	516	16.1	9.2
Chemical industries				
(gas, oil, etc.)	2	23	11.5	11.5
Sugar refineries	9	558	62.0	42.9
Preserved food				
industries	13	535	41.2	39.6
Alcohol industries				
Vinegar	6	18	3.0	3.0
Other	12	22	1.8	1.0
Cereal industries				
(flour, biscuits, etc.)	9	193	21.4	6.0
Textile, leather, and				
clothing industries	146	4,126	28.3	10.0
Household industries				
(candles, brushes, etc.)	26	226	8.7	4.0
Other	453	5,768	12.7	8.9
Total	744	13,868	18.6	8.9

Note: This includes the suburbs of Doulon, Chantenay, and Basse-Indre in addition to the commune of Nantes.
Source: Ministre de l'Agriculture et du Commerce, *Statistique de la France* (Paris, 1850), vol. III.

the exclusive property of the state, could be considered an industrial city in its own right, with lodgings for its personnel, schools, a hospital, and several churches. The factory that manufactured the marine engines was the largest of its kind in France, hiring 2,000 men in the early 1870s. Across the river, at Basse-Indre, the Compagnie Langlois (founded in 1821) was reportedly smelting and rolling 35,000 kilograms of iron daily, to be used mainly by the shipbuilders.[30]

Thus, Nantes' old shipbuilding industry generated two important new affiliates, machine construction and iron; and all three, though heirs of the city's early commercial might, had now broken loose and, under their own momentum, had created a new source of wealth.[31] In this particular instance, it was as if Nantes were pressing for an entirely independent business that would cut ties not only with its deficient trading sector but also with the one natural resource that remained: shipbuilding at Nantes had nothing directly to do with agriculture.

However, this was certainly not the case for Nantes' two other major industries, preserved foods and sugar. Like shipbuilding, they both owed their origins to Nantes' former commercial glory. The curing of beef, ham, and bacon had developed in the seventeenth century out of the necessity to provide mariners with food that could keep. Sugar refining had arisen only a little later because Nantes' most accessible trading partners were the Caribbean islands. But unlike shipbuilding, neither stood aloof of the city's commercial sector. Nor did they ignore local agriculture. Commerce played an especially important role for the refineries because they continued to rely on the delivery of a high-quality cane sugar from overseas. In 1874, three-quarters of all the sugar processed came from the French colonies and most of the remainder was supplied by the British Caribbean islands.[32] In 1892, of the 38,000 metric tons of sugar that passed through the refineries, 89 percent was supplied by the French colonies, 3 percent by the British, and the final 8 percent was made up by homegrown sugar beet.[33] The main reason for the refineries' disdain for sugar beet was undoubtedly its inferior quality and the fact that most of it, anyway, had to be shipped from northern France. Sugar beet was not a major crop in any part of the Loire Country, largely because of soil conditions but also because other crops brought in a much better return.[34]

Local agriculture played a far more significant role as a provider of the materials that went into the refining process than it did in what was actually refined. White sugar, the highest of luxuries in the eighteenth century, became an increasingly important part of the popular diet in the nineteenth century. The only known means of producing it was to filter the raw product through calcinated animal remains. This resulted in two products: the first was the sugar itself; the second was a smelly, sticky, black substance, formerly regarded as totally useless. But in the early decades of the nineteenth century, this animal charcoal (or *noir animal*) was found to contain one extremely valuable element, nitrogen, which makes up the base of most fertilizers. So, not only did the Nantais supply the refineries with the means of processing sugar – livestock farming was a major activity in the *bocages* – but it also got a very practical product in return; 151 stores were selling fertilizer in the Nantais in 1853, and of them, 42 were supplying animal charcoal. That meant that, in an area that included only 96 communes, practically every corner was to some degree or another provided with the material.[35]

The preserved food industries were in an even closer liaison with agriculture. First, the interests of the livestock farmers in the *bocages* and those of the curing houses at Nantes were bound to coincide. More important, however, was the development of a novel technique in the preservation of foods that revolutionized the industry's organization. In France, tinned foods can be dated back to the first years of the Restoration, although they were not, at that date, too reliable – roughly one-quarter of them spoiled. In the 1820s, a M. Colin, resident of Nantes, succeeded in producing a tin can that assured the preservation of its contents. Henceforth, Nantes was to be the central producer of France's tinned foods. Colin's factory alone was turning out 100,000 tins annually in the 1830s. These included 36,000 tins of sardine and 15,000 of vegetables, of which 10,000 were prepared peas "that only needed to be reheated," ran a contemporary report, "to taste as good as the season." The rest was made up of ready-cooked meats. At the same factory, 80 bullock, 400 calves, and 200 pigs were slaughtered every year. "A bullock enters [the factory] at four o'clock in the morning and, thirty hours later, has been completely packed into reliable tins and expedited" – so it was said in the 1830s.[36] The old curing industry had already been showing signs of giving way to the new method,[37] and by the end of the century had all but disappeared.[38] We must add that the tinning industry was ideally situated at Nantes. Not only could it make use of a well-established distribution network (laid to serve the old commercial needs of the city), but it had a supply of fresh meat and vegetables right on its doorstep: whereas the *bocages* produced the livestock, the Loire Valley had an undeniable advantage in vegetables.

There were other large-scale industries, the flour steam mills at Richebourg and the textile factories at Chantenay being the most important. But none were an exception to the general pattern just described. In the nineteenth century, Nantes developed an industrial sector in spite of, and in many ways because of, its declining commercial position. Let us not oversimplify the picture. We cannot, as I said in the last chapter, assume that an entire urban population is geared to identical pursuits. The preceding account would, in fact, suggest not one Nantes, but several. Shipbuilding and its affiliate industries in the western part of the city formed a Nantes somewhat detached from the countryside and other sectors of the city. The food industries, scattered along the river banks, made up another Nantes, which had a number of important links with the hinterland.[39] In the northern and eastern quarters, we find yet another Nantes of artisans and small shopkeepers. And the situation, we shall see, was even more complicated than that.

The important thing to note at this juncture is that Nantes was not isolating itself. Nantes' industries did not become secluded boroughs in a marshland of idle commerce and agriculture. Far from it. Nantes, forever renovating the old trading house, had thrown its doors wide open.

Orléans

The decadence of Orléans' commerce and industry was the subject of a long lecture delivered to the city's Société Royale des Sciences, Arts et Belles-Lettres on 5 September 1828. The speaker, M. Sevin-Mareau, pointed out all Orléans' old strengths. This city used to gather, he said, merchandise into the heart of a kingdom that had no means of communicating directly with maritime ports. The latter, as a result, were chiefly occupied with colonial trade and the fitting out of their ships; they had neither the time nor the capital to be concerned with inland commerce. But, continued Sevin-Mareau,

> today a more prompt means of navigation . . . has led to another division of business. The maritime cities are no longer confined to external trade. Some houses have been set up there for the provision of inland consumers and have become our rivals. Thus, through their commercial travelers, Bordeaux and Lyon supply goods to departments found in the old provinces of Limousin, Berry, the Nivernais and Burgundy. Even Nantes, most detrimental to our contacts, supplies, by means of fast boats, the towns and villages bordering the Loire, and even some of our own city's retailers . . . Her overland expedition, such as to Paris and Rouen, have been favored in the region around Chartres and in Perche, which formerly addressed their demands exclusively to us.[40]

Orléans' chances of enjoying another century of prosperity had come up against two snags – the natural wiles of the river Loire and the presence of some very competitive neighbors. Throughout the nineteenth century, all efforts were put into overcoming both, but, like Nantes, this was done not by making a complete break with the past but by cussedly insisting upon what was felt to be the lasting qualities of the city's old strengths. Unlike Nantes, this obsession with the past, instead of bringing about novel activities, led Orléans down a path of prolonged depression.

A look at some of the reasoning behind the establishment and maintenance of Orléans' first general customs' warehouse will serve as an example. The city council held that the warehouse would be bound to attract commerce by the simple fact of its presence.[41] Sevin-Mareau put forward virtually the same idea: a warehouse would bring colonial goods and spices back into Orléans, first, by providing the retail merchants of the region with a ready supply of commodities and, second, by making speculative ventures more profitable.[42] But this was a largely circuitous argument. One swallow does not make a summer. Commercial centers require warehouses; but warehouses are the result, not the cause, of commerce. Paris, at this time, had been laying plans for a direct railway line to Nantes via Chartres, Tours, and Angers, bypassing Orléans by about 80 kilometers and thus threatening the small profit that might have been gained from the new warehouse. Orléans immediately objected that the plan ignored the significant role it could play as middleman at the head of both westward- and southward-going traffic if the rail were to pass through its city.[43] The diversion was agreed upon, but the results, as we shall shortly see, were the very opposite of those intended: the new rail obliterated whatever remained of the historic commercial crossroads

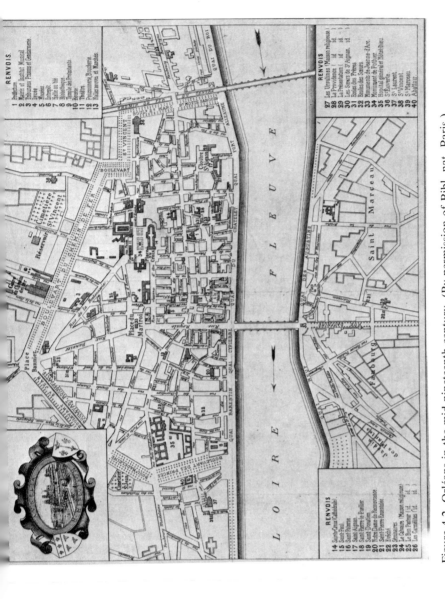

and, thus, the need for a warehouse. By the 1850s it was clear the warehouse's lure to trade was not working and the chamber of commerce, mindful of maintenance expenses, began moves for its demolition. This, however, provoked 60 wholesale merchants to send a petition, declaring, "No, Orléans' commerce is not decaying. Orléans is still and will always be an essentially commercial city; its [geographical] situation *wills it thus*" [my emphasis].[44] So the merchants kept their warehouse, money continued to be poured into its maintenance, and business continued to dwindle. The moral: warehouses do not outlive their usefulness.

There was, however, one feature of Orléans' past economic makeup that the nineteenth century did not see alter: its industries were still dominated by small-scale establishments. Table 4.4, from the same source as employed for Nantes, gives the breakdown of workers by industry in Orléans in the mid-nineteenth century.[45] Orléans had an average of 17.8 workers per establishment against Nantes' 18.2, but the median was only 2 as compared with 8.9 in Nantes (see Table 4.3). Again, as in the case of Nantes, averaging has undoubtedly caused the estimate of the overall median to be somewhat higher than it was in fact; out of a total of 116 establishments, the original source gives only 56 categories of industry.

Most striking, in terms of the comparison with Nantes, is the very low total number of industrial establishments at Orléans. There were, for example, only two establishments involved in metalwork, both manufacturers of tools, one hiring 80 workers, the other hiring 30. It's tempting to think of metalwork as part of Orléans' "large-scale industries" because there were only ten establishments – two in the household industries, seven in textiles and one in sugar – that employed more workers than either of these two. But their influence does not seem to have been that great. Metalwork gets very little attention in the contemporary literature. The only reference I found is in the previously mentioned merchant's petition to the chamber of commerce, in which it was held that "the metal industries have grown since the building of the rail"; but they were probably referring to two establishments set up in the 1840s outside Orléans, at Saint-Jean-de-Bray and Meung.[46]

Otherwise, Orléans secondary sector seems small, traditional, and confined to a very narrow range of occupations. The major industries were vinegar and textiles, both dating back at least as far as the sixteenth century and both largely controlled by artisanal associations. This was especially true of vinegar. Although the *Communauté des maîtres vinaigèriers* was officially abolished with the anticorporation laws of 1791, its rules on training and manufacture continued to be observed. Furthermore, association within the industry was preserved by a series of

Table 4.4. *Breakdown of workers by industry in Orléans, ca. 1847*

Industry	Total establishments	Number of workers Total	Mean	Median
Construction				
Naval	0	0	0.0	0.0
Machine	0	0	0.0	0.0
Building	8	33	4.1	5.0
Metalwork	2	110	55.0	55.0
Chemical industries				
(gas, oil, etc.)	4	29	7.3	1.0
Sugar refineries	1	30	30.0	30.0
Preserved food				
industries	0	0	0.0	0.0
Alcohol industries				
Vinegar	60	120	2.0	2.0
Other	4	12	3.0	2.0
Cereal industries				
(flour, biscuits, etc.)	0	0	0.0	0.0
Textile, leather, and				
clothing industries	21	1,412	67.2	16.0
Household industries				
(candles, brushes, etc.)	11	244	22.2	15.5
Other	5	74	14.8	6.0
Total	116	2,064	17.8	2.0

Note: This includes the whole commune of Orléans.
Source: Ministre de l'Agriculture et du Commerce, *Statistique de la France* (Paris, 1850), vol. III.

ritual meetings, the most important being the *fête patronale* celebrated since 1806 on the first Monday after Assumption Day (15 August).[47] In 1880, the vinegar producers again came into formal association to protect their traditional methods and interests from growing outside competition. According to Courtin-Rossignol, their president, the new association gave the industry cause for optimism: "Some good days are coming [for] our old Orléanais product whose reputation is still alive in France and in the whole world."[48]

The textile industries were subject to greater changes. Their origin lay in the rather curious business of woolen Turkish skullcaps, a boon in the eighteenth century when Orléans supplied customers in every part of the eastern Mediterranean. But in the nineteenth century, Austria entered the market and, because of the more favorable geographical situation, soon controlled it. Nevertheless, hatmaking seems to have held its own in Orléans and to have even developed into a fairly large-scale industry by the mid-nineteenth century. Contemporary accounts are somewhat contradictory on this. Guilbert's *Histoire des villes de la France,* published in 1845, indicates that the last manufacturer of oriental caps had already closed its doors.[49] If so, the practice might have been shortly reestablished. The merchants' petition of 1857 mentions the existence of "our *bonneteries* pour l'Orient." However, *bonneteries,* if today's acceptance of the term is anything to go by, should be taken to mean the hosiery business rather than hatmaking. According to the petition, two were "of the greatest importance."[50] The minister of agriculture's publication, used in Table 4.4, identifies four *bonneteries* in all, employing a total of 985 workers – one factory alone hired 750.

The same source lists 12 separate manufacturers of woolen blankets, engaging 209 workers. This was a growing new trade that was to overtake hatmaking in total output later in the century. The diarist Ardouin-Dumazet, on passing through Orléans in 1890, found that an entire district of the city was dedicated to the supply of blankets to the French army as well as to the Russians, Greeks, and Rumanians.[51] There are shades of Orléans' past Levantine trade in this odd eastern European market. Are we to suspect that the same artisans, deprived of a job in hatmaking, had turned their skills toward the weaving of blankets? If this were the case, it would be easy to conclude that textiles, like the vinegar industry, continued to carry the stamp of tradition, but did so, in this particular instance, by altering the nature of its product. What was the number and what was the history of those who attended the annual *fêtes patronales* of the blanket makers in the 1890s?[52] The pitiable wartime destruction of Loiret's archives renders a definite answer impossible.

We can be much more confident in ascribing a reason for the industry's survival. Its primary resource, wool, could be easily procured from the neighboring Beauce, where sheep raising, albeit vital to the subregion's economy, was practically the only known form of animal husbandry. The blanket makers, therefore, did not have to rely on Orléans' shaky commerce in order to continue production. The same can be said of the vinegar industry, which could find a ready supply of low-quality wines, especially white, in the Orléanais Loire Valley. A glance at Table 4.4 will confirm the same situation for most of the other industries listed. There had never been a shortage, in the Orléanais, of clay for the potteries or tallow for the candle factories, the two trades that largely constituted the household industries; the four beer distilleries were amply supplied with barley from the Beauce and the Valley; and the city's builders had only to rely on the quarries of the Forêt d'Orléans. It seems that the sole enterprises depending on outside supplies were four chemical businesses (the largest being a gas company with 25 employees) and a sugar refinery. But gas was a necessity for any town that wanted to have its streets lit at night. Which leaves the refinery. The prestigious

Sucres royaux were all that remained of an industry that could boast of 32 establishments in the 1790s and still possessed 14 in 1828.[53] However, a good name does not appear to have sufficed: sugar refining is notably absent from Adolphe Joanne's survey of Orléanais industries made in 1874,[54] and it receives no attention in Ardouin-Dumazet's journal of 1890. One presumes its disappearance.

So Orléans' industries, as a result of commercial stagnation, was forced not only to lay a stake in the immediate rural hinterland but also to make a complete break with commerce. It speaks of a much graver recessionary wave than that at Nantes, where *both* the hinterland and commerce were being exploited.

This heavy reliance on the hinterland gave Orléans a pervasive rural character. For example, Les Aydes, a suburb lying within the commune of Orléans, is described in 1869 as "an agglomeration of winegrowers, wine merchants, wholesale traders and landowners."[55] Vineyards were, in fact, so widespread in the commune that, even after the phylloxera crisis of the 1880s, they could be found in the suburbs of Saint-Marceau, Saint-Laurent, Madeleine, Saint-Jean, Saint-Vincent, Saint-Marc, Bourgogne, and Bannier – suburbs that were all within two kilometers of the city center. It is indicative of the importance of wine in the city's economy that every October or November, throughout the nineteenth century, the city council imposed a *ban des vendanges*, laying down the earliest date that the grapes could be harvested. Furthermore, it seems likely that some form of cultivation was practiced even among the poorest families of Orléans. Thus, one working-class family, analyzed in 1894 in Frédéric Le Play's journal, *La Réforme sociale,* was found to own 3½ "perches," or, presumably, about two square meters, of garden and to raise rabbits and chicken – the former living off grass plucked from the roadside – which gave the family some variety in their diet.[56]

It all makes a significant contrast to Nantes, whose workers, it was said, never practiced agriculture because "it is impossible . . . to work twelve hours a day and then busy oneself in cultivating."[57] Orléans had no "industrial city," like that of Indret, and there was nothing comparable to Nantes' urban sprawl; Orléans' built-up area was largely confined within the six boulevards that followed the lines of the city's ancient fortifications, the last remnants of which were removed only in 1850.[58]

There was something symbolic about the demolition of these old walls: a gesture to the countrymen without to collect their wares and enter. Wasn't it in 1841 that the citizens of Orléans saw erected before the Hôtel de Ville a statue of Jeanne d'Arc in prayer? And, with the walls destroyed, didn't a statue to the same peasant savior, now triumphant on horseback, go up in Place Martroi? The city of Orléans understood her plight well – it had only the country to turn to.

2. The communications network

The extent of exchange possible between populations depends, quite obviously, on the communications network. In this respect also, the Nantais had an advantage over the Orléanais. The official statistics, published regularly since the 1870s, indicate that four rivers and their tributaries, or between 80 and 100 kilometers of natural waterway, excluding the 80 kilometers of the Loire, were being used for commercial transit in the Nantais.[59] The Sèvre-Nantaise supplied Nantes with the wines and spirits of Sèvre-et-Maine; boats carried fodder from the Loire Valley up the Erdre to the Nantais Plateau and returned to Nantes with dairy and other animal products; and the Bourgogne together with the Achenau performed the same sort of service for Retz–Vendée. Around the turn of this century, a number of these waterways were allowed to clog with silt, but, even then, they were still quite widely used. This is what a roving reporter of one of the local newspapers had to say to his readers after arriving at the port of Saint-Même on the tiny river Tenu in April 1903:

[There were] two boats, between 130 and 140 tons, at the quays, the *Navarin* and the *Château-Renault* . . . While sauntering about the quays, I met a young ship's boy from the *Navarin,* dressed in blue naval smocks. I approached him and said, there's still boating at Saint-Même? "Yes, monsieur," he replied politely, "but only in the winter . . ., in the summer we don't have enough water and have to stop at Port-Saint-Père."

The reporter was at once introduced to the boy's boss.

After emptying an old bottle of a local Saumurois wine to loosen up his tongue, my sailor told me about his problems. "In the old days, monsieur, we came to Saint-Même much more often, we had water at all seasons. There were at Saint-Même ten, twelve, fifteen boats from the Brandais up to the stream, le Prieuré. Today there're only two or three of us mariners, always the same ones – we've kept the old faithful customers who have a horror for the railways. If the river bed were dredged, this activity would pick up. I'm one of the regulars at the port. Winter: lime, sand, wool, coal. Summer: hay from the lower Loire islands at Nantes. . . . The Tenu is unknown in high places, but it exists; many canals don't have its tonnage; fifteen thousand tonnes a year on the Achenau and its tributaries, the Tenu included.[60] Ah! monsieur, if you could see the port of Saint-Même in the months of February or March! Long queues of wagons, of all sorts, wait their turn to fill up with lime, with sand. Where do all these wagons come from? From La Maine, Touvois, Paulx, Saint-Etienne [-de-Mer-Morte], Falleron, Machecoul, Bois-de-Coué, Bonin, Fresnay, Saint-Cyr, Bourgneuf."[61]

"The Tenu is unknown in high places, but it exists." There must have been many like it.

Not so in the Orléanais. The limestone plateau of the Beauce had no surface streams at all and the stagnant waters that had formed on the impervious clays of the Sologne, left alone, could scarcely have served the needs of boat traffic. The only navigable natural waterway in the Orléanais besides the Loire was the Loiret, which emerged from its underground course just a little south of Orléans and flowed about three or four kilometers before joining with the main river. But the Loiret was used more as a river harbor than as a means of communication. That left the 75 kilometers of the Loire. The navigation hazards on this section of the river were graver than in the Nantais. Sand, carried straight down from the Massif Central, piled up at the bend in the river at Orléans. There were also some unpredictably strong currents. In May 1836, a steamboat laid on at Orléans to carry passengers to the inauguration of a bridge at Sully, 50 kilometers upstream, set sail at 8 A.M. with plans to reach Sully by midday. But, failing to get even halfway by 2 P.M., the captain was forced to put in at Jargeau "to satisfy the desires of wanting stomachs," and then return to Orléans.[62] From August to October, every year, the Loire was closed to all but the lightest traffic, owing to low waters. In the winter, ice became a particularly severe problem – ice in a river practically always forms in the same spot and Orléans happened to be one of those spots.[63] During the hard winter of 1835–6, both banks of the Loire were lined with trapped craft that had failed to make it to the more protected waters of the Loiret.[64]

The Orléanais was, therefore, especially dependent on the establishment and maintenance of man-made routes of communication. The region already had roads, some of which dated back to the Roman Empire and beyond, and in the nineteenth century, it was really just a question of their improvement and upkeep. Both banks of the Loire were paralleled by roads. A major thoroughfare from Paris to Orléans ran via the Beauce, entering the Orléanais at Artenay and then cutting through the western limits of the Forêt d'Orléans at Cercottes. One road leading to Vierzon and Bourges, though hardly the pride of the land, even passed through La Ferté-Saint-Aubin in the Sologne. This network was improved by a series of laws passed during the Restoration and the July Monarchy. But these laws placed a heavy burden on the village communes (labor, horses, bullock, and carts were demanded of the residents) and were not specifically favorable to the Orléanais (they were applied to all of France). Some roads, in fact, actually deteriorated. Complaints of the declining of roads in the communes of Patay, Saint-Péravy, and Coinces, all in the Beauce, were reported to the *Journal du Loiret* in 1832.[65] The parliamentary report of 1848 observed that Jouy-le-Potier, a poor village in the Sologne, completely lacked the means of maintaining the two major roads that crossed the commune.[66]

Again, the situation seems to have been generally better in the Nantais. "Numerous *Routes royales* and *départementales,* as well as strategic roads, cut across [the department's] surface tying the principal centers of population," wrote an agricultural report in 1843.[67] The roads were originally built for military reasons (a consequence of the Vendée Wars). However, Drs. Guépin and Bonamy, writing in 1835, evidently felt these were not enough:

This part of the West, which extends from Nantes to Parthenay and beyond, under the name of Bocage, still does not belong to our epoch. It is a country to be conquered by the power of civilization. Since 1810, our peasants have still continued to live in isolation, as before '89, under the influence of the presbytery and chateau. . . . With easy transport of products in the Vendée, there would be new channels of trade, leading to commerce and industries hitherto unknown. Industry would appeal in the midst of our countryside, to the friends of peace and partisans of liberty . . .; commerce would bring our peasants frequently into the towns where they would meet people more enlightened than themselves. . . . Such was the opinion of Napoléon when he laid out roads in the Vendée . . . But these roads, and even those that have since been laid, do not satisfy all needs. High transportation costs on our major roads considerably reduce their utility. . . . Canals and railways are thereby absolutely necessary if one is going to bring commerce into this part of the West.[68]

There is a flaunting of urban prejudices here, but the good doctors were not without their reason. (Three years before, the Vendéens had once again taken up arms.[69]) Nevertheless, these remarks do place an emphasis on an urban, even national, initiative in the laying of a transport network, which raises some serious questions about the kind of benefits that could be derived by the countryside. The aim expressed here was one-sided: to carry industry (Nantes' industry?) into the countryside; to "bring our peasants frequently into the towns where they would meet people more enlightened than themselves"; to spread, in a word, the kind of industrial economy that we have already described as developing in Nantes throughout its hinterland. But Nantes' industries lay on two foundations, one of which was its hinterland. So was it Nantes' intention, and would it even have been possible, to eradicate a rural tradition without causing a general dislocation of its own internal economy? The risks would be enormous: Nantes' sugar and preserved food industries, not to mention many of the city's smaller industries, depended on the welfare of the rural economy.

The risks would have been even greater for Orléans, where the countryside made up practically the sole base of its industries. All the same, when it came to actually developing routes of communication, the interests of the countryside do not seem to have overly concerned either Orléans or Nantes. It was the memory of the past, rather than the reality of the present, that obsessed both cities. We thus find that the two greatest communications projects of the century, the canal and the rail, were treated, first and foremost, as a means of reestablishing the cities' old roles in international trade and not directly as a means of serving the industries that were developing at that time.

The ill-fated *Canal latéral à la Loire* is a case in point. The projected 350-kilometer waterway remains one of the most ambitious navigational schemes in French history. It was initiated by a private citizen of Orléans, Laisne de Villevêque,[70] who, in the late 1820s, had conducted, largely at his own expense, a survey of the entire stretch of the Loire between Orléans and Nantes. With the studies completed in 1829, the struggle began to get the project authorized by the government. There was a great deal of delay because, Orléans and Nantes claimed, the government felt its designs for the Seine as the capital's major channel of trade threatened. As the *Journal du Loiret* had earlier remarked, " Orléans would be to Nantes and Bordeaux what Rouen is to Le Havre. . . . Orléans will rediscover its old prosperity."[71] Finally, on 17 June 1836, de Villevêque was authorized, "at his cost, risks and peril," to go ahead. The canal was to be built in three sections – the stretch from Angers to Nantes was not included – and work had to begin within three years for the concession to remain in effect. The entire project had to be completed by 1850.[72] Nantes expressed relief at the thought that this new opening to the Loire Valley would revive its waning commerce and began to push the government to also authorize the final stretch;[73] Orléans must have felt one step closer to realizing an ambition expressed two years earlier of "becoming the indispensable warehouse of more than one-third of France, and of even Switzerland and Germany."[74]

The actual country on the Loire's right bank through which the canal was supposed to be dug received very little attention. In the autumn of 1829, Lorin de Chaffin, an influential landowner at Beaugency, claimed that the inhabitants had not even been consulted and that, if they were, the results would not be all that favorable because

one would be forced to leave a certain extent of land between the canal and the Loire. I would like to ask MM. *les entrepreneurs* [i.e., contractors] what they intend to do with this land, and if they are going to be able to persuade a proprietor to keep his vines, meadows or his enclaved woodlands within the space of an inappreciable island.

He concluded that they would not and that, instead of threatening the livelihood of thousands, they should dig their canal in the Sologne – a very practical suggestion for the improvement of this miserable land, but hardly one that could serve commerce.[75] A little over four months later, an anonymous letter was sent to the *Journal du Loiret* complaining that workers on the *Canal de l'Essonne,* which was supposed to eventually join up with the *Canal latéral,*

staked out a considerable stretch of land between the Loire and the forest . . . cutting down hedges in full sap, trampling wheat and other sown corn crops, and knocking off vine buds with their frequent coming and going – all this without having forewarned any of the owners, not even those whose properties were surrounded by walls and high hedges.[76]

It was, therefore, perhaps a relief for the countryside's inhabitants that the project was never actually executed. Although interest for it lingered,[77] not a spade had been put to the soil by 1850, the supposed completion date; Orléans and Nantes had by that time turned most of their attention to the possibilities of rail, though not, in any sense, with the same degree of enthusiasm. Orléans' attitude was strictly determined by its own port, and it could see no future in a line that would divert the flow to other destinations. The railway, from this point of view, was to complement existing patterns of distribution, not to revolutionize them. Orléans therefore opposed the Paris plan to make the line to Nantes pass through Chartres rather than Orléans on the grounds that "the commercial relations between Nantes and Orléans, to which this enterprise ought to give new impulse, fix imperatively at Orléans one of the capital points of the route,"[78] and likewise rejoiced when the chamber of deputies finally voted in Orléans' favor: "The vote on this rail means the salvation of Orléans, which, without it, was falling into the state of a village and which, thanks to it, is going to again take up her rank as a city, allotted to her by her magnificent position."[79] For a brief period after the opening of the Paris–Orléans stretch, this is precisely what happened. The quays of Orléans became overcrowded with merchant shipping; the number of steamboat companies expanded; and the warehouse was, for the only time in its history, overflowing. But already in June 1843, less than two months after the rail's inauguration, remarks were being made about "the harm that will be brought to Orléans' commerce once the rail to Tours is established, once merchandise is transported directly from Paris to Tours."[80] There was no celebrating in Orléans in 1846 when that line was opened.

The railway at Nantes, on the other hand, was always a welcome innovation. Even when the main preoccupation was the *Canal latéral,* Nantes was insisting that a rail should be built on the strip of land dividing the canal from the river in order to carry light, expensive goods.[81] Yet the city had to wait another 20 years before the first locomotive steamed into the Gare des Mauves from Paris, during which time, Nantes complained, the Channel ports were getting all the advantages of an earlier rail outlet.[82] Nantes had no reason to sport the same fears as Orléans: the rail was built for it; it was, effectively, at the end of the line. There was nothing to suggest despair when an extension of Saint Nazaire was considered a necessary partner once ocean-going vessels had grown to a size that made the waters at Nantes unnavigable. The rail was, therefore, a complement to Nantes' commercial interests in a much fuller sense than at Orléans where, once the Paris–Nantes line had been entirely laid, there was not even the need to unload goods.[83]

Our knowledge of the countryside's reaction to all this rail construction is again marred by a lack of hard evidence. There are some indications that the initial response was negative. Obviously, in the Nantais, some of the old-time river haulers, such as the one whose interview we cited earlier, and those who worked part-time in water transport must have felt that their livelihoods were threatened. In the Orléanais, we find evidence of resentment among the neighboring populations of the once well traveled roadways paralleling the Loire. "Three communes," ran a report from the canton of Cléry in 1848,

are crossed by a road upon which there are situated inns, especially at Cléry, where many wagoners would lodge, together with a large quantity of oxen. This road is now deserted; the innkeepers, the wheelrights and the farriers, particularly, followed by the butchers, bakers and other merchants have seen their trade and sales decline in a terrible manner. The hay of the natural grasslands, forming one of the principal products of the country, was once sought after by the postmasters and innkeepers on the Paris road. . . . [One is] obliged to recognize that the establishment of the railway can and must have caused this decay. Sieur Bondu, innkeeper at Cléry, insists that the rails be asked no longer to transport merchandise and livestock.[84]

But the transport by rail of merchandise and livestock could be equally advantageous to those areas of the countryside where there were no jobs to be lost. Some residents of the Sologne, for example, became especially critical of Orléans' deliberate obstruction to further rail construction in the 1840s:

Orléans regards the extension of the railway across the Loire as being unfavorable for her. She would have liked to have remained at the head of a line, collecting from south, east and west all consignments by land and the Loire. But a rail extended to Vierzon will snatch all the overland southern traffic away from her. . . . The Sologne, through which this railway will have to pass, has realized that the line was not designed for her; [but] lucky, in some sense, to find her desert separating the rich provinces of Berry and the Orléanais, she has now the chance to profit from it. . . . If she asks for support from Orléans, this town replies that she does not favor the prospect. If she turns to Berry, this province replies that the destination of the rail is all that counts and that the actual route it takes is of little consequence. The route, on the contrary, means everything to the Sologne; but who will speak on behalf of this country? Who should take care of her interests? . . . Signed: A Solognot.[85]

The Vierzon line was, in fact, to open to traffic even before the Orleáns–Tours line had been completed.[86] By the end of the Second Em-

pire, nearly 400 kilometers of track had been laid in the department of
Loiret, cutting through every subregion that surrounded Orléans. As a
result, the Beauce had found new outlets for her cereals,[87] and some
noticeable improvements had been made in the territories of the Sologne
that neighbored the rail.[88] But the very scarcity of documents conveying
specific demands by the countryside for more rail points out that this network should not be attributed to local initiative – all the more so, when
one considers the evidence of Orléans' lukewarm attitude toward construction. Railways in the Orléanais were built because of the region's
proximity to Paris. All the lines were classified in the official statistics as
rails "of national interest"; even as late as 1914, no rail in the department
of Loiret was reported as being "of local interest." All routes lead to
Paris, and the Orléanais, being so close, could not avoid having a few of
them pass through its territory.

This is largely why, at the beginning of the Third Republic – by which
time most of France's national network had been laid – Loiret had such a
marked superiority over Loire-Inférieure in total rail outlay. Adolphe
Joanne attributes 407 kilometers of rail to Loiret in 1873, whereas Loire-
Inférieure, a department of approximately the same area, is mentioned
as having only 204.[89] But in the 40 years that followed, when the main efforts of rail builders were directed toward regional connections, Loire-
Inférieure very quickly got the upper hand (Table 4.5). In 1902, Loire-
Inférieure had over 700 kilometers of rail against Loiret's 592; by the outbreak of World War I, Loire-Inférieure's total outlay had grown to 790
kilometers, or one-third as much as that of Loiret, whose figures were
virtually unchanged. Of those 790 kilometers, Loire-Inférieure had 117
classified as being of local interest; Loiret, as we have already said, had
none. It seems, in general, that the Nantais had better systems of local
communication than the Orléanais, both in terms of what nature had
supplied and in terms of what was built in the nineteenth century. It had
natural waterways, which the Orléanais lacked; for largely political
reasons, it had gained a network of first-class roads; its many rivers had
reduced the dependence on canals, so there was less threat by the switch
in interest to rail; and it benefited from a city that bore no prejudice
toward the rail, which was probably one of the major reasons why the
local lines came into being. At the same time, there is no conclusive
evidence, in either region, to show that the countryside had contributed
in any significant way toward the development of this communications
network, and there is even some evidence that it did the exact opposite.
One must therefore assume, for the nineteenth century at any rate, that
the means of transport, albeit vital to the rural economy, was imposed
from the outside, either by the commercial interests of the cities or by a
predetermined national policy.

Table 4.5. *Kilometers of rail, Loiret and Loire-Inférieure, 1879–1912*

Year	Rail in Loiret			Rail in Loire-Inférieure			% more rail in Loire-Inférieure than Loiret
	National interest	Local interest	Total	National interest	Local interest	Total	
1879	474	0	474	409	0	409	−14
1884	573	0	573	473	0	473	−17
1888	581	0	581	599	0	599	3
1893	555	0	555	599	44	643	16
1898	555	0	555	614	44	658	19
1902	575	0	575	643	74	717	25
1907	592	0	592	643	108	751	27
1912	591	0	591	673	117	790	34

Source: Statistique générale de la France, *Annuaire statistique* (Paris, 1880–1913).

3. Markets and fairs

Markets and fairs could not be established at whim. In both the Orléanais and the Nantais, their place and time had to be authorized at several levels of administrative bureaucracy in the hope of giving the departmental capitals effective control. For example, in 1861, the general council of the department of Loiret passed a law granting itself the power to establish, suppress, or change the dates of fairs and markets within the department, although to do so it had to first receive a formal request from the village council concerned and then consult the city council of Orléans. The opinion of these last two bodies had to be accompanied with precise information on the population of the commune, the population of the neighboring communes, the nature and quantity of products to be marketed, and the state of the fairs and markets that already existed within a radius of 10 to 15 kilometers. The neighboring communes had also to be consulted.[90] The deliberations of municipal councils indicate that similar laws, of varying severity, existed in the Orléanais and the Nantais for most of the century.[91]

Clearly, the most important marketing in the two regions occurred in their capitals, even if we take into account the bias that a reading of the city council deliberations will obviously create. In Orléans, there seems to have been a large number of markets scattered around the outskirts of the city, especially westward of the faubourg Bannier or crowded into two small districts north and south of the cathedral in the city center. Most of these markets traded in vegetables, fruits, poultry, and other small livestock.[92] The exchange of large livestock (cattle, sheep, pigs, etc.) was generally confined to the fairs, which were held only once a year.[93] Apparently, by the second half of the century, if we are to judge by the number of complaints coming before the council, all these facilities, fairs and markets included, were not sufficient for the livestock raisers in the outlying regions. In the 1870s, the city council therefore authorized another regular livestock market, but either for lack of publicity or because the complaints had been exaggerated, the market failed to attract the animals.[94]

There are far fewer references to markets and fairs in the deliberations of the city council at Nantes. One reason for this could be the fact that the effective limits of the city fell outside the actual commune of Nantes and thus outside the council's jurisdiction. If the same geographical pattern existed at Nantes as at Orléans, many markets would therefore not be of immediate concern to the council. However, one does not even find a marketing district in the town center, or at least anything quite as remarkable as the two in Orléans. Makeshift stalls were always to be found at Place du Bouffay and there were stands to be found on the right bank of the Erdre, downstream of Pont Morand (today all filled in to form the boulevard des Cinquante Otages). There were two important fairs, one held twice a year at Place Bretagne, and another held several times a year at Place Viarme. Orieux and Vincent, writing in the 1890s, say that the fair at Place Viarme was held 15 times a year, which suggests that the fair was playing as much a role as the market at Nantes.[95]

This is significant. Markets were held on a regular basis throughout the year, and it is only logical to assume that they brought in people from the countryside regularly, throughout the year. Fairs, on the other hand, were held only during specified periods within the year and therefore did not give countrymen reason to make the trip to town as frequently. Markets were largely limited to the exchange of commodities. Fairs involved a good deal more. They were a news forum and they were a meeting place, a place of reaffirming friendships and ties of kinship. They were a pleasure ground and, for youth in particular, a place of rivalry and hobnobbing. Small wonder some have argued that fairs were, as institutions, the most effective guardians of peasant customs.[96] From the city's point of view, Nantes, being less dependent on its hinterland, did not need as many regular markets as Orléans. From the country's point of view, the seasonal fair was an "event."

This is something classical economic theory cannot explain. It bewildered administrators of the day. Nantes and Orléans, like most other French cities in the nineteenth century, made several attempts to centralize the distribution of agricultural products. For instance, in 1829, Nantes established a public abattoir and outlawed private slaughtering and tallow manufacture.[97] All this achieved was an enormous growth in the slaughtering of animals in the countryside before delivery to Nantes. By 1893, a member of the city council was reporting that 89 percent of all meat consumed in Nantes was slaughtered outside the commune.[98] Orléans acquired an abattoir 10 years earlier than Nantes, and it had approximately the same effect. At about the same time, construction was started on a *halle au blé*, or covered wheat market, with the intention of bringing all the grain supplied from the Beauce to a single spot. "We cannot hide from the fact," argued the *halle*'s advocates,

that for several reasons a distance exists between us and the cultivators of the Beauce . . . [But] if we provided them with a building that would protect them and their wheat from the weather [and] that would permit a more thorough surveillance . . . thus giving them a security and an easy means of making sales, then it is certain that the prosperity of Orléans' market would only grow and the city's revenue would increase.[99]

During the 30 years that followed, activity in grains does appear to have been given a new impetus – there was always a large section in the city's budget devoted to receipts gained thereby. But in the second half of the century, direct references to the *halle* became increasingly rare and the brief remarks that were made followed the same line; business was not at its former level.

The progress made in transportation since the Second Empire obviously shared part of the blame for the cities' lack of success. An abattoir or a *halle au blé* was no longer a necessity once agricultural products could be speedily dispatched to their destination, and these establishments suffered the same sort of demise as Orléans' warehouse. But that is not what was on the minds of the council members. Instead, they became obsessed with the growing number of markets and fairs in the countryside. There had always been a certain number of them. In the Nantais, the most important were at Clisson and Ancenis; in the Orléanais, they were to be found at Beaugency, Jargeau, and, in the Beauce, at Patay, and Artenay. But after about 1840, there seems to have been an increase in the number of small communes demanding either the establishment of a market (or fair) or the extension of what they already had. This was perhaps less the case in the Nantais where the city council usually gave a favorable recommendation for the demands, except where they directly conflicted with Nantes' own interests (such as when market dates coincided).[100] In the Orléanais, these demands came much more frequently before the city council, whose opinion, influenced by a constant feeling that there were too many markets and fairs in the region, was more likely to be negative. Thus, in July 1856, the council recommended that a weekly market should not be established at Chevilly as requested because it believed

that the exaggerated number of fairs and markets is one of the principal causes of depression in each one of them; that the spread of communications . . . makes local meetings less and less useful . . .; that cultivators are wasting their time and increasing their expenditures, without any compensation, by going too frequently to markets . . .; [and] that the village of Chevilly is surrounded, within a radius of 4 or 5 leagues [16 to 20 kilometers], by communes that have at least one market every day of the week.[101]

In the first half of the century, attempts at centralization were further aggravated by heavy taxes imposed on all products brought into cities. Consider, as an example, the following petition addressed to both chambers of the national government in 1829 by a group of winegrowers, merchants, and vinegar manufacturers from the arrondissement of Orléans:

Orléans, practically ruined by the feebleness of her commerce in colonial goods, by the reduction of her refineries, by the abandonment of most of her factories, ought to at least find in the product of the many vineyards bordering the Loire a compensation for her losses, a source of prosperity. [However,] all too often she finds in them a new cause for misfortune and suffering. . . . Taxes collected on entering towns above certain population size are imposed not in proportion to the taxpayer's fortune but according to where he lives. [The taxes] are in no way related to the value of the commodities upon which they are imposed: a person producing 100 hectoliters of wine at three francs pays one hundred times as much in taxation as a person producing a hectoliter of wine at 300 francs.[102]

But the tax reforms of the Second Republic largely stifled these complaints. Taxation could only have been a secondary factor in the disruption of the cities' centralizing schemes, which clearly received their most serious challenge in the second half of the century. More important was what was going on in the countryside itself. Nantes, by resting its industries more heavily on supplies from the countryside, and Orléans, by developing an almost total reliance on the hinterland, had created new opportunities for the two regions. As communications improved, these economies began to develop their own momentum, which urban administrators could not, or would not, understand. The number of small properties increased, production intensified, and the demands for more local markets grew louder. It seemed economically so inane.

4. Several Nantes; one Orléans

At the outset of this chapter, I noted that we would be looking for basic patterns in the social space of the Orléanais and the Nantais. What has so far emerged? We have numerous pointers. Let me summarize those I consider most important. One of the issues felt in all the major cities of the Loire Country throughout the nineteenth century was the river's declining hold on national and international commerce. This affected the way the region as a whole, and in its parts, regarded the world beyond. We have concentrated on the responses of Orléans and Nantes, and have discovered some important differences. Most notably, Nantes developed a major industrial sector, whereas Orléans did not. At the same time Nantes, like Orléans, strengthened its ties with the countryside. So Nantes found itself playing the dual role of international industrialist and rural marketer. Orléans was almost solely devoted to the latter – even where there was industry, it was totally reliant on local resources. Nantes' activities went in so many directions that it is impossible to think of it as a single town. Orléans, though its inhabitants followed many different trades, seems to have had but one goal: to extract from the country what it could to reestablish a former prestige.

We have to be careful with the words "become" and "develop," "former" and "latter." Despite enormous change, when we compare the two towns in 1914 with the two towns of 1800, we find this geographical distinction holds true. Nantes had its hinterland, but it also had an international clientele. Orléans was more limited. This was reflected in its obscurantist attitude toward communication improvements. It also had an effect on regional marketing arrangements: the Orléanais markets were more frequent, but the Nantais fairs were more permissive.

5　The connectors

Now that we have an idea of the differing regional potentialities for exchange, we can start to look at the actual processes by which exchange was accomplished. Here is the key to the social structure of the two regions. As I pointed out in Chapter 3, the survival of the household as a unit of production – the major feature of a peasant economy – is tied to a mode of exchange that allows the household to choose from a definite range of alternative means of self-exploitation. An acquaintance with the mode of exchange in the Orléanais and the Nantais should, therefore, enable us to gauge the possibilities and strengths of a peasant economy within these two regions. But, as was also pointed out in Chapter 3, we have to go beyond the mechanics of the market, beyond the classical economic model, if the mode of exchange is to be used as a reliable signpost to social structure. Exchange, Jean Duvignaud reminds us, is a global activity:

Systems of exchange could take diverse forms, not only in archaic societies, but also in historic and contemporary societies. Not in the rather naive form that Mauss gives (the distribution of wealth by way of social insurances, etc., . . .) but as a global reality in collective life and covering the totality of our modes of life.[1]

Marcel Mauss, by regarding exchange in archaic society as a system of gifts and countergifts, had opened ethnologists' eyes to religion and ethics as equal determinants of social structure. Claude Lévi-Strauss, more than anybody else, has widened this vista to include, among other subjects, cooking, table manners, and art. The revival of interest, in the 1950s, in Fernand Saussure's works on linguistics led to the interpretation of language as yet another part of the total system of exchange. In fact, language has become, for some, the principal object of investigation. The view that all "objects" exchanged – whether material goods, abstract gestures, or even human beings themselves (such as in marriage) – are linguistic symbols that, once deciphered, can open the way to understanding social structure, has probably been the single most important contribution that anthropology has made to the social sciences in the last 30-odd years.

In history, this is still a novel approach, and it can be contrasted with the more traditional anthropological model that limits the idea of exchange to the workings of the market. This is not to say that everything but commercial transactions are excluded from the model; many different forms of exchange are often considered, but their operation is described, explicitly or not, as analogies to market action. We can thus find ourselves talking about such odd phenomena as "a market of ideas," "a market of religions," *ad infinitum*. The immediate result of this sort of approach (and it stands as the hallmark of the market mentality) is a narrowing of the numbers considered as participants in exchange and the classification of whatever society is under study as a strictly linear group hierarchy with those most involved in exchange (or the "market") at the top and those least involved, or not involved at all, at the bottom. Redfield's "mediator" class, playing a role in both national society and the local community, is one widely used example of this. Here, the idea is pinned to a faith in not just a hierarchy of society but also a hierarchy of space with its highest position reserved for the urban settlements. Contact between the urban settlements and the local rural communities, lower down the scale, is made possible only through the dual role inferred upon this very specific class.[2]

It should be clear by now that one of the major concerns of this study has been to avoid such rigid compartmentalization. We are seeking a definition of the structure of the society and economy, within our two regions, as a whole, not as a succession of parts. Our attitude toward exchange is therefore more closely related to the first approach rather than the second: exchange will be regarded as a universal phenomenom that assumes several different forms, some standing out more clearly than others, but all being of equal importance. I shall call those who participate in this exchange "connectors."

In effect, all members of a given society are connectors, and the transformation of the exchange activity of any one of them will imply a transformation of the others. But in history, our records are limited to the broad range of activities of a few or to a very specific activity of the many. Is it not these records, rather than the society, that led historians to restrict their view of exchange activity between "community" and "nation" to a select elite? Those who stand out in the records are the large landholders, the propagators of religion, and the educators. They are the visible connectors. Their activities are pointers to the action of society at large, and because of the abundance of materials on them, they make a good subject with which to begin any study on rural society. But they are not an end in themselves. In Chapter 6, I shall show how this same exchange activity is to be found in the whole of society, defining its structure and giving it that special character we identify with the "imperfect peasant economy."

1. Connectors on the land

On a Sunday morning in July 1875, a religious service was held in the small country church at Mareau-aux-Prés, a village on the left bank of the Loire, 10 kilometers west of Orléans. It was to mark the beginning of an agricultural show that had been held annually by the *Comice agricole de l'arrondissement d'Orléans* for the preceding 40-odd years in various parts of the Orléanais to encourage the spread of new techniques of cultivation and livestock raising. Several locally prominent individuals were present at the service: Petau, parliamentary deputy for the department; Pinson, vice-president of the *comice;* three mayors from nearby communes; and the department's council member for the canton of Cléry. The *Courrier de la Campagne,* which reported the service one week later, listed a total of 26 names that it felt were worthy of note.[3] One fact, above any other, seems to have persuaded the paper to single out these names: the majority of them belonged to some of the largest landholding families of the region. The Pinsons, for example, owned 1,983 hectares in the Beauce, according to the first cadastre of the Orléanais (1822–37),[4] making them the fourth largest propertied family in the region at that time (the fifth if one includes the Duke d'Orléans). Timothée des Francs, the *comice's* secretary, was closely related to a family that the second cadastre (1913) records as controlling 2,958 hectares scattered about every subregion of the Orléanais save the Forêt d'Orléans – it was the largest family property of that time.[5] Five of the names mentioned in the *Courrier* – Peteau, Pinson, Timothée des Francs, the Vicomte d'Orsanne (mayor of Mezières), and de Geffries (mayor of Lailly) – are among the top 40 landholding families at the time of either the first or second cadastre. Six other names – Rabourdin (treasurer of the *comice*), du Roscat, de la Rocheterie (mayor of Dry), Nouël, Lefebvre, and Boucheron – belong to families that are recorded in either one of the cadastres as owning at least 75 hectares; in fact, only one of them, Rabourdin, had less than 100. This list would undoubtedly be longer if our data on landownership were drawn from a cadastre that was closer to the actual date of the church service; for instance, three *propriétaires* mentioned in the *Courrier* have not been found in either of the two cadastres surveyed.[6]

It was clearly not landownership alone that brought these individuals together. Like markets and fairs, the annual agricultural show was a symbolic manifestation of the way rural society viewed itself and the world that surrounded it. Though not a novelty, the show had come into its own during the middle decades of the nineteenth century, supplementing and even superseding the entertainment that the fair and market provided.[7] It was, every bit as much as the fairs and markets of an earlier era, a political event. All levels of the French governmental system, from the national chamber of deputies to the tiny, local village councils, were represented at that service at Mareau. Since the July Monarchy, agricultural shows in the Nantais as well as in the Orléanais had presented, whether willingly or not, a platform for political speeches and comment simply because this was the one time in the year that one had simultaneously the grassroots of village society *and* the upper echelons of the state administration as a public. The agricultural show was also manifestly a religious event; the shows always began with a service in the local church. And it is not without significance that we find among the list of celebrities at Mareaux-aux-Prés that ever-conspicuous later nineteenth-century lay cleric, the village *instituteur,* the primary school teacher. We should likewise look upon the agricultural show as an economic event; it brought to notice not only the best products of the countryside but also those resources that could be most easily developed. The show was, in this sense, a sort of advertisement of wares, a means of publicizing the material output of the rural community.

But what is most remarkable about all the brief accounts we have of agricultural shows, such as the one at Mareau, is the public attention the large landowner managed to hold in all these essential social activities. There were obviously more than 26 people attending the religious celebration, but it was the large landowners who received the bulk of the *Courrier*'s attention to the following week. The major political figures there were also the major landowners. And it was a matter of mathematical certainty that it would be the largest landowners who would walk off at the end of the show with the biggest prizes. "To make us compete with them on the grounds of absolute equality is to condemn us, in advance, to have nothing at all," wrote an unusually outspoken small cultivator in the *Journal du Loiret* at the time of the show at Artenay in 1844.[8]

The large landowner turns out to be the most conspicuous connector within our two regions. Historical source material on large landowners abounds. They were rural society's most articulate members in the contemporary journals, reports, and administrative minutes, and as a result, they were also the most written about. The large landowner therefore makes the easiest starting point in the analysis of rural societal structure.

The cadastre provides the best means of identifying the large landowners and of determining the extent and whereabouts of their properties. We have already pointed out that two cadastres were made up within the period of this present study. In both cases, the cadastre was undertaken in every commune detailing the number of land parcels belonging to each propertyholder, the extent of each parcel, its value, and the use to which it was put (plowland, vineyard, marsh, woodland, etc.) at the time of the survey. It took several years to complete the first cadastre in our two regions: in the Orléanais, the earliest volumes (not counting the first primitive attempts made during the Empire) are dated 1822, the last, 1837; in the Nantais, the volumes run all the way from 1821 to 1844. The second cadastre, on the other hand, was completed in both regions within a single year, 1913. All volumes relating to the first and second cadastres in the Orléanais have been consulted (save the commune of Orléans). Such a comprehensive study has, unfortunately, not been possible for the Nantais, owing to the large number of properties found within each commune and the fact that none of the volumes (save the small number deposited at the Archives Départementales) had been classified at the time the study was undertaken. Instead, we have had to make do with a sample of 52 communes taken from the first cadastre and 43 communes from the second. Most of the information gathered from this study will be presented in the chapter on propertyholding patterns in general (Chapter 8); here I will confine my comments to the large properties.

The *matrices cadastrales* – the only part of the cadastre that concerns us – in addition to listing details on each parcel of land, have, at the head of each folio, the name of the propertyholder, his residence, and, very infrequently, his occupation. At the end of the last volume of each commune (in the Orléanais, there are usually three or four volumes per commune; in the Nantais, there are seven or eight), there is normally a recapitulation, which gives the total area of each property, its evaluation in francs, and the folio in which it has been recorded. The recapitulation has enabled us to build up a very accurate picture of the extent and whereabouts of large properties in our two regions. Every entry in the recapitulation of over 50 hectares has been recorded and then matched with the original folio so that the name, residence, and, if possible, occupation could also be noted. This was done for every commune in the Orléanais. In the Nantais, some of the communes sampled from the first cadastre were found to have no recapitulations – especially the communes of Sèvre-et-Maine and the Loire Valley upstream of Le Cellier – and in these cases the survey of large properties had to be abandoned. Thus, for the first cadastre, our information on the Nantais is based on only 35 communes, or data gathered on 247 families, but for the Orléanais, with the entire region surveyed, I have managed to collect data on 437 families. I have drawn, from the second cadastre, data on 209 families in the Nantais and 433 families in the Orléanais.

In order to facilitate comparison with the Orléanais, I have had to assume that the communes sampled in the Nantais are representative of their subregion and have then weighted them on the basis of their area in proportion to the total area of each subregion. On these grounds, I have estimated that there were a total of 591 families in the Nantais with properties of over 50 hectares at the time of the first cadastre and 509 families at the time of the second. The Nantais is slightly larger than the Orléanais and not all the communes sampled are touching one another (producing an overestimation of the total number of large properties). It would therefore seem that the total number of large landowners in the Nantais was about the same as in the Orléanais.

However, it cannot be assumed that the influence of the large landowners was the same just because their numbers were equal. If the areas occupied by the properties of over 50 hectares are compared, the large landowners are shown to carry much more weight in the Orléanais than in the Nantais. In the first cadastre of the Orléanais, over 153,000 hectares (or 63 percent of the whole region) were owned by landowners possessing more than 50 hectares, whereas, in the Nantais, there were about 87,000 hectares (or about 35 percent of the region) held under the same condition; in the second cadastre, these large properties were still taking up more than 131,000 hectares in the Orléanais (54 percent of the region) and only about 73,000 hectares in the Nantais (29 percent of the region). Large landowners therefore controlled about twice as much more territory by proportion in the Orléanais than they did in the Nantais.

This capital fact was at least partially the result of the difference in the quality of soils and the kind of agricultural possibilities – or lack of possibilities – that the soils afforded. As B. H. Slicher van Bath tersely puts it, "The type of soil decides what crops can be grown, the water supply settles the question of whether tillage or stock farming shall be the chief source of livelihood."[9] Most of the large properties of our two regions were to be found in the areas of waterlogged sands and clays: Retz–Vendée in the Nantais and the Sologne in the Orléanais. Here no crops could be grown save the poorest variety of cereals, such as millet or buckwheat; the land was either used for raising livestock (though never of a very high quality) or was just left as waste. The Sologne had by far the greatest quantity of uncultivated land. The first cadastre indicates that 48 percent of its territory was covered by wood, heath, marsh, or pond, whereas the same accounted for only 12 percent of Retz–Vendée, certainly the poorest subregion of the Nantais. Intensive farming (the small cultivator's only means of survival) was simply not feasible in the Sologne. Instead, vast, unproductive properties sprawled out across a thankless country that could only be of benefit to those in search of a *pied-à-terre,* a rural retreat, and, especially, a place for the hunt. Here were the inactive large landowners that had so angered that providently minded Englishman, Arthur Young, when he had traveled through the region in 1787. "The fields are scenes of pitiable management," he had written in disgust. "Heaven grant me patience when I see a country thus neglected – and forgive me the oaths I swear at the absence and ignorance of the possessors."[10] Properties like those of de Laage, Geffries, and Michel de Gruillard would absorb up to half the area of a commune. It was always the same rule in rural France: poor lands were held by large landowners.[11]

The Sologne was not the only part of the Orléanais to be hampered with bad soils. The Forêt d'Orléans was also covered with heavy clays, so here again the large landowners predominated. The largest of them was the Duke d'Orléans, although, because his name was so closely affiliated with that of the French government, one could hardly consider his holdings private property. The domain, extending for some 25,000 hectares in all four arrondissements of Loiret, had been confiscated by the state at the time of the Revolution and was returned to the Duke only with the Restoration. In 1832, it was incorporated into the royal civil list and, following the Revolution of 1848, the state once again took over complete control of the royal properties. The first cadastre indicates that about 8 percent of the Orléanais surface belonged to either the state or the crown.[12] The French government never owned the entire forest. Large private properties, such as those of Dessoles, which spread over five communes, or of Ligneau, which covered nine, still accounted for a large part of the subregion, 50 percent of which was uncultivated land.

There was nothing comparable in the Nantais to those vast Orléanais estates. Although most large properties were to be found in Retz–Vendée, the very largest were in the Nantais Plateau, such as those of Poydras, Charette, or de Sourches de Tourzot. These were some very big names, but, though it cannot be said with absolute certainty (because not every commune of the region has been verified), it seems doubtful that even these families owned more than 2000 hectares. De Sourches de Tourzot is the only family shown in our survey of 35 communes from the first cadastre to own more than 1,000 hectares; in the Orléanais (106 communes), we found 29. A more reliable statistic is the average size of holding for all properties over 50 hectares, calculated on the basis of our absolute figures for the Orléanais but on weighted figures for the Nantais. The final result confirms the same regional distinction: the average property of over 50 hectares was 349 hectares in the Orléanais as against 148 in the Nantais; in the second cadastre, these averages had fallen to 303 and 144, respectively.

Better soil might also have persuaded the owners to remain on their estates. Figure 5.1 illustrates that absenteeism was rarer in the Nantais than in the Orléanais during the first half of the nineteenth century. We have calculated that approximately 53,000 hectares out of a total of about 87,000, or roughly 60 percent of the land held by large landowners, was managed by families who had at least one member living on their property at the time of the first cadastre. In terms of actual individuals, this translates into 348 resident large landowners out of a total of 675: more than one landowner out of every two possessing over 50 hectares of land lived on his own property. In the Orléanais, only 35 percent of the large landowners (or 175 out of 491) were resident; only 45

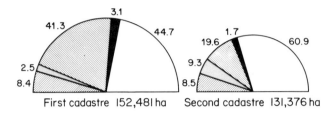

The Orléanais (total area 242,057 ha)

First cadastre 152,481 ha   Second cadastre 131,376 ha

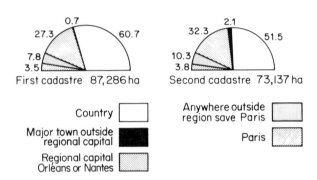

The Nantais (total area 253,114 ha)

First cadastre 87,286 ha   Second cadastre 73,137 ha

Country

Major town outside regional capital

Regional capital Orléans or Nantes

Anywhere outside region save Paris

Paris

Figure 5.1. Percentages of properties over 50 hectares by residence.

percent of the total area owned by large landowners (68,326 hectares out of 152,481) was managed by resident families. It is important to note that most of these resident landowners are those whose properties are to be found *exclusively* within the Beauce, the most productive subregion in the Orléanais outside of the Loire Valley. Furthermore, the great land improvements that were to be undertaken in the Sologne during the Second Empire appear to have been a compelling enough invitation to the landowners to establish their residence on their properties so as to exert a closer control over these activities – by the time the second cadastre was drawn up, 48 percent of the large landowners in the Orléanais [13] were living on their properties, the main growth owing to the larger number of resident landowners in the Sologne.

But soil productivity only partially explains the distribution and residence of the large landowners; it was, after all, the landowners themselves who contributed most to the Sologne's increased productivity. The agricultural sciences, founded in the eighteenth century by a narrow circle of physiocrats, had developed into a cult among the large landowners of the Loire Country by the mid-nineteenth century. The pages of the *Journal du Loiret, La Sologne, Le Breton, Le Colibri,* and *L'Union*

Bretonne – newspapers that we know, through their published correspondence, had many landowners as subscribers – were studded with articles on new fertilizers, agricultural equipment, methods of stock-breeding, irrigation, and drainage. And the large landowners were clearly the ones responsible for introducing these sciences into the countryside. Like Hourdequin, Zola's *grand fermier* of the Beauce, they understood the future of their extended type of properties as going "in the very direction of science and progress with the growing employment of machines and the heavy investment of capital."[14]

A good supply of capital was especially important for anyone aspiring to set himself up as a large landowner and manage to survive. Such, at any rate, is suggested by the few professions recorded by the cadastre as being exercised by the large landowners (see Table 5.1).[15] Besides the obvious category of *propriétaires/rentiers,* which really says very little about how the landowner actually maintained himself, the occupations that come out strongest are those normally associated with an urban, capitalist class – the merchants, the lawyers, and doctors account for 34 percent of all the professions given in the Orléanais, 30 percent in the Nantais. These were not necessarily urban residents, but it certainly would not be wild speculation to suggest that this group had contacts with the regions' towns and their hands on a certain amount of urban capital. Furthermore, it is highly probable that the amorphous group of *propriétaires* and *rentiers* were also in some way associated with the towns, either directly through the possession of an urban property[16] or indirectly by marriage into these urban classes. Hourdequin, in *La Terre,* had been obliged to marry a notary's sister in order to secure enough capital for himself in spite of the fact that he had inherited 200 hectares of land from his father.

What is remarkable about this whole aspect of urban influence is the enormous role that the regional capitals performed in comparison to the practically negligible parts played by the regions' other major towns. In the first cadastre, landowners residing at Beaugency, Meung, Jargeau, and Chateauneuf held only 3 percent of the large propertied territories, whereas the residents at Orléans held 41. The landed residents at Indre, Rezé, Clisson, and Ancenis held under 1 percent as against 27 percent controlled by Nantes' residents. Approximately the same is true of the second cadastre (see Figure 5.1). The overwhelming size of the regional capitals is obviously one reason for this, but if that were the entire story, why did Orléans, the smaller of the two cities, control so much more of its hinterland than Nantes? and what is the cause of the apparent rapid drop in Orléans' influence – 41 percent to 20 percent – between the first and second cadastres?

We have to go back to the conclusion drawn in the preceding chapter. During the nineteenth century, Orléans – by which we effectively mean

Table 5.1. *Professions of the owners of over 50 hectares of land*

Profession	The Orléanais cadastre				The Nantais cadastre (weighted)			
	1st	2nd	Combined	%	1st	2nd	Combined	%
Propriétaires/rentiers	26	62	88	35.9	89	55	144	48.6
Cultivators	9	12	21	8.6	0	0	0	0.0
Merchants	17	25	42	17.1	17	27	44	14.9
Lawyers	13	19	32	13.1	6	12	18	6.1
Medical doctors	2	8	10	4.1	7	19	26	8.8
Armed services	5	13	18	7.3	4	29	33	11.1
Artisans	1	2	3	1.2	0	0	0	0.0
Others	14	17	31	12.7	22	9	31	10.5
Total	87	158	245	100.0	145	151	296	100.0
Missing data	377	362	739		488	431	919	

Source: Matrices cadastrales.

those residents of Orléans who had control over the city's capital wealth – developed an almost total reliance on its surrounding hinterland. Nantes, on the other hand, had a dual interest in both agriculture and commerce: the former never took on that singular importance that it did for Orléans. It should not, therefore, be very surprising to find that it was Orléans rather than Nantes that invested most in its hinterland. At Nantes, money was still being diverted into commerce, a fact that might account for the relatively large proportion of such "un-urban" professionals as the men of the armed services among the Nantais' large landowners (though our weighted statistics for the Nantais are, here, hardly the scientist's proof). Nor should any eyebrow be raised on the discovery of the great agricultural works undertaken in the Sologne during this century; the landowners were merely improving simultaneously upon their own investment and upon the chances of Orléans to pull out of its debilitating slumber. It seems that these landowners became so obsessed with their work that they actually moved residence to their country properties. "Once taken over by this passion [for land improvement]," remarked Ardouin-Dumazet, "the most convinced Parisian becomes a Solognot to the core."[17] How much more true this must have been for the residents of Orléans. The number of large landowners residing on their properties thus rose (and because some of these properties were only partially included in the Orléanais, the number of residents outside the region also rose), whereas the number of landed residents of Orléans actually declined.

Land improvement was one of the most important contributions that large landowners made to the countryside. It was done through a combination of urban capital and scientific know-how (which was also essentially an urban import). Later in this study we shall have the chance of looking at some of the actual ways in which these improvements were made, at the means by which the large landowner channeled this capital and knowledge into his own rural properties, thus providing one of the essential links between town and country that were to make up the economy and society of our two regions. After establishing a more general picture of this structure, we shall be in a better position to point out some of the other important "connecting" activities performed by the large landowner, especially the political role that was played by the less urban-oriented landowners of the Nantais. But in order to build up that picture, we must first look at another group of participants in social exchange, the educators.

2. Connectors in spirit

Teachers of religion and teachers of secular knowledge; in the nineteenth century so many of France's political leaders stressed the differences between the two that it probably seems a little odd to anyone familiar with this period to consider them both under the same title. Political parties were made and broken up by the position taken in the national struggle over who should be given the direct responsibility for primary education: should it be left to the *curé,* the religious leader of the local community, or should it be wholly passed on to the *instituteur,* an officer of the state who would not be subject to the prejudices and dogma of the Catholic church? The lines were drawn clearly enough on the political front at Paris,[18] but as is so often the case, they became increasingly blurred and indistinct the further one withdrew into the countryside. A shortage of funds and qualified personnel bred some curious alliances in rural France.

The one major feature common to both the *curé* and *instituteur* was the large number of different duties that each had to perform for the rural community. In no part of France outside the cities was there a well-defined division of labor between the two posts. The *curé* had for centuries been the only individual responsible for the education of his parishioners, merely because he was the only one capable of taking on the job; he was the most literate member of the community and, as Charles Tilly remarked, he often had the largest library in the village.[19] The *curé* also played an important psychological role by inspiring hope and confidence during times of emotional stress; his familiar figure stood over all the family *rites de passage,* from birth to death; and at times of disaster (e.g., war or epidemic), he made it his duty to be with those who were most in need. When a contagious disease broke out in Pithiviers in 1803 and spread throughout the surrounding countryside, we read that the sole comfort for the inhabitants lay in the consolations of their priests;[20] during the disastrous floods of 1856, the bishop of Orléans wrote to the minister of religious affairs on the devotion shown by the rural clergy;[21] and at the time of the Prussian invasion of the Orléanais (autumn 1870), we are told that the *curés* also "showed an admirable devotion – several were shot by the Prussians for having attempted to defend their parishioners."[22] The *curé* also had a number of more mundane functions to perform, such as the writing of recommendations for those hoping to rent land outside the community, the announcement of land auctions (often made after Sunday mass), and the making of appeals to government agencies and the press.[23]

The *instituteur,* a creation of the Revolution, was ostensibly independent of the church, though his job was in fact based on the precepts of the Catholic religion (under Napoleon I this was intentional). Anyway, the national ideal of a lay, primary education did not even have the full support of law until 1833, so there was little restriction on what the few *instituteurs* scattered about the country could actually teach – and little restriction on the clergy, too. Enough has been written about the laws of Guizot, Falloux, Ferry, and Combes. National governments followed a slow but deliberate course in "freeing" the primary school from clerical influence. That policy sets a neat pattern for those partial to simple, developmental histories. But is that what we are looking for? What went on in the provinces?[24]

There is little doubt about the close association between school and church in nineteenth-century France.[25] Two of the commonest supplementary duties of the *instituteur* were church cantor *(chantre)* and bell ringer, which would usually account for one-quarter of his total earnings (amounting to a national average of about 500 francs – the Orléanais and the Nantais were no exceptions). Thus, the *instituteur* was publicly on view every week in church, in front of his pupils, their families, and, most important of all, the master of ceremonies himself, the village *curé*. But there was another side to the *instituteur*'s customary duties: in practically every rural commune by 1850, it was he who performed the task of secretary to the mayor, a job that brought him another quarter of his total income. And then there were those additional activities and favors that could push him into direct confrontation with the *curé:* he was the legal adviser to many, an entertainer, a medical man, and an informed counsellor on agricultural matters.

The multiple functions of the *curé* and *instituteur* thus contained the seeds of both collaboration and conflict. How their relations developed and what kind of respect each commanded depended not so much on what was written in the lawbooks as on the spirit of those they served. The law itself was simply substituting one intellectual spokesman for another – whoever had the upper hand still had to fulfill the many subsidiary duties demanded of him by the local inhabitants. Thus, as Barnett Singer found, "The emancipated teacher qua notable of the Ferry-Combes generation actually seems closer to his church-ridden predecessor than to the person who today in France essentially teaches and does nothing else."[26]

The crucial factor was religion. Obviously it would be easier for an *instituteur* to act independently in a community where religious fervor was low than where it was high – in the former situation we would expect his role as mayor's secretary to be more important than his church functions, whereas the opposite would be the case in the latter. All Frenchmen were Catholic,[27] but, as Orwell might have put it, some were more Catholic than others.

There is no simple means of measuring the intensity of religious belief. The best gauge is language. But, though in France this kind of research has got off to a highly promising start,[28] it was decided that this would be far too time-consuming for our own specific purposes. We can steer a less tortuous route by following in the tracks laid down by that master sociologist of religion, Gabriel Le Bras. Moreover, for the dioceses of Orléans and Nantes, our burden has been significantly lightened by the painstaking research undertaken by Christiane Marcilhacy and Marius Faugeras, both of whom rely heavily on Le Bras' methodological approach.[29]

Le Bras' assessments of religious intensity were based on a survey made during the 1930s and 40s on church attendance – particularly for the weekly Sunday mass and the annual Easter communion – in practically every parish of France. The survey provided an accurate measure of intensity, he argued, because open, public worship was an essential part of the true Catholic's life; a high attendance rate would not *necessarily* indicate a sincerity of faith, but it would at least *suggest* that this was the case.[30] As for our own concern with clerical influence in rural society, church attendance is of course critical because it brought the public face to face with their *curé*. Within northern France, Le Bras' researches exposed an important difference in the rates of attendance between east and west. He decribed it this way:

A line of 300 kilometers, which generally follows the border of the *bocage,* sometimes the banks of a river on the side of hills, separates the faithful kingdom of the West's interior and the kingdom of indifference of central France: the traveler who from Constances heads for Les Sables-d'Olonne via Alençon, La Flèche and Parthenay, looks to the right at immense territories where four-fifths of the rural inhabitants are observers, to the left at even larger territories where four-fifths of the rural inhabitants are [only] seasonal conformists. Anyone walking from Chaillet to Belleville leaves a land where observers are in the majority for a land where observance is reduced to a tenth and where seasonal conformism retreats before paganism.[31]

This central, "irreligious" zone stretched from the Channel coast through Paris and all the way south to Toulouse. The diocese of Orléans was thus placed right in its middle – statistics cited by Le Bras for six parishes within the diocese suggest a weekly attendance rate of about 10 percent of the total population.[32] The diocese of Nantes, on the other hand, lay in the heart of the "faithful kingdom of the West's interior . . . The countryside remains generally faithful"; the weekly attendance rate was upward of 90 percent of the population.[33]

Evidently, the situation had not been very much different during the nineteenth century. Mgr. Dupanloup, bishop of Orléans (1849–79), recorded that "when I arrived, 20,000 to 25,000 celebrated Easter out of 360,000 inhabitants. There were parishes where there was no longer an Easter service."[34] It was perhaps this extremely low rate that moved the bishop to maintain some of the most thorough records on the moral state of his parishioners ever kept in a French diocese. Drawing her information from these records, Christiane Marcilhacy has established that only about 4 percent of all males over 20 went to Easter communion in 1852 as against 23 percent under 20; among the women, 20 percent of those over 20 attended the service as against 67 percent under 20. All in all, less than one-quarter of the entire population of the diocese (it shared its borders with those of the department) turned up for communion on that Easter Sunday.[35] Some areas had a much worse record than others. The arrondissement of Pithiviers, a large part of which incorporates the Beauce, had only a 12-percent attendance rate as against 30 percent for the canton of La Ferté-Saint-Aubin in the heart of the Sologne. Attendance in the Loire Valley tended to reflect the patterns of the neighboring subregions; the parishes next to the Beauce on the right bank of the Loire west of Orléans had an attendance rate of 19 percent, whereas Jargeau, on the left bank, had a rate that was close to 30 percent.[36]

The attendance records for the diocese of Nantes are inexact. Nevertheless, a study of the *curés'* reports made to the bishop at the time of his pastoral visits (usually conducted every four or five years) gave us reasonable grounds for believing that the rates were just as high in the diocese in the first half of the nineteenth century as they were when Le Bras undertook his work in the 1930s.[37] Fernand Boulard expressed surprise at the stability in the rates between 1851 and 1891. The 94 parishes that made up the Nantais were zealously Catholic, although the pattern was not entirely uniform. Marius Faugeras draws attention to the 16 communes (7 in the Loire Valley, 4 in the Nantais Plateau, 3 in Sèvre-et-Maine, and 2 in Retz–Vendée) where there was apparently less than full attendance at the weekly mass.[38]

The generally high attendance rate gave the *curés* of the Nantais a degree of social prestige and power that was absolutely unknown in the Orléanais. The pulpit was not just the stand for religious sermons; it had become a general platform for news and information simply because it was known that once a week the vast majority of the rural population would be present. What better time than after the Sunday mass to brief cultivators on where to get the best government-approved fertilizers?[39] Practically all public pronouncements made in the community, from political speeches to announcements on changes in the dates of the local market or the news of a forthcoming marriage, were made on Sunday, during or immediately after the church service. For the rural inhabitants of the Nantais, the village church symbolized the beliefs, the work, and the life of their community, and the *curé* stood, *de facto,* as their material and spiritual spokesman. "In our Catholic countries," remarked the Bishop of Nantes in a letter to Paris,

some intimate relations link the population to the priests who are devoted to their service. Each parish is a family in which the *curé* is the father. In times of suffering, he must necessarily talk with this family about the misfortunes it endures and the relief that he would like to bring it.[40]

A public memory that went back to the turbulent days of the Revolution had inspired a sense of confidence in their *curé*; the population knew only too well the extent of his past sufferings. And those sufferings had been real. Consider the story of Garnier, ex-*vicaire-général* of Nantes, whose religious career had begun in the last years of the Old Regime:

I obtained at the age of twenty-seven a post as *curé* [which] I managed for twelve years; these were the most beautiful years of my life because at that time I tasted to its fullest and without any exception the good fortune of loving and of being loved. Then came the period of '92. After a certain amount of anxiety I devoted myself to the cause of duty and misfortune. Wandering, outlawed, inscribed upon the *liste des émigrés,* cast out of my patrimony, I managed to save myself in the capital where I lived, unknown during the Terror. Around the end of '95 M. de Boischollet, late bishop of Sées, then *grand-vicaire* of Nantes, charged me to come back to my post as *curé*. At the time, the situation appeared peaceful. I took up again my functions as *curé*. But soon the civil war restarted and, if I enjoyed the support of the Royalist party, in which one of my brothers . . . was a commander, I was, on the other hand, exposed to the fury of the Republicans. I spent one year like that, exposed to the rigors of poverty, eating the bread of the poor and sleeping on the ground in the middle of the woods, always preaching the Gospel to the men of peace. Finally I, with a colleague, was taken by surprise by a band of Republicans. We gave ourselves the last rites for our own execution. Our resignation gave us favor in the eyes of our executioners; they granted us our lives and allowed us to take flight. Under the cover of night I managed to slip away to Nantes [where] I again found asylum and a lot of work. Up until 1803 I fulfilled with zeal and without respite the functions of the . . . missionaries, working all day, going out only at night, continually exposed to the loss of life and, what was worse, [the possibility of compromising the lives] of the Christians who had given me asylum. . . . In 1803 there was the organization of the clergy. I was granted amnesty (that is to say, crossed off the *liste des émigrés*) and later nominated *grand-vicaire*.[41]

Obviously, not every *curé* became *vicaire-général,* but the essential elements of the story were repeated to one degree or another in practically all the parishes of the region. Between 1790 and 1814, the total number of ecclesiastical posts in the diocese of Nantes had declined by one-third. Yet the sacrifices made by the clergy during this period of bloody civil war had given the village *curé* a special place in the hearts of his parishioners; like a Resistance hero of the twentieth century, he had become one of the most honored personalities of the community.

All this made the *instituteur* look very small next to the *curé*. He might have gained esteem as village "notable," but only through the *curé*'s good graces. The reports of mid-century called the *instituteur* incompetent, with "peu d'aptitude."[42] He was incapable, so they ran, of the most elementary teaching duties, leaving the *curé* the only one able to fulfill them. That was why the Loi Guizot, which relied heavily on the clergy for the success of the act, had been greeted with great enthusiasm in the Nantais. "To openly call on the clergy," wrote one school inspector at the time, "is the most powerful, surest means of attaining the goal that the government has in mind." Most of the primary schools were set up in the presbytery, and the *instituteur,* always under the *curé's* watchful eye, devoted his time to the teaching of the catechism and the preparation of his pupils for their first communion, which, taken usually at the age of 12 or 13, was the signal to the parents to withdraw their children from school and get them to work in the fields.

There is absolutely no myth to the *curé's* overpowering influence in education in these western parts of France. The *instituteur's* "little aptitude" was continually being compensated by the efforts of the rural clergy. Thus, in Riaillé in 1833, we are told of the *instituteur's* "very bad writing" and yet of the model handwriting of his pupils, "traced with care, neatness and principles." How was it possible? *M. le curé* came every day to give the pupils a lesson in writing. He was also "actively involved in the other branches of teaching in the school, and so as to encourage the *Instituteur* and *Institutrice* to receive as many free pupils as possible, he distributes to them the bushels of wheat that the inhabitants of this commune are in the custom of giving every year to their *curé.*"[43]

But in addition to exerting a tremendous influence in the running of the state schools, the clergy also encouraged the spread of private religious schools. By 1858, there were 54 such schools in the Nantais as opposed to the 148 state-run schools; roughly 12 percent of the male school population were attending religious schools as against 59 percent of the females. As the century proceeded, these proportions increased. One *instituteur* at Ligné became so frustrated by the trend that he dispatched a curtly worded letter off to the arrondissement's school inspector. It read:

Of the seven pupils who attend my school today, only one (who's free) lives in the commune of Ligné, and even he is a child from the hospital taken in for care by this commune . . . Do not be surprised, *M. l'Inspecteur,* at seeing the *école communale* so deserted and abandoned . . . *M. le Vicaire* [a term usually used in reference to the *curé's* assistant who would himself eventually become *curé*] is exercising his moral influence on the children and even on the parents to get them to go [to the religious school]. As the pupils abandon me, the parents tell me, "*M. le vicaire* wants them to go to the other school and we are frightened that if we left them with you they would not go to communion."[44]

There were no such complaints in the Orléanais. Here, it was rather the *curé* and his associates who were made objects of displeasure. For example, the inspector's report of 1858, though finding the general level of teaching satisfactory (with writing standards being singled out for special praise), commented that "it is regrettable to see several religious schools remaining backward and thus losing their pupils; [they took] no part in the intellectual exercises so necessary for [the pupils'] instruction and education."[45] The religious schools in the countryside were designed exclusively for girls; there were only 5 religious schools for boys in the region in 1858, and they were all in the city of Orléans.[46] The schools were not set up in the presbytery, but rather in the *mairie* itself or in a nearby annex; the *instituteur* was therefore physically independent of the *curé* and was thus in a much easier position than his counterpart in the Nantais to exert his own personal influence within the community. "The public *instituteurs* have known how to win the confidence of all the families," ran the report of 1858, "and the private teachers who have tried to set themselves up beside them have failed."

It would be simple and even tempting to argue that the *instituteur*'s prestige in the Orléanais was a result of the exclusive interest that Orléans had in its hinterland: Orléans, one might want to say, had been forced by its own economic needs to bring civilization and reason to country folk. The argument would have to rest on the assumption that a "rationalism" – of the kind that Le Bras speaks of as embodying "the crowds enlightened by the towns and factories"[47] – pervaded the spirit of the rural population, encouraging it to break loose from the traditional ties of the church and take on the *instituteur* as their intellectual and moral spokesman. The problem here is that there was nothing very rational about the Orléanais countrymen: they might not have held much love for the *curé,* but their lives were governed by superstitition.[48]

This could take the form of idol worship, as was the case of the old wooden madonna standing by the altar at Notre Dame de Cléry.[49] When, in 1836, the *curé* of the parish attempted (in a most undemocratic fashion) to replace it with a rather smartly dressed plaster version, there was a riot. "What have you done with our good Virgin, *M. le curé?*" cried the crowd at the gates of the church, "Bring us back our good Virgin!" *M. le curé*, accused of selling the original to Chartres for 40,000 francs, managed to slip out a back door, but his vicar received a number of bruises in the assault. The mayor intervened, the police were brought in, and the crowd dispersed. But it was only after the old madonna was returned, again under the mayor's initiative, that real peace was restored.[50]

Marcilhacy has placed a great deal of emphasis in her work upon the superstitious nature of the rural population in the region. In all parts of the Orléanais, particular physical objects such as the church candles, Easter palms, the water of certain fountains were considered to be endowed with mystic powers of healing, of controlling the harvest, or of affecting the chain of future human events. In the Beauce, there was widespread belief in the supernatural powers of certain individuals in the community to influence the health of others and even change their own physical appearance – werewolves stalked at night through the open farmlands.[51] Some women, known as *voyageuses,* made a profession of going on pilgrimages for the sick. Even if the client was himself capable of doing the trip, he would pay his *voyageuse* to do it for him out of the conviction that she possessed a unique power of communication with the saints. For some diseases, several saints would have to be called upon and thus several pilgrimages (or *voyages*) would have to be undertaken. In the Sologne, the subregion most prone to superstition, an enormous yule log consecrated to the child Jesus was burnt in every household on Christmas Eve. The head of the household would spare nothing in his search for the largest possible log; to neglect or minimize this ritual meant certain catastrophe for the family concerned. There were elements of mysticism to be found in all parts of the Orléanais; it suggests what some psychologists might call "individuation," a personalization of the religious myths that followed the whims of the community and developed completely independently of the church's formal creed. It is interesting to note within this context that Le Bras, when describing the state of religious belief in central France, speaks of Catholicism retreating before paganism, not rationalism.[52] Paganism, the dictionary tells us, is a cult, belonging to none of the great Western religions (Christianity, Judaism, Islam), that generally involves the worship of many gods. The term itself is derived from the Latin word *paganus*, meaning rural inhabitant, or, to use the English derivative, "peasant." Did this motley array of beliefs, faiths, and superstitions still represent such an ancient, polytheistic tradition?

One thing to be sure: it neither represented nor pleased the likes of the village *curé*. Nor can we very well imagine the *instituteur*'s attachment to such irrational views. The superstitions of the rural population of the Orléanais seem to have been independent of both. Whereas the *instituteur*, by his evident control of local educational affairs, was more important than the *curé*, neither had managed to attain the level of influence that the *curé* in the Nantais was accustomed to exercise. There was not much love lost between peasant and school in the Orléanais. "It is a great error to imagine," wrote a village mayor in 1830, shortly after the establishment of an *école normale* in Orléans, "that the peasant has the least thirst for instruction. He does not understand it, he does not like it and he certainly does not want to pay for it."[53] And in 1881: "Our peasants are very irritated about the new law of compulsory primary education. . . . They say, 'The government can build the prisons, they will never be large enough to take us all.'"[54]

All the same, in the early years of the nineteenth century, literacy rates were somewhat higher in the Orléanais than in the Nantais (corresponding to the more general contrast between the Paris Basin and the West). Between 1827 and 1830, 44 percent of those recruited by the army from the department of Loiret could both read and write, whereas only 24 percent of the recruits from Loire-Inférieure could do the same. However, by the outbreak of the First World War, we find only 1.4 percent of the recruits from Loire-Inférieure illiterate. Judging from marriage signatures (or the lack of them), most of that increase in literacy occurred during the middle years of the century, particularly the 1850s and 60s.[55]

The Orléanais' higher rates can be simply explained. Orléanais schools served communes whose total populations were often under 500, whereas in the Nantais, most communes had over 1,000 inhabitants and frequently two to three times that number. Population pressure alone could account for the generally lower school attendance rates in the Nantais along with the shorter average amount of time that each pupil could expect to spend in school. Both the statistics and the inspectors' reports confirm these last two facts. In 1833, pupils attended primary schools in the Nantais for 2 to 3 years, in the Orléanais, 4 to 5 years. "Children do not attend the schools long enough," wrote an inspector from Ancenis in 1857, "nor, especially, regularly enough; they come to class at the age of 8 or 9 and often leave before 12." Even in 1884, the regional contrast remains, although the most remarkable thing about these more detailed statistics is that, by this date, the teacher/pupil ratio was almost identical in the Nantais to that of the Orléanais (see Table 5.2).[56]

The *curé* and *instituteur* were an embodiment of the rural mentalities of each region. Weren't these the shamans and psychologists of this imperfect peasant economy?[57] The *curé* owed his power in the Nantais to a devoutly Catholic population. The *instituteur* found relatively greater prestige in the Orléanais that lacked such a singular, united faith – he was not nearly as powerful as the Western *curé*.

It is this dependence on the rest of the population that defines the character of the social connector. It marks out his role in the entire integrated structure of society. The large landowner, the *curé*, and the *instituteur* cannot be separated from their society and analyzed in isolation. They cannot be considered a class unto themselves. All this chapter has done has been to bring to light a few of the major contrasts that existed between the Orléanais and the Nantais, contrasts that must have been felt through the entire fabric of society. Which leaves us with some very important questions: how could Orléans afford to place a near total reliance on its hinterland whereas Nantes could or did not? Why was the Nantais so much more attached to Catholicism than the Orléanais? What, in general, gave the rural population of the Orléanais that degree of autonomy from both the *curé* and *instituteur* that was so obviously lacking in the Nantais? To answer all this we have to widen our vision of the social connector.

Table 5.2. *Primary school attendance in the Orléanais and the Nantais, 1884*

Region	Schools	Instituteurs/ Institutrices	Pupil/teacher ratio	% absent (5 April 1884)	% under 6 years	% over 13 years
Orléanais						
Beauce	50	61	54	6.3	17.9	3.3
Sologne	25	36	55	11.7	17.0	6.6
Forêt	37	57	52	4.8	16.4	2.9
Valley	87	140	50	5.8	20.3	4.1
Boys	81	122	54	4.8	8.8	6.2
Girls	80	130	47	7.0	14.1	2.8
Mixed	24	24	56	11.0	14.3	2.8
Infant	14	18	77	7.7	89.1	0.0
Regional total	199	294	52	6.5	18.6	4.0
Nantais						
Plateau	36	58	60	12.1	3.7	2.1
R–V	55	98	53	12.0	7.1	2.6
S-et-M	33	67	55	5.7	6.6	2.5
Valley	52	92	54	8.2	12.6	2.2
Boys	96	169	62	10.0	4.0	2.5
Girls	75	141	45	8.3	7.8	2.3
Mixed	1	1	35	74.3	11.4	0.0
Infant	4	4	112	13.9	100.0	0.0
Regional total	176	315	55	9.6	7.9	2.4

Sources: AN F^{17*} 2927, 2929, 2930, 2935, 2936, Ministère de l'Instruction Publique, *Statistique sur la situation des écoles primaires en 1884.*

6   The rural economy in toto

In switching our attention from particular groups to the social whole, we must restrict ourselves to a more specific kind of social activity. No history can outline all types of social exchange. The most exhaustive investigation would still only give a fragmentary picture of the total circuit of human dialogue that brought individuals and communities together. We get, for instance, from historical records, only the faintest reflection on the means by which traditions, habits, and social behavior were either spread or abetted by word of mouth – a rather serious blindspot if we recognize the two regions as being comprised of mostly oral cultures. Even in so "hard" a subject as rural economics, where records are most abundant, we have no way of knowing how many commodities were passed from hand to hand, household to household, without ever having been recorded by the local statistician. The historian is left with a sample of the kinds of social exchange practiced; and a very biased sample at that because it must rely so much on the *written* record.

Exchange consists of giving and receiving (or in Saussurian terms, an active part and a passive part). But who is to say who are the givers and who are the receivers? The more successful political leaders of the French Revolution, literary men for the most part, assigned voting rights in accordance with their view of a social reality: "active" and "passive" citizenry corresponded to a society of those who contributed and those who did not. In their eyes, France was divided into two unequal camps, a minority of givers and a majority of receivers; and it was surely no small coincidence that this majority consisted of those who could not read.

The notion of the "social connector" denies this sort of blanket classification of givers and receivers. Giving and receiving are viewed as integral, *inseparable* elements of the same act. No individual can give without being at the same time the object of some kind of receipt, and vice versa. The very presence of an individual within a society is itself an act of giving that can, even if he were to do nothing else, exert a profound effect on the structure of society (a point that should become clearer when we discuss the historical demography of our two regions). So, if one finds evidence in the written records of one element of social exchange, one might assume that the other element also took place.

But whatever approach one adopts, historical enquiry must always be selective. For this very reason, it is essential to establish, in as explicit a manner as possible, the kinds of sample one plans to make. The most common type of document in the French National Archives or in the

94

local departmental archives is related either directly to agricultural production or to the organization of the population within the context of
agricultural production. There is also the mass of material on local
politics, the major part of which deals with those directly involved in
local political life – samples from these records would be biased in favor
of one social group. The analysis that follows is therefore aimed in the
direction of goods and services (and more on goods than services, again
because of the documentation). Here we also have the advantage of a
theory that can act as a control to any bias that might seep into our
analysis from the use of one document.

The question by now should be obvious: how did the half million individuals who inhabited the Orléanais and the Nantais in the nineteenth
century maximize the means of their survival?

1. The means

Man without commerce (if he ever existed) relied on local resources.
Social space was then determined by the amount of land required to support his number and his habits of consumption. In the Loire Country,
consumer products had been exchanged over great distances for centuries. Did that break down the regionalism of the area? Did it destroy
society's identity with the land? Historians have suggested that commerce
severed the ties between man and his local territory by giving him a
wider, independent view of his international world.[1] Many studies of "industrialization" and "modernization" have argued that the process has
accelerated in the last two centuries. Does this hold true for the Loire
Country?

The last two chapters have already begun to depict a society that was
becoming increasingly *dependent* upon the land, suggesting that commercial growth is not a process solely destructive of human geographical
regions. In fact, geographers have for a long time pointed out that,
however commercially advanced a society, there always exist some
elements in the operation of that society that tie it to its home territory.
In economics, the major tie has been food (a fact that remains true even
in the present-day United States). Thus, over 50 years ago we find the
French geographer Vidal de La Blache writing:

Among the connections tying man to a certain milieu [which he had defined largely in terms of the land], one of the most tenacious . . . is food. Clothing and
weaponry are much more likely to be modified by commerce than the diet by
which different groups, according to the climate in which they live, satisfy the
necessities of their system.[2]

A major result of the broadening patterns of commercial exchange had
been to force the cities of the Loire Country to rely more and more on the
resources of their hinterlands; food had become the area's most impor-

tant asset. Commerce had thus reinforced the ties between man and the land; it accentuated the regional differences by encouraging local specialization. The nineteenth century saw the Loire Country develop into the vineyard, market garden, and granary of France. (Though it would be an exaggeration to claim that the Loire Country was the only area in France to evolve in this way. In fact, France, as a whole, so developed its agriculture that it remains, to this day, western Europe's number one producer of foods.)

The regional variety of the Loire Country – clearly the area's most outstanding feature if contrasted, say, with the northern parts of the Paris Basin – has already been described in general outline (Chapter 2). My concern here is to give a more specific idea of what this actually meant in terms of agricultural production in the nineteenth century. This is not a difficult thing to do because, since 1852, statistics on agricultural production were drawn up every 10 years for each canton in France. The most complete enquiry still existing on the Orléanais and the Nantais is that of 1862 deposited at the national archives.[3] Most of the information that follows is taken from that source.

Tables 6.1 and 6.2 and Figures 6.1–6.3 give a very clear picture of the sort of agricultural variety found in the two regions. Two essential facts present themselves: Cereal production was generally more important in the Orléanais than the Nantais, while livestock rearing was of greater importance in the Nantais. On the other hand, intensive cultivation (vines, vegetables) appears to have been of almost equal importance for the two regions, though the Nantais did have the upper hand in vegetable production. Such broad observations confirm the general contrast, noted earlier, between the fertile lands of the Paris Basin (represented here by the Orléanais) and the heavier soils of the Massif Armoricain (the Nantais), as well as the unifying aspect of the rich river valley.

The cereals

But we obviously cannot stop with that. Specialization in a particular agricultural commodity in one region clearly did not altogether exclude its production in the other. Cereals were a case in point. Some areas of the Nantais devoted large parts of their territory to the production of grains. This was particularly true of the alluvial flatlands bordering each side of the Loire where the major cereal was wheat. But by the nineteenth century, even the *bocage* country of the Nantais Plateau and Retz–Vendée had extensive areas planted in grains and, again, the major crop among them was wheat. Always enclosed by hedges of hawthorne or gorse (more common on the Plateau than in Retz–Vendée), these grain fields had been developed largely thanks to the new fertilizers produced by the sugar refineries at Nantes and the valuable alkalines manufactured by the numerous lime-burning ovens that had sprung up throughout the region during the Restoration and July Monarchy. What was most remarkable about this development was the tremendous priority given to the production of wheat, which, outside the Valley, seemed to have been cultivated in utter disregard of the natural restraints imposed by the acidic quality of the region's soils. According to the 1862 enquiry, over three-quarters of the total area planted in cereals in the Nantais was devoted to wheat. A high proportion of wheat to all the other cereal crops existed in all the cantons neighboring the Loire, although the highest proportion was actually in the two cantons directly south of the Lac de Grandlieu, Machecoul and Legé, where wheat was practically the only cereal cultivated (though it, alone, took up almost half the total surface of the canton of Legé). In the Orléanais, only a little over one-third of the area cultivated in cereals was dedicated to wheat.

There are two possible reasons. In the first place, the rotation of crops followed a much stricter pattern in the Orléanais than in the Nantais. If there were any pattern at all in the Nantais, one might say that a biennial rotation predominated in the lands of the left bank whereas a triennial rotation was the more common practice on the right bank. But the contrast was not nearly as distinct as the textbooks on rural France often imply. In answer to the question "What is the most widespread form of rotation?" in the 1862 enquiry, many of the cantonal commissions replied that crops were "rotated without regularity," "rotation is no longer practiced," or "there is no regular rotation." Fodder crops were frequently introduced in the Valley after two or three years of wheat, but this followed no formal pattern. It seems that if the decision had been made to cultivate a certain plot of land in cereals, that cereal would be wheat, and wheat would be harvested for as long as the soil and fertilizers would permit. The 1862 enquiry is really only a snapshot of agricultural production taken at a specific instant in time; it is hardly surprising, given the apparent priority placed on wheat and the lack of regulation in crop rotations, to find wheat so predominant among the cereals recorded for the Nantais.

In the Orléanais, every canton is reported to have favored a triennial rotation, with the exception of the cantons of Orléans Northeast (where biennial and triennial rotations were practiced), Beaugency (quadriennial), Cléry (biennial), and Jargeau (undetermined). Thus, only 2 cantons out of a total of 12 practiced a crop rotation involving less than three courses. Documentation on the systems of rotation employed in this region prior to 1862 are extremely rare, but if our secondary sources are anything to go by, the universal adoption of the triennial rotation in the Orléanais seems to have been a phenomenon confined to the nineteenth century. At an earlier date, the biennial rotation is reputed to have

Table 6.1. *Cultivated land, percentage area, 1862*

Canton	Subregion[a]	Cereals	Potatoes	Other vegetables	Natural and artificial grasses	Vines
Patay	B	53.9	0.5	0.2	18.5	1.1
Artenay	B,F	46.4	0.4	0.0	18.2	0.8
Meung	B,V	52.4	0.7	0.3	10.5	10.3
La Ferté	S	15.3	0.7	0.1	11.0	0.0
Jargeau	S,V	37.0	2.3	1.1	11.8	12.7
Neuville	F	32.7	1.2	0.2	13.2	1.4
Châteauneuf	F,V	25.4	1.7	0.5	11.3	0.4
Orléans NE	F,V	25.1	?	0.5	13.6	4.3
Orléans NW	V,F	27.8	1.6	2.3	9.4	23.3
Orléans S	V,S	32.8	2.1	0.3	11.2	19.5
Cléry	V,S	25.3	1.9	1.9	13.4	10.4
Beaugency	V,B	46.2	1.1	2.4	17.1	13.9
Orléanais		35.7	1.3	0.5	13.9	8.1
Riaillé	P	29.8	0.8	0.3	23.6	9.8
St. Mars La J	P	26.3	1.7	0.2	16.7	0.2
La Chapelle s/E	P,V	31.2	1.0	1.0	5.8	0.5

Machecoul	R	24.3	0.8	1.0	26.2	4.4
Légé	R	49.2	1.0	10.2	30.4	12.1
St. Philbert	R	19.4	?	4.2	19.0	8.4
Aigrefeuille	R	28.6	2.7	1.6	15.9	7.5
Clisson	SM	?	?	?	?	?
Vertou	SM	17.2	2.8	1.6	17.7	24.2
Vallet	SM	19.1	2.2	1.2	14.8	22.4
Le Loroux	SM,V	?	?	?	?	?
Bouaye	V,R	18.8	1.1	4.4	18.4	18.6
Nantes	V	22.5	5.6	8.9	19.5	6.5
Carquefou	V	34.3	4.6	3.9	27.1	6.1
Ligné	V,P	25.7	1.4	0.5	18.5	8.8
Ancenis	V,P	25.6	1.2	1.1	21.8	9.5
Varades	V,P	35.0	2.4	2.7	24.9	4.8
Nantais		26.8	1.7	2.5	20.2	8.6

Note: ? – Data not available. Subregional code: B, the Beauce; S, the Sologne; F, the Forêt d'Orléans; P, the Nantais Plateau; R, Retz–Vendée; SM, Sèvre-et-Maine; V, the Loire Valley. The same code is employed throughout this study.
Source: Agricultural enquiry, 1862 (AN F^{10} 2705).

Table 6.2. *Livestock per square kilometer and per household, 1862*

Canton	Subregion	Horses		Cattle		Sheep		Pigs	
		per km²	per household	per km²	per household	per km²	per household	per km²	per household
Patay	B	6.0	0.7	15.3	1.8	126.0	15.1	4.8	0.6
Artenay	B,F	6.7	0.8	22.3	2.5	109.3	12.4	5.8	0.7
Meung	B,V	6.4	0.5	17.5	1.3	112.6	8.5	5.3	0.4
La Ferté	S	3.0	0.7	11.0	2.5	78.5	17.9	5.3	1.2
Jargeau	S,V	5.2	0.4	21.8	1.8	79.9	6.5	6.8	0.6
Neuville	F	5.4	0.5	23.1	2.1	41.4	3.7	3.8	0.3
Châteauneuf	F,V	3.7	0.4	17.5	1.9	25.6	2.7	5.1	0.5
Orléans NE	F,V	4.8	0.3	23.5	1.3	42.2	2.3	9.5	0.6
Orléans NW	V,F	9.8	0.4	20.8	0.7	32.7	1.5	7.4	0.4
Orléans S	V,S	6.9	0.4	19.5	1.2	81.1	4.5	11.4	0.6
Cléry	V,S	6.2	0.5	19.3	1.6	34.8	2.9	9.4	0.8
Beaugency	V,B	5.9	0.3	34.6	1.5	67.7	2.9	13.8	0.6
Orléanais		5.6	0.5	20.0	1.6	72.1	5.9	7.1	0.6
Riaillé	P	2.6	0.2	57.1	4.7	52.5	4.4	11.8	1.0
St. Mars La J	P	2.4	0.2	62.6	4.6	24.8	1.8	8.2	1.0

La Chapelle s/E	P,V	1.0	0.1	32.1	2.0	8.8	0.5	8.8	0.5
Machecoul	R	4.7	0.4	54.6	4.3	20.8	1.7	5.6	0.4
Légé	R	1.8	0.1	38.0	2.1	9.5	0.5	5.2	0.3
St. Philbert	R	2.2	0.2	42.3	3.4	8.8	0.7	4.0	0.3
Aigrefeuille	R	1.?	0.1	56.3	3.0	0.0	0.0	7.8	0.4
Clisson	SM	?	?	?	?	?	?	?	?
Vertou	SM	5.7	0.2	38.2	0.2	0.7	0.5	13.2	0.0
Vallet	SM	3.8	0.2	33.0	1.6	1.6	0.1	11.1	0.7
Le Loroux	SM,V	?	?	?	?	?	?	?	?
Bouaye	V,R	6.3	0.2	37.0	1.2	9.6	0.1	9.6	0.3
Nantes	V	10.1	0.5	52.5	2.5	0.2	0.0	179.6	8.4
Carquefou	V	6.2	0.3	42.7	2.0	5.8	0.3	9.2	0.4
Ligné	V,P	2.5	0.2	49.0	3.3	31.7	2.1	10.3	0.7
Ancenis	V,P	3.9	0.2	34.9	1.7	24.7	1.2	9.0	0.4
Varades	V,P	6.8	0.4	49.4	2.8	15.1	0.8	14.0	0.8
Nantais		3.8	0.2	43.7	2.4	15.7	0.9	15.7	0.9

Note: ? means data not available. Subregional code: B, the Beauce; S, the Sologne; F, the Forêt d'Orléans; P, the Nantais Plateau; R, Retz–Vendée; SM, Sèvre-et-Maine; V, the Loire Valley. The same code is employed throughout this study.
Source: Agricultural enquiry, 1862.

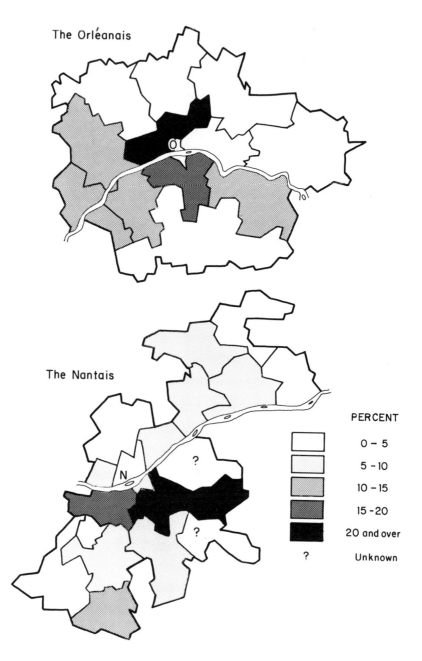

The Orléanais

The Nantais

PERCENT

0 – 5

5 – 10

10 – 15

15 – 20

20 and over

? Unknown

Figure 6.1. Vines, percentage area, 1862.

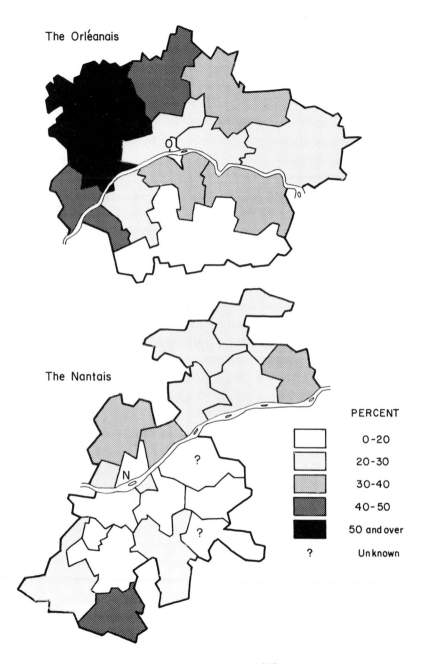

Figure 6.2. Cereals, percentage area, 1862.

103

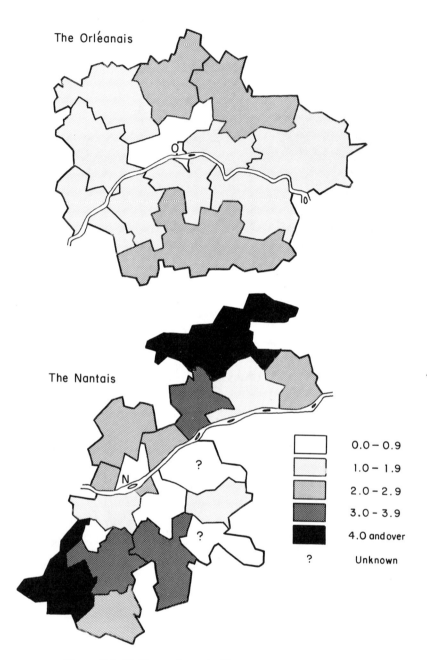

The Orléanais

The Nantais

	0.0 – 0.9
	1.0 – 1.9
	2.0 – 2.9
	3.0 – 3.9
	4.0 and over
?	Unknown

Figure 6.3. Cattle per household, 1862.

been the common practice on the left bank of the Loire.[4] The triennial rotation normally followed in the Orléanais was a winter wheat, a spring cereal (oats, barley, or spring wheat, the last two being practically unknown in the Nantais), and fallow (or, in some parts of the Valley, a fodder crop). Any enquiry, because it is fixed in a given moment of time, would indicate a smaller proportion of wheat being grown in areas where this kind of rotation was being practiced by comparison to areas, such as the Nantais, where it was not.

The second possible reason for the relatively low proportion of wheat cultivated in the Orléanais is the very poor soil found in two of its subregions, the Forêt d'Orléans and the Sologne. In the Sologne, particularly, the cultivation of wheat was practically impossible except in the areas bordering on the Valley.[5] In the canton of La Ferté-Saint-Aubin, according to the 1862 enquiry, only 14 percent of the total area planted in cereals was devoted to wheat – the lowest proportion found in any of the cantons within our two regions. This figure is almost equal to that of buckwheat, cultivated in no other part of the Orléanais and only very infrequently north of the Loire in the Nantais. The major cereals in La Ferté-Saint-Aubin were oats and rye, the latter making up a higher proportion of the total grain crop than in any other canton in the two regions.

All the same, poor soils seems a weak second explanation for the lack of wheat sown in the Orléanais. Even in the Beauce, the proportion of wheat to other cereals was quite small when compared with the Nantais. In Artenay, 46 percent of the area planted in grains was devoted to wheat; in Patay, the figure was as low as 39 percent; whereas for the entire Nantais, the *average* was 78 percent (the Orléanais' average was 37 percent). If we take the cantons of Patay and Artenay together, add the area left to fallow[6] to that of cereals, and then consider the proportionate area devoted to each crop, we come up with the interesting result that 32 percent of this area was planted in wheat, 31 percent in oats, and 17 percent was left to fallow: elegant testimony of the triennial rotation.

The vine

One crop that was never subject to rotation and, indeed, had the almost unique characteristic of not having to be replanted each year was grapes. The vineyards of the Orléanais and the Nantais produced a gross revenue that came second only to that of cereals, even though they accounted for less than 10 percent of each region's total area. As noted earlier, there was not a significant difference between the two regions in terms of the area planted in vines (7.2 percent for the Orléanais, 8.5 percent for the Nantais). Nonetheless, there remain two important regional distinctions that must be made within the context of wine production.

The first pertains to the quality of the product. Up until the end of the Second Empire, and even beyond, the catalog of grapes grown in the Orléanais was very long. The region produced both red and white wines. The reds were, without question, the better-quality wines with the Gris Meunier being the foremost among them, though the Gascon, the Gros Noir, and the Gamay were cultivated extensively in some areas. The white wines generally found their way to the vinegar factories of Orléans and the Valley (in fact, a large proportion of the reds were also bound to the same fate). The most important white wine grape was the Meslier, followed by the Pineau Blanc, the Gouais, and, in a few rare instances, the Chasselas. None of these wines had any reputation in France. This was partly because the Orléanais, situated at the northernmost limit of the river Loire, had a natural disadvantage vis-à-vis the other regions of the Loire Country. Nevertheless, there was room for improvement. Jules Guyot, France's most preeminent specialist in viticulture during the Second Empire, pointed out that, besides the Meunier and the Meslier, the grapes were not suited for the region and they were also picked too early. It would be far better, he argued, to adopt the vinestock and techniques of the Rhine and Burgundy – a theme that he had doubly stressed by placing his review of the department of Loiret in the volume that included these two areas, not the Loire Country.[7] The Orléanais thus had, in the mid-nineteenth century, a number of different wines, which were all very ordinary in quality and, it seems, rushed to the market before they were fully matured.

The Nantais specialized in two white wines, the Gros Plant and the Muscadet, both ideally suited to the region's pebbly soils. To the extreme east, in the communes of the canton of Varades, which bordered the river, were also found a number of vineyards planted in the Pineau grape, which reputedly produced the finest white wines of the region. However, outside Varades, this grape was extremely rare. The Gros Plant is a classic example of a French *vin ordinaire*. "The Gros Plant," noted a report from the prefecture in 1807,

produces a sour wine with a disagreeable taste. It is preserved only with difficulty beyond one year, and if it did not redeem these disadvantages with some great advantages there is no doubt that the culture would have been abandoned long ago.

Its advantages, needless to say, were great.

It is suited to all soils, all kinds of exposure . . . Its produce is more reliable [than that of Muscadet]; it is affected less by frost . . .; it is less subject to insects' destruction of the bud, it produces more . . ., yielding one-fifth as much as the Muscadet. In general, owners of small vineyards prefer to cultivate it.[8]

The wine was consumed in Brittany, Vendée, and even in Anjou. It was the most common drink in Nantes. Large quantities were sent to Paris

where it was mixed with the popular red wines of the Midi and sold as
Burgundy.[9] Jules Guyot noticed that the wine was "snatched up by
Bordeaux for the blending and manufacture of red wines because it is
neutral and youthful [frais]."[10] The Muscadet, on the other hand, was
not a popular wine – "the drink of the bourgeois," remarked Guyot.[11]
During the Second Empire, this plant would have been expected to yield
35 hectoliters of wine, or less, per hectare, whereas the Gros Plant could
achieve up to 50. It was much more vulnerable to frost and disease, as indicated by the report just cited. Consequently, it occupied about one-half
the acreage of that cultivated in Gros Plant. All the same, the rewards
were often good for anyone willing to take on the risks: as a smooth,
slightly fruity wine, Muscadet sold at about twice the price of Gros
Plant.

Thus, in terms of the quality of their wine product, the Nantais differed significantly from the Orléanais. Whereas the Orléanais was ex-
pending energy on a large number of wines of no national repute whatsoever, the Nantais was specializing in both a popular wine sold
throughout the country and a quality table wine.

The second major regional distinction was the actual geographical
distribution of the vineyards – a factor that was obviously closely related
to the quality of the wines. The most important vineyards of the
Orléanais were found in the communes bordering the Loire. Vines were
grown outside the Valley, but they only accounted for about one-
twentieth of the total wine-growing area. The 1862 enquiry records only
8 hectares of vineyard for the whole canton of La Ferté-Saint-Aubin; the
canton of Neuville, which consisted largely of woodland, possessed just
under 300 hectares; and in the Beauce, if we consider the two cantons of
Patay and Artenay combined, there existed a little less than 400
hectares.[12] These vines were cultivated for local use and were rarely ever
marketed. The most notable vineyards within the Valley either surrounded Orléans (the communes of Saint-Jean-de-Braye, Saint-Jean-de-la-
Ruelle, and Ingré were especially important) or were spread along the
right bank of the Loire, downstream of the city. On the Loire's left bank,
the canton of Cléry-Saint-André possessed some vineyards of note;
Jargeau and even more so Olivet had a significant amount of land
planted in the Gascon grape. The right bank of the Loire, upstream of
Orléans, was the area least fit for wine growing because the heavy soils of
the Forêt extended practically all the way to the river banks (very much in
contrast to the wide alluvial plains that separated the river from the
Sologne at Jargeau). The canton of Châteauneuf was the only part of the
Orléanais to have the Gamay Blanc, a normally tough and resistant vine,
grafted to an otherwise very varied stock.

In the Nantais, roughly two-thirds of the area cultivated in vine lay *outside* the Loire Valley. The only subregion really lacking in vineyards was the Nantais Plateau, although even here one could have found vines planted haphazardly in the enclosed fields that spread across the country. In Retz–Vendée, the Gros Plant was grown in practically every commune, especially those belonging to the cantons of Bouaye, Saint-Philbert, and Legé. Sèvre-et-Maine was the natural domain of the Muscadet; it extended across the cantons of Vallet and Vertou, at times entirely dominating the subregion's hilly landscape. Almost half the surface of the communes of La Chapelle-Heulin, Le Pallet, La Haie-Fouassière, and Saint Fiacre were cultivated in grape. In the canton of Le Loroux-Bottereau, in addition to Muscadet and Gros Plant, were found, in the first half of the nineteenth century, the only red wines of the region, the Gros Noirs, although they were of a very mediocre quality. The Loire Valley itself was relatively denuded of vines; it was really only upstream of Le Cellier, in the arrondissement of Ancenis, that they occupied as great a part of the land surface as in the Orléanais Valley.

The market gardens

The proportionately low quantity of vineyards in the Nantais' western half of the Valley should not, however, be taken to signify a general lack of intensive cultures. It really meant quite the reverse. As indicated earlier, during the nineteenth century, Nantes developed a growing interest in fruits and vegetables, products for which the flat Valley floor was in fact much better suited. Small fields cultivated in beans, peas, carrots, asparagus, artichokes, and 100 other kinds of vegetable were concentrated within a radius that included the whole of Nantes, half of La Chapelle-sur-Erdre, most of Carquefou, as well as, to the south, the two communes of Rezé and Bouguenais. Their produce fed the preserved food industries at Nantes or was exported. Any traveler approaching or leaving Nantes by road could not fail to be impressed by this great cluster of unenclosed plots of land that, together, amounted to one huge market garden.[13]

However, the degree of intensity of these cultures was obviously not strictly defined in terms of circles around the major regional towns. The actual physical characteristics of the Loire Valley dictated a pattern of cultivation that appeared to a greater or lesser extent in every part of the subregion, including the immediate vicinity of Nantes.

The classic Valley pattern consisted of four zones: the bordering hills, planted in vines and rising to more than 30 meters above the valley floor in some eastern parts of the Nantais Valley; the moist flood plain, varying in width and usually devoted to rich natural or artificial grasses (though as the century proceeded, the vine occupied an increasingly important place); a narrow dryer zone neighboring the river levées, which was put to intensive cultivation and the growth of fruit trees; and the riverside itself, where grassland was once more the norm. No area entirely conformed to the pattern. Within the radius of Nantes, just described, market gardening spread out across the flood plain. Still, meadows predominated at the river's edge and on the islands, even on those within the actual commune of Nantes such as the Ile Gloriette. Upstream from Nantes, wide stretches of rich pastureland were more common. But, east of Le Cellier, on the right bank of the Loire, where the Valley narrowed, intensive cultures spread all the way from the riverside to the bordering hills. In this case, one could find certain crops being grown within each of the different zones. The textile plants were important in the arrondissement of Ancenis: flax cultivated on the hills, hemp on the plain.

A similar pattern existed in the Orléanais Valley even though there was less variety in the actual crops grown there. The most intensively cultivated part of the Valley was downstream from Orléans, the cantons of Meung and Beaugency being particularly important. Upstream, grasslands were much more prevalent. Market gardening was also less extensive in communes surrounding Orléans than those around Nantes partly because, as previously pointed out, their major interest lay in the viticulture. However, immediately to the south of Orléans, in the suburb of Olivet, there was a considerable array of tree and flower nurseries. They had put Ardouin-Dumazet in mind of a forest in Lilliput as he crossed this part of the river plain:

The fruit tree is the principal branch of trade. Pear, apple, plum, quince and cherry tree seedlings are produced by the million . . . [But,] of the number of trees cultivated in the plain of Olivet, the most prestigious are the forest trees, the landscape trees for city plantations and the ornamental trees and shrubs. All the parks planted in Spain, Italy and most of the American countries are tributaries of Orléans.[14]

Nevertheless, taken as a whole, there was much less land dedicated to this kind of market gardening in the Orléanais than in the Nantais. For example, outside the Valley, root crops, such as the sugar beet of the Beauce or the potatoes of the Sologne, began to be cultivated on a large scale only after 1870. In the Nantais, on the other hand, fruits and vegetables were grown in all four subregions even at the beginning of the century. One should take special note of the cider apple trees of the Nantais Plateau, which in the course of the century spread to the left bank, and the cabbages, largely employed as livestock feed, which were cultivated extensively in Retz–Vendée.

Livestock and agriculture

The relationship between the raising of animals and the cultivation of the land has intrigued students of the countryside for many years now. It is usually presented in either of two ways. The first is most frequently found in analyses in which the primary interest is in agricultural regionalism. It follows a single, basic theme: where the land cannot be cultivated, animals are let out to graze. This leads logically to a two-poled contrast in the form of cultivated regions versus livestock-rearing regions, *pays de culture* versus *pays d'élevage* (which is often used to imply rich regions versus poor regions). The second comes out of studies that are more interested in the processes of production and follows a theme along the line: cultivated land needs livestock to provide fertilizer, livestock needs cultivated land to produce foodstuff, therefore cultivated land and livestock are interdependent. The two themes are somewhat contradictory. In their simplest forms, the first implies that the cultivation of land without livestock (or vice versa) is feasible, the second implies that it is not. A solution of this contradiction is crucial to the understanding of the range of production possibilities existing within a given rural economy. In the Loire Country, this essentially means establishing the extent to which artificial fertilizers and an advanced means of transport (see Chapter 4, Section 2) had loosened the bonds between cultivation and livestock rearing so that each could be pursued in the regions for which they were best suited. In other words, given the technological advances, the question is how much should the first theme be given preference over the second? Is the distinction between cultivation and livestock rearing the most regionally valid one that can be made for the Orléanais and the Nantais?

A correlation analysis (Table 6.3) on 10 variables, representing the major forms of culture and livestock in the two regions, gives us a more precise means of answering this question than a simple review of the raw data.[15] Because these statistics are calculated from data representing a single point in time, they are purely measurements of variations in space. Specifically, they measure the variations that existed between 24 cantons of the Orléanais and the Nantais (data for Clisson and Le Loroux-Bottereau are missing) at the time of the 1862 enquiry. Any coefficient below + .35 and above − .35 should be rejected as statistically insignificant on the grounds that one could arrive at such figures by chance alone.[16] This leaves 17 significantly correlated pairs out of a possible total of 45. Eleven are between cultures and livestock, 4 are between different livestock, and only 2 are between different cultures.[17]

This suggests that the type of culture grown within a given canton was much more affected by the presence (or lack) of livestock than by the presence (or lack) of another culture. The correlations between different cultures are indicated in Table 6.3 above the rectangle. The correlations between different kinds of livestock – to the right of the rectangle – also appear to be generally weak. With the exception of one pair, all significant correlations include poultry – poultry, this seems to say, were found

Table 6.3. *Pearson correlation analysis of cultivated land (percentage area of canton) and livestock (per household), 1862*

	Grass	Cereals	Vines	Potatoes	Other vegetables	Cattle	Horses	Sheep	Pigs	Poultry
Grass	1.00									
Cereals	+.13	1.00								
Vines	−.04	−.17	1.00							
Potatoes	+.16	−.31	+.16	1.00						
Other vegetables	+.50	+.03	+.20	+.48	1.00					
Cattle	+.41	−.09	−.53	−.12	−.06	1.00				
Horses	−.20	+.29	−.31	−.14	−.26	−.12	1.00			
Sheep	−.25	+.36	−.37	−.47	−.42	.00	+.80	1.00		
Pigs	+.06	−.16	−.12	+.62	+.49	+.10	+.20	−.07	1.00	
Poultry	+.42	+.32	−.44	−.41	−.12	+.54	+.40	+.50	−.01	1.00

Source: Agricultural enquiry, 1862.

wherever there were livestock. But the strongest correlated pair is between sheep and horses.[18]

Sheep were allowed to graze in the Beauce on the fallows and grain fields after harvest. They were also found in the shrublands of the Sologne. They were hardly suited for intensively cultivated areas and thus were rare in the Orléanais Valley and most parts of the Nantais. According to the 1862 enquiry, horses were the primary draft animals in the Orléanais, a job that was left to oxen in the Nantais. This would explain the strong correlation between horses and sheep as they were both numerous in the grain-growing parts of the Orléanais. (Horse breeding, on the other hand, was commoner in the Nantais, particularly the western half of the Valley and the reclaimed lands of Machecoul. Many of the horses of the Beauce were Breton in origin – undoubtedly a good number came from the pays Nantais).

Most of the correlations between cultures and livestock – the figures within the rectangle – are negative. But of the 11 statistically significant coefficients, 5 are positive, suggesting a close association between certain livestock and cultures. We should therefore not speak of a simple opposition between livestock and culture but of regional contrasts based on *types* of livestock and culture.

We can distinguish three types of culture. In the areas of intensive cultivation (represented here by vines, potatoes, and other vegetables), the number of livestock per household was obviously quite low; the only animal with which these cultures were not negatively correlated was the pig, and pigs we know from the enquiry were found in every part of our two regions.

We should draw a line between cereals and grasses, though in the case of grasses we have to make a further distinction between the artificial and natural. The artificial grasses (clover, sainfoin, lucern, rye grass, etc.) were of major importance in the Orléanais, accounting for 69 percent of the total grass-growing area. In the Beauce, there were no natural pastures; only artificial grasses that fitted so well into the triennial rotation pattern. Only four cantons had a proportionate area of artificial grasses that fell below the region's average: Châteauneuf (with 51 percent of its grass-growing area), Beaugency (16 percent), Cléry (33 percent), and La Ferté (10 percent). All of these, with the exception of Châteauneuf, had at least one commune in the Sologne where artificial grasses were clearly of little importance. The natural pastures found scattered about the Forêt d'Orléans accounted for the relatively low percentage of artificial grasses at Châteauneuf. In the Nantais, on the other hand, the only artificial grass of any significance was clover, cultivated along with cereals on the Nantais Plateau. Elsewhere it accounted for roughly 10 percent of the total area devoted to grass. The region's average was only 23 percent. Thus, artificial grasses were largely found in the cereal-producing regions. As previously noted, the most important animals to be associated with cereals were sheep and horses.

The natural pastures of the Nantais and the southern and eastern parts of the Orléanais were the most common habitat for cattle. In the mid-nineteenth century, the Nantais was raising a large number of cattle for meat. The English Durham had already made its appearance and was often crossed with the Nantais' two most important indigenous breeds, the Choletaise and the Parthenaise. The last were good working beasts and for this reason were almost the only animals employed in the region for plowing. The indigenous breeds of the Orléanais were leaner and of a generally poor quality. Like the horses, the best cattle of the region had been introduced from Brittany and Normandy and were kept in stables in the Valley and, to a lesser extent, in the Beauce. The so-called Solognote, which was allowed to graze freely among the scrub of the Sologne, never aroused much interest in the cattle and meat markets outside that one subregion.

In conclusion, the tremendous regional variety that existed both between and within the Orléanais and the Nantais can be reduced to three broad-based *agricultural types:* an "intensive type" (vines and market gardens associated with few livestock), a "cereal type" (cereals and artificial grasses associated with sheep and horses), and a "pasture type" (natural grasses associated with cattle). These types were distributed among the eight subregions under study in the following manner:

The Orléanais	1 The Beauce: cereal
	2 The Sologne: pasture
	3 The Forêt d'Orléans: pasture (some cereal)
	4 The Loire Valley: intensive
The Nantais	1 The Nantais Plateau: pasture (some cereal)
	2 Retz–Vendée: pasture (some intensive)
	3 Sèvre-et-Maine: intensive
	4 The Loire Valley: intensive

There was obviously some diversity within each type. We have seen that the intensive cultures in the Nantais were not only more widespread than in the Orléanais, they were also more varied and were held in higher national repute. Furthermore, one hardly needs to be reminded that the scrub and thicket of the Sologne and the Forêt were very much inferior to the grasslands of the Nantais. Nevertheless, the schema does give a general idea of the production possibilities open to the inhabitants of each subregion. How did they exploit this?

2. The effort

Tables 6.4 and 6.5 give a general idea of the way in which society in the Orléanais and the Nantais was organized around economic production. The statistics have been drawn from the original manuscript lists made up in every commune for the 1851 census. Lists were found for all but three of the communes in the Nantais.[19] On the other hand, those of the Orléanais that were deposited in the departmental archives were destroyed in 1940 (as were the census returns for all other years), and we have had to turn to the lists conserved in the village *mairies*. Only eight of these lists have actually been consulted, so that, although they represent communes evenly distributed throughout the region, they cannot give us more than an approximation of the situation in each sub-region.[20]

With this caution in mind, our first impressions are something of the order: (1) that the agrarian professions and activities were of far greater importance in terms of numbers than the nonagrarian, although the latter's percentage did tend to be above the regional average in (a) areas of an intensive type of agriculture in the Nantais, (b) areas of a cereal type of agriculture in the Orléanais (but we might also note that the absolute percentage of the active population to the total population is smaller in these same areas); (2) that the percentage of full or part owners of the soil was greater in areas of the intensive type than in the pasture type, and conversely, there was a greater percentage directly dependent on others for their livelihood in the pasture type – Table 6.5 also indicates that dependent labor was widespread in the cereal type. At a more general level, we should further note that the distinctions between occupations as well as between subregions were less remarkable within the Nantais than within the Orléanais.

In the remainder of this chapter, I shall attempt to determine the validity of these initial observations. Our main interest here is to establish the extent to which the household played a productive role in the economy. We want to know how far the two regions deviated from the model of a peasant economy as presented in Chapter 3. I shall begin with an evaluation of the importance of nonagrarian activities in the two regions, then turn attention to the problems of land ownership and exploitation, and conclude with a review of dependent labor. Because nonagrarian activities and land ownership appear to be associated with an intensive type of agriculture, we can also expect to start by concentrating on the intensive type and finish with the pasture type.

Nonagrarian activities

Nonagrarian activities form an important part of the "connecting" bond in a rural society. Indeed, the traditional kind of anthropological model

Table 6.4. *Occupational distribution of the active population in the Nantais and the Orléans, 1851*

Subregion	Active population (% of total population)	% of active population						
		Agriculture	Industry and Commerce	Rentiers	Liberal professions	Household domestiques	Miscellaneous	No known profession
Nantais								
Plateau	66	85	11	1	1	1	0	0
Retz–Vendée	70	84	9	2	1	1	1	2
S.-et-M.	56	76	16	1	3	2	1	1
Valley	62	68	22	3	3	3	1	1
Nantais	63	78	15	2	2	2	1	1
Orléanais								
Beauce	51	65	20	9	2	1	0	2
Sologne	71	86	4	5	1	5	0	0
Forêt	64	88	8	2	1	0	0	1
Valley	57	84	11	2	2	1	0	0
Orléanais	58	81	11	4	2	1	0	1

Note: Nantes and Orléans were excluded from these calculations. Statistics for the Orléanais derived from only eight communes: Saint-Péravy, Tournoisis (Beauce); Ardon (Sologne); Trainou, Bouzy (Forêt); Baule, Darvoy Dry (Valley). The subregional percentages have been weighted in calculating the grand averages for the Orléanais.
Source: Listes nominatives, états récapitulatifs 1851.

Table 6.5. *Occupational distribution as percentages of the total population active in agriculture, Nantais and Orléanais, 1851*

Subregion	Owner-cultivators (%)	Fermiers (%)	Part fermiers and part owners (%)	Part fermiers and other (%)	Métayers (%)
Nantais					
Plateau	15	26	9	1	11
Retz-Vendée	16	20	8	1	11
S.-et-M.	28	20	6	0	4
Valley	17	34	12	4	7
Nantais	18	25	9	2	9
Orléanais					
Beauce	7	8	2	4	0
Sologne	0	13	0	0	0
Forêt	13	14	4	2	6
Valley	69	6	0	0	0
Orléanais	41	9	1	1	1

Note: Nantes and Orléans were excluded from these calculations.
Source: Listes nominatives, états récapitulatifs, 1851.

of peasant society – garbed in its paraphernalia of market analogies – views these activities as the sole prerequisite for a broadly extended, differentiated society; without them, it is implied, men would be reduced to a narrow world of autonomous, face-to-face communities. This approach leads inevitably to a tantalizing paradox (if not just a plain contradiction): if nonagrarian activities are so unique, then how do they create the popular reciprocal basis for the exchange so vital to the operation of a total society? The usual answer is that they cannot: nonagrarian activities are practiced by an isolated minority that forces its unifying, consolidating principles upon the remaining rural majority, often by means of violence.[21] The rural masses are thus once again reduced to the role of passive citizenry, they become once more an *âme damnée,* the receivers in this unequal social equation. I do not accept this argument. In my view, the nonagrarian activities were not a unique link in rural society but, instead, closely resembled the systems of exchange practiced throughout the main body of that society.

Nonagrarian activities were defined in the 1851 census under three rubrics, "industry and commerce," "the liberal professions," and "domesticity." The last two were evidently closely tied to agrarian life even though the professions themselves could be considered nonagrarian. By far the largest category among the "liberal professions" were the *rentiers,* men or women living off the income of their own properties (they are indicated as a separate category in Table 6.4). One assumes that

Part métayers and part owners (%)	Part métayers and other (%)	Journaliers (%)	Part journaliers and part owners (%)	Part journaliers and other (%)	Farm domestiques (%)	Woodcutters and charcoalburners (%)
3	1	16	1	0	16	0
2	0	24	4	1	13	1
1	0	26	1	0	15	0
2	0	12	1	0	12	0
2	0	20	2	1	14	0
0	0	65	0	0	12	1
0	0	56	0	0	31	0
0	0	34	3	1	19	5
0	0	10	7	0	7	0
0	0	29	4	0	13	1

most of them were the large landowners already described in the preceding chapter. Lawyers and doctors, members presumably of the urban, capitalist class whose role in rural society has also been previously described, made up the rest of the liberal professions (see Chapter 5, Section 1). "Domesticity" covered household servants, small in relative numbers (with the exception of the Sologne) and who anyway were usually hired only on a temporary basis.[22]

It was in industry and commerce that one was most likely to find isolated islands within the broad ocean of rustic activity. A mid-century enquiry into the state of French industry[23] indicated that industries were widespread in the Nantais. Outside Nantes itself, the region is recorded as having 2,257 establishments, or about 75 percent of the total number of establishments with Nantes included. On these grounds, industry would appear to have been less important in the Orléanais, where only 529 establishments are recorded outside Orléans. Nonetheless, this accounted for over 80 percent of the total. The larger absolute number of establishments in the Nantais does in fact corroborate the earlier evidence (Table 6.4) of an association between nonagrarian activities and intensive agriculture, which was practiced in a far greater area in the Nantais than in the Orléanais. Furthermore, about 65 percent of the establishments of the Orléanais, outside Orléans, were to be found in the Loire Valley.[24]

Large-scale establishments were, however, very rare. There were only

24 in the Nantais operated by more than 10 individuals; in the Orléanais, there were only 11. The largest of those in the Nantais were the coal mines of Mouzeil (the Plateau), which together employed almost 600 persons. All of them were wage earners and most, one suspects, had started at a very early age (more than 100 of the employees are classified in the official statistics as children). Here, then, there was a community that could very well have been isolated from the general cycle of rural exchanges, though this should not be exaggerated: although production was regular throughout the century, the contemporary documents emphasize that a practically permanent state of depression hung over the industry. It was never expansive because its product was of such poor quality that it could be used only to fulfill the local needs of the region. The lime burners, who themselves would only operate in small groups of two or three, were its most important customers.[25]

The stone quarries at Fay-aux-Loges in the heart of the Forêt d'Orléans constituted the industry closest to mining in the Orléanais. The parliamentary enquiry of 1848 indicates that the industry employed 300, although they are described at that time as being "without work"[26] – the published *Statistique générale* does not even mention them.[27] An enquiry made 40 years later does, however, take note of the importance of the quarries and especially the stonemasons' yards clustered together in this commune. They were all wage earners and "their parents exercised the same profession." They worked for 8 to 12 hours a day beginning at five or seven in the morning "according to the season." For lodgings they rented, for 90 to 150 francs, two-roomed cottages "ordinarily with a yard and a small garden," which were about a kilometer away from their work. Like the coal miners of the Nantais, this was a tight-knit community with little communion with the outside rural world besides the sale of their products.[28] The only other industry in the Orléanais that could possibly be considered isolated consisted of the two iron forges at Meung and Saint-Jean-de-Bray, which were set up in the 1840s to provide supplies for the new rail. Together they hired about 200 persons in 1850.

Otherwise, industries were largely family undertakings and were closely associated with the main occupation of the rural economy, agriculture.[29] A total of 1,450, or 93 percent, of the industrial "establishments" recorded by the *Statistique générale* for the Nantais, outside Nantes, were operated by two or fewer persons; in the Orléanais, there were 450, or 85 percent. These included tilers (especially widespread in the Sologne and the Forêt d'Orléans), tanners, and shoesmiths, who often worked at their profession for only a part of the year.

But easily the most important of the small-scale household industries was textiles. The Nantais was part of a vaster territory in the West including a large part of Brittany, Maine, and Anjou that had been for a long time heavily involved in the production of cloth. It seems that the industry owed its origins to the cultivation of textile plants, particularly hemp, which had become increasingly widespread with the gradual intensification of agriculture during the seventeenth and eighteenth centuries. However, as the industry developed, it depended more and more on imported raw materials, first linen and then, in the nineteenth century, cotton. Tilly has insisted that in the Mauges (directly east of Sèvre-et-Maine) the dependence on the outside for both raw materials and a market isolated the textile workers from the generally subsistent kind of agriculture that dominated the region. There is no part of the Nantais that could be described as subsistent. Furthermore, the majority of textile workers – spinners and weavers – were found in Sèvre-et-Maine and the eastern parts of the Loire Valley, thus confirming once again the association between the intensive type of agriculture and industry. But, in spite of the large number of textile "establishments" recorded in 1850 (234 in all), only 13 of them – all manufacturers of spun wool – employed more than 10 persons;[30] the production of linen and cotton cloth was still in the hands of small-scale household enterprises scattered throughout the countryside.[31]

The textile industry was less important in the rural areas of the Orléanais. Orléans itself appropriated the lion's share of the business with its hat and blanket manufactures (see Chapter 4, Section 1), leaving the countryside only a small fragment of an already depressed regional market. It is one of the paradoxes, exposed so clearly by comparative study, that Orléans' near total reliance on local resources had deprived its hinterland of the opportunity of household manufacture, or the luxury of economic choice open to the Nantais rural inhabitant, thus increasing the risks of agricultural intensification. The textile industry certainly reflected this narrow, local aspect of Orléanais manufacture. The *Statistique générale* records that in 1850 no part of the countryside produced cotton yarn or cloth;[32] except for the three establishments at Meung that specialized in hemp (grown within the canton), all the textile manufacturers worked with wool, the Beauce contributing by far the largest quantity. As in the Nantais and following the example of Orléans, wool manufacture in the Orléanais tended to be found in workshops rather than in single households. At Patay, in the middle of the Beauce, four such shops employed almost 150 workers. Thus, even in the case of rural textile manufacture, the industry did not have nearly as pervasive a domestic, household character as it did in the Nantais.

This brief survey of the nonagrarian activities of our two regions does then point to one vital aspect about their relationship with the regional capitals. Evidently the regional capital that relied entirely on its hinterland was obstructive to the development of dispersed, household industries in the countryside, whereas the regional capital that had an autonomous branch within its manufacturing sector actually encouraged their development, not the reverse. In fact, the survival of the household – that is, essentially the family – as a unit of economic production is closely tied to such a dual-based economy in the regional capital. But here we are anticipating.

Land ownership

An examination of the dominant household-type rural economy must inevitably lead to a consideration of land ownership and exploitation. The discussion and definition of a peasant economy in Chapter 3 has already shown how intricate the relationship between the household and the landholding was (see Figure 3.1). We can look at this in two ways. In the first place, we can examine the network of relationships that bound each individual household to the land. In the second, we can examine the whole "household society" and ask how it formed the various groups that exploited the land. The first represents an analysis from a *mechanical* point of view; the second represents a social, *functional* point of view. Further, this distinction between the individual and the whole can be seen to correspond to the Chayanovian distinction between micro- and macro-economic analysis. Here we are concerned largely with the latter. In Chapters 7 and 8, the emphasis will be more on the individual, micro-economic aspect of the peasant household.

Our first problem is to establish the actual proportion of the population that directly exploited the land to satisfy their own personal needs; this is indispensable if we are to demonstrate the existence of a subjective peasant economy in our two regions. Table 6.5, based on the 1851 census, indicates a particularly high proportion of owner–cultivators in the Loire Valley of the Orléanais. Given the fact that more than half the Orléanais rural population lived in the Valley, this would lead one to suspect that the general proportion of owner–cultivators to the total population active in agriculture was greater in the Orléanais than in the Nantais. And in fact in the published statistics for the entire Loiret department – which included another segment of the Forêt and the whole infertile Gâtinais – one does find that 22 percent of the population active in agriculture were owner–cultivators, whereas in the Nantais – which had a far larger area devoted to intensive agriculture – there were only 18 percent.[33] The addition of part owners (that is, those who were also renting a part of their exploitation or were working for others) does not change this contrast one bit; in fact, it even reinforces it, especially if we look at the differences between the Loire Valley of the two regions: in the Orléanais Valley, three-quarters of the population active in agriculture owned some land in comparison with less than a third in the Nantais Valley.

A far larger proportion rented the land they exploited in the Nantais. Thus, if we add the various kinds of tenants to the propertyholders, the difference between the two regions is much less remarkable: 57 percent of the agricultural population of the Nantais exploited the land for their own benefit in the capacity of either propertyholders or tenants; we would put the Orléanais within a range of 55 to 65 percent, that is, slightly lower than the Nantais. Furthermore, the subregional differences in the Nantais were evidently smaller than in the Orléanais so that even if the general proportion of small propertyholders was very low they were all spread out evenly across the region – they accounted for 28 percent of the Plateau's agricultural population, 30 percent of Sèvre-et-Maine's, and 32 percent of the Valley's. By contrast, they accounted for 76 percent of the Orléanais Valley's, only 20 percent of the Forêt's, 9 percent of the Beauce's, and none at all of the Sologne's. The 1851 census therefore tells us that small propertyholders were virtually confined to areas dominated by the intensive type of agriculture in the Orléanais, whereas they were represented equally in all agricultural types in the Nantais. Thus the census keeps well in step with the general contrast Paul Bois makes between the divided, varied society of the middle Loire and the homogeneity of the West.[34]

The contrast, however, was probably not as great as the census suggests. The 1862 agricultural enquiry, for a start, presents a less uniform picture of the Nantais. Propertyholders made up less than 20 percent of the agricultural population in the two cantons of the Plateau (Riaillé and Saint-Mars-la-Jaille); all cultivators, tenants included, accounted for only 45 percent. Retz–Vendée and Sèvre-et-Maine appear to have had a greater proportion of propertyholders and tenants than indicated by the census, whereas the proportions for the Loire Valley do, by and large, agree. On the other hand, responses from the cantons of the Orléanais indicate a more homogeneous situation than the census. We do find a large proportion of propertyholders in the Valley and virtually none in the Sologne, but almost twice their proportion in the Forêt. The two sources differ most on what they report for the Beauce: although the census limits propertyholders to about 10 percent of the agricultural population and the total number of cultivators to about 20 percent,[35] the enquiry indicates 35 and 50 percent respectively. Thus, the enquiry, contradicting the census, suggests that small propertyholders and tenants were common in the cereal type of agriculture as well as the intensive type in the Orléanais.

However, the 1862 enquiry is not a very dependable source. Several commissioners admitted themselves that the absolute numbers given in their responses fell far short of the total agricultural population – an underestimate, it would seem, of between one-third and a half of the actual total. We would even be tempted to ignore this section of the 1862 enquiry were it not for the fact that so many qualitative sources support its conclusions rather than those of the census. Among the most notable is the 1848 parliamentary enquiry, which, although confirming a large number of propertyholders in the Orléanais Valley and a large amount of dependent labor in the Sologne, hints of a quasi-egalitarian society in the Beauce. Here is an extract from the response from the canton of Artenay:

There are about 15 farriers in the canton, the same number of wheelwrights, 5 or 6 masons and the same number of carpenters. They either employ no workers at all, or they employ only during certain seasons of the year. There are even fewer workers and *compagnons* than masters. . . . All the other workers [*travailleurs*] are involved in the industry of agriculture. It would be useless to enumerate them as they make up practically the entire population of the canton. One cannot divide the workers involved in agriculture into masters and workers. The great majority of cultivators work alone or they have recourse to outside assistance. [Work] is almost always done by establishing an exchange of services in which one becomes, in turn, master and worker. As for the most important *chefs d'exploitation,* the landowners and *fermiers,* they have under their orders domestics who mostly rent their services for a long period but who cannot be considered workers. One can consider as such only the *journaliers* and cultivators employed irregularly and temporarily for certain works, such as digging ditches, as well as those employed at certain seasons when there is a greater than normal demand for hands, such as during the harvest. The latter are for the most part foreigners to the canton who stay only as long as there is the work in question. . . . The cultivators are in the habit of rendering services for certain jobs on a reciprocal basis, one for the other. Those who have horses do the plowing and carrying for their neighbors who pay back with other services. Even the domestics who are engaged for a fixed period often rent several acres of land that they cultivate for themselves. They work for themselves when they are not occupied with their masters, sometimes reserving two or three days a week.[36]

We shall be defining some of the terms used shortly. It is quite clear that the author of this report felt that only a minority was totally dependent on others for a livelihood and that most work on the land was done either by individual cultivators for their own gain or through an informal system of mutual aid. Even the domestics, the most common form of permanently hired labor, were reported as having exploited small plots of land for their own ends. Nor should we assume that this individual form of exploitation was confined to the land. Many cultivators in the Beauce raised their own livestock. Grenadou, an old-time cultivator of the Beauce, reminiscing in the 1960s about life in his village in the days prior to World War I, reported that all houses save the poorest had one cow and an ass. "Ça occupait la femme pendant que le mari travaillait."[37]

In fact, whatever the subregion, most qualitative sources indicate that there was a larger proportion of cultivators (*exploitants*) in the agricultural population than suggested by the census. At Fay-aux-Loges, the same commune of the Forêt in which the stone quarries were to be found, it is reported that the majority of the agricultural population consisted of "petits exploitants."[38] And this is just as true for the Nantais. In the same enquiry that reported those conditions at Fay, we find the Comice Agricole of Loire-Inférieure stating that "propertyholders form the majority, then come *fermiers,* then wage earners, *métayers* and finally piece workers [*tâcherons*]."[39]

There is actually only one way of establishing, with any degree of certainty, the proportion of the agricultural population that directly exploited the land for their own benefit. That is a comparison of the number of propertyholders given in the census with the number of propertyholders registered in the cadastre. Table 6.6 presents a comparison of the crude totals found in communes for which both the 1851 census and the first cadastre are available.[40] It indicates that in both regions there are about 1 ¾ times as many propertyholders registered in the cadastre as in the census. Even if one makes allowance for the fact that some of the properties from the cadastre were put to nonagricultural use, the difference is large enough to affirm an underestimate in the proportion of propertyholders given by the census. One might conclude that full and part owner–cultivators formed at least 50, and probably over 65, percent of the agricultural population in the Nantais; in the Orléanais, the overall percentage could well have been as much as 80 percent or more. The cadastre does confirm a more general spread of small properties in the Nantais than in the Orléanais, although, as indicated by the 1862 enquiry, the distinction between the pasture-type agriculture of the Plateau and Retz–Vendée and the intensive type of Sèvre-et-Maine and the Valley was much more important than the 1851 census suggested. The former puts the propertyholders within a range of 40 to 50 percent of the agricultural population; the latter, somewhere between 70 and 80 percent (less in the Valley than Sèvre-et-Maine). In the Orléanais, the distinction between the intensive-type agriculture of the Valley and the pasture type of the Sologne is quite marked; in the Valley, propertyholders account for practically the whole agricultural population, whereas in the Sologne, they form a negligible part. Together with the 1862 enquiry and the qualitative sources, the cadastre presents clear evidence that the cereal-type agriculture of the Beauce was the domain of small properties.

Tenants

These rough figures do not include all cultivators, although the proportion of tenant–farmers who did not at the same time own some property must have been much smaller than the 1851 census indicates. As pointed out earlier, tenantry was more common in the Nantais than in the Orléanais. Nevertheless, in both regions, there existed two major forms of

Table 6.6. *Comparison of the total number of propertyholders in the 1851 census and the first cadastre*

Subregion	Number of communes sampled	Total population active in agriculture	Total propertyholders recorded in the 1851 Census (a)	First cadastre (b)	b/a
Plateau	9	10,645	2,963	5,187	1.75
Retz–Vendée	11	12,845	4,638	7,317	1.58
S.-et-M.	6	6,287	3,398	5,298	1.56
Vallcy	9	9,864	3,192	7,436	2.33
Nantais	35	39,641	14,191	25,238	1.78
Beauce	2	455	43	480	11.16
Sologne	1	369	0	26	—
Forêt	2	1,074	215	437	2.03
Valley	3	1,770	1,340	1,779	1.33
Orléanais	8	3,668	1,598	2,722	1.70

Sources: Listes nominatives, tableaux récapitulatifs, 1851, and *matrices cadastrales.*

it: *fermage à prix d'argent,* based on a fixed money rent, and *métayage,* or sharecropping. *Fermage* was easily the most common of the two, in spite of the frequent references in contemporary documents to *métairies* and *métayers.* Bois has drawn attention to a loose use of those terms in the West dating back to the eighteenth century – they had "nothing to do with the system of rent, only with the size of the exploitation."[41] A nationally known dictionary of the nineteenth century defines a *métayer* as a "1. *Fermier, fermière qui donne pour fermage la moitié des fruits . . .* 2. *Abusivement. Fermier en général . . .*"[42] A dictionary of place names for the department of Loire-Inférieure, published in 1857, defines *métairie* as "an area of rented land of over fifteen hectares" in contrast to the *borderie* of under 15.[43]

Evidently contemporaries felt that the area of exploitation was more important than the mode of exploitation. However, we obviously cannot ignore tenantry altogether, given the fact that the most precise statistics available are confined to property and that all additional forms of direct exploitation[44] were based on rent of one kind or another.

The terms of a *fermier*'s lease were varied and, on paper, normally contained a number of minutely detailed obligations. The lease often laid down the kind of crop rotation to be followed as well as the amount of the harvest to be set aside for seed. In the open cereal country of the Orléanais, it restricted controls on the construction of barriers, whereas in the *bocage* of the Nantais, it stipulated how the hedgerows were to be maintained and how often they were to be replanted (usually every seven years). But, as Bois has again pointed out, these terms were written more as a guarantee of good maintenance of the landowner's property than as strict regulation of farming practices. They were guidelines. For a lease that ran for at least six years, one could hardly have expected the terms to be followed to the letter. The irregular system of crop rotations in the Nantais indicated that they were not.

Leases tended to be shorter in the Nantais than the Orléanais. The 1862 enquiry reports that in some of the eastern parts of the Valley (the cantons of Ancenis and Varades) there was land being rented for only three years. The norm, however, was a six- or nine-year lease, the latter being commonest in the Plateau and Retz–Vendée, subregions with a predominant pasture type of agriculture. No part of the Nantais reported having leases of longer than nine years. By contrast, in the Orléanais, almost one-quarter of the farms recorded had leases of 15 years or more. The rest were practically all rented for 9 years. Leases of 6 years or less accounted for less than 10 percent of the farms and were found almost exclusively in the Forêt d'Orléans. The longest leases were to be found within the intensive agricultural area of the Valley, in other words, quite the reverse of the Nantais. It is also interesting to note that rents tended to be one-third as high in the Orléanais for lands comparable in quality to the Nantais, whereas the venal value was about the same. One should keep in mind the fact that large landed properties were much more extensive in the Orléanais than the Nantais and that, in the first half of the nineteenth century, absenteeism was also more common (see Chapter 5, Section 1). During this period, even though capital was beginning to shift away from Orléans' decaying commerce into the land, there were few attempts to oversee the results directly. The 1862 enquiry was made at a time when the large landowners were beginning to move out of the city into the countryside. However, the long leases and high rents suggest that they were still more interested in a steady fixed return without taking on direct responsibility for their investments. Conversely, the shorter leases and lower rents of the Nantais suggest a greater direct involvement of landowners in their properties.

This direct involvement is further suggested by the more widespread practice of sharecropping, which involved not only *métayage* but also a system quite unique to the Nantais, the *complant*. *Métayage* tended to be practiced in areas dominated by a pasture type of agriculture. Thus the only parts of the Orléanais where it was to be found was in the Sologne and the Forêt, and even there it accounted for less than 10 percent of the agricultural population. It existed in all areas of the Nantais but was most common in the Plateau and Retz–Vendée. An agricultural report of

1855 notes that it was practiced in the cantons of Machecoul, Bouaye, Ligné, and Varades.[45] According to the 1862 enquiry, it was most common in the cantons of Legé (22 percent of the agricultural population), Saint-Philbert (11 percent), Carquefou (9 percent), and Ligné and Saint-Mars-la-Jaille (both 6 percent). The enquiry also indicates a surprisingly high proportion (24 percent) in the canton of Nantes. In the 1851 census, we find approximately twice the proportion of *métayers* in the Plateau and Retz–Vendée than in the Valley and Sèvre-et-Maine (see Table 6.5). The intensive type of agricultural subregion, Sèvre-et-Maine, had the lowest proportion.

The terms of the *métayage* system were even more varied than those of *fermage*. About half the harvest would be turned over to the landowner in payment of rent, though this differed from property to property. The landowner would normally supply half the livestock and the rest would be the exclusive property of the *métayer*. In some instances the landowner would also supply seed, in others this would be the responsibility of the *métayer*. All these conditions discouraged absenteeism: for the landlord to avoid the risks of fraud, he almost had to stay on his property.[46] *Métayage* was being abandoned in the Orléanais for this very reason.[47]

The *complant* also included a payment in kind. It was a form of land lease that was found only in the vineyards of the Nantais, concentrated largely in the cantons of Le Loroux, Vertou, and Vallet – in other words the best Muscadet vineyards of Sèvre-et-Maine. In fact, it was traditional for the nineteenth-century agricultural reports on Loire-Inférieure to make a distinction between the *vignes franches* exploited by owner–cultivators or rented out to *fermiers* and the *vignes à complant* rented out to *colons*[48] for an indefinite period of time. The *colon's* legal rights in this contract remained ambiguous throughout the nineteenth century. Although he rented the land from a proprietor (the *bailleur*), he owned not only all the built-up property – the house, sheds, roads, wells – but also most of what was planted on the land – the hedgerows, grass, and, most important of all, the vines. The length of the lease was tied to the life of the vine so that as long as the *colon* maintained his vines, he had control of the exploitation and even had the right to pass it on as an inheritance. Poor maintenance or the destruction of the vine were the sole grounds of dismissal. All the proprietor possessed besides the land itself were the trees "strong enough to support a ladder": woodland trees and chestnut groves. The rent would be collected at the time of the grape harvest, which would be surveyed by either the proprietor himself or by his representative, the *écarteur*, to assure payment of one-third or sometimes a quarter of the crop.

It is difficult to say what the exact origins of this system were, though one can be fairly certain that they lay in the late Middle Ages when land-owners, short of capital, required their tenants to bear the costs of planting their domains in vine. It closely resembled the *domaine congéable* practiced in Lower Brittany where the tenant possessed all built-up property, hedges, and other barriers on the land. As long as the vines continued to produce and the proprietors continued to live close to their properties, the *vigne à complant* offered definite advantages to both parties of the contract: to the proprietor it guaranteed an income without exacting a heavy outlay of capital; to the *colon* it gave a form of assurance that his work would not be wasted. It was an ideal system for the pebbly soils of Sèvre-et-Maine, where an intensive form of viticulture was practically the only feasible form of exploitation. But if the vines failed, the whole system was called into question. Did the *colon* forfeit all his rights? Could the proprietor lay claim only to the land and trees? Prerevolutionary documents had stated that the *colon*'s rights had been "ceded forever," and for the greater part of the nineteenth century, the *colon* assumed that this was so; he lived as if he were a propertyholder with the sole proviso that an annual rent be paid in kind. However, despite a number of court cases and an even greater number of general legal debates both at Paris and Nantes, the respective property rights of the proprietor and *colon* were never explicitly defined during the lawmaking years of the Revolution and Empire. Thus there was no real legal sanction behind the operation of the *vignes à complant*. It was a system of family exploitations founded more on a traditional accord between the actual proprietor and the exploitant than on the code of law. Consequently it was going to be one of the first systems to suffer during the crisis years of the late nineteenth century (see Chapter 9).[49]

Dependent labor

A survey of the active rural population cannot be complete without consideration of those who neither owned nor rented any land at all, those who lived solely by the work they did for others, the dependent labor force. They were a minority, although they did make up a greater proportion of the population in the Nantais than in the Orléanais and were especially important in areas where a pasture-type agriculture was practiced. Full-time wage earners are not strictly part of a peasant economy because of their relative dependence on outside employers as opposed to their own families. Dependent labor can be better analyzed within the objective terms of the market, and its presence should be understood as an important qualifying factor in our model of the peasant economy.

As in practically every other part of rural France, there were two kinds of dependent labor in the Loire Country, the *journaliers* and the *domestiques*. The *journalier* was employed by the day, the *domestique* for a term of several months or the year. The *journalier* was easily the most common kind of wage earner in the Orléanais and the Nantais, though clearly the conditions of his employment implied that he was not working full time in this capacity. A response from the canton of Aigrefeuille (Retz-Vendée) to the 1862 enquiry notes that the majority of *journaliers* rented several parcels of land that they cultivated when not employed. Most *journaliers* probably did exploit some land for their own benefit. There is evidence that some of them turned to nonagricultural pursuits during the "dead season," the two or three winter months when there was no agricultural work to be had. The 1862 enquiry suggests that this was more common in the Orléanais than in the Nantais: in the Forêt d'Orléans, they were employed in the stone quarries; in the Sologne, they were employed as sawyers and terrace builders; the only mention of nonagricultural employment of the *journaliers* in the Nantais is in the responses from the extreme eastern part of the region where some worked, for their own account, as spinners or weavers during the winter months. Some of them also probably found work in the towns. In normal times, the summer was a busy season for the *journalier*. The demand for labor was so great that some areas, particularly those with a cereal-type agriculture, had to call on outside help. In the Beauce, these outsiders were known as *aoûtrons*, or *oûtrons*, and came from as far away as Brittany and even Belgium.[50] They returned every year, carrying their own implements, to be employed by the same person. The wealthier farmers of the Beauce sometimes even applied to the prefect to have soldiers sent to help in the harvest when there was a particularly heavy crop to be taken.[51]

The greater area planted in cereals combined with the lower number of *journaliers* resulted in higher wages in the Orléanais than in the Nantais. A *journalier* could earn 3 francs or more a day in the Beauce at harvest time. Even in the Sologne, he was reportedly earning over 2 francs during those crucial summer months, and this did not include the food and drink supplied by the employer. In the Nantais, the highest harvest wage that one could expect was 2 francs, paid within the canton of Nantes. Otherwise, wages ranged in the Nantais between 1.25 and 1.75 francs during the harvest, 0.75 and 1.00 francs at all other times. In all areas of the Orléanais, the off-peak wage was over 1 franc. A general comparison of *journaliers'* wage rates given in the 1862 enquiry, taking into account seasonal fluctuations and the nonpecuniary advantages (which essentially meant food), indicates that they were one and a half times as high in the Orléanais as in the Nantais.

Domestiques were, as the Latin origin of the term implies, workers hired to do work for the household. In its narrowest sense, the term was applied only to those who actually lived in the same house as their employer, did a variety of jobs on the farms, and ate at the same table as their master. This close personal contact was undoubtedly the main reason behind the 1848 parliamentary enquiry's remark that *domestiques* in the Beauce "cannot be considered as workers."[52] The 1862 enquiry indicates that the feeding and clothing of *domestiques* were practiced in all areas of both regions, even though these supplies were scarcely objects of luxury. From the canton of Saint-Philbert, we read: "The *domestiques* who receive something in kind are very numerous, but these objects are only a few clothes of insignificant value, 12 to 15 francs at the most." And from the canton of Vertou: "The *domestiques* are paid exclusively money wages; some have many supplementary effects – clothing, shirts, wooden clogs – which hardly attain a fifteenth of the total wage."[53] Many documents, especially the manuscript census returns (which we shall be discussing in the next chapter), extend the term *domestique* to all workers hired for a rural household for a period of several months, whether they actually lived with their employer or not. Cowmen, carters, and shepherds were frequently lodged in the stables. But their employer usually supplied them with food and drink. Furthermore, the stables were nearly always next door to the main farmhouse, if not an actual part of it, as in the case of the enclosed farmyards of the Beauce. In several instances, the stables were the warmest, most comfortable part of a cultivator's home.

Domestiques – and we are using the term in its widest sense – were normally hired for a year in the Nantais. In the Orléanais, they were commonly hired for a period of either four or eight months. These shorter terms were particularly frequent in areas with a cereal-type agriculture, where it was necessary to keep as flexible a labor force as possible. *Domestiques* were hired on a fixed date. The most common were Saint John's Day (24 June) for the four-month term and All Saints' Day (1 November) for the eight. The hiring would take place at the main square of the major towns in each region with the candidates assembled into groups according to their specialty. The prospective employers conducted all their interviews in the open square. When the employer decided to hire, he would pass the candidate a coin, as an assurance that the contract would be kept. There was never any written contract.[54]

Taken as a whole, the wage earners are the most vaguely defined social group that we find in the rural parts of our two regions. It seems probable that the major part of the *journaliers* and *domestiques* recorded by the census only worked in this capacity part time. Certainly, most of the *journaliers* exercised some other "profession" for a part of the year, whether it was cutting wood, an artisanal pastime, or working on their own small parcels of land (which the cadastre suggests were quite widespread). The *domestiques* were, of course, more likely to rely on a steady wage income, but even they were subject to seasonal unemployment during which time they either tended their own land or, like the *journalier,* pursued some nonagrarian activity. The very vagueness of the documentation on this dependent labor force is itself significant. As one browses through the governmental enquiries, one again and again gets the impression that the administration was seeking information on a social class, a working class, that didn't really exist. Columns upon columns of questions asking the total number of workers, the workers' wages, the workers' expenditures, the workers' standard of living are left unanswered not solely because of the respondent's indolence (though this was undoubtedly sometimes a factor) but because there was simply no answer to give. Nowhere in the rural parts of our two regions could one find a large number of permanently employed wage earners working for a single agricultural production unit. The only production units that did employ large numbers were the nonagrarian establishments previously described. The center of the whole rural economy remained the household: the wealthier households supplemented their own family's effort by hiring others to help; the poorer households supplemented their family income by going out to work for a wage.

3. The imperfect peasant economy

To sum up the main points made so far, we should go back to Chapter 4, which dealt with the potentialities for exchange created by the capital cities of our two regions. The analysis revealed that both cities were suffering from a relapse in commercial activity but that they reacted in different ways. Nantes developed a dual-based industrial economy that relied equally on national, even international, commerce and local agriculture, whereas Orléans' industries became totally dependent on local agriculture. Nantes' interest in national commerce gave it a greater initiative to adopt new modes of transportation than Orléans, which stubbornly resisted all innovations that threatened its old role as a commercial warehouse. On the other hand, Orléans was more regularly in contact with its hinterland: the most common form of commodity exchange with the country in Orléans was the weekly market; Nantes showed greater interest in the seasonal fair. In Chapter 5 we made our first observations on the processes of social exchange by focusing attention on two groups that could be easily documented, the large landowners and the educators. The large landowners were found to be more influential in the Orléanais than the Nantais, whereas the educators, embodied in the person of the village *curé,* were more influential in the Nantais. The landowner's strength in the Orléanais was related to Orléans' near total reliance on its hinterland; the *curé's* strength in the Nantais was related to the Catholic fervor of the region. Do these two separate observations have a common explanation? We left the question open.

In this chapter we turned attention to the whole of the two regions and concentrated on a specific topic, the economy. Two general facts have been brought to light. The first is the continuing importance in both regions of the subregions. Each subregion was dominated by a certain agricultural "type," for a combination of various agricultural resources, which were themselves correlated to a degree with certain forms of social organization. But one finds that the organization of rural society cannot be entirely explained by the agricultural type. The second fact to emerge from this chapter has to do with each region as a whole, not its parts. Namely, the region whose capital had developed a dual-based economy had a more integrated, homogeneous society residing in its hinterland than the region whose capital relied almost totally on its hinterland. In the Nantais, household industries were more widespread, landowners more involved in the management of their leaseholds, and the small owner-cultivators more dispersed than in the Orléanais. Nantes, directing its gaze simultaneously to sea and to land, permitted a freedom of action in its hinterland that could never be matched in the Orléanais. This city provided the rural economy with sizable outlets but in no way monopolized it. Orléans not only supplied fewer outlets but also had full control of industries that, in the Nantais, would have been scattered throughout the countryside. Thus the potential optimum level of agricultural intensity must have been higher in the Nantais than the Orléanais.

It seems that the Nantais was, throughout the nineteenth century, more intensively cultivated than the Orléanais. A weighted sample taken from the first and second cadastres of almost 7,000 properties (excluding all properties with buildings occupying more than one-third of their total area) indicates a mean property size of 2.82 hectares in the Nantais, 5.58 hectares in the Orléanais. The median – a more telling statistic given the extremely skewed distribution – was 0.48 and 0.62, respectively. There are no precise figures available on the exploitations. Data provided by the 1862 enquiry, for what they are worth, actually suggest a greater intensity of agriculture in the Orléanais than the Nantais (74 percent of the exploitations in the former being under 5 hectares against 53 percent in the latter). But, as the commissioners themselves readily pointed out, these statistics ignored the smaller exploitations. There are 1¼ times as many cultivators (or *exploitants*) as exploitations recorded in the enquiry, and we already know that the total number of cultivators was grossly underestimated.

The large proportion of the rural population that exploited the land directly for the benefit of their own households is the basis of our contention that these two regions can be described as peasant economies. From all the information previously presented (qualitative and quantitative), we would estimate that these cultivators made up at least 75 percent of the total population active in agriculture in either region. But these are imperfect peasant economies because (1) some areas of the countryside, though not very extensive, were dedicated to large-scale, nonagrarian activities (the mines of the Nantais, the stone quarries of the Orléanais) and (2) many cultivators both hired and worked as wage earners. The vast majority of wage earners only worked part time. Thus, wage labor was not a direct challenge to the household as the major unit of production. Rather, wages were an important supplement to the household budget and only heightened the optimum level of agricultural intensity.

We must not forget Chayanov's lesson. This optimum level is determined by a subjective labor–consumer balance – the household's subjective evaluation of its needs against the effort required to fulfill them – and not the absolute terms of the market. How did they labor? How did they consume?

We know from the enquiries that most of the agricultural population, in either region, worked from "dawn until dark" – during the harvest they even worked while it was dark. But for the same amount of work, a cultivator in the Nantais got less on his kitchen table than in the Orléanais. Table 6.7 gives the average adult's daily diet in 1862. The figures are only very approximate and are based on the averaging out of data provided by the cantonal responses to the enquiry of that year. The agricultural population is divided into four groups: well-to-do cultivators, small cultivators, *domestiques*, and *journaliers*. ("Cultivators" refers to owner–cultivators and *fermiers* alike.) It can be readily seen that there were no major differences in the diet between these groups, with the exception of wine. Wine was a cash crop that the smaller cultivators preferred to sell than consume themselves; it was served to *domestiques* and *journaliers* only during the peak of the harvest season. The greater difference between the groups in the Nantais than in the Orléanais is a reflection of the greater marketability of the Nantais' wines. Cider and other fruit alcohols were drunk in both regions; cider, in fact, was virtually the only drink consumed in the Nantais Plateau. Another alternative drink was a brandy (*marc*), distilled from the pomace of grapes and often a variety of other fruits and then mixed with a lot of water – a drink that the cantonal responses from the Nantais identify as *boite*.

As for food, the main diet in both regions was bread, soup, and vegetables (mostly potatoes). Residents in the Orléanais also used to enjoy a daily serving of meat, usually pork, but occasionally beef. La Ferté-Saint-Aubin, in the Sologne, had the lowest rate of meat consumption, but even there every adult, whatever group he belonged to, is reported to have eaten 165 grams a day. In the Nantais, 100 grams or more were the

Table 6.7. Daily diet of average adult cultivator in the Orléanais (O) and the Nantais (N), 1862

	Well-to-do cultivators			Small cultivators			Métayers			Domestiques			Journaliers		
	O	N	O/N	O	N	O/N	O	N	O/N	O	N	O/N	O	N	O/N
Bread (gm)															
Wheat	513	640	0.80	463	601	0.77	800	580	1.38	429	620	0.69	408	573	0.71
Wheat and rye or barley	550	300	1.83	650	338	1.92	592	246	2.41	808	167	4.84	763	233	3.27
Barley	8	0	–	13	0	–	0	0	0.00	13	0	–	13	0	–
Rye	0	8	0.00	0	8	0.00	0	8	0.00	0	8	0.00	125	8	15.63
Buckwheat	0	123	0.00	0	138	0.00	0	142	0.00	0	142	0.00	0	131	0.00
Total	1,071	1,071	1.00	1,126	1,085	1.04	1,392	976	1.43	1,250	937	1.33	1,309	945	1.39
Soup (cl)	59	115	0.51	74	90	0.82	73	95	0.77	73	106	0.69	83	88	0.94
Milk and dairy prod. (cl)	20	39	0.51	20	32	0.62	28	33	0.85	19	35	0.54	17	36	0.47
Meat (gm)	237	161	1.47	226	93	2.43	236	76	3.11	251	75	2.35	210	71	2.96
Vegetables (gm)	198	244	0.81	225	190	1.18	275	230	1.20	242	250	0.97	278	245	1.13
Cheese (gm)	74	0	–	94	0	–	84	0	–	101	0	–	105	0	–
Other Food (gm)	19	73	0.26	19	?	?	50	88	0.57	27	90	0.30	27	96	0.28
Wine (cl)	65	78	0.83	54	108	0.50	38	70	0.54	35	46	0.76	32	17	1.88
Other drink (cl)	81	73	1.11	100	86	1.16	108	100	1.08	131	96	1.36	125	85	1.47

Note: ? means data not available.
Source: Agricultural enquiry, 1862.

normal daily consumption in only the Plateau and the cantons of Carquefou and Nantes. Elsewhere, meat consumption was low, probably
even lower than reported. In the canton of Vertou (Sèvre-et-Maine), it
was noted that the *métayers* ate meat only 20 times a year. The rural
population made up for their lack of meat by eating more soup and dairy
products. The *galette,* found in all parts of Brittany, was also a popular
dish. Furthermore, the bread consumed in the Nantais was probably of a
better quality than that of the Orléanais, where the strict system of crop
rotations obliged the population to mix wheat flour with either rye or
barley. In the Nantais, almost everybody ate a pure wheat bread – the
lack of meat must have been one of the main incentives behind the
widespread cultivation of wheat that one found in the Nantais. And
where did all the meat go that was not consumed in the countryside? It
went, of course, to Nantes.

Nantes made it possible for such an intensive form of peasant economy to survive in the countryside. This might have resulted in a lower absolute standard of living in the Nantais but it meant that the household-
type structure of the economy – which is, after all, what we are mainly interested in – was more secure in the event of crisis than in the Orléanais,
where the economic alternatives open to the rural population were considerably less varied. Here we have a key to understanding the greater
degree of rural "autonomy" in the Orléanais that we noted in Chapter 5.
This was the upshot of an insecurity felt throughout the rural population
that made them turn their mentality inward, one result being the
prevalence of superstition. Such a worldwide institution as the Catholic
church was strongly distrusted; the rural population had no means of
identifying with it. Catholicism in the Nantais, on the other hand, was a
local phenomenon. In this tight-knit, more homogeneous society, it was
easier for the rural inhabitants to accept the *curé* as one of them, whereas
in the Orléanais, he was viewed as an outsider.

This element of insecurity, the development of crisis, and the way in
which crisis was reflected in as well as created by the household structure
of the peasant economy can only be understood within the context of
time. All we have done to this point has been to contrast the two regions
and their subregions by discussing the functions of the various social
groups that lived within them. It has been largely an analysis over space.
In the third and final part of this study, we introduce the notion of time.

Part III
Time

7 Peasant family and peasant population

Ideally, if space is to be defined in terms of social exchange between individuals, time should not be taken here as the objective measure of the calendar that can be chopped up into years, weeks, hours, and minutes but as the individual experience of each connector, which, when compounded with the experience of others, adds up to a social sense of time. The *measurement* and *experience* of time are not at all the same thing.

This distinction is frequently made in studies of rural societies because a countryman is much more exposed to the natural cycle of the seasons than the citizen (which is not to deny its validity in an urban setting). As the rural sociologist Henri Mendras puts it, the traditional concept of time in the countryside has not been as "a pure quantity, homogeneous in all its parts, always comparable to itself and exactly measurable. . . . The units of time are not units of measurement but units of a rhythm, where the alternation of diversities are periodically brought around to the similar *[l'alternance des diversités ramène périodiquement au semblable]*". . . . In other words, one could say that time was less an abstract notion allowing a dimension to be given to human life than a *succession of lived experiences*. . . . Thus *lived time* is never completely synchronous with calendar time" [my emphasis].[1] This is time seen from a thoroughly Bergsonian perspective — "that fluid mass, that moving mysterious, grand and powerful ocean."[2] It describes time as a mediating experience between the conscience of each individual connector and the others around him, the objects that make up his environment, and the play of chance that pulls him in as an active member of the rural society. In this sense, time *is* the social order.

There are certainly grounds for supposing that the "lived-time" within the very dense populations of the Orléanais and the Nantais had a certain character of its own, a character defined by the human environment of high labor intensity, where most of that labor was expended by families directly exploiting the land for their own benefit. One might even guess that the difference in the possible levels of intensity between the two regions was in some way tied up with a difference in the experience of time. But the historian, unlike Mendras, has no opinion poll to go by. There was no IFOP in nineteenth-century France to sound out the attitudes that the country folk had toward time. Our sources are, as always, the written records, the vast majority of which are, as always, administrative records. The possible range of our enquiry into time thus has exactly the same limits as our enquiry into space.

So, we cannot hope to recreate each individual experience of time nor even the general social temporal attitude that existed during this period. But there are documents available that do give some indication as to how the individual stood in relation to others and how that relationship changed over time, both for the individual and for the population as a whole. Obviously, the information contained in these documents is not going to be the same as a description of the experience itself, but it is the closest we can get. The two most suggestive documents are the census nominal lists (*listes nominatives*) and the cadastre. The nominal lists itemize the name, age, occupation, family situation, and, in some instances, the birthplace of every individual in the population. The cadastre[3] provides the names of every propertyholder, his residence, the quantity of property possessed, the dates of purchase and sale, together with information on the individuals with whom these exchanges were made. Both the nominal lists and the cadastre are complete in these details (with a few minor exceptions to be discussed later) from the July Monarchy up until the outbreak of the First World War or within a few years thereof. It is therefore possible to outline the individual experience within the population structures and property structures of the two regions over an 80-year period – more than three generations. Because it has now been established that approximately four-fifths of the active agricultural population in either region owned land and exploited it almost entirely through the enterprise of their own families, we can claim with some confidence that an analysis of these documents is going to provide a powerful insight into what the average individual experience of time for the major part of rural society must have been. Obviously, the answers that we generate will be heavily economic and materialistic in nature but that, after all, is the prime emphasis of this study.

We can say a bit more. When discussing a theoretical definition of the peasant economy in terms of an interplay between population and property, we made a point of dividing the analysis into "microeconomic" and "macroeconomic" levels (see Chapter 3). A study of the nominal lists and the cadastre demonstrates, in a very practical way, how the two sides of this interplay – population and property – operated in actual fact. Using these sources, we can build up a rough picture of what was really happening at both these analytical levels as well as indicate what sort of impact the microeconomic structure might have had on the macroeconomic, and vice versa. All this turns on the experience of time: the time it took the individual to inherit property, to disinherit it, to buy, to sell. There is no way of knowing at this point how these individual experiences were woven into the full fabric of rural society, what sort of effect a change in that individual experience might have had on the society and, conversely, once such a social change had been effected how this in turn would have further influenced the experience of the individual. But that is precisely what we intend to find out.

These are enormous sources, so, instead of setting out all their analysis in a single sweep, we decided to divide the presentation into two chapters. The first will deal with the questions related to population and the second with property. At the end of the second chapter, there will be a summary of our findings before proceeding onto Chapter 9, which will be concerned with the phenomenon of "agricultural crisis" (as defined in Chapter 3) within this same context of the individual experience and the society that it created.

Why population before property? In theory, there is no real reason at all except insofar as the density of population defines the options available to its members (see Chapter 3, Section 1); but the population density is itself the product of decisions made on earlier options. It should be clear by now that this study is seeking a definition of the structure of relationships within the peasant economy, not some *primum mobile* that sets the whole system in motion. However, given the historical sources, there are some very good methodological reasons for considering population first. By limiting its survey to propertyholders, the cadastre cannot provide sufficient information for reconstructing the entire life experience of the individual, and there are certainly no other sources on landed property that can provide it. Short of a complete reconstitution of families from the vital registries – quite impossible for this scope of study – the nominal lists offer the best possible means of mapping out the kind of experience, from birth to death, that most individuals would expect to have had in the Orléanais and the Nantais during the nineteenth century. Furthermore, there are other demographic sources, particularly those vital registries (*états civils*), that can be used in addition to the nominal lists to build up a picture of the entire demographic composition of the rural society. In other words, a study of population provides the surest, most complete way of fathoming out how the individual experience was related to society at large. Thus, corresponding to the more general micro- and macroeconomic analytical levels we have discussed primarily in theoretical terms, there is a micro- and macrodemographic approach that can be taken when inspecting the actual data at hand.[4] Having examined these population patterns, we shall be in a far better position to evaluate the part, albeit important part, that landed property played in the lives of the rural inhabitants.

1. Microdemography: the developmental cycle

In the perfect peasant economy that Chayanov had described, the number and age of the family members were the major determinants of the point of equilibrium in the labor–consumer balance at any given moment of time. Chayanov made his initial demonstration of this with a simple model that took as consumers every family member and as workers only those over 14 years of age. Then, on the assumption that the husband was 25 and the wife 20 at marriage and that a surviving child was born to them every 3 years of the fertile period, he proceeded to calculate a consumer–worker ratio. He found that the ratio reached its peak (1.94:1) in the fourteenth year of marriage and then began to fall off. He was, in fact, describing the developmental cycle in its most elementary form: in a society in which the conjugal family unit (father, mother, children) is the main producing unit, an individual's social position (consumer or worker) is determined by his demographic position; the structure and productivity of the family is determined by the given length of its existence.[5] As already noted in Chapter 2 (Section 1), in Chayanov's theory, the changing labor force and consumer demands of the family through this cycle directly determined the amount of land that it exploited. But Chayanov made a major qualification to this general rule at the end of his discussion of the cycle:

In a number of countries where nonpartible inheritance is the rule . . . the pressure of the biological development of the family undoubtedly *can not influence the amount of land for use.* This is expressed predominantly in *changes in the relationship of own and hired labor* serving the particular production machine and *to the extent to which its own surplus labor goes off to work elsewhere.* [My emphasis][6]

In a most remarkable study of an eighteenth-century census of the north Austrian village of Heidenreichstein, where nonpartible inheritance was the law, Lutz Berkner has demonstrated (though I find his statistics a weaker proof than he claims) that there was indeed a relationship between hired labor and the stage that the family employers had reached in the developmental cycle and that this relationship could also be extended to include resident kin outside the conjugal family unit.[7] To what degree does this relationship hold when the limitation on the extension of property is not so much the law as the density of the population itself?

Scattered remarks in the administrative enquiries and reports that we have used in earlier chapters do hint at the existence of some sort of developmental cycle in our two regions. They are mostly references to the ages that children began their apprenticeship – if it were a question of some rural trade – or the age at which they began work in the fields. The information has, of course, an intrinsic significance inasmuch as trade is considered a vital part of the peasant economy and the age at which one began one's trade or field work is the point at which one became an active producer within the family unit (whether the child's own or another's). All these reports indicate that one's role as a "worker" began at 13 or 14, in other words the same age Chayanov had noted for early twentieth-century Russia. The 1848 enquiry for Artenay (Orléanais) points out that the age of apprenticeship was between 13 and 14; in Cléry, the school-leaving age is put at 13 and 14; apprenticeship for girls in the canton of Ancenis (Nantais) began at 12 and lasted two years, whereas boys began a three-year apprenticeship at 15; the reports from Bouaye and Legé indicate the same ages.[8] Apparently the situation was not very different in 1884: school-leaving age 13 or 14 in the cantons of Chécy and Mardié (Orléanais); 13 for the whole department of Loire-Inférieure.[9]

These figures are too cut-and-dried. Presumably it was not uncommon for children to assume work in the fields at an earlier age, and school and apprenticeship (especially in the earlier years of the century) were not everybody's experience. More important still, none of these reports indicate what happened to these individuals after that age or even what kind of family status they had when they began their work. That sort of information can only be found in the nominal lists.

Method of study

There is no point in going into any great detail on the methods used in studying these lists because they correspond, by and large, to standard practices found in any demographic textbook.[10] Except when noted, the terminology on household matters is the same as that adopted by the *Cambridge Group for the History of Population and Social Structure*.[11] So the comments here will be limited to the method of abstracting our data from the manuscript lists (because there is as yet no recognized standard practice) and to any other aspect of these data's compilation that could otherwise be the cause of later ambiguities.

Our data have been drawn from the nominal lists of 17 communes that were compiled every five years from 1836 to 1911.[12] All individuals enumerated are listed by *household* (i.e., all those under a single head of household) and by *houseful* (all households within the same set of premises, or house – everybody living under the same roof) with the exception of the lists for 1836 and 1841, when only the households are given. From each quinquennial list, we have usually sampled 14 or 15 housefuls. In the case of Ardon, we have sampled 30 per list because this is the only commune we found to represent the Sologne. In the case of the communes of the Loire Valley, we have sampled fewer housefuls per list (usually 10) because the subregion in both the Orléanais and the Nantais is represented by three communes. These samples were taken from microfilms of the documents and not from the original documents. In order to avoid excessive expense, not every page of the lists was photographed – in many cases our films include only every other page or even every third page. The sampling was done in two stages: first, the photographed pages from which the sample was to be made were selected (e.g., if we wanted 10 housefuls per list and we had (unlikely) only 5 photographed pages, we would take 2 housefuls per page; with 10 pages, 1 houseful per page; 20 pages, 1 houseful every other page, etc.); then the housefuls themselves were seleced. If precautions had not been taken, a bias could have crept into the sample at this second stage because there was no way of knowing whether the first and, especially, the last housefuls on the photographed page were actually complete. The first and last housefuls were therefore never sampled. Sampling from the remaining housefuls was based on a descending order of selection. Thus, if one selected the second houseful on the first page, one would select the third houseful from the second page, and so on until one had sampled the second-to-last houseful, after which one would start again with the second houseful.

Through most of the following analysis, the houseful is to be taken as the statistical "case," containing general information on the commune and year, as well as the number of households and number of residents within that particular houseful. We also had enough space to record details on up to 11 residents. These details include each resident's age, sex, occupation, and, if he is outside the first conjugal family unit, his relationship to the first head of household. For 1872, 1906, and 1911, we also have been able to note the resident's place of birth. The entire sample contains information on over 3,600 housefuls and more than 15,000 individuals.

A roughly equal number of housefuls have been taken from each subregion in order to get a fair gauge of variance within each one of them. However, for the purpose of interregional comparison, we have had to weight the data. This has been done in such a fashion that the weight factors, when multiplied out for the entire sample, are equal to unity – in other words, the total *weighted* number of cases adds up to a little over 3,600, or the same as the total *unweighted* number of cases. The weighting is determined by two criteria. The first is based on the assumption that the communes selected may be considered typical of their subregion. The proportion of the housefuls within each subregion has therefore been weighted according to the proportion of the populaton within these subregions. Second, an additional weight factor has been applied to assure that the total number of residents within the sample for each subregion grows at the same rate per five-year period as the population of that subregion. For example, if the population of a given subregion were to grow from 10,000 to 12,000 between 1851 and 1856 and our actual sample from the two communes representing this subregion contained 100 residents for each year, the cases for 1856 would be multiplied by a weight factor of 1.2 in relation to the cases of 1851. Obviously, this is going to produce some distortion at the level of the subregion if one were to concentrate on a brief period of a decade or so, but it has been assumed that within the broader context of the following analysis these haphazard errors will smooth themselves out.[13]

Enough! Other methodological problems can easily be discussed during the analysis.

Household and houseful

Is the distinction between household and houseful a useful one for the rural economies of the Orléanais and the Nantais? It most certainly would be if there were any evidence that several families frequently did live together in one house. Guy Thuillier has described at some length just such a situation among the *métayers* of the southern parts of the Nivernais. He traces this to the *bordelage* system of tenure of the Old Regime whereby land was returned to the owner if the tenant died without heirs, thus encouraging the tenants to form joint family holdings (*communautés*). South of the Morvan, this remained the general rule until the first decades of the twentieth century, even though all laws supporting the system had been nullified during the revolutionary era.[14]

Although we know that *métayage* was not very widespread in the Orléanais, the possibility should be considered of some kind of parallel arrangement in those parts of the Orléanais with a pasture-type agriculture and closest to the Nivernais, especially in the Sologne. Our sample indicates, however, that multiple households were rare – if there were any eighteenth-century province with which the Orléanais could be compared, it would have been less the Nivernais than the Ile-de-France, where, after Jacques Dupâquier, the general rule was "one house, one household."[15] Only 7.7 percent of all the housefuls sampled in the Orléanais had more than one household; in the Nantais, we found only 6.7 percent. Curiously, this proportion showed a slight tendency to increase over time, with a high point being reached, in the Orléanais, somewhere between 1872 and 1886; in the Nantais, the main increase appears to have occurred after 1891.[16] It is possible that this increase reflected the same sort of gradual trend toward more complicated systems of cohabitation that Michael Anderson and W. A. Armstrong have noted in some of the urban areas of Victorian England.[17] But the idea should not be pushed too far: the proportion of multiple households is low at all times, and even though there are some signs of change, the overall effect on household structure must have been slight indeed. As we shall see shortly, this corresponds to a stability found in most of the other forms of living arrangements recorded in the nominal lists.

Space, in fact, accounts for much more of the variation in the number of households per houseful than does time. Thus we find that the slightly greater proportion of multiple households in the Orléanais is largely due to their relatively high percentage in the two subregions with a pasture-type agriculture – 10.3 percent in the Forêt d'Orléans, 15.7 percent in the Sologne. Again, in the Nantais, it is the pasture-type subregions that have an above average proportion – 8.3 percent in the Plateau, 8.8 percent in Retz–Vendée. In other words, multiple households were not the mark of areas with tightly agglomerated populations (i.e., what might be considered the more "urban" subregions) but of areas where the population was dispersed, where the isolated farmstead with its open yard was most common. In the light of what has been written about rural joint families in other parts of France, one would expect to find that a large proportion of the multiple households was made up of relatives of one sort or another (constituting what the Cambridge Group would call "multiple family households"). But in actuality, the percentage of multiple households with at least one relative in the second household was significantly lower in the Orléanais (43.0 percent) than in the Nantais (86.9 percent); it was lowest of all in the Sologne (20.1 percent).

Do these figures imply that it was the occupation of the household members rather than their blood ties that caused them to share their house with another household? *Journaliers* and artisans made up roughly one-third of the active members of these multiple households in the Orléanais. Most of the other occupations listed are cultivators of one kind or another. These proportions are representative of all the member households, whether listed first or last, so that, considering the large proportion of *journaliers* and artisans found here as compared with the Orléanais at large (where they accounted for somewhere between 15 and 20 percent of the total), it does seem that the multiple households were established by farming families in need of a supplementary income. We know that there was significantly less opportunity for rural industry in the Orléanais than in the Nantais, so the motivation to combine one's talents with another's in the production of a commodity for which there was relatively little demand must have been correspondingly that much greater in the Orléanais. In the intensive-type agricultural areas of the Valley, where houses were closely grouped together, there was hardly any need for one family physically to move in with another, but in the pasture-type areas, where housing was much more dispersed, there almost certainly must have been.

The multiple households of the Nantais, which largely consisted of relatives, had a much smaller proportion of *journaliers* and artisans among their members – they made up roughly 10 percent of the total. In fact, one-quarter of the active members are recorded as exercising no occupation at all. Furthermore, there is a sharp distinction between the occupations of the members of the first household listed and of those following it. The members with no occupation are generally found in the latter. If the multiple households of the Nantais are compared with single households with relatives living outside the conjugal family unit, no statistically significant difference can be made in their occupations, nor in their various kinship ties.

Thus, to return to our original question, we should note that the distinction between household and houseful has a certain utility in the Orléanais inasmuch as it can be considered a rough index of hidden unemployment in the economies of the pasture-type agricultural subregions. But, with the exception of the Sologne, the proportion of multiple households was very low. More than 85 percent of an even lower overall proportion of multiple households in the Nantais could be looked upon as simply another form of the extended family in which the members outside the first conjugal family unit lived in such a manner as to be considered by the census enumerators as a separate household. It is quite possible that this small proportion of multiple households was the result of nothing other than a peculiar quirk in the local methods of census taking. What is certain is that, in both the Orléanais and the Nantais, the general rule *was* "one house, one household."

Mean household size

Let us first consider a few simple descriptive statistics on these households before going about the more complicated task of assessing the effects of the developmental cycle. To begin with, households tended to be somewhat smaller in the Orléanais than in the Nantais: the means of the household size for the entire period were 3.76 and 4.16, respectively.[18] Variation over time was clearly not very great. Table 7.1 suggests a drop from 4.33 in 1836 to 3.16 in 1906 in the Orléanais and from 4.40 to 3.78 in the Nantais, and as in the case of the increasing trend found in the proportion of multiple households, the main development appears to have occurred later in the Nantais than the Orléanais. However, the analysis of variance presented in this table indicates that, at least as far as the Orléanais was concerned, the differences in mean from one year to another could have been just as much due to the luck of the draw as any real trend (although we do know that this decline did correspond to a national trend).[19] Again, space explains much more of the variation than time. Households were smaller in the intensive-type agricultural subregions than in the pasture type, although it is important to note that even the Nantais Valley had larger households than any subregion of the Orléanais – yet another indication of the greater opportunities available to the Nantais' population.

Composition of the household

For an analysis of the actual makeup of these households, we have to take into account a few of what the anthropologists like to call "basic principles." As an economist of peasant society, Chayanov chose to build

Table 7.1. *Mean household size (MHS), 1836–1911*

Year	Orléanais MHS	$N_w{}^a$	Nantais MHS	$N_w{}^a$	Subregion	MHS	$N_w{}^a$
1836	4.33	78	4.40	128	Beauce	3.97	277
1841	3.99	84	4.55	120	Sologne	3.90	157
1846	3.76	92	4.11	142	Forêt	4.03	226
1851	4.01	90	4.64	126	Valley (O)	3.57	741
1856	3.88	91	3.97	154	Plateau	4.44	434
1861	3.97	87	4.14	145	R–V	4.18	592
1866	3.78	91	4.38	139	S-et-M	4.06	514
1872	3.78	90	3.95	154	Valley (N)	4.04	728
1876	3.73	87	4.09	149		4.01	3,670
1881	3.53	96	4.60	139			
1886	3.77	93	4.20	147	df n_1		7
1891	3.74	89	3.87	152	n_2		3,662
1896	3.79	90	4.07	136	F		9.088
1901	3.56	96	4.03	140	sig .05		Yes
1906	3.16	103	3.78	153	.01		Yes
1911	3.48[b]	46[b]	3.98	144	.001		Yes
	3.76	1,401	4.16	2,268			

	Orléanais		Nantais				
df n_1	15		15				
n_2	1,385		2,252				
F	1.530		2.560				
sig .05	No		Yes				
.01	No		Yes				
.001	No		No				

	MHS	$N_w{}^a$
Orléanais	3.76	1,401
Nantais	4.16	2,268
	4.01	3,670
t	5.919	
sig .05	Yes	
.01	Yes	
.001	Yes	

Note: Only the first household is considered where there is more than one household per houseful.

[a] N_w is the weighted number of cases.

[b] No communes of Orléanais Valley represented.

Source: Listes nominatives.

his analytical schema upon the relationship between husband and wife because it was they who determined the size and structure of the household and thus the levels of production and consumption within the household unit. He deliberately ignored "semiclan" and "semifamily" organizations because, he claimed, these fell outside the realm of peasant economy.[20] Anthropologists today tend to lay less stress on the sexual bond between the parents than on the mother–child bond, "which has to survive for the species to survive," whereas "it is not *strictly* necessary for any adult males to be in constant association with the mother–child bond unit."[21]

But the anthropologist here is attempting to uncover a *universal* structure. Within the specific context of the peasant economy, where the decision has already been made that the conjugal family unit is the best survival unit, it *is* necessary for the adult male to live in constant association with the mother–child bond. The maintenance of the conjugal family as an economic unit of production has to be added to the more general principles of gestation, impregnation, and the avoidance of incest if one intends to understand the structure of peasant populations. Evidence of adult males being continually out of contact with the mother–child bond would be conclusive proof that a peasant economy did *not* exist. The economic principle of the conjugal family also brings into focus another, looser kind of bond that the generalist frequently overlooks. A need for flexibility in household size that cannot be fulfilled by controlling the number of children causes others, outside the conjugal family unit, to be brought into the household. Whereas some sort of blood tie between these outside members and the conjugal family unit is possible, this is secondary to their economic function as consumers or workers. If the conjugal family opts for a change in the labor–consumer balance or its own members take up economic functions formerly performed by the outside members, this bond will be the first one to break.

The household in the peasant economy is thus made up of three kinds of human bond: the sexual, the mother–child, and the economic. The frequency distributions given in Table 7.2 indicate the relative importance of the latter two in terms of the absolute number of children and members outside the conjugal family unit. Roughly one-quarter of all the households sampled had no children, two-thirds of them had no members outside the conjugal family unit. The larger number of children and outside members in the Nantais obviously accounts for the larger households in this region. Developments over time have again been found to be only slight: a trend in the direction of decline in the number of children and outside members is more marked in the Orléanais, although the variation between one year and another is actually greater in the Nantais.[22] This is our first indication that there was a greater flexibility within the households of the Nantais, corresponding to the greater number of economic alternatives open to them. Outside members were found more frequently in areas with a pasture-type agriculture than a cereal or intensive type[23] It ought to be kept in mind that a larger proportion of the rural population owned the land they exploited in the cereal-

Table 7.2. *Frequency distributions of children and household members outside the conjugal family unit (CFU), 1836–1911*

	Number of children per household with at least one parent (%)		Number of household members outside the CFU (%)	
	Orléanais	Nantais	Orléanais	Nantais
0	29.4	20.1	71.0	62.3
1	23.4	24.7	15.0	20.7
2	21.4	24.3	7.6	9.3
3	12.6	15.7	3.2	3.6
4	6.5	7.4	1.5	2.1
5	4.0	4.2	0.7	0.8
6	1.8	2.3	0.4	0.5
7	0.6	0.9	0.3	0.3
8	0.3	0.2	0.1	0.1
9	0.1	0.1	0.1	0.1
10	0.0	0.1	0.0	0.1
11	0.0	0.1	0.0	0.0
12	0.0	0.0	0.0	0.1
13	0.0	0.0	0.0	0.1
Total	100.1	100.1	99.9	100.1
N_w	1,402	2,273	1,402	2,273

Source: Listes nominatives.

and intensive-type subregions and that the need for workers outside the family was, at the most, only seasonal. It is a well-known fact that work in a pasture-type agricultural economy is less susceptible to these seasonal fluctuations: the care of livestock is a year-round occupation. Furthermore, we have been at pains to point out that none of these agricultural types were characterized by a single resource, but rather a specific combination of resources exploited in such a fashion as to provide the best possible means for the peasant household's survival. If the household was to remain the pivot of the rural economy in the pasture-type areas, it had to maintain a flexibility among its member workers in order to do the odd jobs (woodcutting, ditch digging, the construction and maintenance of barriers, etc.) that were so vital for the exploitation of the land's meagre resources – a flexibility that was not as important for the households that could rely, or thought they could rely, on their annual crops to bring in a steady income. The economic bond between the outside member and the conjugal family unit was thus that much stronger in the pasture-type subregions.

The exact nature of the sexual bond is a tricky one to establish. As anyone who has delved into the subject knows, the annals on human sexuality are few and far between.[24] If the disapproving comments of the local clergymen are anything to go by, premarital intercourse was widespread in the Orléanais, but until we know how widespread and, more particularly, about the degree of emotional involvement that could have pulled these knaves away from the hearth, there is no way of telling how this might have affected the structure of the household, if at all.[25]

The nominal lists do provide information on the married couple, but even here it is not as complete as we would like. For instance, the birthplaces recorded in the lists do give some indication of how far away it was customary for an individual to find his or her mate. But only the 1906 and 1911 lists give birthplace by commune, so it is impossible to analyze this geographical spread over time or even, because of the low number of cases, to do a breakdown by subregion. The statistics that can be obtained (Table 7.3) show that marriages were less common in the Orléanais between persons born in the same commune than was true in the Nantais. But neither parts of the tables are suggestive of endogamy – the higher proportion of couples from the same commune in the Nantais could merely be a reflection of the greater chances of finding an unrelated partner in communes that were often twice as populous as those of the Orléanais. All the same, one obviously cannot simply infer from these statistics that cousins didn't marry. It is quite certain that, with over 80 percent of both the husbands and wives hailing from either the same commune or the neighboring one, the motive to go far afield for one's mate was not a very strong one in the Nantais. On the other hand, in the Orléanais, a significantly larger proportion of wives came from neighboring cantons and even neighboring departments.

Were women, in Lévi-Strauss's sense, "objects of exchange?"[26] We won't find the answer here – perhaps a detailed study of the marriage contracts, now heaped up in the departmental archives, would provide the clues. The difference between the two regions does at any rate point to a tighter, communal – I hesitate to use "village" for the *bocage* country – community in the Nantais; a fact that ought to be added to our observation of the region's greater homogeneity. Of course, one could argue the reverse: that a greater geographical spread in the couples' birthplace would signal a more homogeneous society. But this would be ignoring the *opportunities* for exchange that we have been emphasizing as so important for the peasant economy's survival. A greater geographical spread meant less opportunity at home.

The most significant fact arising from the comparison of the husbands' and wives' birthplaces is the consistently lower proportion of "outsiders" among the husbands, which indicates that it was the husband's property, not the wife's, that determined the couple's residence. Established husbands had no need to marry older women (Table 7.4). The propor-

Table 7.3. *Birthplace and urban origins of spouses in percentages, 1906 and 1911 combined*

	Orléanais		Nantais	
Origins	Husband	Wife	Husband	Wife
Birthplace				
Commune	54.4	44.0	67.2	59.2
Neighboring commune	25.3	19.2	19.3	23.7
Canton	1.9	2.4	0.0	0.0
Neighboring canton	9.0	19.2	11.1	12.9
Region (Orléanais or Nantais)	0.0	0.0	0.0	0.0
Department	3.8	4.1	0.0	0.6
Neighboring department	4.0	9.4	1.0	2.2
France	1.7	1.2	1.3	1.4
Abroad	0.0	0.4	0.0	0.0
Total	100.1	99.9	99.9	100.0
Urban origins				
Country	93.3	93.9	88.6	87.0
Canton capital	4.5	4.8	9.3	11.5
Arrondissement capital	0.0	0.0	0.0	0.0
Department capital	2.3	1.3	2.1	1.5
Paris	0.0	0.0	0.0	0.0
Total	100.1	100.0	100.0	100.0
N_w	116	120	276	261

Source: Listes nominatives.

tion of older wives remains at around 20 percent of all the couples sampled, whether one is making the comparison over time or over space. On average, the husband was three years his wife's senior, which means that, with the female singulate mean age at marriage varying between 23 and 24 in the Orléanais and 26 and 27 in the Nantais, the mean age for men was between 26 and 27, and 29 and 30, respectively.[27] Actually, the most significant thing about these age differences was their spread (indicated by the standard deviation), which was slightly higher in some of the pasture-type subregions – notably the Sologne and the Plateau – and showed a marked decline over time. This might have been in correspondence to the much-talked-about nineteenth-century phenomenon of declining singulate mean ages at marriage (although it should be noted that departmental figures show this tendency only to have been very slight in the Orléanais and absolutely negligible in the Nantais).[28]

Summarizing, the sexual bond, insofar as it is quantifiable on the basis of the nominal data on married couples, developed within narrower geographical limits in the Nantais than the Orléanais. It caused women to move more often than men, and as time passed, it occurred increasingly

Table 7.4. *Age differences between spouses (years husband older than wife), 1836–1911*

	Mean	Median	Mode	Standard error	Standard deviation	% wives older than husbands	N_w
Husband born:							
Orléanais							
Before 1846	2.99	2.73	0.00	0.22	6.15	21.7	785
1846–65	3.45	3.32	3.00	0.28	4.00	14.5	203
After 1865	3.30	3.16	3.00	0.55	4.25	18.4	59
Nantais							
Before 1846	3.43	2.50	0.00	0.20	6.77	23.1	1,207
1846–65	3.35	3.19	2.00	0.30	5.72	18.1	366
After 1865	2.31	2.50	4.00	0.43	4.58	24.0	111
Beauce	3.15	3.36	5.00	0.36	5.04	20.5	194
Sologne	2.79	3.48	5.00	0.57	6.30	21.6	123
Forêt	3.58	3.16	0.00	0.43	5.63	17.4	173
Valley	3.00	2.80	3.00	0.25	5.80	20.5	557
Orléanais	3.10	2.96	3.00	0.18	5.70	20.1	1,046
Plateau	3.69	2.96	0.00	0.39	7.07	25.8	323
R–V	2.68	2.41	2.00	0.29	6.09	22.4	435
S-et-M	3.09	2.41	2.00	0.34	6.54	23.5	374
Valley	3.83	2.95	1.00	0.26	6.21	18.6	553
Nantais	3.34	2.66	2.00	0.16	6.44	22.0	1,685

Source: Listes nominatives.

frequently between couples of a similar age. It ought to be added, just in case there has been any doubt, that the sexual bond was far and away the most common kind of human tie found at the head of the household. Only 5.1 percent of all the households sampled from the Orléanais were headed by bachelors or spinsters; only 3.1 percent in the Nantais. Those headed by widowers made up another 6.2 percent and 7.9 percent; by widows, 9.0 percent and 10.7 percent. Thus, well over three-quarters of the households were managed by married couples. The sexual bond was the bond of governance in the peasant economy.

Lived time: the mother–child bond

The mothers have the children. Table 7.5 gives some indication of the kind of birth experience women did have in our two regions. Calling this table "age-specific fertility rates" is perhaps a little bold. The rates are based only on those individuals actually recorded in the nominal lists – no account has been taken of migration. Women emigrated most frequently between the ages of 15 and 30 and especially in their early twenties.[29] Thus it is quite possible that the fertility estimates for women of this age are either too low (if the emigrants were mainly married) or too high (if they were mainly single). Ignoring infantile mortality has undoubtedly had a much more distorting effect and this is compounded by the fact that, as we shall very shortly see, a number of living infants had not been recorded in the lists. The combined effect of these three factors has almost certainly been an underestimation of the real fertility rates. However, the table does present the extent to which women actually brought new, surviving members into the household, and that is what we are really interested in.

We should also note that the estimates are based on the division of live births by the total number of woman-years lived. The numerator is derived from the total of children between 0 and 4 who have mothers, giving us an estimate of the total number of live births between one census and the next. This is all broken down by the mother's age at her child's birth. The denominator, or total woman-years lived, is based on the number of years that every woman recorded in the lists experienced within each of the five-year age groups during the last intercensal period. One obviously cannot use as a denominator a simple breakdown of women by their ages *at the time of the census* because, through part of the intercensal period, they could have belonged to a different age group. Thus, a woman aged exactly 32 at the moment the census was taken, would have lived, since the last census, two woman-years in the 30–34 age group and three woman-years in the 25–29 age group. If she had a child of three, that child would be added into the numerator of the 25–29 age group.

This program was run twice, once using the normal weighting procedures, and a second time without them so that we have been able to add in parentheses the actual unweighted number of woman-years upon which each estimate is based. The low number recorded in some instances (like zero!) is the result of a decision to break the results down by generation (for those with a military mind, it can be called "cohort") instead of by census year. Where the number of woman-years is zero, we have substituted a "guestimate" – anyone willing to redo the simple calculations actually presented in the tables will see that a change in these figures will have no major effect on the overall results. Generational analysis seems more appropriate in a section on microdemography where our concern is with the real individual experience of time. So as to give a clearer idea of chronological developments, a column with the *recorded* years of each generation's fertility period (assumed to be 15–40 years of age) has been added. There is a gap between 1836 and 1840 because the 1841 census did not record ages.[30] The Total Fertility Rate (TFR) is calculated by summing up the rates for each age group and multiplying the result by five; it is an estimate of the total number of children born to the average woman of a given generation or subregion throughout her whole fertile period.[31]

Does all this tell us anything about the mother–child bond? I, of course, think it does. Compared with what we know about the rural communities of Crulai, Lourmarin, Colyton, or even Sennely in the Sologne during earlier times,[32] the 17 communes sampled here indicate that children were rather rare. Better put, the experience of childbirth was rare; rare in both regions, all subregions, and for every generation recorded. This low fertility rate was especially notable in the two Valley subregions. But there was no clear relationship between agricultural type and fertility: the intensely farmed Sèvre-et-Maine had the highest rate in the Nantais. And would Zola ever have imagined that his Beauceron peasants were among the most fertile of the Loire Country? The data seem to suggest that a greater premium was placed on children in a cereal-type agriculture than anywhere else. Work was certainly more predictable in the Beauce than, say, the Forêt or the Sologne, so the unpaid child could have been economically more desirable than the domestic.

But this sort of reasoning is tentative at best. We simply do not know what went behind that decision to have a child or even the role that the mother played in it. What we do know is that her natural capacity as child-bearer had been drastically curtailed. With each succeeding generation, fewer and fewer women had children once they reached the age of 30. A target of somewhere around three or four children had been set and, with that attained, no more childbirths. So, in the Orléanais, increasing rates in the 25–29 age group were countered by declining rates in

Table 7.5. *Age-specific fertility rates, 1831–1910*

	Years of fertility recorded	15–19	20–24	25–29	30–34	35–39	40–44	45–49	Total Fertility Rate
Generations born, Orléanais									
Before 1810	1831–1835, 1841–1859	.010 (0)	.048 (43)	.138 (79)	.206 (116)	.111 (139)	.064 (226)	.009 (247)	2.93
1811–1840	1831–1835, 1841–1889	.017 (380)	.133 (370)	.191 (437)	.169 (467)	.125 (570)	.084 (452)	.007 (406)	3.63
1841–1865	1856–1910	.029 (427)	.145 (423)	.208 (383)	.180 (335)	.128 (348)	.049 (373)	.007 (259)	3.73
1866–1895	1881–1910	.037 (422)	.132 (277)	.179 (191)	.113 (165)	.047 (65)	.070 (13)	.008 (0)	2.93
Total		.028 (1229)	.134 (1113)	.140 (1090)	.169 (1083)	.117 (1122)	.066 (1064)	.008 (902)	3.56
Generations born, Nantais									
Before 1810	1831–1835, 1841–1859	.041 (0)	.041 (30)	.200 (99)	.177 (131)	.175 (169)	.081 (220)	.015 (321)	3.65
1811–1840	1831–1835, 1841–1889	.041 (381)	.096 (406)	.159 (459)	.198 (448)	.149 (447)	.070 (478)	.009 (429)	3.61
1841–1865	1856–1910	.043 (484)	.052 (467)	.188 (449)	.177 (430)	.159 (409)	.060 (344)	.007 (339)	3.43
1866–1895	1881–1910	.042 (545)	.083 (381)	.164 (290)	.150 (236)	.036 (113)	.045 (72)	.006 (0)	2.63
Total		.042 (1410)	.074 (1284)	.174 (1297)	.179 (1245)	.143 (1138)	.067 (1114)	.010 (1089)	3.45

Subregions

Beauce	.054 (291)	.170 (238)	.270 (232)	.202 (253)	.140 (302)	.086 (240)	.009 (230)	4.66
Sologne	.035 (367)	.147 (366)	.240 (312)	.149 (301)	.123 (296)	.026 (298)	.013 (288)	3.67
Forêt	.054 (294)	.136 (298)	.201 (291)	.173 (280)	.121 (273)	.078 (268)	.007 (220)	3.85
Valley (O)	.017 (274)	.113 (227)	.162 (261)	.152 (249)	.105 (251)	.064 (262)	.008 (214)	3.11
Plateau	.045 (375)	.052 (385)	.199 (339)	.186 (289)	.140 (296)	.091 (287)	.016 (308)	3.65
Retz–Vendée	.039 (368)	.061 (320)	.171 (312)	.188 (324)	.134 (319)	.060 (291)	.006 (228)	3.30
Sèvre-et-Maine	.040 (262)	.099 (300)	.160 (301)	.234 (288)	.172 (280)	.067 (217)	.016 (236)	3.94
Valley (N)	.044 (405)	.084 (309)	.171 (360)	.134 (333)	.142 (272)	.059 (332)	.007 (327)	3.21

Note: The total unweighted number of woman-years are given in parentheses.
Source: Listes nominatives.

the 30–34 age group. The Nantais, indicating yet again that greater flexibility, had a much wider spread in its age-specific rates; but a tight control on the total number of births was undoubtedly being exercised.

Obviously, the question of whether this strengthened or weakened the mother–child bond is rather speculative. The old argument is that mothers became more emotionally attached to their children as contraceptive practices expanded and the idea of "necessary wastage" gradually disappeared.[33] Recently, it has even been suggested that the high infantile mortality, the human "wastage," of earlier centuries was actually the result of the lack of emotional attachment of the mother to her baby.[34] Whatever way we want to look at it, a conscious effort at controlling the number of birth experiences is identified with a growth in the affection and empathy that mothers felt for their children. There is surely some truth in this. But that does not necessarily mean that the mother–child bond as a "basic principle" in demographic *structure* was strengthened; and until we know more about the more fundamental physiological aspects of the bond, we shall never be sure. My own hunch is that the structural principle that ordered the population around the biological tie between mother and child, if anything, weakened as the total number of births per woman declined.

There are some grisly tales of infanticides and child concealment scattered about the newspapers and police reports of the Orléanais (never it seems in the Nantais), which might suggest something wrong in the "emotional investment" theory. This is a typical example, taken from the *Courrier de la Campagne:*[35]

Cours d'assises du Loiret
Présidence de M. Pelletier
Audience du 24 octobre
1re affaire – Suppression d'enfant

1° Marie-Ermance-Pauline Ringuedet, *femme Renard* aged 30 years, winegrower, living at Bou 2° Adélaide – Florence Ringuedet, aged 54 years, also living at Bou, are accused of child concealment in the following circumstances:

On the twelfth of last August, the police of Jargeau learned by public rumor that *la femme Renard,* winegrower at Bou, must have clandestinely given birth around the twenty-first of the preceding July. They went to the house to question . . . *la femme Renard* and *la fille Ringuedet* who lives with her. After several denials, they both had to admit that the birth had taken place on 21 July around 2 P.M. They asserted that the child had lived for two days and that it died of convulsions on 23 July. The body was discovered, following their directions, under a heap of manure where *la fille Ringuedet* admitted to having hidden it on 24 July. The autopsy of the child established that it had lived. Its birth had not been reported to the *mairie* and its registration had been prevented by a conspiracy between *la femme Renard* and her mother. Both are bastard children. *La femme Renard'*s husband was condemned in 1875 to forced labor for life. However, she has already given birth in 1877 to a child who died after three months. . . . Pronounced guilty with the admission of extenuating circumstances, *la femme Renard* and *la fille Ringuedet* were together condemned to five years' imprisonment.

But the exception proves the rule. In this case, as in so many of the others, infanticide is related to illegitimacy, which we know was rare, even if on the increase. And convict husbands were not in abundant supply.

Evidence in support of a weaker mother–child bond comes rather from the age distribution of children living with their mothers (Figure 7.1). Although not necessarily an index of affection, I believe the distribution does tell us something about the degree to which the mother–child bond could affect the structure of the rural population. There are two facts that emerge from the distributions. First, children tended to move out of the household earlier in the Orléanais than they did in the Nantais. The flatter curves of the Nantais are proof that a significant number of children stayed on after their twentieth birthday and even after their thirtieth. The difference between the rates at which men and women left their first homes does not appear to have been very important here. But in the Orléanais, the curves are noticeably steeper for men between the ages of 8 and 28 and for women between 11 and 23. The fall-off in female children is particularly important after 15 years. The fact that women moved out quicker than men corresponds to the greater geographic mobility of this sex that we found in the Orléanais. The faster overall house-leaving rate of the Orléanais as compared with the Nantais corresponds to the narrower age limits within which women had their children. If the household is to be seen purely in terms of an economic unit, an explanation of this contrasting pattern is simple: there was less of a premium placed on children in the Orléanais than in the Nantais. But the possibility – and that is all we can say with the present evidence – that the greater restraint on births in the Orléanais actually weakened the biological tie between mother and child, thus upsetting one of the barriers to geographic mobility, should not be discounted. Birth control could one day prove to be a major destabilizing factor in the household economy.

Psychologists, pediatricians, and anthropologists agree that the most formative period for the child, and one might assume the mother–child bond, is the child's first three years: from conception to the weaning and perhaps a little beyond. The second fact arising from an analysis of the children's age distribution is the under-reporting of infants of precisely these ages. It is almost as if the census enumerators had decided that they would keep the greatest secret of the countryside, the nature of the mother–child bond, forever guarded. There is no possible life-table function that could account for the low numbers recorded for these ages – there are fewer children under three than there are at four or five. Hun-

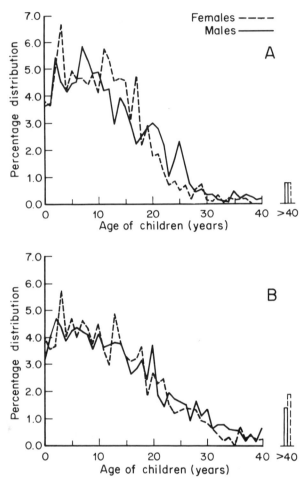

Figure 7.1. Age distribution of children living with their mothers in (A) the Orléanais and (B) the Nantais, 1836–1911.

dreds of children seem to have simply disappeared or, rather, not yet to have appeared. There is some reason to suspect a systematic under-estimate of certain sections of the population, especially in the earlier censuses, which were taken on a *de jure* basis excluding all transients.[36] Even when the *de facto* principle was officially introduced in the 1840s, it is not at all improbable that the local enumerators continued with their old practices. But this sort of explanation only begs the question of how infants under three could have possibly been considered transients.

A transient infant,[37] one might assume, was an infant who didn't live with his own mother, an arrangement that must surely have weakened the mother–child bond. Arnold van Gennep – a pioneer in the study of the individual life cycle – saw the placing of an infant in the care of another woman as a transitional rite that the infant had to undergo in order to be accepted as a member who played a part in the day-to-day functions of the household. Until that had occurred, he was looked upon as a stranger, somebody from a foreign environment who had to be isolated or put, as it were, in quarantine.[38] Now, wet-nursing and the putting out of infants is a gray area in French social history, and in rural history it is an almost entirely black expanse. The general view held today is that, at least until the Revolution, it was practiced by the urban population, the rich having a nurse in residence and the poor sending their offspring out to the farmer's wife who needed the extra income.[39] After the Revolution some argue that it declined,[40] others that it increased.[41] That it was the *poorer* urban populations who put their children out is confirmed by Guépin and Bonamy in their 1835 report on Nantes: "There are fewer individuals [between 0 and 1 years] in the poor streets than the rich quarters, most of the poor mothers sending their children to wet nurses so as to be free for work."[42] This practice might have been abandoned by the time birthplaces were being recorded; our sample from the 1906 and 1911 censuses includes only three nurslings from Nantes and one nursling in the Orléanais from Paris.[43] But, then, the *entire* sample has only 20 nurslings in all. Transient population?

For the best answer, one would have to turn to the infant deaths recorded in the vital registries that normally do give the birthplace and family situation (i.e., whether a nursling or not) of the deceased.[44] But still the nominal lists provide evidence of one important fact: whether or not the *urban* populations put their infants out (either for nursing or other reasons), there was certainly, in the nineteenth century, a proportion, perhaps a sizable proportion, of the *rural* population that did. Part of this pattern is revealed by an analysis of the infant household members outside the conjugal family unit (see Figures 7.2 and 7.3). They are not the answer to the riddle of the missing children because their total number, if added to those infants living with their mothers, gives only an extra 0.50 to 0.75 percent to this age group in the frequency distributions of Figure 7.1 – clearly one would expect more. But they do provide some clues.

First, it appears that it was more common for infants outside the conjugal family unit to be in some way related to the head of the household. The usual relationship, if noted in the lists, is "grandson," "granddaughter" or "nephew," "niece."[45] It would be an unusual coincidence to find a relative "in milk" just at the moment that one's own child required suckling, especially if that relative was one's mother or, better still, one's mother-in-law. This would at least suggest that a number of children born

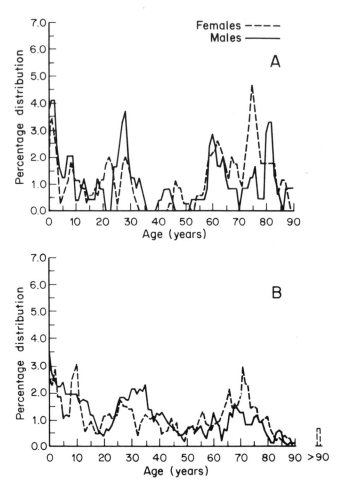

Figure 7.2. Age distribution of related household members outside the conjugal family unit, in 3-year running means, in (A) the Orléanais and (B) the Nantais, 1836–1911.

in our two regions during the 75 years under discussion were never breastfed. This could account for the extended period of time that some of these infants were boarded out: the function of the foster parents was not so much to suckle the child as to hold it until it could be incorporated into its own household – a function closely akin to that described by van Gennep. It is important to note that although fewer infants were put out in the Nantais (if one is to judge from the smaller apparent number of missing children), those that were put out stayed out for a much longer period of time than in the Orléanais. In fact, the data suggest that many

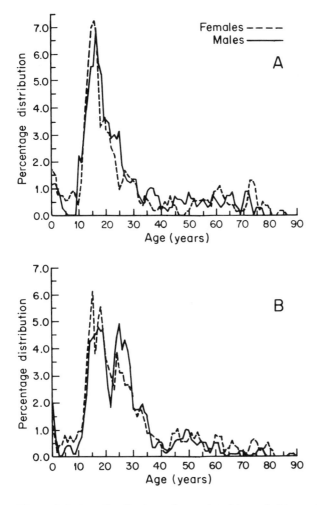

Figure 7.3. Age distribution of nonrelated household members outside the conjugal family unit, in 3-year running means, in (A) the Orléanais and (B) the Nantais, 1836–1911.

of the infants, especially the males, spent the rest of their childhood with their foster parents, whereas the infants in the Orléanais were quickly dispatched to their own parents' household at the end of their first or second year.

My own way of interpreting such a pattern is this. The mother–child bond was the principal bond of the peasant household: "It is the husband who carries the stones, but the wife who builds the house" runs an old French proverb that would have made Freud sit up in his chair.[46] The mother produced the new members of the household, the new workers, which, in an earlier epoch of high infant mortality, must have been very time consuming; it was, at the very least, a frequent biological event that was absolutely essential for the survival of the population. The household itself was simply an effective means of assuring the impregnation of the woman and the economic requirements for the mother's and child's survival. There were certainly other forms of organization that could have been adopted, but they weren't. With the decline in infant mortality, the mother was no longer required to be full-time procreator of the species, and the major biological tie that had been the reason behind the household as an economic unit slackened. But that certainly did not sound the death knell of the household economy. *Natura non facit saltus!* – Nature makes no jumps; nor does nature have any foresight. Although there was no particular reason for this peasant household economy to go on functioning, there was no particular reason either why it should not. Except for the economic situation in the city of Orléans. Orléans had robbed its hinterland of its industry, thereby leaving its inhabitants only the option of controlling their numbers. The members of each household were locked in a struggle, not with an outside class of rural exploiters, but with themselves: their sexual needs were pitted against their economic needs. The Orléanais became a region of introverts.[47]

This could go a long way toward explaining the relative "autonomy" that we have found in the Orléanais. Instead of the economy becoming more integrated, the very opposite occurred, with each household looking out for its own subjective interests in a delicate situation: fewer workers on the farm, fewer options to exploit. That left little room to move in. If a child was born, he was kept at home, or if the situation really demanded it, he was sent away to board. But the willingness to adopt permanently another woman's child was rare; even where the tie of sympathy was greatest, between kin, children were sent to their mother's homes as soon as the main drudgery of childcare had been completed. Children were thus not only deprived of their mother's milk but of the possibility of identifying with a foster mother. Hence one might suspect a weakened mother–child bond in the Orléanais. At 15, if the occasion arose, the child would be amply willing to move out and even, in the process, travel some distance. Because of the property arrangements, which we discuss later, women had a greater opportunity to move than men.[48]

It would be wrong to take any of this too melodramatically. The struggle was the result of a multitude of factors acting on the individual experience of life, and that particular individual was probably not even conscious of what was happening. But something was happening. And we only know that because we can see that it was *not* happening in the

Nantais, 350 kilometers downstream. Because of the larger number of options that the household could exploit, the Nantais had a much more integrated kind of rural society. We have already seen this in its more homogeneous economic structures, discussed in the last chapter. Now we have evidence to suggest that the mother–child bond, central link in the household economy, was stronger in the Nantais than the Orléanais. Births were not limited to a decade in the mother's existence but were much more spread out through her fertile period. As in the Orléanais, families did have the option of sending the newborn out to board, but unlike the Orléanais, if a child were sent out, it was less likely that he would ever come back; children were permanently adopted by their foster parents, thus allowing the child to develop in the environment with which he had learned to identify during his first three critical years of life. This could be part of the reason why children stayed on longer in their first homes.

Lived time: the economic bond

Leaving the household implies entering another. In several cases, this of course meant setting up a new household. But one could also enter a household that had already been established. Practically all household members outside the conjugal family unit had at one time or another lived in a different household. They had entered the present one out of economic necessity. Obviously, *every* member of the household was associated with the others by an economic bond, in the sense that they consumed the products of their work together – they all ate from a common pot. But the economic bond was the principal bond only for the household members outside the conjugal family unit. Their prime purpose of joining the household was to participate in its meals, and that is why we regard the economic bond as the weakest of the three bonds tying the household together. Consider another of van Gennep's observations, this time on the rite of eating and drinking together:

[It] is clearly a rite of incorporation, of physical union, and has been called a sacrament of communion. A union by this means may be permanent, but more often it lasts only during the period of digestion. Captain Lyon has noted that the Eskimo consider a man their guest only for twenty-four hours. Often the sharing of meals is reciprocal, and there is thus an exchange of food which constitutes the confirmation of a bond. When food is exchanged without a common meal, the action falls into the vast category of gift exchanges.[49]

Earlier we saw that the "vast category of gift exchanges" defined the outer limits of society. Now we also have an economic bond that defined the outer limits of the household, although it obviously could not be the bond that held the household together.

If we consider relatives and nonrelatives together (Figures 7.2 and 7.3), we notice that there were three periods when one was most likely to move out to this unstable fringe of the household unit: infancy, adolescence, and old age. Outside of these periods, one was tied to the household by the stronger mother–child or sexual bonds. Here, I will refer to anybody within those stronger bonds as being in a certain social "state." One might even say that social states would include those with no bonds at all – essentially a condition of nonlife. In this way, infancy, adolescence, and old age can be regarded as periods of transition from one social state to another: from the prenatal state to the state of recognized personhood, from the asexual state to the sexual state, from the state of life to the state of death. Let us emphasize the part social recognition plays because, although an individual's state might well coincide with a certain biological condition, it was not necessarily that biological condition that determined the state. Thus, it was certainly possible for an individual to be sexually active even though he or she was regarded as being in an asexual state; it was what others expected of him that actually counted. Also, we have to be aware of the degree of uncertainty in this whole system. The small number of members outside the conjugal family unit (see Table 7.2) suggests that not everybody in the nineteenth century went through the transitional periods. Take Zola's La Grande who, at 88 had not yet passed into the "period of old age." And one can be absolutely certain that not everybody experienced all the possible social states. Once born, the only inevitable state was death.

The evidence (Table 7.2 and Figures 7.2 and 7.3) suggests that a larger proportion of the rural population in the Nantais went through the transitional periods and that the periods were more prolonged than in the Orléanais. In fact, these periods are sometimes so extended – as in the case of "adolescence" between 10 and 30 – that one hesitates to label them "transitional." There is a quasi-permanence about them. But that is not the point. Even if these individuals remained within a transitional period for the rest of their lives, theirs was not the bond that held the household together. It is the fragility of their bond that classifies the period through which they were living as "transitional." Thus the significance of the prolonged transitional periods in the Nantais is that the household tended to be delimited by a larger number of members in fragile bondage.[50]

One can really look upon these members as making up a buffer zone around the structural nucleus of the household. As we have implied earlier, they lent a certain flexibility to the operations of the household. This is best understood by checking what the outside members were actually doing in the households (Figure 7.4): 52.4 percent of them were relatives in the Nantais; 34.0 percent of them were relatives in the Orléanais. There was, therefore, a positive correlation between the proportionate number of outside members staying with relatives and the

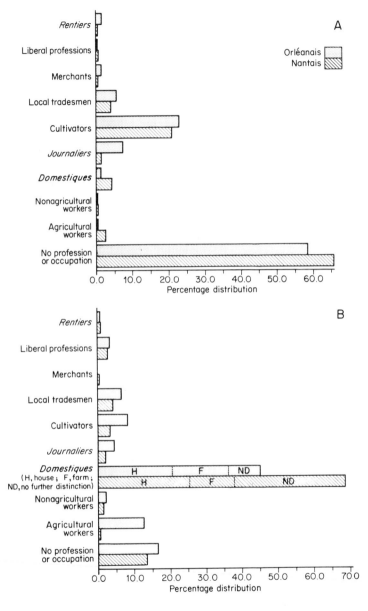

Figure 7.4. Occupational distribution of household members outside the conjugal family unit in (A) the Orléanais and B) the Nantais, 1836–1911.

length of the transitional period. Around 60 percent of the related outside members had no profession or occupation recorded beside their
names. That did not mean that they did nothing. All it meant was that
the census enumerators could not think of any "profession" to describe
their functions adequately. They were the odd-job men and women of
the household. If they were given any profession in the lists, it was usually *cultivateur*,[51] a very nondescript term in the nineteenth century, which
referred to anything between a farmer in possession of 50 hectares of
land and a humble *journalier*. We do not know what sort of financial arrangement existed between the outside members and the head of household, but one imagines that a much more informal kind of agreement
would have been made with those who were related than those who were
not. This could have further contributed to the flexibility of action in the
Nantais. Again, compare the regions. There were more *journaliers*
among the related outside members of the Orléanais than the Nantais,
and a *journalier* was, by definition, somebody who was paid a daily
wage.[52] Turning to the nonrelatives, we find that most of them were
domestiques, but also that the Nantais had a far larger proportion of
them than the Orléanais. And the listing of "domestique," without any
further distinction, was more common in the Nantais. Take this information at its face value: it probably meant that the enumerator could not
make any further distinction; in the Orléanais, he could because the
situation was less flexible. This is further illustrated by the Orléanais'
larger proportion of *journaliers* and the significantly greater number of
agricultural workers – shepherds, swineherds, carters, threshers, etc.[53]

Actually, it was all these outside members, relatives and nonrelatives
alike, who made up the real "working class" of the countryside in the
sense that they were the least in control of their own destinies, they were
the most expendable. In the event of an agricultural crisis, they were the
first to lose.

But then, given the comparatively greater number of outside members
in the Nantais, wouldn't that contradict our earlier inference that family
ties were stronger in this region? Not necessarily. First, the longer periods that the outside members spent with their host families indicate that
they were less threatened and, second, the much larger proportion of
relatives among them illustrates just how far the family bonds were being
extended. On the other hand, the psychologically isolated families of the
Orléanais, if they had to share their pot with anyone at all, clearly
showed a preference for somebody who was not related. And the families
certainly did not keep them on for very long. This is particularly notable
during adolescence, quite evidently the most important transitional
period in terms of its impact on household structure. For most of the
people who experienced it, this transitional period would have begun between the ages of 10 and 13; there is in fact a marked rise in the numbers

after the age of 11. This is true of both regions. But, in the Orléanais, the numbers reach their peak in the mid-teens (15–16 for women, 16–17 for men), then fall rapidly off, and slow down a little in the 20s. There was almost no one over 30 who was still in this transitional period; one assumes that most of them have moved into the sexual state. By contrast, the curves peak later in the Nantais and the drop is only gradual, with a significant number of individuals over 30 still in the transitional period: people were slower in moving out to set up their own households; they were marrying later.[54]

Lived time: the sexual bond

There is not much to be added to what has already been said on the sexual bond, except to underline the fact that marriages were taking place, on average, three years later in the Nantais than in the Orléanais. Historians are inclined to argue that marriages were delayed because the young lacked the economic means to marry. But that is only part of the story. In the Nantais, where we assume family ties to have been stronger, the offspring were encouraged to stay at home longer. It must not be forgotten that this is what the majority in fact did do. If, for some reason, the children had to leave their homes, they would be adopted into another household where they would remain *as if* they were with their own parents. In encouraging later marriages, in postponing sexual bonding, and in prolonging the transitional periods, the stronger family ties made it possible for the household to respond to many more kinds of economic situations: the Nantais household was more flexible than the Orléanais household. This made intensive agriculture a less risky affair. Therefore it would be wrong to argue that intensive agriculture was a *cause* of late marriages in the Nantais; rather, late marriages made an intensive agriculture possible.

Lived time: household structure

By now we should have a rough idea of what time meant for most household members in the rural parts of our two regions. We should also have some very elementary ideas about the structure of their households: the vast majority were headed by married couples who usually had a few children and the odd relative or domestic living with them. But we have yet to show how the individual experiences of time influenced this structure, and that is really what the developmental cycle is all about. The degree to which household structure was determined by the cycle can be assessed in terms of the relationship between the following six variables:

1.   Age of the head of the household
2.   Occupation of the head of the household
3.   Total number of kin
4.   Total number of servants

5.   Mother's age at birth of first recorded child
6.   Total number of children

The first two variables are derived from the first individual listed in each household; the third is a total of all members outside the conjugal family unit whose surname is the same as that of the household head or as his wife's maiden name; and the fourth is a total of all unrelated outside members between 15 and 55 (the broadest possible definition of "servant"). Historians have frequently emphasized the effect that the wife's age at marriage can have on the total number of children born to a family. This statistic is not provided by the lists, so in its place we have substituted the fifth variable based on the mother's age at the time of the census less the age of the first child listed. The sixth variable is straightforward. The order in which these variables have been presented is dictated by common sense. Obviously it would be ludicrous to propose that the total number of children could affect the age of the head of household, whereas the reverse is perfectly tenable. Similarly, although it is impossible for occupation to determine age, age *can* determine occupation. In fact, the only ambiguity in this ordering is between the third and fourth variables and the possible effect that the sixth could have on them.

In addition to assessing the effects of the developmental cycle, the analysis that follows also includes an evaluation of the possible changes in the pattern over *historical* time. The cycle might have had a different character at the end of the nineteenth century from what it had at the beginning. Historical contrasts in family structure are essentially contrasts between one generation and another. Thus, the year of birth of the head of household would be the ideal measure of historical time. Unfortunately, there are certain inherent complications in the use of this variable, if derived from nominal lists,[55] so, throughout most of the following analysis, we have adopted the census year as the measure of historical time.

It has to be noted right from the start that the overall variation in household structure was slight. We have already seen what a low proportion of households had more than one outside member and how rare it was to have more than three children in a family (Table 7.2). Added to that was the low variation in the types of occupation practiced by household heads[56] as well as a remarkably low variation in their ages – approximately two-thirds of the house-heads sampled were aged between 35 and 55 (Table 7.6). Thus, whatever factor one might want to pick as an explanation for differences in household structure, whether it be developmental cycle or something else, it must first be realized that the differences themselves were simply not very great.

Table 7.7 gives some indication of what the developmental cycle actu-

Table 7.6. *Means and standard deviations of variables used in analysis of developmental cycle, Orléanais (O) and Nantais (N), 1836–1911*

Variable	Region	Mean	Standard deviation
Age of head of household	O	44.03	10.59
	N	48.00	12.05
	O and N	46.65	11.73
Occupation of head of household	O	53.36	12.33
	N	50.14	10.67
	O and N	51.23	11.36
Total kin	O	0.09	0.30
	N	0.16	0.45
	O and N	0.14	0.41
Total servants	O	0.27	0.71
	N	0.23	0.57
	O and N	0.24	0.62
Age of mother at birth of first child	O	27.11	6.00
	N	29.17	7.02
	O and N	28.47	6.76
Total children	O	2.43	1.43
	N	2.40	1.45
	O and N	2.41	1.44

Note: The total combined weighted number of cases sampled was 2,354, 799 from the Orléanais, 1,555 from the Nantais.
Source: Listes nominatives.

ally meant in terms of the number of children, kin, and servants per household. The absolute number of households in each age group has been replaced by a proportionate number always totaling 1,000. As one would expect, the total number of children per household appears to reach its peak in the 35–44 age group, with the Orléanais showing a significantly narrower distribution of children by the head's age than the Nantais. This is particularly noticeable in the age groups above 54, where one finds a far larger proportion of households without children in the Orléanais than in the Nantais. The same regional contrast can be made for the number of kin and servants. However, there is no apparent pattern in the accommodation of outside members into the household; their distribution seems haphazard. This is reflected in the low "gammas," reproduced here in order to reveal any association not immediately apparent to the naked eye (the first order gammas are measures of association for both regions, controlling for the differences that existed between them). If the gammas tell us anything, it is that the household head's age

Table 7.7. *Total number of children, kin, and servants by age of head of household, 1836–1911*

Age of head of household	Number of children								Number of kin					Number of servants					N_w
	0	1	2	3	4	5	6+	Total	0	1	2	3+	Total	0	1	2	3+	Total	
Orléanais																			
Under 25	504	423	0	0	0	0	73	1,000	898	29	0	73	1,000	1,000	0	0	0	1,000	8
25–34	194	363	272	123	27	18	3	1,000	935	59	5	1	1,000	835	126	19	20	1,000	214
35–44	90	184	251	210	151	73	41	1,000	871	129	0	0	1,000	822	116	27	35	1,000	303
45–54	189	220	240	166	69	71	45	1,000	925	69	6	0	1,000	824	112	29	35	1,000	307
55–64	422	241	220	66	27	18	6	1,000	923	67	10	0	1,000	852	93	39	16	1,000	214
Over 64	768	154	47	11	17	3	0	1,000	901	70	29	0	1,000	927	44	26	3	1,000	190
	297	232	213	127	66	42	23	1,000	909	82	9	0	1,000	848	101	27	24	1,000	1,237
Conditional gamma	−.34								.00					−.09					
Nantais																			
Under 25	500	300	100	100	0	0	0	1,000	733	0	267	0	1,000	1,000	0	0	0	1,000	10
25–34	184	344	282	92	56	38	4	1,000	845	129	26	0	1,000	835	102	60	3	1,000	243
35–44	111	189	281	196	124	52	47	1,000	827	146	24	3	1,000	812	139	35	14	1,000	531
45–54	128	232	235	230	79	55	41	1,000	866	117	13	4	1,000	841	112	35	12	1,000	533
55–64	243	268	219	133	58	43	36	1,000	893	86	16	5	1,000	849	112	25	14	1,000	429
Over 64	399	300	185	58	34	4	20	1,000	874	77	31	18	1,000	803	146	45	6	1,000	339
	199	252	241	157	76	41	34	1,000	859	112	23	6	1,000	829	123	37	11	1,000	2,087
Conditional gamma	−.19								−.16					−.06					
Zero-order gamma	−.24								−.10					−.07					
First-order gamma	−.23								−.13					−.07					

Source: Listes nominatives.

was more likely to have an effect on the number of children than the number of kin or servants but that all three tended to decline as the head got older.

Part of the randomness in the distribution of kin and servants, and even of children, could have been due to the intervention of another variable, such as occupation, which obscured the real effect that the head's age was having. The age's effect on the number of children would be diminished where, for example, *journaliers* systematically had their children later than winegrowers and both of the occupations were very common. To find out age's real effect, one would have to control for occupation. The same might go for the subregions – children could have been born to younger households in one subregion than in another. But controlling for occupation and subregion is not a simple matter because the coding of these variables is, unavoidably, somewhat arbitrary, particularly in the case of the subregions. Table 7.8 indicates the codes that have been adopted. Numbers have been assigned to each of the subregions without speculating on any special order. For occupation, we have worked on the assumption that the various agricultural classifications had been loosely employed, whereas the mention of a particular trade or profession (doctor, lawyer, etc.) was more specific. This conforms to the general theme of the last chapter. Thus there is only a 6-point difference between owner–cultivator and *journaliers* and there is a 20-point difference between the liberal professions and the local traders and artisans (butchers, bakers, shoemakers, weavers, dressmakers, etc.). It has been difficult to concede to any particular order here because the notion of linear group hierarchy runs totally against the grain of our whole social analysis (see the introductory comments to Chapter 5). But in part of the following analysis, we shall have to make some sort of assumption about ordinality. So, with a brief bow to convention, we have placed the liberal professions "above" merchants, merchants "above" artisans, artisans "above" cultivators, etc. Hence, the effects of the statistical adjustments made for occupation should, theoretically, be treated with caution.

The information presented in Table 7.8 does not rely upon an assumption of ordinality; the order of the categories is assumed to be purely arbitrary. The table gives an idea of the effect that occupation and subregion had on the number of children in each household. In spite of its awesome title, it should be fairly easy to read. The first column gives the means of each category expressed as deviations from the grand mean, 2.52 children, without controlling for the effects of the other variables. In the second column, these category means have been adjusted for the effects of the other "factor," i.e., the column gives the category means for occupation holding subregion constant and for subregion holding occupation constant. Each successive column represents the adjustments

Table 7.8. *Analysis of covariance of the number of children adjusted for factors and covariates, both regions, 1836–1911*

Code	Factors	Unadjusted	Factors (occupation or subregion)	Plus age of head of household	Plus mother's age at birth of first child	Plus year of birth of head of household	Plus total kin	Plus total servants	N_w
	Grand mean = 2.52								
	Occupation of head								
10	Rentiers	+1.02	+0.39	-1.59	+0.12	-2.71	-2.76	-2.69	0
	Liberal professions								
20	Miscellaneous	-0.47	-0.42	-0.32	-0.37	-0.30	-0.33	-0.32	14
23	Government, police, army	+0.08	+0.04	+0.15	+0.17	+0.21	+0.21	+0.21	25
27	Church	0.00	0.00	0.00	0.00	0.00	0.00	0.00	0
30	Merchants	-0.22	-0.21	-0.24	-0.41	-0.38	-0.38	-0.39	35
40	Local tradesmen	-0.08	-0.07	-0.10	-0.12	-0.13	-0.13	-0.13	233
	Cultivators								
50	No further distinction	+0.11	+0.15	+0.19	+0.18	+0.18	+0.18	+0.17	710
51	Propertyholders	-0.04	-0.03	-0.06	-0.26	-0.25	-0.25	-0.26	114
52	Winegrowers	-0.19	-0.18	-0.22	-0.27	-0.26	-0.26	-0.25	144
53	Part owner, part *mét.* or *ferm.*	-0.18	-0.69	-0.62	-0.94	-0.79	-0.77	-0.77	3
54	*Fermiers*	+0.23	+0.18	+0.24	+0.17	+0.20	+0.21	+0.20	47
55	*Métayers*	+1.34	+1.47	+1.71	+1.49	+1.43	+1.41	+1.39	9
57	*Journaliers*	-0.22	-0.29	-0.31	-0.16	-0.17	-0.17	-0.15	176
	Domestiques								
60	No further distinction	-0.50	-0.72	-0.73	-0.68	-0.59	-0.58	-0.55	9
63	House	0.00	0.00	0.00	0.00	0.00	0.00	0.00	0
67	Farm	-0.52	-1.12	-0.41	-0.46	-0.70	-0.69	-0.66	1
70	Nonagricultural workers	-0.10	-0.05	-0.11	+0.02	+0.03	+0.03	+0.04	54
80	Agricultural workers	+0.26	-0.14	-0.09	-0.03	-0.09	-0.08	-0.07	38
90	No profession or occupation	-0.01	+0.04	-0.42	-0.33	-0.36	-0.38	-0.37	6
	Beta	.13	.14	.15	.16	.16	.16	.16	

Subregion

Subregion									N
1	Beauce	+0.48	+0.60	+0.53	+0.53	+0.52	+0.53	+0.52	123
2	Sologne	−0.19	−0.06	−0.14	−0.15	−0.15	−0.15	−0.17	76
3	Forêt d'Orléans	+0.03	+0.03	+0.04	−0.09	−0.09	−0.08	−0.09	107
4	Valley (O)	−0.13	−0.02	0.00	−0.02	−0.04	−0.04	−0.04	305
5	Plateau	+0.26	+0.24	+0.11	+0.28	+0.28	+0.27	+0.27	185
6	Retz–Vendée	+0.10	+0.03	−0.05	+0.03	+0.04	+0.05	+0.05	255
7	Sèvre-et-Maine	−0.04	−0.15	−0.15	−0.05	−0.05	−0.05	−0.05	226
8	Valley (N)	−0.21	−0.25	−0.11	−0.25	−0.24	−0.24	−0.24	340
	Beta	.14	.16	.11	.15	.15	.15	.14	
	Multiple R^2		.04	.05	.12	.13	.13	.13	

Note: Only households in which the head was aged 25–54 have been considered.
Source: Listes nominatives.

made for an additional variable until, in the second to last column, the means have been controlled for the effect of six separate variables.

It is perfectly clear that subregion and occupation had very little effect on the number of children per household. The largest deviation from the grand mean within the subregional categories is a paltry $+0.52$ in the Beauce – a confirmation of the Beauce's higher rate of fertility noted earlier in this chapter. As for occupation, no category mean, with an N_w of over 50, deviates more than 0.30 from the grand mean.[57] Therefore we may assume that, even if we adopt a linear hierarchy in the measurement of occupation, this is hardly going to affect our assessment of the interaction between the other variables.

But our problems are not over. One cannot just blithely assume that whatever relationship existed between the other variables must have been linear. This would completely contradict the idea of a *cycle*. Figure 7.5A illustrates the absurdity of such an assumption. The dashed line represents the closest a straight line can describe the distribution of the total number of children by the age of the head of household. Like the gammas of Table 7.7, this line is telling us that the total number of children per household had a slight tendency to decrease as the head of household got older. But what in the world does that mean? That a head of household aged 15 tended to have more children than one of 35? Obviously we have to find another model. The simplest is the parabola, which has a single curve built into it, thus allowing one to account for the major increasing *and* decreasing trends in the total number of children as the head of household got older.[58] The solid line is the closest-fitting parabola for this particular distribution. But, in order to weigh the effect of the head's age against the effects of the other variables on the number of children, the shape of this parabola has to be adjusted for the other variables' effects and also standardized (Figure 7.5B). The conventional method of standardization is to transform the numerical values of all the variables in question so as to give every variable a mean of 0 and a standard deviation of 1. Figures 7.6A–J illustrate the same standardized curves for every other pair of variables for which the formula of a parabola has been used.

Now at last we can begin to assess the effect that the developmental cycle had on household structure. This can be done diagrammatically by tracing out the paths of each of the cycle's constituent effects. The path diagram presented in Figure 7.7 is based on data drawn from both regions; its structure is determined by the intrinsic causal ordering of the six variables. The seventh variable, census year, is really a gatecrasher; it is a measure of historical time and has nothing to do with the developmental cycle *per se* – that, of course, is the reason for the dashed lines. The inclusion of nonlinear relationships makes this a rather unconven-

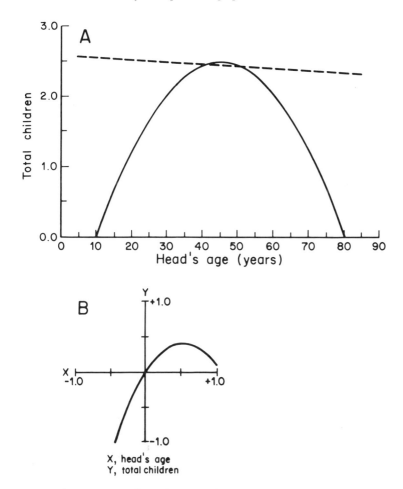

Figure 7.5. Total number of children on age of head of household, from (A) linear and parabolic regressions and (B) standardized parabolic regression line in both regions, 1836–1913.

tional path diagram and creates some difficulty in interpretation.[59] Where the relationships are assumed to have been linear, it is easy to understand the meaning of the path coefficients. For example, an increase in 1 standard unit in the total number of kin would tend to bring about an increase of only 0.04 standard units in the total number of children. Thus, the relationship between total kin and total children can be described as highly *in*elastic. Generally speaking, the larger the coefficient, the steeper the line and the greater the elasticity of the relationship between the two variables. Unfortunately, no single coefficient can describe a curved line. Two have to be employed, one describing the part

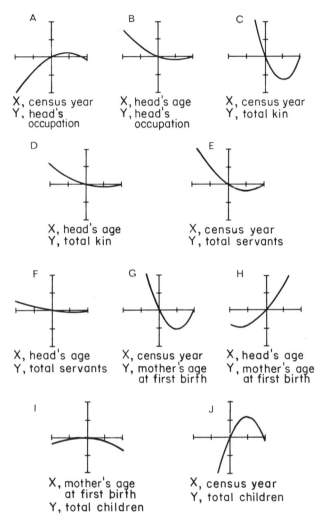

Figure 7.6. Standardized parabolic regression lines in both regions, 1836–1911.

played in the parabola's equation by the independent variable when it has not been squared, the other describing its part when it has been squared. One can, in fact, adopt the same rule of thumb as applied to the linear equations – the larger the coefficients, the steeper the curves. But there is no satisfactory way of imagining the design of these curves without actually seeing them (Figures 7.5B and 7.6A–J).

So, what is the shape of the beast that emerges from this statistical jungle? One thing to be sure, if we hadn't been looking for him, he would

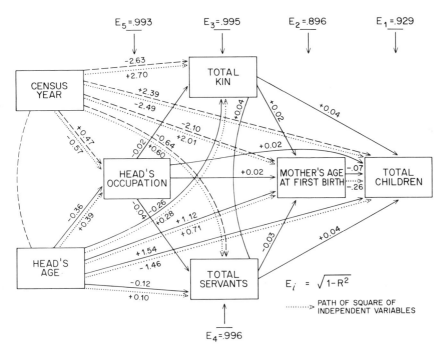

Figure 7.7. A path analysis of the developmental cycle in both regions, 1836–1911.

have got away without ever being noticed. The numbers at the top and the bottom of the diagram ($E_1, E_2, E_3, \ldots$) are the disturbance terms. They may be looked upon as latent, independent variables that account for the variation not explained by the model. Square these terms and one has the *proportion* of variation not explained by the model. Thus, 98.6 percent of the variation in occupation remains unexplained by this model, or put the other way round, only 1.4 percent of the variation in the household head's occupation is explained by his age and the year of the census. The census year, the head's age, and occupation explain under 1 percent of the variation in both the total number of kin and the total number of servants. The model explains 19.8 percent of the variation in the mother's age at the birth of the first recorded child and 13.7 percent of the variation in the total number of children.

We get approximately the same results when this analysis is done for each of the two regions separately, with a slightly larger proportion of the variation being explained in the Orléanais than in the Nantais. The only paths in the general model that explain more than 1 percent of the dependent variable's variation are between (1) the head's age and the mother's age at first birth (19.0 percent), (2) the mother's age at first birth and the total number of children (8.4 percent), and (3) the head's age and the total number of children (4.7 percent). As for the outsider, historical time, it never accounted for more than 1 percent of the variation in any of the variables in the model.

One would expect the head's age to explain a large proportion of the variation in the mother's age at the birth of the first *recorded* child; husbands and wives, if they are lucky, grow old together and their first born will one day leave them, at which point their second will move up to first place, until he leaves. . . . . . This, of course, accounts for the greater positive elasticity in the relationship between the two variables as the ages increase (Figure 7.6H). Controlling for this effect, one notes that the mother's age at first birth still accounts for a comparatively large proportion of the variation in the total number of children. However, this is quite an inelastic relationship (Figure 7.6I). That leaves us with the weak tie between the head's age and the total number of children, which is really the only perceptible cyclical effect in the whole model.

Thus, even when the effects of the other variables have been controlled and all the possible nonlinear relationships have been taken into account, one finds that the developmental cycle played no significant role in the household head's occupation or in the total number of kin and servants in the household. It was only within the family nucleus that the cycle had any structural effect: the birth and the eventual departure of children from their parents are the only elements of a cycle detectable here; marriage and death, not included in the analysis, presumably had their part too. But even within this nucleus, the cycle accounted for only a small portion of the total variation in its structure. And that was true throughout the 75-year period under study.[60]

Marshall Sahlins has described the household-type economy as a "species of anarchy."[61] Certainly, the apparent lack of order in household structure would seem to confirm such a characterization. Should one even try to explain the variation not accounted for by the above model? Historians traditionally have a horror of the empty, of effects without cause. But this simply might be a case in which the vast proportion of variation cannot be explained, whatever kind of rational model one picked. Consider, for example, a model that stressed the division of labor as a prime determinant of household structure. Quite obviously, the analyses done on the correlation between occupation and the other variables (Table 7.8, Figure 7.7) indicate that one would end up with roughly the same result as the earlier model. The point is that there is little relationship between the variables; the ruling factor is chance.

But let us not try to distort Sahlins' position. For Sahlins, as for Chayanov, there is an order in household structure. The anarchy of the economy is not evident *within* each producing unit but rather *between* them. Thus Chayanov would have undoubtedly agreed with Sahlins that no social or material relationship can be established between the households except that they are alike.[62] The present inquiry has failed to detect any particular order in household structure – it has failed to uncover any "laws" defining the household's formation and development. But the main problem here is that the analysis is based on a comparison *between* households. If, instead of taking the household as our most fundamental social unit, we took the individual, then the disorder of household structure would be far less apparent. Indeed, we have already found patterns in the various forms of social bonding that the individual experienced through time and have even noted some important points of contrast between the Orléanais and the Nantais. One fails to account for much variation when comparing across households because they were so alike; and they were so alike because of the effort made by individuals to control the number of children born, the number of outsiders admitted into the household, and the length of time these members were permitted to stay.

If there were a single variable that could best explain the enormous proportion of variation still "unexplained" by the model, it would probably be "control" – we are really trying to explain why there was so little variation between the households to start with. But again we run up against the old phenomenological problem of studying generations now dead. Did all this represent a *conscious* control of the number of children? a *conscious* control of the number of outside members? Given the exceedingly small number of children being born and the striking similarity between all households, it would probably be correct to say, yes, it was. But we will never find any direct evidence of what affected that decision to control. My contention, of course, is that it was largely determined by the level of agricultural intensity reached in this peasant economy (an argument that will be elaborated in Chapter 8). But whatever was behind that decision, the control itself had produced a curious contradiction in demographic structure. It is one of the great paradoxes of this study that a disciplined regulation of household size had led to the establishment of chance as the ruling factor in the variation of household structure. To the extent that one is willing to accept the thesis of Piaget or Lévi-Strauss – that structures detected "out there" in the measurable universe of social actions and relationships are reflections of the innate mental structures existing within the individual actor – each household member was caught between the ordered vision of his own individual experience of time and the disordered vision of the group in which he was to perform.

2. Macrodemography: population movements

Our analysis of the individual experience has already revealed that
demographic controls were more restrictive in the Orléanais than the
Nantais, a fact that has led us to the hypothesis that psychological tensions were generally greater in the Orléanais. Put in the perspective of
our model of a peasant economy (Chapter 3), these tensions are to be
understood in terms of the range of economic options open to society's
members: I have repeated, almost to the point of sounding redundant,
that the range was narrower in the Orléanais than in the Nantais. A study
of the population movements throughout both regions promises to give
some indication of how much narrower the range of options was in the
Orléanais. But it has to be remembered that population is not an isolated
factor. Both these regions were densely populated. It was proposed in
Chapter 3 that there were four alternative ways in which a peasant
economy could avoid a "crisis" situation: a further intensified use of the
land, a higher rate of mortality, a conscious effort to control population
(birth control and emigration), and cooperation in production. By ex-
amining population movements, we can get an idea of the extent to
which rural society as a whole adopted the second and third
alternatives.[63] But the first and last will have to be considered later.

The population movements in our two regions largely conformed to
the national trends amply documented in the literature on nineteenth-
century French demography. Mortality and fertility declined; rural
emigration increased. An analysis of the departmental statistics given in
the government publications would lead to needless repetition of an
already familiar story. Instead, we shall concentrate on some of the less-
known details of local movements in an attempt to find out how each
agricultural subregion contributed to the general trend and the way in
which movements in the countryside were related to movements in the
city. To do this we have had to go back to the original vital registries.
Recapitulative tables were made up annually by the prefectures, but unfortunately most of the preserved tables on the Nantais include only
departmental figures with the occasional breakdown by arrondissement.
Figures by commune are extremely rare.[64] As for the Orléanais, all the
recapitulative tables were destroyed in the fire of 1940. The vital
registries (états civils) consist of annual and decennial lists. The annual
lists provide much more information than the decennial lists but they are
very bulky; a systematic study of the lists for the 200-odd communes
within our regions would have required more time than we had available.
The decennial lists give only the names of those born, married, and dead
during the respective 10-year period. However, that in itself is valuable
information.

The method of analysis was simple. By relating these lists to the population totals of each commune, we were able to estimate the annual crude birth, marriage, and death rates for every commune in the two regions, and this, in turn, provided the means of estimating net migration rates. The calculations were made as follows. First, the decennial totals of births, marriages, and deaths were made up for each commune[65] and placed alongside the quinquennial population totals drawn from local publications.[66] Second, annual totals for births, marriages, and deaths were calculated by dividing the original totals by 10; annual population totals were calculated by linear interpolation (i.e., if the population totals for a given commune were 200 for 1851 and 205 for 1856, one would estimate a total of 201 for 1852, 202 for 1853, etc.); and migration rates were calculated from the differences in total population not accounted for by births and deaths. Obviously the results are not to be trusted on a year-to-year basis. But they do give an indication of local secular trends. In order to detect such trends, the final estimate of the annual rates was based on 9-year running means (i.e., an estimate for the crude birth rate for 1860 would have been calculated by dividing the total number of births between 1856 and 1864 by the estimated *average* population total for this period and then dividing the result by 9 and multiplying by 1,000). These calculations were performed in two runs. All the communes were blocked first by region and then by subregion. Estimates for Orléans and Nantes were done separately.

The results have been plotted on the graphs presented in Figures 7.8–7.11. There is one caution we ought to make at this point. Vital rates expressed simply in terms of the number of events per thousand head of population measure more than just the inclination of a given population toward those events. For example, a crude birth rate is a function of the population's age distribution and the proportion of women married as well as marital fertility. Age distribution also influences the marriage, death, and migration rates – something to be kept in mind during the following analysis.[67]

Our first observations confirm our original expectations: Birth and death rates declined from a point somewhere in the 30s down to the level of the low 20s or even the upper teens; marriage rates remained stable at around seven, eight or nine, and rural emigration tended to increase over time. However, these were not all steady trends. Notably, the decline in death rates appears to have leveled off at some point in the 1850s and, in the Orléanais, to have even increased. With the 1870s, the rate of rural out-migration picked up momentum (although it ought to be noted from the start that these migration rates do not indicate a countryside being "emptied" of its population at any point in the nineteenth century). Obviously, any kind of periodization is somewhat arbitrary. All the same,

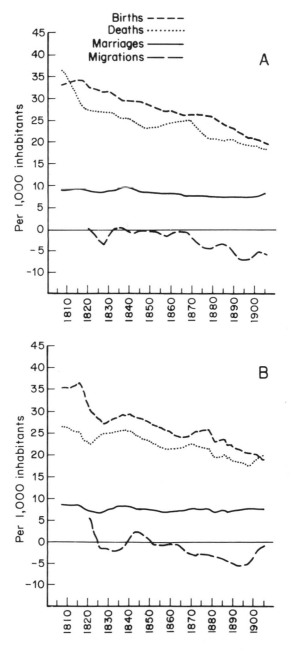

Figure 7.8. Births, deaths, marriages, and migrations per 1,000 inhabitants, in 9-year running means, in (A) the Orléanais and (B) the Nantais, 1807–1906.

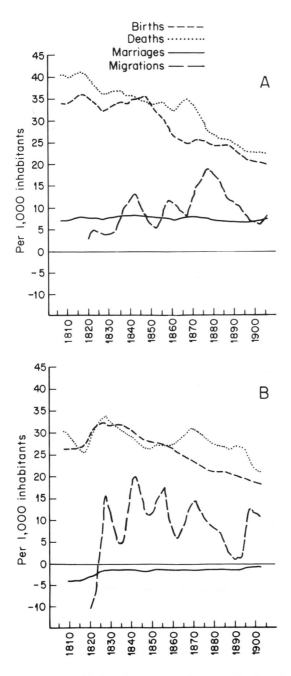

Figure 7.9. Births, deaths, marriages, and migrations per 1,000 inhabitants in 9-year running means, in (A) Orléans and (B) Nantes, 1807–1906.

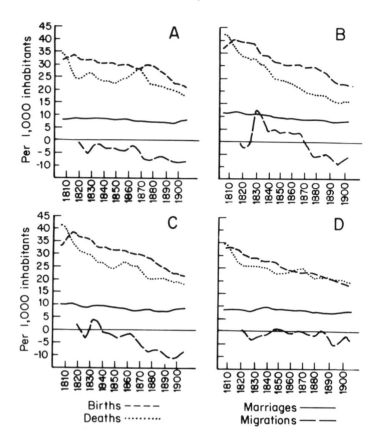

Figure 7.10. Births, deaths, marriages, and migrations per 1,000 inhabitants, in 9-year running means, in (A) the Beauce, (B) the Sologne, (C) the Forêt d'Orléans, and (D) the Orléanais Valley, 1807–1906.

the analysis will be made easier if we can speak of the first half of the nineteenth century as being generally a period of declining birth and death rates, the 1850s and 60s as a period when the decline in mortality slowed down (at least for one region), and the last quarter of the century as a period of increased out-migration and further decline in the birth and death rates. That gives us a basis for more detailed comparisons.

Mortality

The decline in the death rate was a Europeanwide phenomenon that had its origins in the eighteenth century. Its cause has not been clearly established – it was probably due to a multiplicity of factors.[68] But it is a fact that many of the lethal infectious diseases of earlier times had, by the first decades of the nineteenth century, either entirely disappeared from the continent of Europe or were showing signs of abating.[69] In ad-

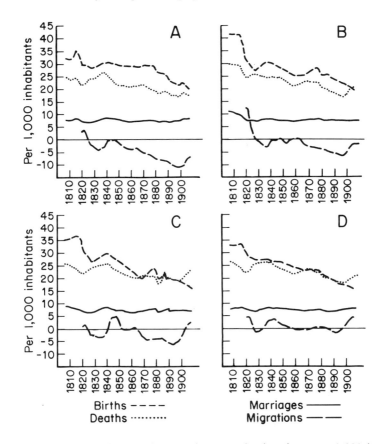

Figure 7.11. Births, deaths, marriages, and migrations per 1,000 inhabitants, in 9-year running means, in (A) the Nantais Plateau, (B) Retz–Vendée, (C) Sèvre-et-Maine, and (D) the Nantais Valley, 1807–1906.

dition, the old type of "subsistence crisis" in which large proportions of the population died as a result of poor harvests was occurring less frequently.[70] None of this suddenly happened. In the Orléanais and the Nantais, as must have been the case in most parts of Europe, the elimination of disease and undernourishment was, even in the nineteenth century, slow and irregular. Thus, in a detailed inventory of the major causes of death in the city of Nantes for the year 1870, smallpox and typhus were still being reported among the major killers.[71] And anybody thumbing through the regional papers of the July Monarchy and Second Empire will very swiftly discover that the sentiment of the local populace was less of joy at the victory over old maladies than of fear of nature's new war hammer, cholera.

There were six major cholera epidemics in France during the nineteenth century, 1832, 1849, 1853–4, 1865–6, 1873, and 1884, all of which were felt, with varying degrees of severity, in our own two regions. Each epidemic followed a fairly standard pattern: the first outbreak was usually in a southern French port, the next in the capital, and hence into the provinces. The Nantais, like many of the western parts of France, was sometimes afflicted before Paris because of its seaport.

The most complete newspaper accounts still available for both the Orléanais and the Nantais are on the 1849 epidemic. That year, cholera is reported to have broken out in Paris on 7 March.[72] As was typical of the other years of epidemic, it only took two or three weeks for rumors to spread that the disease was already taking its toll in the Orléanais.[73] Typical also was the minor outbreak of some other disease prior to the start of the epidemic – this time smallpox at Saint-Denis-de-l'Hotel, a small rural commune on the right bank of the Loire about 20 kilometers east of Orléans.[74] But it was not until 2 June that the *Journal du Loiret* declared:

Cholera is among us. A relief bureau has been organized at the town hall. But that is not enough. Sweep the streets and water them twice a day, that is what the normally executed prescriptions lay down. . . . We plead our citizens to carry out the decree from the town hall punctually and to thoroughly wash the gutters two or three times a day. Cleanliness of the air is one of the best protections against cholera.[75]

Actually, Orléans was not the first part of the region to be affected. It seems that the first outbreak occurred at Patay, the small agricultural market town in the middle of the Beauce. It had begun in mid-May in a household run by two sisters, novelty merchants, who had received their mother from Paris, where she had recently lost her husband following the contraction of the disease.[76] But most of the stories in the *Journal du Loiret* dealing with the epidemic concentrate on the city of Orléans – coming from a newspaper that had the habit of reporting events on a regional rather than urban basis, this would seem to be evidence that Orléans was the worst hit. Between 1 June and 15 September, the epidemic claimed 227 victims in Orléans.[77] By the end of September, the epidemic had run its course. No figures were published for the surrounding countryside – one assumes they were too low to have attracted any attention.

The pattern was significantly different in the Nantais. Here, a minor outbreak of what was probably another disease or even a spate of diseases occurred the preceding autumn in Ancenis. In October 1848, *Le Colibri* was reporting:

One dies very frequently at Ancenis in these times and the causes of the maladies do not seem to be known. What is certain is that the month of October will carry off more from our town than commonly die in three months.[78]

And a week later:

> Still sickness and deaths in our town. Among others, a young woman of 36 is dead leaving her husband seven young children. Such misfortunes are feared at the moment; and if the reports are not lies, no less than 500 sick are to be counted in the town.[79]

On 21 April 1849, the first victims of the cholera epidemic were reported in the city of Nantes. By 2 July, 517 citizens had died as a result of the disease; another 84 victims had been claimed in the rest of the arrondissement of Nantes.[80] In the meantime, the only communes to be affected in the arrondissement of Ancenis were those bordering the Loire. But the toll in these communes was high. Ancenis alone, with a population of 3,800, lost 82 persons between 13 May and 24 June, or, as the official medical report put it at the time, a proportion of 1 death for every 46 inhabitants.[81] The rural communes were not spared. Montbert, in Retz-Vendée, lost a particularly large number of inhabitants in the first week of the epidemic; Anetz and Varades, east of Ancenis, likewise suffered:

> In the communes of Anetz and especially Varades the disease had announced itself with such swift intensity as to throw the population into a state of terror. Fortunately, the gravity of these threats was not realized and the disease, after a few weeks, was suddenly and completely terminated having taken about 20 victims.[82]

The severity of the epidemic dwindled during the month of July but picked up again in August, with the countryside following the same cycle as the city.[83] Deaths from cholera declined in early September only to increase once more in the last half of the month.[84] It was only in late April 1850 that the epidemic was finally declared to be at an end.[85]

I have recounted the details of this epidemic because it reveals a certain pattern of mortality in our two regions. First, from a general point of view, the manifestation of other diseases prior to the onset of cholera suggests that the populations had an especially low resistance to sicknesses of any kind at that particular time. The low level of the population's resistance rather than the presence of a specific type of bacteria would then seem to be the cause of the epidemic. Indeed, an analysis of cause-specific mortality tables of the nineteenth century would indicate that there were nearly always some deaths ascribed to cholera. But a second observation seems to contradict the first, and that is the identity of waterways as carriers of the disease. Even contemporaries were aware that the worst-hit areas were those with an abundant supply of flowing water.[86] Surface streams, as we already know (see Chapter 4, Section 2) interlaced the Nantais whereas in the Orléanais, they were practically nonexistent beyond the Loire and Loiret, which would explain the greater severity of the epidemic in the Nantais, its longer duration, and its wider sphere of influence.

The contradiction between the first and second observation is really only apparent. Although the presence of waterways might explain the epidemic's varying degrees of severity, it does not explain why the epidemic began. The first observation provides a better solution to this problem, although, conversely, it gives no satisfactory account of the epidemic's severity. There is no reason to believe that the larger number of victims in the Nantais meant that the Nantais had the weaker population.

This point should be considered within the context of the long-term trends plotted out in Figures 7.8–7.11. The death rates were, on average, lower in the Nantais than the Orléanais. During the first of the three periods just outlined, these rates remained somewhere in the region of 25 deaths per 1,000 and only began to decline in the 1840s. It is quite possible that mortality failed to decrease before this date because of the presence of contaminated waters, although it is unlikely that cholera contributed much to the general trend. Dysentery, enteritis, and the other recurrent intestinal ailments were more plausible determinants. By contrast, in the Orléanais there was a steady drop in the death rates from a high that in some subregions reached as much as 40 per 1,000 in the early years of the century down to a level roughly equivalent to that held in the Nantais. Between about 1830 and 1850, the curves of the Orléanais and Nantais Valley subregions are almost identical, thus attesting to the lower limits of mortality in areas crossed by a major waterway.

The long death rolls that came in from the communes of the Sologne and the Forêt d'Orléans were the main cause of the generally higher rates of the Orléanais during this first period. And, in this case, it was stagnant water rather than streams that had created such a sickly environment. Ponds and marshes were the breeding grounds of mosquitoes that carried a whole host of diseases. But if the presence of stagnant water were the sole cause of high long-term mortality rates, the same pattern should have been found in the Nantais Plateau and Retz–Vendée – and it evidently wasn't. The explanation must be of a regional nature. In the Nantais, even the most waterlogged subregions had been able to develop products for which there was a demand in the regional capital, whereas subregions of the same agricultural type in the Orléanais had been forced into a state of quasi-isolation by virtue of Orléans' stagnation (a fact that is further demonstrated by the high death rates, relative to those of Nantes, recorded within its city limits). Thus, prior to 1850, there existed, in at least two subregions of the Orléanais, an unhealthy environment inhabited by an undernourished population. Death was one of the few "options" left open to them.

To summarize the pattern for the first period, short-term fluctuations related to the dispersion of bacteria via contaminated water were more murderous and more widespread in the Nantais than the Orléanais. But the secular trends indicate a higher mortality in the Orléanais, largely due to the combination of poor lands and human poverty.

Sometime during the 1840s or early 1850s, the pattern was radically altered. In the Nantais and, for a brief spell, in the Orléanais, death rates began to decline gradually. The universality of the phenomenon suggests that for some reason or other the floor of these rates had been removed and they were now falling to a new, undefined point of equilibrium.[87] But in the Orléanais, something very curious happened. Mortality began to pick up again, first in the Beauce (and to a lesser degree in the Forêt d'Orléans) and then in the Loire Valley. By the end of the second period, (around 1870), it was the richest, not the poorest, agricultural subregions that were the leading cause of the Orléanais' high death rates. In other words, there had been a complete reversal of the pattern of the first period: whatever had been the main factors behind the earlier high rates, there was now clearly another at play. We should note the existence of a similar trend during the 1860s in the Nantais, especially marked in the Loire Valley, once more, and Retz–Vendée. But the height and duration of the increase were significantly more limited than in the Orléanais.

The third period opened with a rapid decline in the death rates of the Orléanais until the regions caught up with levels already attained in the Nantais. Both regions then followed the same steady decline that had begun in the Nantais at midcentury. There are some minor fluctuations present in the Nantais' curves during this period, but they could be just apparent, arising from the fact that the rates after 1882 are calculated from the incomplete data.[88] This, however, could not account for the sudden rise in the death rates of the Nantais in the first decade of the twentieth century. Rather, the phenomenon seems to be closely related to a simultaneous rise in the rate of rural in-migration.

Before proceeding to the other aspects of the population movements, a brief comment on the reliability of our data is in order. It is possible that the low death rates recorded in the Nantais during the first years of the nineteenth century were due to underregistration. This was often deliberate: the countryside was still in rebellion against the state, in spirit if not in fact (see Chapter 9, Section 1). However, with the Restoration, this form of revolt probably diminished. Furthermore, if there had been an underregistration of deaths, there would logically have been the same for births and this was not the case: Retz–Vendée, one of the most rebellious subregions, had the highest recorded birth rates in the region. As for the effects of a changing age distribution, it is true that declining birth rates would have led to an aging population and hence higher crude death rates. But this could not account for the *decline* in mortality. If anything, it was steeper. And it most certainly could not explain the sharp rise in the mortality rates of the Orléanais during the 1850s and 60s and the even sharper fall in the 1870s. We therefore believe that the employment of more sophisticated measures of mortality would merely confirm the same general patterns just described.

Children and marriage

Crude birth rates and marriage rates are more liable to be misinterpreted than crude death rates because they can be affected by so many more factors (a changing age distribution is only one of them). It would therefore be unwise to attempt to add any new facts about fertility and nuptiality to those already presented in the first part of this chapter. But we ought to at least note that there is nothing unexpected in the shape of these curves. The flat and practically dead straight lines of the marriage rates corroborate the evidence that the average age of marriage and the overall proportion married did not change much during the nineteenth century. The wider fluctuations in the Nantais' birth rates correspond to the greater variation we observed in the region's age-specific rates, whereas the uninterrupted drop in the Orléanais' birth rates confirms the existence of a stricter pattern of control. In fact, the Nantais shows the same degree of indifference to historical trends in its birth rates (most notably in the 1830s and 1870s) as it showed in the proportion of multiple households, the mean household size, and the average number of outside members per household. Birth control was one of the major options open to a peasant economy; it was always exerted in the Orléanais, whereas it was periodically relaxed in the Nantais.

Migrations

A comparison of the migration rates with the birth and death rates will show that to leave one's home was considered an option only of the last resort. Certainly, it would seem logical that a cultivator, faced with the choice of either controlling births or emigrating, would choose the former. But why he would choose death rather than emigrate is a bit more puzzling. Many of the contemporary commentators on migration would probably not have even believed this. The *exode rural* was one of the great scandals of the second half of the century. Local journalists showed almost as much distress about this subject as they did about the Panama Canal, Boulanger, and Dreyfus. Seen from their urban offices, the rural population had ample reason to break camp: urban wages were higher than in the country and there was, in the journalists' opinion, a better chance for self-improvement. There were also, to use the pet phrase of the day, "the pleasures of the town" that countrymen had met through that baneful necessity, the military draft. It would undoubtedly have been denied that the cause of migration was the wretchedness of the country rather than the attractions of the city. Several journalists, in fact, took it upon themselves to write fruity encomiums on the peasant farm and the inevitably happy, self-satisfied family that exploited it.[89] The reason why they did this was almost surely political (countrymen, in theory, are easier to govern than citizens).[90] But, politics notwithstanding, they succeeded in propagating – either through their elegance or sheer verbosity – a myth still affirmed in many quarters today: there was a whole army of eager folk out there in the country waiting for the first opportunity to move into the city.

Prior to 1870, migratory movements could not have had any significant effect on the total populations of the two regions. Even in the 1890s, at the height of the rural exodus, the overall rate for either region (Orléans and Nantes excluded) was less than -10 per 1,000. Thus it would be perfectly justifiable to argue that Orléans and Nantes grew as slowly as they did on account of the reluctance of people in the surrounding areas to leave their farms. Low migratory rates and low rates of urban growth obviously go together. Figure 7.9 indicates that the net annual rate of in-migration into Orléans reached a high in the 1880s of + 18 per 1,000, which would be the equivalent of an annual growth rate, *ceteris paribus,* of 1.8 percent; net migration rates remained below 10 throughout most of the century. Rates of in-migration into Nantes were appreciably higher than into Orléans during the first half of the century, although Nantes' high point, which was reached in the early 1840s and which was twice that of Orléans' rate for the same period, was still only + 20. The rates seemed to have remained below + 10 for most of the second half of the century, i.e., even lower than in Orléans. Until the 1880s, death rates were substantially lower in Nantes than in Orléans[91] and this contributed to the fairly rapid rate of growth of the city during the first half and middle decades of the century (Table 7.9). Still, Nantes' average annual rate of growth between 1831 and 1906 was identical to Orléans', that is, 0.94 percent. Low rates of in-migration, then, meant low rates of growth, especially after 1860 when the death rates of both cities continually hovered above their birth rates. We do not know from where this trickle of immigrants came. There is some evidence suggesting that most of Nantes' newcomers were from Lower Brittany, the south of France, and even Italy.[92] Orléans, with its total economic reliance on its hinterland, probably had a larger proportion of local immigrants. This is borne out by the fact that, whereas Nantes' main period of growth (the 1850s and 60s) coincided with the national trend,[93] the most steady period of growth for Orléans was during the third period (or after 1870) when rural out-migration in the Orléanais was at its height.

Of course we are speaking here only of net migrations, and it is possible that there was more movement than our figures would suggest. One

Table 7.9. *Population growth of Orléans and Nantes, 1831–1911*

Year	Orléans		Nantes	
	Total population	Annual percentage growth	Total population	Annual percentage growth
1831	40,161	–	77,992	–
1836	40,272	0.1	75,895	– 0.5
1841	42,584	1.2	83,389	2.0
1846	45,788	1.5	94,194	2.6
1851	47,393	0.7	96,362	0.5
1856	46,922	– 0.2	108,530	2.5
1861	50,798	1.7	113,625	0.9
1866	49,100	– 0.7	111,956	2.1
1872	48,976	0.0	118,517	1.0
1876	52,157	1.6	122,247	0.8
1881	57,264	2.0	124,319	0.3
1886	60,826	1.2	127,482	0.5
1891	63,705	1.0	122,750	– 0.7
1896	66,699	0.9	123,902	0.2
1901	67,311	0.2	132,990	1.5
1906	68,614	0.4	133,247	0.0
1911	72,096	1.0	170,535[a]	–
1831–1906		0.9		0.9

Note: The vast increase in Nantes' population between 1906 and 1911 is largely due to a change in the city's boundaries (absorption of the communes of Chantenoy and Doulon).
Sources: Annuaire du Loiret and INSEE.

of the most remarkable facts to emerge from the subregional breakdown of the data is that there were several areas in both regions that, over certain stretches of time, actually recorded net rates of *in*-migration. In the Orléanais, this occurred during the first period within the pasture-type agricultural subregions, with the Forêt d'Orléans experiencing a high of about + 4 per 1,000 in the 1830s and the Sologne, about + 12. The Sologne registered net rates of in-migration all the way to the third period, when the rates suddenly dropped off. In the Nantais, it is in the intensive-type agricultural subregions that one finds net rates of in-migration. For the first period, Sèvre-et-Maine rose to a rate of + 5 in the 1840s; the Nantais Valley appears to have held on to nearly this level since the 1830s. The rates fell in both subregions with the beginning of the second period but rose again rapidly toward the end of the third. It also ought to be noted that at no point during any of the three periods did the Nantais Valley have a net rate of out-migration of more than – 2.

Rural in-migration is a phenomenon not widely appreciated by historians of the nineteenth century.[94] Yet it certainly existed and probably played a vital role in the migratory movements of the period. For a start, it was almost certainly less traumatic for an individual to migrate to another rural area than to move into the city. It was common enough for people to move from one commune to another in order to get married. If times were rough, why not move to a neighboring subregion where land was cheap or the chances of making a living were greater? One could still preserve the basic values, the basic subjective sense of cost and profit, effort and satisfaction, which were the heart of the peasant economy. The presence of cheap, sparsely populated land in the Sologne could thus have provided a sanctuary for destitute cultivators from other parts of the Orléanais (and, of course, the neighboring regions), which might itself partly explain the lower death rates in the wealthier subregions during the first period as well as the rapid improvements that occurred in the Sologne after 1850 (see Chapter 8, Section 2). Around 1850, population density in the Sologne had reached an optimum and, if the subregion were to continue accepting in-migrants, agricultural improvements would *have* to have been made; the sudden rise in mortality in the Beauce and the Orléanais Valley during this period suggests that rural migration was no longer conceived as a real option. By the 1870s, rural in-migration in the Orléanais was definitely at an end.

The evidence showing people in the Nantais migrating into the intensive-type agricultural subregions instead of the pasture type is one more indication of the greater opportunities in the region. The movements were certainly not made for cheaper land – which is probably why the in-migration rates never reached the dramatic heights of the Orléanais. But rural migration remained an option in the Nantais right through the nineteenth century. The Nantais, for instance, was accepting in-migrants in the 1890s and 1900s, a time at which the whole of France was alight with talk about agricultural depression.

Should the idea of a rural exodus be rejected outright?[95] The graphs undermine a lot of the inflated rhetoric, in the first place, by demonstrating the reluctance of the population to leave the countryside: practically every case of increasing rural out-migration is preceded by a period of high mortality (the exceptions are the increases in out-migration in the Sologne after around 1870 and in Retz–Vendée and Sèvre-et-Maine after around 1865). The rates of the Orléanais during the second period are particularly striking; they are literally saying that the rural inhabitants preferred to die than leave the countryside. It took at least 10 years of rising mortality (perhaps as many as 20 in the Beauce) before migratory patterns began to change. Once they had, the death rates dropped. But even after 1870, the net rates of out-migration were scarcely world shattering. The rates for the Orléanais as a whole were not much more than those of the Nantais − − 77 and − 6 are the respective low points in the two curves. The lowest point reached in the eight subregional curves is − 11 for the Forêt d'Orléans and the Nantais Plateau in the late 1890s, the only two cases in which the rates fell below − 10.

There remains a possibility that the rates presented in the graphs do not adequately describe local movements, even when broken down by subregion. The two maps of Figure 7.12 should relieve that worry. They are a visual representation of net migrations, by commune, over the 30 years of greatest migratory movement (1881–1911) expressed as rates per thousand inhabitants living in each commune at the beginning of the period.[96] As one would expect, the maps show the Orléanais to have been the most affected by rural emigration. Net in-migration is found only in the immediate vicinity of Orléans and in a few of the outlying canton capitals – Patay and Artenay in the Beauce, Beaugency in the Valley, and La Ferté-Saint-Aubin in the Sologne.[97] Meung, on the right bank of the Loire west of Orléans and one of the most densely populated communes in the region, registered the largest rate of out-migration. Beyond that, the Sologne and the Forêt d'Orléans (especially its eastern limits) appear to have been the most affected. In the Nantais, by contrast, one is struck by the large areas that had an overall net rate of in-migration: virtually the whole of the right bank of the Loire west of Ancenis, together with some of the richest winegrowing regions of Sèvre-et-Maine (the cantons of Vertou, Vallet, and Clisson). The subregion most touched by out-migration in the Nantais was the Plateau.

It has to be kept in mind that all these rates are based on a 30-year period. A rate of − 400 per 1,000, though it might appear great, is equivalent to an annual rate of only − 13. All the same, when that sort of rate is combined with low birth rates, a population will no longer be able to replace its numbers, as can be demonstrated by an elementary simulation. With constant annual death rates of 20, birth rates of 25, and net migration rates of − 13, a population of 1,000 would be reduced to 920 after 10 years and 760 after 30. Even with a migration rate of only − 10, the population would fall to 950 and 850 after the same respective periods. This is what was happening in several of the rural communes of the Orléanais after 1870. Small wonder the concern about depopulation! But it was not solely due to out-migration (which was itself quite small): the region was exercising every possible means of repressing its numbers.

Repression has been the single most important theme to emerge from this chapter. Significant, if hardly overwhelming, changes in mortality, fertility, and migration over historical time coexisted with the general stability of peasant family structure, of the peasant sense of "time." The extent of repression that this required in the two regions is a fundamental

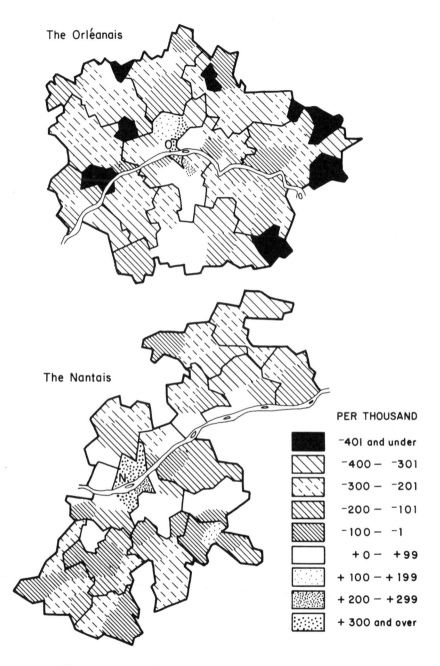

The Orléanais

The Nantais

PER THOUSAND

−401 and under
−400 − −301
−300 − −201
−200 − −101
−100 − −1
+0 − +99
+100 − +199
+200 − +299
+300 and over

Figure 7.12. Net migrations for the period 1881–1911 per 1,000 inhabitants (1881–6) in (A) the Orléanais and (B) the Nantais.

point of contrast. An individual born in the Nantais at any time during the nineteenth century was more likely to grow up in an environment of stronger social bonding than in the Orléanais; he was also more likely to perpetuate that strength by directing himself through each transitional period in his life and toward each recognized social state according to his own impulse. There was less variation in the lives of the Orléanais' inhabitants. They had purged themselves of all superfluous affects that threatened the peasant economy's survival. One was rushed through the transitional periods of infancy and adolescence; family size was more strictly controlled; individuals were more isolated. The recorded behavior of the Orléanais' population is an outline of the behavior of a peasant population that had reached an optimum, and we see the choices before it: birth control, death, and emigration, in that order of priority.

8   Peasant properties

Small, intensely cultivated plots of land were, we have seen, a major feature of the Loire Country's landscape, a major part of its economy too. Consider here the example of Beaugency:

> The industrial life of Beaugency rests almost entirely on its markets whose importance is increasing every day. Their progress is the result of several causes, and principally the fragmentation of property. While at the beginning of the century a hundred cultivators were enough to feed our markets, one has today more than five hundred coming in every week carrying with them the various products of their farms. . . . It is without any doubt, in our eyes, that the result, so advantageous for our town, is due to the large number of properties sold one after the other over the last thirty years.[1]

That was one journalist's opinion, writing in February 1860. But this is another on the same area seven years later:

> See the windings in the country of the [river] Lieu, the greenness of its banks, the splendid foliage of the swaying trees, the elegant clock tower of the village [Tavers]; the Fontenis with their springs unceasingly gushing forth onto the sand. . . . But it is a walk whose charms will not take long to disappear. The cool shades no longer exist; for I can hear from here the hatchet of the woodcutter. . . . Most of the trees have been sold to active and intelligent traders. Adieu Fontenis! Adieu walker's paradise! Adieu! All the poetry departs, it is no more! Here it has made way for hay, lucern, wheat or other crops. This time, agriculture has destroyed the eclogue.[2]

What had been said about Beaugency was being said in one form or another about many other regions throughout France. These small properties were seen as either the fount of the nation's well-being or the root of its troubles; the *mal français* in the nineteenth century was, in the countryside at least, a problem of property structure. Thus Balzac would attribute the breakdown of morality and order in rural society to the relentless drive of the peasantry to possess the land: "Le paysan n'a pas d'autre passion, d'autre désir, d'autre point de mire que de mourir propriétaire."[3] *Les Paysans* concludes with the depiction of an old Burgundian estate divided up into "more than a thousand plots" resembling "a tailor's sample card."[4] It hardly required any great stretch of the imagination to suppose that if properties were being broken up in this way, the same thing was happening to the families that possessed them. The problem was to find a cause. The civil code was the main culprit in Le Play's books – if France was going to compete successfully with its greatest economic rival, England, it would have to abandon those terrible laws

that forced the partition of family properties and adopt a more stabiliz-
ing, more "English" system of testamentary liberty to assure the continuity of the patrimony.[5] For Edmond Demolins, one of Le Play's young
acolytes, the trouble lay with the French notion of the home: for a
Frenchman the idea of home is represented by a property and the attachment is to the place, "home" is a material thing; for an Englishman it is a
moral thing, an abstraction for which comfort is the first consideration.
There is no French equivalent, noted Desmolins with insight, to the Saxon word "home." "This Saxon word evokes an idea less material and
definitive than our own word *le foyer*, 'the hearth'. It means rather the
interior arrangement, the comfort of every-day life, which is characteristic of the Anglo–Saxon home, whether in the farmhouse, town dwell-
ing, or workman's cottage."[6]

Giving this a more rustic frame of reference, French property was not
simply a unit of production but the ideal symbol of one's own identity in
society; an exchange of property was therefore, in the very fullest sense
of the term, a social exchange. As evidence, we might point to the fact
that at the same time as France developed a comprehensive census of its
population, it developed, unlike England, a cadastre that included all
(landed) properties within its frontiers together with their entire history
from the time they were first recorded. Beyond its simple function as a
tax register, the cadastre provided a concrete means of recognizing an individual's existence, every bit as much as the *état civil*.[7]

In the last chapter, we noted some of the difficulties of self-identity experienced by the Orléanais' inhabitants, in contrast to the Nantais', as the
direct result of population pressure. Utilizing the cadastre, we are able to
get an idea of how the same pressure affected the structure of property
and the patterns of its exchange over time. We can make the same
distinctions of time as in the previous chapter. Hence, to the extent that
one can consider property as part of the attendant trappings of an individual's identity there will be a "property cycle" that will evolve as that
identity evolves; within the context of "lived time," an analysis of property must turn around the questions "how long was it possessed?" and
"how much?" At the level of "historical time" and paralleling the population movements previously discussed, there are the general movements of
property that can be used as a second pacestick on the evolution of society at large.

I intend to discuss this more general element of property structure
first. But before even doing that, there is the question of method.

1. A property census

Very few studies of the cadastre have been published, probably because
of the respectable hugeness of the *matrices* or because property itself is

simply not a very sexy issue. To my knowledge, nobody has attempted to trace the outlines of the property cycle from the cadastre.[8] The method of abstracting and analyzing the data presented in this chapter has therefore had to be developed practically from scratch. We are already familiar (Chapter 5, Section 1) with the main features of the *matrices cadastrales*: their folios listing details on the area, culture, and estimated value of each property and the recapitulation at the end of the last volumes.[9] The recapitulations only give the total area and total estimated value, together with the folio number of properties existing at the date of origin of the cadastre (1821–44, depending on the matrices) or at the date of revision (1913). They therefore cannot be used in the study of property development. We should also note the existence of an alphabetic list of names and folio numbers, some added and others crossed out, as the century proceeded, which has been useful for sampling. Finally, the folios themselves. This is where most of our data have been gathered; they give the name, residence, and, infrequently, the occupation of the propertyholder; they also supply, by parcel,[10] information on area, culture, and estimated values. When new land was acquired, it was added to the list of parcels along with the date of its acquisition and the folio number of its previous owner. Similarly, land yielded was crossed out, and the date and folio number of the new owner marked.

Our own survey consists of two batches of data: a general sample of properties[11] existing at the time of origin of the cadastre and at the time of its revision and a smaller sample drawn from 19 communes for the purpose of studying developments over time. The general sample has been taken from the recapitulations and consists of three variables, the total area of property (found in the recapitulations), the owner's residence,[12] and the total area of built-up land within the property (based on a subsequent analysis of the folios).[13] Sampling was done in the Orléanais by taking 1 in every 20 properties listed in the recapitulations for every commune in the region. In the Nantais, we encountered two major obstacles that rendered this impossible. First, most of the matrices were unclassified and in poor condition – we managed to put together the first cadastre's matrices of 52 communes; for the second cadastre, we managed 42 communes. Second, the large number of properties in each commune made it difficult, and needless, to maintain a 5 percent sample – in a few instances, we dropped the sample to as low as 1 in every 80. Some matrices, especially the very early ones of Sèvre-et-Maine, had no recapitulations and the sample had to be taken directly from the folios. All in all, information was gathered from both cadastres on 4,142 properties in the Orléanais and 2,353 in the Nantais. As in the case of the nominal lists, we have weighted these properties according to subregion, taking into account two factors: (1) the different proportion of sampled properties to total properties listed; (2) the proportionate area selected for sampling in each subregion as represented by the communes selected from each cadastre (thus we have selected 100 percent of the area of the Orléanais but somewhat less than 50 percent of most subregions in the Nantais).

We have been forced to abandon data gathered on occupation and estimated property values. Occupation is missing for more than 95 percent of the total sample in some communes. As for the estimated values, even contemporaries warned that they were arbitrary, varied from commune to commune, and represented much less than their real value.[14] This, combined with the fact that data on the first cadastre are spread over a quarter of a century, led us to believe that the results would be more misleading than helpful. On the other hand, the data on built-up property made it possible to present statistics on purely *agricultural land,* defining agricultural land as all land exclusive of built-up areas and including only those properties with less than one-third of their surfaces built up (hence, striking out all properties that consisted of simply a house and a small garden; that is, between 4 and 7 percent of the sample, depending mainly on the relative population densities).

It has not been possible to take built-up property into account in the smaller sample. However, this sample does provide more information on the identity of the propertyholder (including sex, occupation, and residence) as well as a complete history of the property. A total of 844 properties have been sampled from the matrices of the first cadastre. We have selected two communes from each subregion (practically the same communes as selected for the analysis of the nominal lists) and have sampled for each commune approximately 50 properties taken at random from the alphabetic lists (or from the folios themselves when the lists were missing).[15] All data are derived from the folios. Once more, we have weighted the properties by subregion, deriving the weight factors from the overall proportion of properties per subregion as calculated in the first general sample of the two cadastres.

Data on property history had to be organized in such a way as to assure no excessive use of computer "space" and at the same time to supply enough information to be able to build up a picture of the property cycle as well as developments over historical time. Recording the data by parcel would have been out of the question – some properties had over 100 such parcels. The same was true of the transactions – the sale of a single block of territory could involve as many as 30 purchases. It was decided to limit each property sampled to 20 exchanges. If we define a *transaction* as the changing of hands in land between a single buyer and a single seller (or inheritor and disinheritor), we can define an *exchange* as any series of transactions taking place at the same date provided (1) they are either all purchases or all sales and (2) that all those involved in these transactions belong to the same "code of relationship." The code of relationship is similar to that employed in the last chapter in studying the household members outside the conjugal family unit and essentially is determined by whether or not the buyer and seller have the same surnames.[16] Out of the whole sample, there are only 15 properties with over 20 exchanges and in these cases we have simply combined several exchanges into one. For each exchange, we have recorded the date, the area of land exchanged (+ for a purchase, − for a sale), the number of transactions involved, and the code of relationship.

To facilitate the study of the property cycle, we have had to distinguish, in the style of Goubert's demography, between complete and incomplete properties. A *complete property* is one whose entire history, from first purchase to last sale, is included within the 80-odd years of the matrices. An *incomplete property* is any property whose first purchase took place before the origin of the matrix or whose last sale occurred after 1913. Note that addition of all the areas exchanged will equal zero for all properties sampled, save those still in existence in 1913. Similarly, addition of the areas exchanged up to a given date will provide a picture of property structure at that date.

The acquisition of the titles to property are thus recorded, whence they came, whither they went; we can witness here some of the major events in rural France one century past.

2. Property movements

Two cadastres

Commune by commune, one visualizes the drafting of a map comparing the differences in the absolute number of properties between one survey completed in the declining years of the July Monarchy and another at the eve of the First World War. Its details defy generalization even by subregion. First, the Beauce. Lion-en-Beauce shows an increase of 26 percent, whereas its neighbor Trinay, just this side of the forest fringe, shows 82; Patay, in the center, shows 37 percent and Saint-Péravy, to the southwest, shows 46. But let one step back and watch the cartographer continue his piece – a vague pattern emerges: Neuville, 15 percent; Saint Lyé, 25; Vennecy, 85; Trainou, 96; Ingrannes: 100.0. The map traced to the center of the Forêt d'Orléans, supporter of a pasture-type agriculture and host to the large estates, indicates some of the major property movements in the region. But the most dramatic changes are reserved for the Sologne, where properties were the largest and agriculture the poorest: 113 percent for Sennely (Gérard Bouchard's "motionless village" of the Old Regime), 152 percent at Marcilly. A fourfold increase is sketched into the space left for Ligny-le-Ribault.

And is this not the same pattern in the Nantais? Certainly the movements had been less violent. In the communes of the Nantais Plateau closest to the Loire Valley, the increase is limited to 20 or 30 percent. But to the north, although the variation is as great as elsewhere, one notes communes such as Joué with an increase of 41 percent, Saint-Mars-la-Jaille with 47, and Le Pin with 50. Still greater advances are marked in the communes of Retz–Vendée that encroach upon the *bocages* to the south; Legé, 72 percent, Saint Colombin, 83; and Vieillevigne, 276. Two communes in the marshes bordering the Lac de Grandlieu exceed 50 percent.

Balzac's portrayal of the great estate unable to resist the onslaught of peasant acquisitiveness seems to have been many times repeated in the Loire Country. But the apparent strength of the small propertyholder was no novelty. Even in the eighteenth century, the richest land had been his domain, whereas the large estates were limited to the least fertile subregions (Chapter 5). Here was the historical proof of the first principle of peasant economy – that its subjectively determined optimum level of intensity far exceeded the objective optimum set by the market (Chapter 3). This is not simply idle speculation derived from a Russian theorist; it is an observation frequently made in the agricultural reports of the day, sometimes with admiration, often with scorn:

[The small properties] are generally very productive because the circulating capital used in their cultivation is, relatively, very high. However the same proportion is not reflected in the net product if one is to take into account all the costs of cultivation; the price of labor reimbursed by production does not exceed, on average, sixty-five centimes a day. Thus, the owner–cultivators are ordinarily not well-off. This is particularly due to bad rotations or even more to the absence of rotations which opens the last gate to a limitless fragmentation of property. . . . In the middle-sized farms which include exploitations of ten to forty hectares and sometimes beyond . . . the circulating capital is frequently below the needs of good cultivating . . . As a result, the land does not yield anywhere near what it would be able to yield.[17]

Of the regional reports sent into the minister of agriculture in 1908, both those from Loiret and Loire-Inférieure emphasized the small properties' superior level of productivity, in spite of their inability to acquire the proper farming gear: "The question of equipment is balanced by that of individual effort."[18]

The individual effort had intensified. By the outbreak of the First World War, former areas of scrub, thicket, marsh, and woodland had been taken over by the small propertyholder because the valley glebe could no longer support his number. One watches the design of the map progress. Now the communes in the center of each region are shaded, bringing attention to the corridor of the river Loire and the complex parquetry that takes its form on either side of its banks. The narrow wine-producing strip of land on the right bank, west of Orléans – an area that has already been noted for its high rate of rural emigration (Figure 7.12)

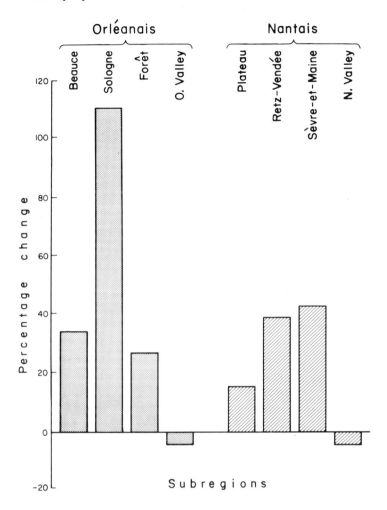

Figure 8.1. Percentage change in total properties recorded in the first and second cadastres, 1821/44–1913.

– registers some serious net losses. In Baule, the total number of properties had dropped by 5 percent, Tavers by 10 percent, and Messas by 23. By contrast, the left bank managed a net gain, no doubt owing its greatest victories to the reclamation of the Sologne; Dry, with almost half its territory lying within the Sologne's limits, scores an increase of 80 percent. In the Nantais, negative percentages are recorded east of Ancenis, whereas there are points of growth to the west. The pattern is never uniform. Some of the most astonishing results are recorded in

Sèvre-et-Maine, already a region of "very divided" properties at the beginning of the century,[19] where we find increases of 67 (La Haie Fouassière) and even as much as 138 percent (Haute Goulaine).

However, a general summary may be permitted once the tabulations by commune are completed and the results added (Figure 8.1). The relationship between property development and agricultural type is not at all obvious, although we ought to note that the Loire Valley, despite the enormous variations, ends up with the same result for the two regions – the area was exploited to its utmost limit. No other region comes close to the kind of progress made in the Sologne; and although the Sologne perfectly conforms to our definition of a pasture-type agriculture, one has to be cautious. Among all the subregions, the second highest figure recorded is that of the intensive agricultural subregion, Sèvre-et-Maine. Of course, this is itself a capital fact. The Sologne, even after improvement, constituted only about one-twentieth of the Orléanais' total population, whereas Sèvre-et-Maine made up a good sixth of the Nantais'. Thus there was still room to expand in the Nantais' intensive agricultures, whereas in the Orléanais there was none.

The comparison of crude property totals between one date and another can tell us little else about this important symbol of rural society. The first thing the historian will want to know, after calculating the differences in totals, will be the extent of change in the size of properties. Here we must refer to our first sample. Because the area distributions are so skewed, no single statistic can give a very satisfactory picture of reality. The mean property size can be influenced by just a handful of large properties and is reproduced here (Table 8.1) only for the purpose of checking the results against other published sources.[20] The best one can do is a statistic that will frequently crop up in this chapter, the "percentile score mean," which, as the name implies, is based on a cumulative frequency score computed by ranking every property in the sample (the two regions and the two cadastres combined and weighted) from the smallest to the highest. (Actually, two scores have been created, one including all properties and another on agricultural land only. Theoretically, the overall mean and median should equal 50.0 for both scores; in fact, they are both slightly above, owing to the extreme skewness of the raw distributions from which they are computed).

The difference created in the sample by taking into account only agricultural land turns out to be very little. Furthermore, repeating the pattern found in the population and family structures, the most important variation is found over space, not time. There is a slightly greater amount of variation between the two cadastres in the Nantais than in the Orléanais, particularly the decline in the percentile score means of the Plateau and Retz–Vendée, but this can be almost wholly accounted for by the smaller sample upon which the results are based. However, one fact that might be pointed out in comparing the two cadastres, keeping in mind the contrast already established in comparing the crude totals of the Orléanais' and Nantais' pasture-type subregions, is that the median property size in the Sologne and the Forêt increases, in the Plateau and Retz–Vendée it declines.

The extremely stable character of the property sizes is fully recognizable once the area distributions are represented graphically (Figure 8.2). The curves of the second cadastre slip over those of the first with virtual glove tightness. Thus, the only way of appreciating the small changes that had occurred is by grouping the properties together into various area "blocks" and then observing the respective changes in the proportion per block (Table 8.2). The main points to be noted in the Nantais are an increase in the proportion of "microproperties" of 10 ares and under, a decline in properties of 26 to 50 ares, an increase over the whole range of small- and middle-sized properties (between 0.51 and 25 hectares), and a decline in all larger properties. In the Orléanais, properties of 5.01 to 25.00 hectares increase to the detriment of all others with the exception of those under 50 ares, whose proportion remains unchanged.

The growth in strength of the middle range has led Dupeux, Bois, and others to speak of an "equalizing" process or even the "democratization of property." We mustn't get carried away with this – the development is barely detectable to the naked eye. Changes, it is true, are a little more marked in some of the subregions. In the Beauce, one notes an increase in the proportion of properties between 11 ares and 2.5 hectares at the expense of those beyond either end of the range; in the Sologne, it is clearly the large properties that made way for the new small- and middle-sized properties. This might be contrasted to the decline in some of the middle-range properties, especially those between 1 and 5 hectares, in the two pasture-type subregions of the Nantais. Here the major increases were confined to the very small. There was no significant change in the area distributions of any of the intensively cultivated subregions, including Sèvre-et-Maine.

We are obviously dealing with some tiny properties. However, two factors could be contributing to an overestimate of the importance in number of these small plots. First, as we have mentioned earlier, many properties were spread over more than one commune – the sample only picks up the fragments by commune. Second, the cadastre frequently registered different members of a single family as being the owners of separate plots of land that were actually farmed as a unit. One notices the existence of such familial properties on perusal of the matrix folios. As in the case of the first factor, there is no other way of evaluating the significance of this second, short of a complete reconstitution of the properties by family name.

Family ties surely had a bearing on the stability of property sizes,

Table 8.1. *Statistical description of area distribution*

Subregion	Cadastre	Area (in hectares)				Percentile score mean	N_w
		Mean	Median	Interquartile range	Skewness		
Total area							
Beauce	1	8.83	0.98	0.26–3.50	16.74	61.5	133
	2	5.23	0.78	0.26–2.94	8.91	59.4	170
Sologne	1	41.94	1.04	0.20–7.20	3.12	63.6	21
	2	30.89	1.55	0.19–8.37	4.29	63.5	42
Forêt	1	10.64	1.26	0.33–4.15	8.04	64.8	73
	2	11.08	1.40	0.36–4.78	12.30	65.7	109
Valley (O)	1	1.74	0.41	0.11–1.34	13.70	48.1	430
	2	2.30	0.37	0.09–1.42	18.43	47.2	476
Orléanais	1	5.43	0.58	0.15–1.86	17.34	53.2	657
	2	5.64	0.53	0.14–2.00	14.97	53.2	798
Plateau	1	6.06	1.43	0.38–4.21	5.14	65.2	188
	2	3.41	0.79	0.27–2.43	10.65	59.1	262
R–V	1	2.74	0.54	0.13–2.04	7.13	52.8	316
	2	2.10	0.35	0.10–1.84	4.45	48.9	448
S-et-M	1	2.57	0.34	0.07–1.04	11.14	43.7	325
	2	1.54	0.29	0.08–1.08	5.51	45.2	372
Valley (N)	1	1.72	0.35	0.12–1.00	9.64	46.6	283
	2	3.12	0.36	0.07–1.39	12.28	46.8	384
Nantais	1	2.99	0.46	0.12–1.68	10.52	50.7	1,111
	2	2.46	0.42	0.10–1.62	17.13	49.2	1,467
Both regions	1	3.90	0.49	0.13–1.73	22.53	51.6	1,767
	2	3.58	0.45	0.12–1.76	21.04	50.6	2,264

Agricultural land only

Beauce	1	8.89	0.99	0.28–3.54	16.68	60.0	132
	2	5.44	0.85	0.29–3.15	8.61	58.9	162
Sologne	1	46.35	1.37	0.35–18.80	2.93	66.9	19
	2	33.98	1.96	0.28–10.16	4.05	66.2	38
Forêt	1	10.73	1.28	0.33–4.15	8.00	63.4	73
	2	11.40	1.48	0.38–5.13	12.12	65.2	106
Valley (O)	1	1.81	0.45	0.13–1.37	13.37	46.7	408
	2	2.45	0.42	0.11–1.49	17.78	46.2	442
Orléanais	1	5.63	0.62	0.17–1.89	17.04	52.0	632
	2	5.98	0.61	0.17–2.11	14.52	52.7	748
Plateau	1	6.28	1.52	0.46–4.24	5.07	65.7	180
	2	3.52	0.80	0.35–2.48	10.47	58.5	252
R–V	1	2.82	0.57	0.15–2.07	7.02	51.8	305
	2	2.17	0.38	0.13–1.97	4.36	47.5	430
S-et-M	1	2.66	0.34	0.09–1.12	10.91	42.0	312
	2	1.62	0.37	0.09–1.22	5.36	44.1	351
Valley (N)	1	1.79	0.41	0.14–1.08	9.45	45.3	268
	2	3.48	0.47	0.14–1.63	11.59	48.3	342
Nantais	1	3.10	0.49	0.14–1.73	10.31	49.7	1,066
	2	2.60	0.47	0.14–1.76	16.66	48.9	1,375
Both regions	1	4.04	0.54	0.15–1.82	22.15	50.5	1,697
	2	3.79	0.51	0.15–1.93	20.44	50.2	2,122

Note: Skewness measures the degree to which cases are clustered to the left (positive skewness) or to the right (negative skewness) of the mean. High positive scores are found in subregions with a large proportion of small properties. Employment of the percentile scores reduces skewness to practically zero.
Source: Matrices cadastrales.

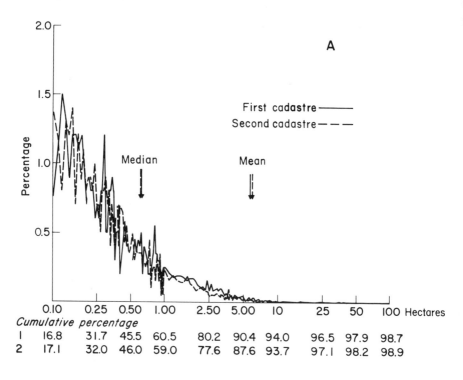

First cadastre ——————
Second cadastre — — —

Median

Mean

2.0

1.5

1.0

0.5

Percentage

0.10   0.25   0.50   1.00   2.50   5.00   10   25   50   100 Hectares

Cumulative percentage

1	16.8	31.7	45.5	60.5	80.2	90.4	94.0	96.5	97.9	98.7
2	17.1	32.0	46.0	59.0	77.6	87.6	93.7	97.1	98.2	98.9

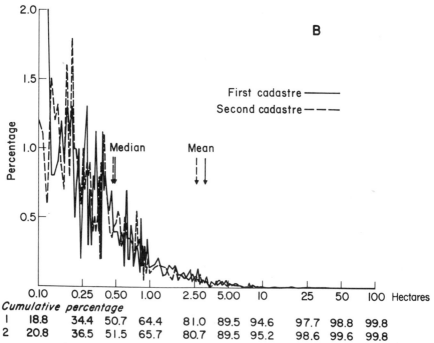

B

First cadastre ——————
Second cadastre — — —

Median

Mean

2.0

1.5

1.0

0.5

Percentage

0.10   0.25   0.50   1.00   2.50   5.00   10   25   50   100 Hectares

Cumulative percentage

1	18.8	34.4	50.7	64.4	81.0	89.5	94.6	97.7	98.8	99.8
2	20.8	36.5	51.5	65.7	80.7	89.5	95.2	98.6	99.6	99.8

Figure 8.2. Area distribution of properties (agricultural land only), first and second cadastres, 1821/44–1913.

prompting one to once more evoke the anthropologist's "basic principles"; one of our tasks must be to explain the essential mechanism that helped maintain the status quo. The stability of size might be seen as the result of a successful effort to preserve the integrity of the patrimony. In this connection, it is interesting to note that in every area where there had been a net increase in the total number of properties there had also been a marked rise in the proportion of the total surface[21] owned by residents of the commune (Figure 8.3), accompanied by a drop in the proportionate surface owned by residents of the towns, particularly the regional capitals (Figure 8.4). It is the very opposite development to the one envisaged by Le Play, where the autodestruction of family properties was to encourage the intervention into the land market of urban interests, forcing the mass of the rural population into wage labor.[22] The amount of land possessed by residents had more than doubled in the Beauce; it was four to five times greater in the Sologne. The same kind of expansion was less marked in the Nantais, partly because the more homogeneous population was already in possession of a large part of the land at the beginning of the century. (The area owned by residents of the communes or of neighboring communes made up almost two-thirds of the total surface sampled from the first cadastre). The expansion nonetheless took place and was especially striking in Sèvre-et-Maine, where the large net increase in the number of properties has already been noted. The only exception was the Nantais Valley. Nantes, concurrently growing industrial city and market town, had extended an arm into the important horticultural districts bordering the Loire.

But the general outcome of property growth, which had been achieved with this extraordinary control of property size, was an extension of the home territory. At the end of our period, a greater part of the hinterlands of Orléans and Nantes could be identified with the people who lived in them. This is where, we shall see, the repressions exercised within the rural home found at least some compensation.

Historical time: annual movements

Measurements of net changes between one date and another, although useful in a preliminary investigation of the cadastre, cannot provide much in the way of understanding how these changes took place. We ought now to turn to the second sample. Because the number of properties analyzed is much more limited than in the last section, the variation due to the luck of the draw is going to be greater. That creates a problem. I shall be concentrating on the annual movements in the number of properties, the percentile score means,[23] and the number of transactions along with some data on the relationship of the transactors. Attempt to arrange these statistics into anything smaller than the subregions and the tireless computer will mete out tables that look like two spilled pots of alphabet

Table 8.2. *Area distribution of properties by subregion*

Subregion	Cadastre	Property area (hectares)					
		0.01–0.10	0.11–0.25	0.26–0.50	0.51–1.00	1.01–2.50	2.51–5.00
Beauce	1	108	114	136	144	166	134
	2	66	152	176	146	172	133
Sologne	1	125	54	70	179	143	89
	2	113	113	113	70	130	104
Forêt	1	78	110	142	115	206	138
	2	95	66	129	110	224	123
Valley (O)	1	206	171	142	157	208	85
	2	234	170	133	134	187	81
Orléanais	1	168	149	139	150	197	101
	2	171	149	140	131	186	100
Plateau	1	59	89	115	145	217	162
	2	89	119	128	218	203	100
R–V	1	178	154	145	130	183	96
	2	223	173	163	114	113	84
S-et-M	1	285	133	196	122	136	75
	2	279	148	145	139	151	83
Valley (N)	1	176	231	175	159	145	34
	2	203	176	155	127	155	89
Nantais	1	188	156	163	137	165	85
	2	207	158	150	142	150	88

Source: Matrices cadastrales.

soup. But we are interested in trends. In fact, one rarely has any reason to want to break down the analysis into units smaller than the subregions and the sample is, in most instances, large enough to be workable at this level. Where it is not, we have had either to group the data by decade or to compute running means.

One ought to note the points of contrast and similarity between these property movements (Figures 8.5–8.7) and the population movements discussed in the last chapter. Of the first period (the first half of the century), we can only observe the last 10 years. But a complete series exists for the second and third periods (third and fourth quarters of the century).

A first glimpse reveals that property movements were less erratic than population movements: nowhere do we see a full reversal of patterns in the style of the Orléanais' mortality between the first and second periods. In general, the profile is simpler: a flux and reflux in the number of properties accompanied by a less-marked inverse trend in the percentile score means, the intensity and timing of both depending on the subregion. The maximum point reached in the number of properties roughly corresponds to the transition between the second and third periods, that is, the time at which rural emigration began to pick up and the high death rates of the second period began to slacken. Furthermore, the stricter

5.01–10.00	10.01–25.00	25.01–50.00	50.01–100.00	Over 100.00	Total	N_w
78	55	30	20	15	1,000	132
72	55	6	12	10	1,000	162
71	18	36	54	161	1,000	19
96	122	26	17	96	1,000	38
69	73	32	14	23	1,000	73
117	66	44	13	13	1,000	106
15	7	4	1	4	1,000	408
41	11	2	3	4	1,000	442
36	25	14	8	13	1,000	632
61	34	10	7	11	1,000	748
92	46	45	26	4	1,000	180
65	57	13	4	4	1,000	252
62	34	9	9	0	1,000	305
84	39	7	0	0	1,000	430
22	20	0	5	6	1,000	312
20	22	13	0	0	1,000	351
47	28	2	3	0	1,000	268
53	23	9	4	6	1,000	342
52	31	11	10	2	1,000	1,066
57	34	10	2	2	1,000	1,375

demographic controls exercised in the Orléanais seems to have born fruit: the overall rate of increase in the number of properties during the Second Empire was slightly less than in the Nantais and there was no major subsequent decline, whereas the number of properties in the Nantais continued to grow until about 1880 and then, after a decade of stability, began to drop. The fall in the percentile score mean was also less significant in the Orléanais – it actually rose during the 1850s.

This was not necessarily a healthy development. Quite plausibly, the Orléanais' unyielding grip on property was the result of its weak economic situation and reflected the stubborn face put on by a population dominated by fear and insecurity. The peasant family could still identify with *le foyer* evoking its "use rights"[24] of the surrounding territory, but far from encouraging a network of exchange with others, this only strengthened each household's devotion to its own interests and thus exacerbated an already oppressive spirit of isolation. It is, after all, perfectly logical that a population, faced with the prospect of rising mortality and/or emigration, should increase its effort to maintain property size.

Ardouin-Dumazet remarked in the early 1890s that the Beauce, traditionally considered a rich and prosperous land, "is the most stricken of all our agricultural regions. . . . The agriculture is still primitive . . . 'Aren't we the granary of France!' reply the cultivators. With impossible

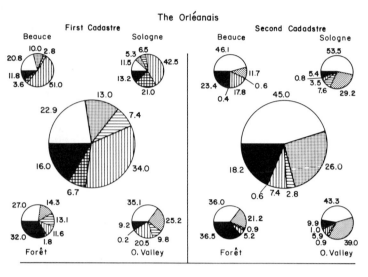

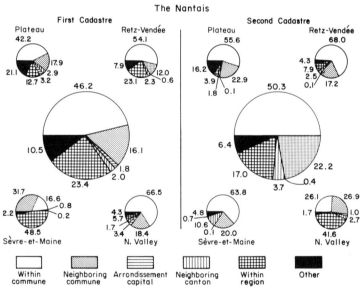

Figure 8.3. Proximities of propertyholders' residence, first and second cadastres, 1821/44–1913.

obstinacy the old methods are kept and ridiculous yields are obtained; the country suffers and loses its population."[25] The Beauce stagnated. That at least is the picture left by the property movements of the two communes selected from the subregion. A dramatic fall in the number of transactions, concomitant with the midcentury surge in mortality, had

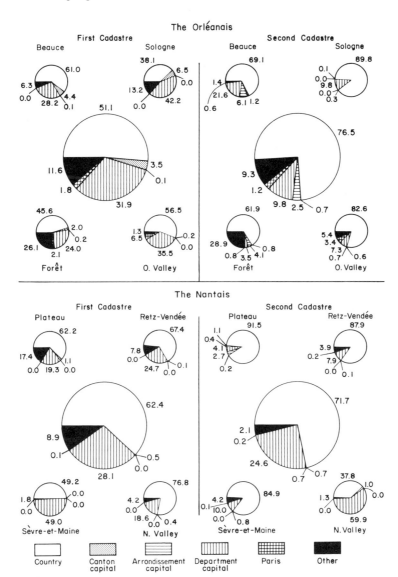

Figure 8.4. Urban residences of propertyholders, first and second cadastres, 1821/44–1913.

probably been the main reason why there was so little growth in the total number of properties. Land was not being exchanged; the inhabitants fastened on to it in the hope of conserving a semblance of their former high standard of living. Likewise, there was barely any growth in the number of properties in the four communes selected from the Orléanais

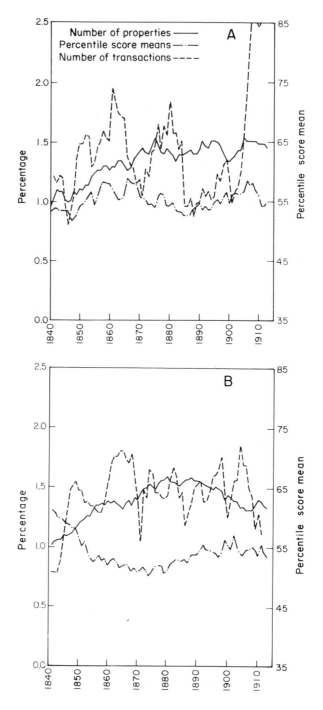

Figure 8.5. Annual distributions of number of properties, property transactions, in 5-year running means, and movement of percentile score means in (A) the Orléanais and (B) the Nantais in 1840–1913.

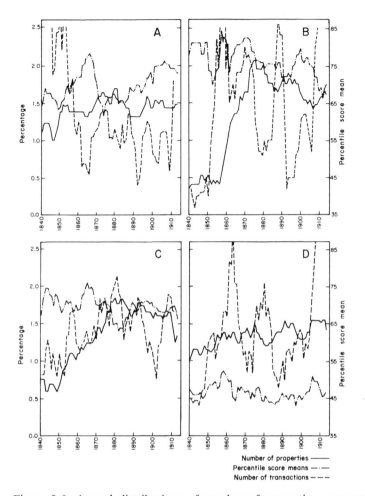

Figure 8.6. Annual distributions of number of properties, property transactions, in 5-year running means, and movement of percentile score mean in (A) the Beauce, (B) the Sologne, (C) the Forêt d'Orléans, and (D) the Orléanais Valley, 1840–1913.

Valley: the only notable movement was in the transactions that quickly multiplied between the late 1840s and early 1860s, then declined to a low point at the time of the Franco–Prussian war, picked up again for a brief spell in the late 1870s and early 1880s, subsequently declined, only to make a snappy upward turn again at the end of the period. But most of these transactions involved the tiniest fragments of land;[26] the essential structure of property, as indicated by the percentile score mean, remained unchanged.

The graphs add further weight to the evidence that the major property movements in the Orléanais were confined to its poorest subregions,

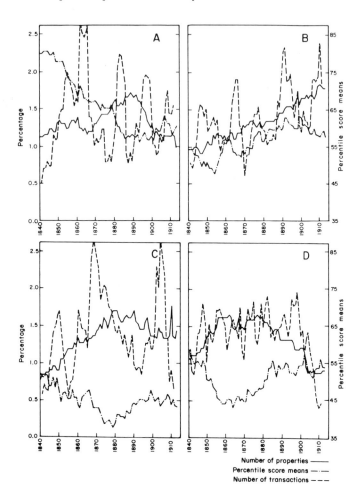

Figure 8.7. Annual distributions of number of properties, property transactions, in 5-year running means, and movement of percentile score mean in (A) the Nantais Plateau, (B) Retz–Vendée, (C) Sèvre-et-Maine, and (D) the Nantais Valley, 1840–1913.

the Forêt and the Sologne. It must be remembered that these were also the only parts, bar Orléans, Beaugency, and some of the smaller towns, that had registered net rates of in-migration at any time since 1830. I have already remarked that the Forêt and, even more, the Sologne afforded the inhabitants of the intensively cultivated districts the option of rural migration, at least in the first half of the century. One can get a good idea, by studying the graphs, of the extent to which either sub-region was able to accommodate the new settlers. The meteoric rise in the number of transactions followed, after a few hiccups, by a similarly impressive growth in the number of properties came abruptly to a halt in the Sologne in the early 1870s. Thereafter their number seems to have actually declined. I shall shortly show that even the massive increases of the Second Empire were only possible because of land improvements that opened up these marginal lands to cultivation. The lack of similar improvements in the Forêt was one of the main reasons why the rate of property growth was slower there and also why it took so much longer to find a new level of stability (i.e., not until the mid-1880s).

The Nantais exhibits once again a greater flexibility. Thus the curve of the percentile score means conveys much more the mirror image of the properties' curve that one would logically expect; a particularly sharp drop in the percentile score mean is to be noted in the Plateau. Growth in the pasture-type subregions generated by land improvements was again important and was, as the comparison of the recapitulative totals already indicated, especially marked in the southern *bocages* of Retz–Vendèe.[27]

Retz–Vendée is the only subregion in the Nantais where the percentile score mean does not form a mirror image of the number of properties, which would suggest that there were, in fact, two kinds of property growth. The first, which, in addition to this particular area of the Nantais, accounted for almost all advances made in the Orléanais, consisted of the clearing and putting into cultivation of new lands, thus making an increase in the number of properties possible without forcing the division of existing properties. Obviously this was the only option open for a peasant economy that had reached an optimum level of intensity in the territory already occupied. The second kind involves fragmentation properly speaking – it is the classic form of *morcellement* that had become the subject of so much debate in the nineteenth century. (In those days, one almost automatically assumed that a multiplication in the number of properties meant fragmentation. This was so widely accepted that one of the major authorities on property developments, Alfred de Foville, failed to note the possibility of these two forms of growth even though he differentiated three realizable types of fragmentation.[28] No doubt the lack of sufficient data on area distributions was the principal cause – the breakdown of properties by area was usually very crude. But, if one is to use property movements to gauge the level of agricultural intensity achieved within a given society, a distinction in the forms of growth is imperative.)

The two communes selected from Sèvre-et-Maine indicate how predisposed the inhabitants were to fragmentation, the second form of growth. It was only in the 1880s, lean years for even the most prosperous, that a spirit of retrenchment set in: the number of properties declined and the percentile score mean rose. The Plateau followed a similar

Table 8.3. *Area distribution of properties by decade in property-years, 1840–1913*

| Decade | Property area (hectares) | | | | | | |
	0.01–0.10	0.11–0.25	0.26–0.50	0.51–1.00	1.01–2.50	2.51–5.00	5.01–10.00
Orléanais							
1840–49	197	137	142	128	226	106	19
1850–59	173	82	158	142	248	126	19
1860–69	176	117	96	137	228	131	33
1870–79	191	126	129	140	172	113	37
1880–89	192	163	130	121	167	122	17
1890–99	199	158	100	104	193	134	38
1900–09	183	159	106	105	166	135	64
1910–13	200	133	164	117	121	130	44
1840–1913	188	136	124	124	193	125	34
Nantais							
1840–49	140	135	108	117	200	110	95
1850–59	211	145	96	135	190	82	63
1860–69	227	161	96	142	158	94	58
1870–79	209	180	111	156	148	91	60
1880–89	157	189	152	151	170	75	65
1890–99	145	168	155	147	177	91	70
1900–09	157	145	157	121	206	114	66
1910–13	178	129	157	138	202	104	69
1840–1913	179	162	128	139	178	94	67

Note: N_t is the true N (unweighted).
Source: Matrices cadastrales.

course (though the absolute size of the properties was clearly somewhat larger). In contrast, the Valley's countrymen were signally inhibited; they had arrested the growth of properties by the late 1850s and by the 1860s were already bringing about the redintegration of property size; this, remember, was the only area where urban interests made a successful bid for the land, not perhaps with some reason. "Notably, for about ten years," wrote a rural sociologist in 1885, "more small propertyholders [in Upper Brittany] may be selling than one sees people buying small grounds."[29] The Nantais had clearly come up against a frontier to growth but this had not happened without, first, an upsurge in fragmentation, something that seems not to have occurred in the Orléanais.

There are undoubtedly a few readers who will take exception to my use of the "percentile score mean" to portray developments in property size. Actually, if these developments are to be demonstrated graphically, one doesn't have much of an alternative. However, I have attempted to assemble, by decade, a more traditional kind of frequency distribution (Table 8.3). By analogy to the "woman-years" used in the last chapter,

10.01–25.00	25.01–50.00	50.01–100.00	Over 100.00	Total	N_w	$N_t{}^a$
32	9	0	4	1,000	646	741
31	11	0	10	1,000	749	896
56	17	1	8	1,000	813	1,104
65	15	3	9	1,000	895	1,327
54	15	11	8	1,000	867	1,296
47	14	11	2	1,000	907	1,317
54	5	11	12	1,000	903	1,267
57	10	11	13	1,000	366	503
50	12	6	8	1,000	6,145	8,451
48	21	18	8	1,000	1,337	1,054
46	17	9	6	1,000	1,608	1,258
35	15	8	6	1,000	1,697	1,318
32	8	0	5	1,000	1,867	1,448
33	8	0	0	1,000	1,930	1,456
40	7	0	0	1,000	1,867	1,445
32	2	0	0	1,000	1,694	1,293
23	0	0	0	1,000	680	516
36	10	4	3	1,000	12,678	9,788

the basic units here are "property-years," or the number of years each sampled property remained within the given size range. (The figures in the last column are the unweighted number of property-years upon which the estimates are based). Lists of numbers quickly become labyrinthine. But careful comparison of each area category will reveal a less haphazard distribution by decade in the Nantais than in the Orléanais. For example, with the exception of properties between 26 and 50 ares, all categories in the Nantais of 1 hectare and under progressively increase in proportion until 1869; thereafter they mostly decline. The opposite trend is noted in the middle range of properties, whereas there is clear evidence of a drop in the proportion of large properties. Barely any trends are detectable in the Orléanais. Thus: flux and reflux in the Nantais' property structure, stability in the Orléanais'. Tables less easy to read than the changes in the percentile score mean bring us to an identical conclusion.

When I say "stability of property structure" I am, of course, referring only to the proportionate distribution of properties by area. It turns out that this kind of stability is associated with agriculture at a maximum level of intensity along with a particular form of property growth. The richest land had already passed into the hands of the small property-holders by the beginning of the century. But, even in the Orléanais, the indomitable urge to possess forced an increase in their number. This had caused the large landowners to stop fretting in public, as they had in the 1840s, about "the lack of beasts and dung" and turn their attention, as they did in the 1860s, to "the lack of hands." "The scarcity of agricultural workers," grumbled one influential gentleman of the Valley, "is as much the result of good workers, on account of the fragmentation of land, buying lots that they cultivate themselves."[30] The increasing severity of agricultural intensity had the direct result of driving small property-holders onto the poorer soils of the Sologne, the Forêt, and Retz–Vendée, at one time almost the exclusive domains of the large. If the traditional areas of intensity could not support further growth, some small propertyholders were going to have to move to untrodden ground.

The Sologne: an agricultural revolution

The unprecedented advances in cultivation that opened the Sologne up to the small propertyholder created one of the most spectacular developments in the Loire Country during the nineteenth century. "Revolution" is a word the rural historian has learned to treat with caution: haven't we seen the fabled agricultural explosion of eighteenth-century Europe turned into a sedate and entirely accountable recovery from a former depression?[31] But the surge in population, properties, and productivity experienced by every commune in the Orléanais south of the Valley is worthy of the title. This was, moreover, a people's revolution. Historians and sociologists, content with limiting the role of initiative in rural society to a class of "mediators," should pay full attention to the facts in the Sologne. The large landowners and the urban capitalists who contributed to the massive improvements of the subregion were bound in their success and timing to the ambitions of the rural mass. If one needs further demonstration of the interdependent character of the "connectors" as defined in Part II, it is to be found in the history of the agricultural revolution of the Sologne.

There is, first, the long delay that elapsed between the drawing up of the initial schemes of improvement and their realization. Various projects had been suggested in the eighteenth century; in 1786, the Royal Society of Physics at Orléans even proposed as the subject of an essay competition ". . . indicate the means of invigorating this sad and languid country."[32] A year later, Lavoisier – better known to us for his chemistry – proposed the construction of an agricultural canal to the provincial assembly at Orléans.[33] The Baron de Morogues (whose estate, managed from his château at La Source, covered over 1,000 hectares of the Sologne) led, in the first two decades of the nineteenth century, a campaign from the offices of the Société d'Agriculture d'Orléans to persuade government and large landowners that the subregion's agriculture could be immensely improved by the use of lime and fertilizers. But these early schemes were largely talk. The only important development before 1848 was the influx of rural immigrants. Our own figures indicate net annual rates of $+11$, $+12$, and $+13$ per 1,000 during the 1830s; no other subregion ever came near that mark (with the dubious exception of Retz–Vendée in the 1820s) (See Figures 7.10 and 7.11). I have suggested earlier that the fall in the rates of immigration apparent in the 1840s was because, without land improvements, population densities had already reached their limits.

It was at precisely this point that government and the large landowners began to take direct interest in the Sologne's agricultural development. On 10 June 1848, the national assembly allocated a million francs for the construction of "a canal intended for the improvement of the Sologne . . . [to be dug] between Blancafort and La Motte-Beuvron, drawing its waters from the Sauldre."[34] The general idea was to provide a cheap means of transporting marl (gold dust for the Solognot) from the neighboring regions. Work was underway within two months. We read that on 12 August "numerous workshops of unemployed laborers from different occupations have been digging for several weeks at a piece-rate, south of La Motte-Beuvron, at the cost of the State."[35] We are not told who these workers were or from where they came. Some were probably from the troubled districts of Paris. But it is fairly certain that others were from the overpopulated and, for the time being, economically depressed Sologne. Thus, the government was responding, consciously or not, to the demographic initiatives of the countryside. But, even then, its efforts in the long run proved to be rather half-hearted. Only one section of the canal had been dug by 1859 when it was abandoned for a whole decade. The entire project was completed only in 1873. Long before then, the inhabitants of Orléanais' part of the Sologne were wondering what possible benefits could be gained from a canal that, without some tributaries being added, was almost as far as (or for some communes actually farther than) the river Loire.[36] As far as I can gather, no such tributaries were ever built.

There were, of course, other means of transport. The railway was important for those lucky enough to be near it. "It is not rare today," ran a report in 1858,

to see, principally in the areas neighboring the rail, properties in which the harvests compete with the best harvests of the Beauce. The Canton of La Ferté-Saint-Aubin supplies magnificent examples of this.[37]

The Orléans–Vierzon line gave one restricted part of the Sologne a marked advantage over the rest: in Figure 7.12, a narrow white strip indicates this to have been a zone of net immigration during the years of agricultural crisis, 1881–1911. But Orléans, jealous guardian of its own commercial interests, was loathe to establish a railway network south of the Loire. Until late in the century, the Orléans–Vierzon line was the only main line to cross the Sologne from north to south. For a long time, the Compagnie d'Orléans refused to reduce its rates for the transportation of marl, rendering it economically unfeasible for anybody but those next to the rail. Local lines, recommended in 1862, were only accorded funds by the general council in 1900; they were opened just a few years before the outbreak of the First World War.

In fact, the most impressive improvement as far as transportation was concerned was neither the canal nor the rail, but the road. The *route agricole* was intrinsically of more value to a small propertyholder than the canal or rail because it gave him the freedom to choose how to transport his small volume of goods (by wagon, by horseback, etc.) and exactly where to take them. Roads corresponded best to the subjective logic of the peasant economy: the cost of transport was not determined by company rates but by the propertyholder's own effort. It is thus highly significant that when the government temporarily abandoned canal construction it directed its attention to the building of roads. Between 1860 and 1869, nearly 600 kilometers of road were laid at a cost of 3.3 million francs, or between a quarter and a third of the total government expenditure in the improvement of the Sologne during the Second Empire.[38]

Transportation was the charge of government but the actual improvement of the land fell to private hands. A comparison of the two cadastres for this subregion shows that, along with a decline of 70 percent in the area occupied by marsh and heath, there had been a 40 percent increase in the area of woodland and 30 percent increase in arable land (*terres labourables*).[39] Two distinct kinds of improvement are thereby revealed. What is more, one will find that it was the large landowners who directed their efforts to the development of woodlands and grasslands, leaving almost all the work in extending the cultivated lands to the small propertyholders. Put another way, two types of property had been operated at two separate levels of intensity.

Obviously, small propertyholders weren't going to be interested in growing trees. Reforestation was nonetheless an important part of the general process of land improvement because trees, in addition to contributing valuable humus to the topsoil, helped mitigate the extremes between summer soil aridity and the winter's humidity. The planting of the great pine tracts that are today the most distinctive feature of the Sologne required heavy capital investments, which could be redeemed only after a long delay. Not even the largest landowners could afford this kind of risk without in some way limiting their liability. This was then the origin of the associations founded in the Sologne during the Second Empire; though the money spent on reforestation came from private funds (estimated at a total expenditure of 4 million francs between 1850 and 1910), the commission of delegates from the *comices agricoles* of the Sologne (founded in 1853) and the more important central committee (founded in 1859) brought the landowners financial guarantees from the government.[40]

Big investments had another effect, not remarked on at the time: they pulled the landowners out of their town houses and into the country. We have noticed this as a phenomenon general to the whole Orléanais and have ascribed it to the decline in Orléans' commerce, leaving land the only profitable sector open to the investor (Chapter 5). But what made land suddenly so profitable? The commercial depression at Orléans had also narrowed the range of economic choice for its rural neighbors (Chapter 6) who, thereupon, initiated the pattern of demographic restraint, part of which consisted of rural migration (Chapter 7). The main surge in the Sologne's population occurred in the early years of the July Monarchy, or 20 years before the founding of the first associations, 30 years before the building of the *routes agricoles,* 40 years before the completion of the Canal de Sauldre. Almost a generation had passed before these little pioneers began to stake their claims to the soil (Figure 8.6). After 1850, the number of land transactions proliferated, engendering the massive growth in the number of properties after 1855. Thus the advent of small property in the Sologne coincided with, if not slightly preceded, the first initiatives of the large landowners to improve the land. It anticipated the major government programs by about a decade. One cannot help but think of Ester Boserup's rural world where population pressure forces the adoption of a new economic order. Immigration and the resultant demographic optimum had created demand for land that had never before existed. The situation snowballed.[41]

The extent to which the large landowners' position was modified is illustrated by a few simple statistics taken from the cadastre. In the first cadastre, one counts a total of 44 families in possession of over 500 hectares. Only 11 of these are recorded as being resident landowners, whereas 29 are recorded as living in Orléans, 1 in Paris. There were 21 properties of over 1,000 hectares, the largest of them all being the estate of Massena, the Prince d'Esling, veteran general of the Empire, whose 4,900 hectares sprawled over three communes. The second cadastre gives a total of 37 names with over 500 hectares; 27 resided on their properties and only 7 lived in Orléans, 1 in Paris. This time there were only 9 properties with over 1,000 hectares and the largest was under 3,000. Hence, in addition to the dramatic fall in absentee landownership, there had been a drop in the absolute number of large landowners as well as a general reduction in the size of estate.

One could, with some reason, consider the encroachment of the small properties onto the large as "fragmentation." But this, I think, would be counter to the essential meaning of the term because the land that the small propertyholders moved onto had previously been barely exploited. These old estates were deserts: they were not cultivated and were grazed only in the most ineffective fashion by the small number of inhabitants that existed at the time; they consisted largely of great stretches of pond, marsh, and scrub.[42] Here, in the northern half of France, was where the medieval jurist had applied his formula, *nulle terre sans seigneur* – all land, even if useless, had to fall under somebody's jurisdiction.[43] And thus it remained, in the Sologne, until the mid-nineteenth century.

Comparison of the two cadastres indicates that some important transfers of ownership had taken place. Only six of the families with over 500 hectares at the time of the first cadastre had retained as much land at the second: Baguenault, Bigot, de Laage, d'Orsanne, Robert, de Tristan. All, save d'Orsanne, had been part of that minority of resident landowners that we found in the first cadastre; it was a minority that had shown an interest for the subregion from an early date. But anyone tempted to believe that the transfer of large properties marked one further step ahead for the rising bourgeoisie should consider a few names of the Sologne's new landlords: de Bellet, Burot de l'Isle, de Durfort-Civrac, de Labeau, Murat de l'Estang. . . . We do find a Goldschmidt, *industriel,* who had bought 519 hectares in Vannes and Tigy, but his voice is without quorum. More typical are families such as the Colas des Francs or the Raguenets, former landowners in the Beauce, who began buying up land in the Sologne during the Second Empire and the early years of the Third Republic.

Land improvement in the Sologne was a response to population pressure. Small propertyholders, although they most certainly had the will, could never have had the kind of capital required to clear the scrub and drain the ponds – the delay of almost a generation between the surge in immigration and the buying up of the land illustrates that. The intervention of the large landowners was therefore a necessity. But did it, at the same time, create a conflict of interests? I shall be discussing the more general question of social tension in the next chapter. Suffice it to say that there is very little evidence of such conflict in the Sologne. Landowners stayed in the areas where the comparative economic advantage of extensive farming was greatest, the poorest lands; the richest lands were bought up, as they were developed, by the small propertyholders. In fact, the only evidence of conflict I have found is not between large landowner and small propertyholder but between small propertyholders and the government. In 1855, engineers, employees of the ministre des ponts et chaussées, started work on a project that was to clear the flow of the river Cosson. Within a year, a lengthy petition was sent to the minister, signed by 16 propertyholders whose taxes represented, according to the engineers' reply, less than 1 percent of the whole valley. The property-holders complained that state funds should be spent on land clearance rather than clearing out small streams. They claimed that the engineers had destroyed the river banks without any reason and that now, 48 hours after any heavy rain, the valley was flooded. Although there is, then, the sign of a conflict between the government's desire to improve the water-ways and the propertyholders' desire to clear the land, the tone of the petition would indicate that the main problem arose from ham-handed planning rather than any intended evil. The fact is that during these early efforts at land improvement the engineers didn't know what they were up to.[44]

The history of the Sologne teaches an important lesson. These lands were not developed by well-meaning investors out of pure love for agricultural improvement; if the population hadn't grown first, it is unlikely that the improvements would have taken place. Of course, there is that possibili-ty. But, given the history of the whole region – the restricted economic opportunities, the growth in mortality rates at midcentury, the rigorous demographic controls adopted – the likelihood of these improvements being due to *independent* entrepreneurial initiative seems slight. One is even tempted to consider the small propertyholders as the real "medi-ators" in this society; after all, if there were any single group that first at-tracted national capital into the Sologne, it was they. But it really would be more accurate to attribute the improvements to a whole series of cir-cumstances that had drawn the Sologne into the clublands of peasant economy.[45]

In the Sologne, we find one particularly extreme aspect of a general consolidating trend induced by population pressure that had developed to one degree or another in both the Nantais and the Orléanais: the cultivation of marginal lands and the acquisition of a growing propor-tion of the regions' territories by the local inhabitants. Can all this be im-agined without the family playing some role?

3. The property cycle

When land is scarce and property (or the usage right) is vested in in-dividuals, the family is confronted with the problem of its continuity. At some point the property must be passed into the hands of the next generation. There are logically only two major types of solution: either one recognizes the equality of siblings and the property is divided up into equal portions (equity) or one advantages a single child, thus maintaining the original dimensions of the property (unity). In actual fact, the parents are presented with an almost infinite number of choices, but they will always fall within the range of these two extremes. Our concern here is with the nature of that choice and the effect it had on the individual's identity with the land.

Under Napoleonic law, parents cannot disinherit their children. The law even lays down the minimum portion of the estate, a "reserve," that must be equally divided among the direct descendants: one-half if there is only one surviving legitimate child, two-thirds if there are two, three-quarters if there are three or more. The parent is free to dispose of the remaining portion in any way he sees fit. Of course the estate involves more than just land, and the various possibilities opened by consideration of both chattels and the disposable portion has given the system enormous flexibility. "By the civil code, beyond the civil code" was the cry of jurists toward the end of the nineteenth century. Indeed, a principal factor in the code's success has been the great liberties taken in its interpretation. Though decreed by government, the code never represented the strict dictate of statutory law the English common lawyer is obliged to observe. Here, in full Cartesian regalia, was written reason, *ratio scripta*, which would have to take into account any given particular situation. And reason founded on tradition. The code's authors (whose average age at the time was, significantly, 60 years) borrowed, left and right, from the customary laws of the country.[46]

It would therefore be wrong to view the civil code as a legal innovation that came into open conflict with time-tested rural practices. By and large, it was sufficiently flexible to allow local populations to follow patterns best suited to their own needs and traditions.[47]

In the area of successions, the Orléanais and the Nantais belonged to separate legal traditions, one found in a central zone of France dominated by the customary laws of Paris, the other situated in a north-western zone that included Normandy, Brittany, and, with some qualification, Anjou and the Touraine. I am not going to enter into any details because the distinctions between the two zones have been well described elsewhere.[48] It is enough to note that their differences were based on the relative weight either zone accorded to two principles, namely, the prohibition of parental preferences and the exclusion from the inheritance of previously advantaged children. This was in turn bound to the degree to which the stability of the marriage contract was favored above the continuity of the lineage, or vice versa. In central France, the emphasis lay on the stability of property settlements agreed upon at the time of marriage and, as a natural corollary, the subsequent exclusion of children thus established. Since the late fifteenth century (in the Orléanais), this rule had been mitigated by an option that gave such children the chance of either restoring their previous allotments to the parental community in order to receive an equal portion of the inheritance or keeping the allotments and thus abandoning all rights to the inheritance. However, the option hardly lessened the opportunity of advantaging the married child. By contrast, the West adhered much more strictly to the principle of equality, even to the extent of ignoring whether children had been previously established or not. On the day of reckoning, all donations that had been made *inter vivos* were compulsorily restored and the family "pool" then divided into equal portions.

These legal distinctions remained in effect until 1794. What is of particular interest for this study is the contrasting notions of the family the distinctions apparently represented. The laws of succession in central France portrayed the family as a household community dominated by the married couple, whereas the laws of the West regarded the family merely as an instrument in the transmission of property from one generation to the next. Jean Yver:

It is because there exists a community of people living within the same "cell," eating from the same loaf and the same pot . . . that the physical break with this group creates for the established child a unit in some way detached, isolated, and henceforth deprived of all rights to the group's patrimony. One imagines that it must have been otherwise in an environment where the rights of each member would be more individualized and likely, as a result, to live just as well outside the group as within its heart.[49]

Now, the isolation and detachment of the domestic community in the Orléanais were one of the main themes to emerge from my last chapter. It is certainly a fascinating thought that a whole legal tradition could have helped exaggerate the differences in the local reactions to population pressure. Laws take their color from culture. The customary laws of central France point to a culture more sensitive to the physical space occupied by the community; the laws of the West suggest a culture more concerned with time, lived time, the time it took to pass the family holding from one generation to the next.[50] Thus the domestic community of the Nantais would not be so much between husband and wife as between parent and child – an interesting complement to the extended transitional periods the individual of this region is observed to have lived through. In the Orléanais, it was the marital bond, the bond of governance, of control, that received greatest attention in the law . . . But just how much in reality?

First, a fact so obvious that one is wary even to mention it: it is frequently overlooked that when we speak of "propertyholders" we are speaking largely of men. Roughly 15 percent of all the propertyholders sampled were women, of whom slightly under half were widows. By law (customary and Napoleonic), women had as much right to a portion of the inheritance as men, but on their marriage, their property was taken over by the husband; the old French legal rule of *puissance maritale* was barely modified before the twentieth century.[51] Thus marriage would seem to be the most likely moment when a man would come into some, if not most, of his property, especially if one takes into account the small number of both bachelor households and households with more than one married couple.

If men held on to their properties until their deaths, then the average length of a "property-life" (i.e., the duration that a property remained in the hands of one owner) should be roughly the same as the life expectancy of a male in his late 20s. We have no accurate life tables for our two regions, but it is unlikely that they differed much from available model life tables with equivalent overall levels of mortality.[52] On this basis, we estimate that a 25-year-old man from the Orléanais could have expected, in 1831–5, using the current mortality rates, 34 more years of life. At the same epoch, a man of 30 could have expected 30 years. Seventy years later, the situation would have been appreciably different. The mortality levels of 1901–5 would give a 25-year-old man 40 more years, a 30-year-old man 36 more years. In the Nantais, the figures would have been something on the order of 31 years for the 25-year-old and 28 years for the 30-year-old in 1831–5, 39 and 35 years, respectively, in 1901–5. Because men do not live acording to current rates of mortality but rather to the rates established over their generation, the average life expectancy for the whole 70-year period would be closer to the 1901–5 figures than those of 1831–5. The age of marriage, I have already indicated, hardly changed during this time – on average, men married at 26 or 27 in the Orléanais, at 29 or 30 n the Nantais. Therefore, if the assumption were correct, the average length of a property life in the Orléanais should have been somewhere between 35 and 40 years; in the Nantais, 30 to 35 years.

In point of fact, the averages were a good bit lower (Table 8.4). Twenty-five years was a fairly standard average throughout the two regions; there is no statistically significant difference between the grand averages of the Orléanais and the Nantais. The direct effect of the variations in age of marriage on the length of property life is proven, as in the case of demographic structure, to have been negligible. One might note the larger number of properties on the lower side of the average in the Orléanais (as indicated by the medians and the interquartile ranges). Part of this could have been due to the high rates of mortality we know to have existed in some of the subregions there. But neither mortality nor marriage could explain the disparity between these averages and the life expectancies previously estimated. The figures suggest, particularly for the Orléanais, that men spent 10 or more years after marriage landless. Immediately after marriage? It's difficult to tell. Again, the nominal lists seem to say that, at marriage, a man took charge of his own house and

Table 8.4. *Length of property lives (in years)*

Subregion	Mean and 95% confidence interval	Median	Interquartile range	N_t	N_w
Beauce	20.7 ± 5.1	11.5	5–36	50	
Sologne	18.7 ± 3.9	17.1	8–21	43	
Forêt	26.4 ± 3.9	28.5	13–35	48	
Valley (O)	25.1 ± 4.5	24.5	9–36	52	
Orléanais	24.2 ± 2.7	22.0	8–35	193	135
Plateau	28.2 ± 5.1	25.5	19–39	28	
R–V	20.4 ± 4.5	18.3	7–31	33	
S-et-M	28.3 ± 5.1	29.8	18–37	34	
Valley (N)	25.5 ± 3.9	23.0	13–36	73	
Nantais	25.4 ± 2.0	24.3	14–36	168	222

Note: All properties with first acquisition occurring before enumeration of first cadastre or after 1884 are excluded.
Source: Matrices cadastrales.

one would assume that, along with the house, came land. Also, we noticed a slight upward trend in the distribution of related outside household members over the age of 60 (Figure 7.2). So it probably wouldn't be too much off the mark to suggest that this landless period was more likely to be spent at the end of one's life rather than the beginning (Zola's old Fouan should be kept in mind). But whether at the beginning or the end, there was fairly certainly some phase in the life of the average peasant spent as a married, or widowed, landless laborer. Unlike adolescence, this would not have been a time of domestic labor because there was, as far as can be judged, no period after marriage, apart from old age, when a man lived under the roof of another household. Old age was an important exception. Could it be viewed as a retirement into labor when father came to live on the son's farm? It is not farfetched to imagine that this marginally run household expected a contribution from the landless old man.

The transitional periods discussed in Chapter 7 were shown to have been significantly more extended in the Nantais than the Orléanais. On the other hand, the population pressure that had shortened property lives in several parts of the Orléanais would have made this the region of more extended landless periods. That was clearly the case of the Beauce and the newly reclaimed marginal lands of the Sologne. Such restrictions on the duration of ownership should be compared with some evidence of growth in the proportion of land transactions between kinsmen. Over historical time, the proportion of transactions between people of the same surname increased (Table 8.5). Most of this increase occurred in the Orléanais prior to 1870, which would conform to a periodization already

Table 8.5. *Relationship of property transactors per 1,000 transactions by decade and by subregion, 1840–1913*

| | Transactions with | | | | | | |
	Coparceners	Propertyholders with same name	Propertyholders without same name	The commune	Others	Total	N_w
Orléanais							
1840–49	0	243	740	3	14	1,000	195
1850–59	0	283	716	1	0	1,000	288
1860–69	0	327	655	18	0	1,000	292
1870–79	5	329	660	0	6	1,000	250
1880–89	0	248	752	0	0	1,000	243
1890–99	0	378	620	0	2	1,000	210
1900–09	0	199	800	1	0	1,000	320
1910–13	0	239	761	0	0	1,000	150
1840–1913	1	280	713	3	3	1,000	1,947
Nantais							
1840–49	0	136	838	23	3	1,000	362
1850–59	10	207	745	23	15	1,000	426
1860–69	5	167	819	2	7	1,000	558
1870–79	3	242	752	3	0	1,000	472
1880–89	0	202	783	8	7	1,000	474
1890–99	3	273	724	2	0	1,000	490
1900–09	2	301	697	0	0	1,000	491
1910–13	10	410	573	0	7	1,000	139
1840–1913	4	228	756	7	5	1,000	3,411
Subregion							
Beauce	2	181	812	2	3	1,000	396
Sologne	0	194	806	0	0	1,000	40

Subregion							
Beauce	2	181	812	2	3	1,000	396
Sologne	0	194	806	0	0	1,000	40
Forêt	3	261	719	15	2	1,000	200
Valley (O)	0	316	680	2	2	1,000	1,311
Orléanais	1	280	713	3	3	1,000	1,947
Plateau	6	208	765	13	8	1,000	670
R–V	8	334	649	6	3	1,000	869
S-et-M	1	172	819	4	4	1,000	1,093
Valley (N)	0	207	783	7	3	1,000	778
Nantais	4	228	756	7	5	1,000	3,411

Source: Matrices cadastrales.

demonstrated in population and property growths. By 1870, the Orléanais had reached its peak. The Nantais, starting with a significantly lower proportion than the Orléanais in the 1840s, shows a continuing advance in transactions between people carrying the same name through the last quarter of the century and beyond. As in property, as in population, the Nantais could afford to be less demure, more gallant. But the breakdown by subregion is confusing. If there were a simple relationship between these proportions and agricultural intensity, why does the Forêt d'Orléans get such a high score? And even more startling, why the very low score for Sèvre-et-Maine?

Part of the problem could be due to the way we are counting. Table 8.5 takes into account neither the quantity of land involved in each transaction nor the timing with regard to property life. This is not at all an easy thing to do. Nevertheless, Figures 8.8–8.10 do represent an attempt. One of the first difficulties is that the length of property life differs from one property to another so that if we were to measure "lived time" in terms of years, we would either have to draw multitudinous graphs corresponding to each different life duration or combine them into one or more graphs in which the constituent properties would end at varying points on the time scale. The alternative is to recode all events from the beginning to the end of the property cycle into a standard length. This is what has been done here. The standard length of life is taken to be 100 property cycle units (PCUs) in a way that the points on the graphs at 50 PCUs represent the average situation for properties half-way through their lives, 25 represents the situation one-quarter of the way through, and so on. To take into account the quantity of land transacted over time with persons of the same surname, we have invented a "kin area index" (illustrated by the dashed line) derived from the proportion of land thus transacted to all land transacted up to a given point in time.[53] To take into account changes in the total property area, we have a "property area index" (the solid line), where the average area for the entire cycle represents the base, 100.[54]

For the regions as a whole, there was definitely a larger part of the properties, on average, exchanged between relatives in the Orléanais than in the Nantais. Therefore, it would seem that the old family tie became more and more of an influence as the population approached its optimum or, put another way, transactions with an unrelated neighbor became a less frequently afforded "luxury." Rural society had been stripped to its essentials. But this wasn't an endorsement across the board, of the family network, for we note that the Orléanais' lead was *entirely* due to the high proportion of family land exchanged in the Loire Valley (even though this represented well over half the region's population). Elsewhere the index is low; in the Sologne, it amounts to practical-

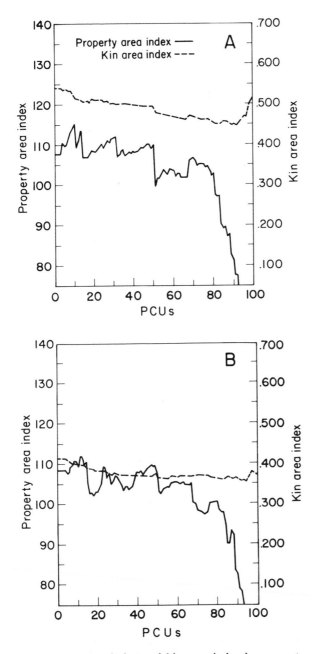

Figure 8.8. Property area index and kin area index by property cycle units (PCUs) in (A) the Orléanais and (B) the Nantais.

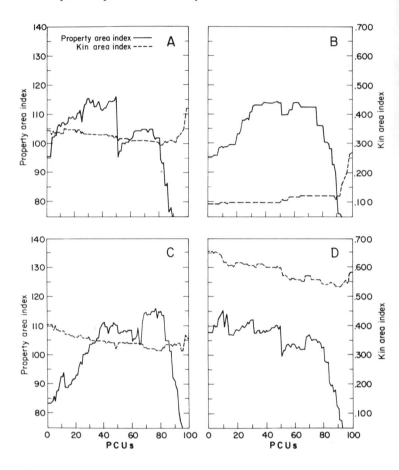

Figure 8.9. Property area index and kin area index by property cycle units (PCUs) in (A) the Beauce, (B) the Sologne, (C) the Forêt d'Orléans, and (D) the Orléanais Valley.

ly nothing until right at the end of the cycle. The migrations probably had a lot to do with this, first in the sense that migration was a less popular option in the Valley than anywhere else (see Figure 7.10) and, second, because, in the areas where migration did occur, it represented a definitive break with the past. The *declining* number of propertyholders living outside the commune shows that there was no desire for these migrants to hold on to former possessions. Anyway, they probably migrated because they had none – their term as propertyholders had either already expired or was so brief that they felt it was not worth the wait. The Beauceron emigrant was, preeminently, the uprooted rustic who found his way to other parts of the countryside or to the city; on the

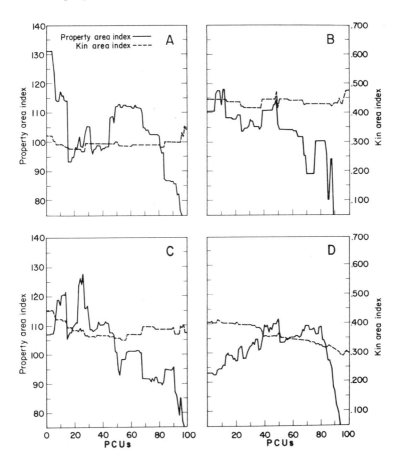

Figure 8.10. Property area index and kin area index by property cycle units (PCUs) in (A) the Nantais Plateau, (B) Retz-Vendée, (C) Sèvre-et-Maine, and (D) the Nantais Valley.

other side of the river, we once more witness an economy of small propertyholders in the making. The old Beauceron was unlikely to leave an inheritance; the new Solognot could hardly expect to come into an inheritance (though the graph demonstrates that, once established, he was more likely to pass the land on to a relative, thus perpetuating his own new kind). The Orléanais would therefore appear to have exercised two contradictory but related options: a reinforcement of the family *property* network that was confined to the Valley (I shall explain the emphasis shortly) and migration.

How much more integrated was the Nantais! Counting by area rather than by transaction, Sèvre-et-Maine is now shown to be slightly above the region's average. In fact, the kin area index is at similar levels in the Nantais Valley and everything to the south of it. The only significant aberration is in the least intensively cultivated subregion, the Plateau, where the scores are somewhat lower.

As far as the actual cycle is concerned, the kin area index follows the same general pattern throughout both regions: from the point of initial acquisiton, it continually drops until the final sale, where it makes a steep upward turn. This is to be expected. Relatives were unlikely to play much of a role in the territorial adjustments following the initial acquisition, but they were obviously considered when the property was wound up. The slope of these curves is slight because there was usually little activity between the first purchase and last sale (5 exchanges on average, including the first and last – only 12 percent of the sample had over 10). The rates of decline are virtually identical for the two regions, but the last minute upward turn is more marked in the Orléanais largely due, it would appear, to the important rise at this stage of the cycle of the properties of the two subregions with the lowest overall average, the Beauce and the Sologne. In the Nantais, the upward turn is not very conspicuous in the two pasture-type subregions; in the two intensive-type subregions, it is negligible. The property area index simply demonstrates how restricted the propertyholder was in both regions (a point that is also borne out by Table 8.6). Not only did property areas in most parts fail to expand over the cycle, in some instances they are actually shown to have been in perpetual contraction. It is readily observed that only the most marginal subregions, the Forêt and the Sologne, had properties that habitually expanded after the initial acquisition.

What does all this say about the previously stated contrast in legal traditions? Obviously a survey of surnames is not going to give a complete picture of the family's role in property transactions. But it does tell us something. The similarity in the rates of the kin area indices' declines shows there to have been no major regional difference in family patterns between the first acquisition and last sale. True, dowries to daughters would not be detected here, but that is the case for both regions. The real differences are found at either end of the cycle and can now be identified as (1) the larger proportion of short property lives in the Orléanais (especially the Beauce and Sologne) than in the Nantais, (2) the larger proportionate area exchanged between relatives in lands of high agricultural intensity (notably the Orléanais Valley) than in lands of low intensity, and (3) the sharper final upward turn in the kin area index in the Orléanais (especially the Beauce and Sologne) than in the Nantais. I have already indicated how all three differences can be explained by variations in population pressure and population movements. But that gives us no reason to ignore the legal traditions, much less the local cultures that

Table 8.6. *Area growth probabilities, Orléanais (O) and Nantais (N) (probabilities of properties growing to X times or more of their area at first acquisition at any point during their property-lives)*

Area at first acquisition (hectares)		X																N_w
		1.5	2.0	2.5	3.0	3.5	4.0	4.5	5.0	7.5	10.0	15.0	25.0	50.0	75.0	100.0	500.0	
0.01–0.10	O	.281	.163	.163	.163	.163	.163	.163	.163	.163	.148	.148	.111	.111	.088	.088	.0	23
	N	.450	.395	.359	.359	.359	.359	.359	.340	.286	.232	.213	.213	.091	.018	.018	.0	48
0.11–0.25	O	.503	.503	.503	.473	.473	.370	.370	.370	.197	.181	.181	.078	.0	.0	.0	.0	21
	N	.469	.420	.372	.372	.372	.340	.258	.231	.200	.167	.134	.048	.016	.0	.0	.0	54
0.26–0.50	O	.518	.489	.376	.290	.279	.279	.222	.222	.148	.074	.074	.074	.017	.017	.0	.0	30
	N	.257	.184	.184	.184	.184	.147	.147	.147	.037	.0	.0	.0	.0	.0	.0	.0	24
0.51–1.00	O	.199	.199	.187	.115	.115	.115	.115	.115	.043	.043	.043	.018	.0	.0	.0	.0	28
	N	.304	.217	.132	.132	.132	.076	.076	.076	.028	.0	.0	.0	.0	.0	.0	.0	31
1.01–2.50	O	.266	.266	.131	.084	.064	.045	.045	.045	.037	.0	.0	.0	.0	.0	.0	.0	17
	N	.250	.167	.061	.061	.023	.023	.023	.023	.023	.023	.023	.0	.0	.0	.0	.0	38
2.51–5.00	O	.240	.055	.055	.055	.055	.055	.055	.0	.0	.0	.0	.0	.0	.0	.0	.0	6
	N	.293	.144	.144	.144	.144	.072	.072	.072	.072	.0	.0	.0	.0	.0	.0	.0	12
5.01–10.00	O	.345	.221	.097	.048	.0	.0	.0	.0	.0	.0	.0	.0	.0	.0	.0	.0	3
	N	.0	.0	.0	.0	.0	.0	.0	.0	.0	.0	.0	.0	.0	.0	.0	.0	5
10.01–25.00	O	.035	.035	.035	.035	.0	.0	.0	.0	.0	.0	.0	.0	.0	.0	.0	.0	4
	N	.0	.0	.0	.0	.0	.0	.0	.0	.0	.0	.0	.0	.0	.0	.0	.0	7
25.01–50.00	O	.119	.0	.0	.0	.0	.0	.0	.0	.0	.0	.0	.0	.0	.0	.0	.0	1
	N	.0	.0	.0	.0	.0	.0	.0	.0	.0	.0	.0	.0	.0	.0	.0	.0	1
50.01–100	O	.0	.0	.0	.0	.0	.0	.0	.0	.0	.0	.0	.0	.0	.0	.0	.0	0
	N	.0	.0	.0	.0	.0	.0	.0	.0	.0	.0	.0	.0	.0	.0	.0	.0	2
Over 100.00	O	.0	.0	.0	.0	.0	.0	.0	.0	.0	.0	.0	.0	.0	.0	.0	.0	1
	N	.0	.0	.0	.0	.0	.0	.0	.0	.0	.0	.0	.0	.0	.0	.0	.0	0
All properties	O	.337	.298	.251	.205	.198	.179	.167	.164	.105	.079	.079	.051	.023	.019	.015	.0	135
	N	.339	.281	.224	.224	.217	.194	.174	.164	.126	.094	.082	.057	.023	.004	.004	.0	222

Source: Matrices cadastrales.

these traditions had represented. We have been consistently opposed to deterministic interpretations. There was not just one possible response to the challenge of overpopulation; rural society was faced with several alternatives and the choice it made was essentially psychological. The psychology of the moment related in part back to that demographic pressure, in part to habit. In the area of property, the social habit had been spelled out in the custumals of each region. Thus, whereas population gives us a good idea of the situation, it tells us only half the story about the one choice adopted.

Take the case of the shorter property lives in the Orléanais. Clearly a limitation on the period of ownership was a way of responding to population pressure, but according to the customary laws of the Orléanais, this had also been a manner of preserving the integrity of the patrimony: gifts *inter vivos* could be made for the purpose of advantaging one child. The sharp upward turn of the kin area index – noted in areas with the shortest property lives – could be related to the same phenomenon. Similarly, the strict egalitarian tradition of the West could have been partially responsible for the closely matching levels of the kin area index throughout the Nantais. I do not think that customary law has much to tell about the strikingly high index score in the Orléanais Valley nor about the generally high levels found in subregions of the intensive agricultural type. Of the three distinctions mentioned, this is the only one to be made within the regions rather than between them. A regional explanation would therefore not be in order.

Rural society would always attempt to eliminate what it deemed superfluous as agriculture intensified. Because the household economy was at stake, land transactions with outsiders would have been considered superfluous (obviously, not in an absolute sense, but too many would have posed a threat). Therefore, the positive correlation between the kin area index and agricultural intensity was not so much due to the strengthening of family ties as to the declining importance of outside exchanges. Moreover, one has to distinguish these *property* ties from the more fundamental biological bonding discussed in Chapter 7. One would even go as far as to say that they were in a negative relationship to one another. Intensity forces the adoption of a whole series of controls that tend to weaken the family bonds; at the same time, it increases the direct influence of families within the realm of property. It is not difficult to imagine how property itself could become, under such repressive circumstances, more and more a projected identity for the domestic community.

As the columnist from Tavers had noted, agriculture may well have destroyed the eclogue. But, for the people who had to make a living out of agriculture, the nineteenth century was rather a story of self-preservation. Remarkably, the area distribution of properties at the eve of the First World War was almost identical to what it had been three generations earlier; the small peasant family plot had been maintained in spite of the growth in population. The last two chapters have shown at what cost. In the Nantais, the inhabitants, although hardly enjoying a life of comfort, had at least the satisfaction of being better equipped than their countrymen further upstream to endure the pressure of their own number. First, the family shows every sign of having been a stronger unit (and, all politics aside, that was a major advantage). Moreover, although one generally spent more of one's life with one's first family, whether natural or adopted, the time spent as propertyholders was frequently longer than in the Orléanais. After marriage, one could certainly expect a shorter period without land. The ownership of property thus became one definite point of reference in the whole individual experience of time. This meant more than security. Like adolescence and marriage, property understood within a temporal framework was something that could be varied to the needs of the individual and the group. It was not an immutable given. Thus, when numbers grew, the small propertyholder showed a willingness to cede. And that is exactly what happened in some of the most intensely farmed areas of the Nantais from around 1830 to 1880.

There was no fragmentation, in our special sense of the term, in the Orléanais. Properties grew because the marginal territories were put into cultivation. The Orléanais family was a more isolated unit. But although it was more quickly broken up, the department young could only look forward to extended periods of landlessness. Property was therefore not such a good index of time; it was more likely to be viewed as a strict "economic" asset, the material dimension of the family exploitation. Under these conditions, one was not likely to cede a piece of the land to others. For those in search of property, the marginal lands were often the only alternative.

But, while fully recognizing the hardships incurred, let's not overlook the overall success of the system. Peasant society had survived. What's more, it had become positively aggressive. Restricted in the area of exploitation, restricted in domestic hired labor, the peasant family farm was driven to a level large landowners could not meet. Urban property actually fell into retreat. In the next chapter, I would like to take a closer look at the phenomenon of the peasantry's success.

9   Crisis and stability: the rural economy through time

The two trends, flux and reflux, detected in property suggest a dual-phased development in the economy over the course of the nineteenth century. So do the population movements, if we think of the third-quarter of the century as a transitional period. Such a pattern was not unique to the century of the railway. It had happened before – specifically, in the fourteenth and seventeenth centuries.[1] And like the nineteenth, these were particularly turbulent times. I am therefore not talking about an economy emerging from a pristine state of tradition, of a changeless Old Regime. The peasant household economy was found intact at the beginning of the nineteenth century precisely because of its capacity to initiate and accommodate change.

This flexibility can hardly be appreciated when the economy is reduced to the stock categories of price, rent, wage, and profit. Profit (in the strict economic sense) was a meaningless notion because cost accounting was unknown to most families.[2] Wages were largely part-time earnings. Rent varied from commune to commune, and most of those who paid it also possessed land of their own. The effects of price fluctuations should certainly not be gainsaid. There is little doubt about the reality of subsistence crises, typified by dizzying leaps in price over a one- or two-year period. Such crises continued to occur until the early years of the Second Empire. But interpretations of long-term price trends are less sure. For instance, without reliable production figures, we can't tell whether an extended period of rising prices signaled boom or depression, growth or "stagflation." The experience of our own times has called into question the enthusiasm of those dyed-in-the-wool optimists who wrote histories one generation ago. But above all, it is surely unreasonable to regard market price as an accurate reflection of real opportunity costs when we know that rural society was committed only sporadically to the principles of market economy.

A peasant agricultural crisis, I have said, occurs when the range of economic alternatives has become so narrow as to prevent the singular efforts of the farming family from ever satisfying its needs. Because the critical level of intensification is determined by neither price, wage, nor profit but by a subjective labor–consumer balance, the crisis must be viewed, in the final analysis, as a psychological rather than economic phenomenon. Judging from available population and property figures, there have been in Europe in the last 700 years, as I have just indicated, three such crises. On each occasion, the demographic cycle of pressure and release was completed. Given the relationship of this to landholding patterns and crop preferences (Figure 3.1), we are able, in the case of the nineteenth century, to identify two broad periods: one of *intensification* (circa 1800–circa 1860), characterized by an increase in the number of small peasant properties; and the other of *extension* (circa 1860–circa 1914), where we witness a *remembrement,* or a consolidation, of land-holdings.[3]

The theme I intend to pursue here is that each period was marked by distinctive outward forms of social behavior. During the first period there were numerous acts of collective violence, whereas the second period witnessed the end of violence and the growth of rural coopera-tives. But both violence and association served, at different points in the cycle, an identical end: the preservation of the peasant economy. We will also find the Nantais consistently putting up a more united front, whether in violence or association, than the psychologically isolated Orléanais.

1. Intensification, ca. 1800–1860

The economy
The economy of the first half of the nineteenth century was, then, one of growing population densities and an ever-increasing number of small properties. This was to bring about important alterations in the land-scape. Intensive cropping spread beyond the traditional limits of the valleys and there was a general expansion of cultivated areas to include, ultimately, infertile spaces like the Sologne and the Forêt d'Orléans.

Vineyards were, of course, foremost among the intensive cultures. Observers readily agreed that the wines of the Orléanais were pretty dreadful; but they were competitive, especially during the bad years. In an average year, the outskirts of Paris used to produce an immense quan-tity of hard, acidic wines that, when blended with wines from the Midi, were acceptable in the city's cafés. In a bad year, these wines were un-drinkable. Under these conditions, the cheap Orléanais wines made a good bargain not only against Parisian plonk but also against wines from further afield (e.g., Cher or the Touraine).[4] However, Bacchus does not seem to have gained much territory during this period, and he might have even lost some in the western parts of the Loire Valley.[5] One of the reasons was that it took up to five years after planting before one could expect the first decent grape harvest – the most productive vines were a good deal older. And plantation was not encouraged by the depression in wine commerce in the years immediately following Waterloo. Whatever the cause, between 1815 and the early 1820s, many cultivators in the Nantais ripped out their vine stock to replace them with vegetables.[6] These included beans, carrots, asparagus, and a new root crop, the potato.[7] All of them were less demanding of space than the vine and could be more easily replaced if conditions warranted it. Thus the Nantais already had an important advantage over the Orléanais.

With the accession of the July monarch, cultivators in the cereal- and pasture-type subregions launched an assault against the fallows, which, at that time, took up as much as one-third of what could otherwise be considered perfectly fertile ground. Agricultural inspectors reported a steady increase in clover and other fodder crops in the north of the arrondissement of Ancenis. This was also the moment that fodder began to take the place of fallow in the old triennial system of the Beauce.[8]

It is tempting to look at France's last king, Louis Philippe, as a sort of Gallic version of Farmer George. It could hardly have been chance alone that accounted for the coincidental spread of artificial grasses and the establishment by royal decree of a general council of agriculture, a new agricultural ministry, and a number of agricultural schools and model farms. As a matter of fact, one of the most celebrated model farms was set up in the Nantais, at Grandjouan, by a mettlesome young farmer, Jules Rieffel, who was to make his mark later as an important regional journalist (*Agriculture de l'Ouest de la France*) and a forerunner of the syndical movement (*Association Bretonne*, 1843). But, like the more general accounts of the ingenious "mediator," histories that limit themselves to a handful of inspired administrators reflect a very narrow, lopsided view of rural change. Farms such as Rieffel's probably played a determining part in the actual crops adopted into the rural economy – lucern, clover, sainfoin. However, that says very little in itself. Why did the population adopt these innovations? and why were the model farms only partially successful? Grandjouan had been organized to encourage "good practices" in livestock rearing and thus to better exploit what seemed to be the Nantais' natural comparative advantage. But it was poorly timed. In the 1830s and 40s, the small peasant farmer's main concern in the Nantais was with improved cultivation, not raising cows. That he should have planted fodder in part of his field merely demonstrates the close affiliation of livestock with cultivation in the pasture-type subregions (see Chapter 6, Section 1). That the quality of livestock should remain poor shows exactly where his preferences lay. This would have even seemed quite logical when prices were as high as they had been in the early 1840s; but the agricultural inspectors were at a loss to explain why cultivated areas continued to grow when prices fell through the floor after 1848. Good Ricardians, the inspectors imagined that the rural inhabitant would at least see the sense in improving his livestock (meat prices fluctuate less than harvest prices). The point was, of course, that demographic pressure was the determining factor, not price.[9]

New crops were a happy aspect of intensification; there was also the darker side. Every 5 to 10 years, a lean harvest would remind the unflagging rustic of the narrow perch on which his livelihood had placed him. Despite various contrary claims, there was nothing actually mathematical about the timing of these subsistence crises. Starting with the Revolution, the worst years seem to have been 1793-4, 1799, 1812, 1816-17, 1829-32, 1840, 1846-7, 1853, and 1857-8. The distinctive characteristics of these years were, as the administrative reports amply testify, starvation and fear. In February 1812, a priest of one of Orléans' suburbs was reprimanded by the prefecture for announcing in church that there wasn't enough wheat to go around. That year the government was forced to reinstitute the *maximum* (price controls); in Loiret, the peasants were reportedly reduced to eating grass and roots. . . . the subsistence crises were no myth. But they were not uniformly bad. The crisis of 1857-8 was hardly comparable to the abysm of 1812, though 1816-17 and 1846-7 (in the Orléanais, at least) approached the same dismal level. Nor were these crises universal. The 1847 agricultural report for the Nantais has a surprise in store for some generalists:

The year 1847 will be rightly cited in the annals of agriculture as one of the most favorable from the double viewpoint of the quality and quantity of products. The wheat and rye are of remarkable beauty and cleanness . . . The area sown in wheat for 1847 is more extensive than normal.

All the same, a July drought had hurt the potato crop, as it had buckwheat, "so important an aid in the feeding of the rural populations, particularly on the right bank of the Loire." (There had been a bumper crop in buckwheat in 1846!)[10]

Subsistence crises were obviously not by and of themselves very effective "positive checks"[11] of demographic growth. The long-term trend was, we have seen, one of declining death rates, which in this period led to greater population densities. They nonetheless had their effect on the psychology and subsequent behavior of the population.[12] Doesn't the fact that 1846-7 were less-wretched years in the Nantais than in many other parts of France throw some light on the region's unusual pacifism during the Second Republic?

Norms and deviants
Rural violence was the second ugly face of intensification. I include here individual acts of violence as well as collective violence. Any discussion of either, or of the hazy frontier separating them, inevitably calls to mind the ancient sociological debate over norms and deviants. Deviant or

criminal acts, Durkheim once said, serve an important social function. Like war, floods, and other emergencies, they bring people together into a common posture of anger, indignation, or despair.[13] The implication is that we should (inasmuch as we are sociologists) worry ourselves less about the deviant act itself than about the attitudes of others toward that act – attitudes, for example, that make the soldier a hero, the murderer a criminal.[14] In fact, the act is not even a necessary precondition of the attitude. A good historical example of an attitude formed without the preliminary deviant act is the Great Fear that swept the countryside in the early days of the French Revolution. The popular conviction that the "brigands" were coming was chronicled in such detail that it has been possible to trace its origin and direction of spread. (The first fear in the country actually began in the Nantais.)[15]

Historians of the nineteenth century have not been as lucky as the historians of the Revolution in documenting such fears. They are, however, suggested in the many references one finds to "brigandage." For instance, the annual and monthly police reports sent in from the departments to the minister of the interior often had a special section devoted to it. "Brigandage" could mean anything from petty theft to armed insurgence. In 1802, the commissioner of Loiret reported the presence of "several *isolated* brigands, not belonging to bands" (my emphasis). But it was also "brigands" in the Nantais who rose in arms against the imperial government of 1815. For those on the receiving end (and they were frequently administrators), all rural crime was committed by "brigands."[16]

We do get the occasional hint that it was not only administrators who were scared of brigands. "Bad spirits" in the countryside normally referred to the spread of popular rumors. These were generally of two kinds, often, but not always, occurring together. The more common seems to have been a belief in the presence of bands, employed by some unpopular authority to threaten one or more of the revered institutions of rustic life. The exact form and purpose of these phantom bands depended on time and place: They were the "republican" bands in the Nantais in 1815 and 1832 who would force the closure of churches and carry off the priests; or the "legitimist" bands in the Orléanais in 1820 who were going to exact the taxes of the Old Regime and force the return of the *biens nationaux*. Then there were the rumors about the approach of foreigners, outsiders, *étrangers*: an English invasion of the Nantais in 1832; Russian deserters in the Orléanais in 1814.[17]

There is a possible psychological connection between these popular fears and the innovations that were made, out of necessity, in agriculture. One is a parody of the other. These rumors and suspicions were not so much the mark of an unalterable tradition as of human creativity; and what else does one expect out of creativity if not some sense of anticipation?[18] The adoption of a new crop out of the conviction that it *will* make the land more productive or the drive to possess the land discussed in the last chapter are both obvious examples. This sort of anticipatory spirit must have benefited agriculture. At the same time, it prompted, in the minds of the population, these imagined foreign bandits running amuck in the countryside, shirking the native conventions of those who tilled its soil. Why native conventions? We note that what was taken as the convention, or norm, in one region could have been viewed as deviance in the other. The contrast in regional attitudes to the parish priest – particularly the refractory – is a case in point: a hero in the Nantais, a threat in the Orléanais. If by some whisk of the wand we could actually poll these people, we would probably find *within* each region several different notions of the "social norm."[19]

Thus, a certain type of social psychology might be associated with intensification. The same frame of mind that led the peasant to plant potatoes and cultivate the fallow had sparked off images that the sober social scientist might dismiss as fantasy. But necessity is the mother of invention. Potatoes and "brigands" had a common parent: the will to live, or, rather, the will to survive.

This is not to underestimate the importance of the criminal act, but it is a really tricky business to establish a historical trend. The populations in our two regions are, even when combined, too small to produce a statistically significant measure. National statistics are not much better either. It has been argued that crimes against persons and property declined over the course of the century.[20] And it has been argued that they increased.[21] "The rate of major crimes against property – theft, robbery, and willful destruction – plummeted down, down, down."[22] Or, "a general rise in property crimes seems likely and a rise in theft rates during the nineteenth century highly probable."[23] Meanwhile, "the rate of major crimes against persons – murder, poisoning, infanticide, patricide – barely changed over the entire period."[24] Or, "violence became more frequent but possibly less serious."[25] It is a draw, with several points on each side. The opportunity for certain crimes could have changed, thus affecting the types of crime committed. To be sure, nineteenth-century French peasants did not commit welfare fraud. Crime can therefore be taken as an index, a rather grisly index, of the opportunities open to society – a useful supplement to our indexes on population and property.

To begin with, we find four *common* features in the criminal behavior of the Orléanais and the Nantais. The first two will not surprise the criminologist. From what can be gleaned from police and newspaper reports, one must conclude that most murders and interpersonal acts of violence were committed within the household (involving direct relations or domestics) and that youth comprised the larger part of criminal offenders. Both are more a comment on human nature than on anything particular to the two regions. However, there was a definite "style" in the murders committed throughout most of the nineteenth century, which was largely determined by the weapons available – poison, axes, hammers, and fire.[26] This little example from the *Journal du Loiret,* 24 February 1877, also demonstrates the nineteenth-century gift for grotesque discourse:

Double assassinat au Gué-de-Bleury [Beauce]

Last Sunday, the milkman who collects milk from *la femme Blanchard's* cow was surprised to find the door locked. [La femme Blanchard was 72, her husband 80] . . . A ladder was set up against the wall of the garden and several persons penetrated the interior of the property. It was evident that a crime had been committed. They entered the bedroom and there a horrible spectacle struck their eyes. Thick smoke filled the room; straw piled up on one of the beds was in the last stages of burning. Everywhere on the paved flooring lay linen thrown out of the opened and half-smashed furniture. On the bed, with his feet up against the wall, with half his side hanging over the edge, his head horribly fractured, an eye entirely out of its socket, there was the body of the unfortunate Blanchard [husband]. . . . They still had to find Blanchard's wife . . . In the bread oven, among the remains of burnt straw, they saw her blood-stained head; she was horribly burned, especially in the legs and the hands. . . . [But] she still breathed, in spite of the horrible torment she had endured all night, in spite of the terrible wounds caused by her burns. . . . The murderers . . . having ransacked all the furniture, had pulled up three stones of the paved floor, suggesting that they were familiar with their victims' habits . . . and that they hoped to find money that they assumed to be in the possession of this unfortunate old couple.

The murder of a close relative out of revenge or for money seems to have been fairly common.[27] There was no lack of young candidates to replay the part of Pierre Rivière. And there is probably some truth to the claim that the atrocities committed by that Norman peasant were, in part, the result of the spectacular growth in family property: an enemy within the household.[28] Judging from the number of incidents reported, patricide, matricide, and infanticide were far more common where the pressures of intensification were greatest, the Orléanais. But, again, this reflects what, the reporter or the act?

The second common feature – that youth had more than their share of criminal offenders – is less interesting in itself than in the way it relates to the remaining two aspects of "deviance" in these two regions. One of the more specifically rural forms of deviant behavior in the nineteenth century was the occasional affray between residents of neighboring communes (or, for that matter, neighboring hamlets). We would expect increasing population densities, coupled with the persistent drive to acquire land, to kindle local tensions and rivalries. But, quite evidently, this was not a direct relationship. At least, it was not the propertyholders who

were involved in village brawls but the youth, that is, the group that was
going through a transitional period in the life cycle, whose principal tie to
the peasant household was economic, and a group that made up the majority of household members outside the conjugal family unit – the
"working class" of the countryside, the "buffer zone" around the family
nucleus (see Chapter 7, Section 1). Frequently the violence would be
sparked off by a harmless act, often during local festivities, such as occurred in the following case in the Orléanais on Sunday, 16 August 1834,
the *fête du pays:*

> The youth of Ingrannes and Sully-la-Chapelle, numbering 50 to 60, turned up in
> [Seichebrières] with the intention of knocking about those from Vitry-aux-Loges
> who, not being on their guard and being less numerous than their adversaries,
> would have been cruelly beaten by these madmen who, armed with very short
> sharp-pointed sticks suitable for dealing several hasty blows, began to strike in-
> discriminately all those they found in their way, even including the forest guards
> and police . . . It appeared that these youths were completely drunk, and that the
> scene had begun by indecent acts committed by them dancing in front of the girls
> from Vitry.[29]

We get, then, an image of youth in carnival exorcising tensions that pervaded the entire society. The harsh repressions of the adult world left
homo ludens acting out a hostile role. From the accounts available, it is
not easy to draw a clear picture of developments over time, but it does
seem that, with the decline in population densities and properties after
about 1860, this kind of violence became less common – or so contemporary observers thought. In 1868, when six inhabitants from Cordenais,
Loire-Inférieure, were arrested for a couple of murders arising from a
brawl with a small gang from Boué, a local journalist wistfully remarked, "One believed that these stupid rivalries from belltower to
belltower or from commune to commune had completely disappeared."[30]

The last important type of violence found in both regions was connected with robbery. The peasants' fear of brigands wasn't totally un-
justified because, up until the Second Empire, they could very well expect the odd uninvited visit. Single-handed robbery of rural households
was rare. In most cases, a band of three or four men, armed with knives
and bludgeons, if not guns, would turn up in the early hours of the morning and demand the most precious commodities of the household, wine
and meat (which would normally mean pig fat). The favorite targets were
the isolated farmsteads of the Beauce in the Orléanais or of the *bocages*
in the Nantais. Farms in the more intensely cultivated subregions were
not entirely immune. On the night of 21 August 1846, several farms in
Vallet (Sèvre-et-Maine) had their vitals filched by a dozen bandits.[31]
Food was also the prime motive of highway robbery. Local administrators were continually asking for more protection for the grain carts that
traveled the main road from Nantes to Angers along the right bank of the

Loire, or the main road from Orléans to Paris across the Beauce, and especially for the barges that plied the forested sections of the Canal d'Orléans. There is little indicating who these bandits were. The police were convinced that they were starving beggars. In their reports, the section on "Brigandage" was almost always followed by a paragraph on the progress made toward the "Extinction de la Mendicité."

All of this – murder, delinquent youth, intercommunal brawls, and robbery – were given coverage in the local papers and official correspondence of the day. We have noted that there were some changes around the middle of the century. The style of murders seems to have been fairly constant and one can always find reports about the delinquency of youth. There was, on the other hand, less concern about village rivalry and the kind of robbery just outlined. Probably this was partly due to a real decline in this form of deviance.

All the same, it would be stupid to ignore the change in attitude that the reports of the Second Empire onward do imply. This is not so much suggested by the disappearance of old vices as by the appearance of a new one, outrages on common decency, *pudeur*. I cannot imagine that Louis Philippe's rural subjects were better practitioners of *pudeur* than their sons and daughters under Louis Napoleon, yet comments on heavy drinking, the prime object of this new concern, multiply after 1860. By the 1870s, complaints about the existence of "too many bars" and the "habitual drunkenness of the population" are a standard part of local police reports.[32] Again, I am not attributing this to a simple flight of fancy; there is in fact evidence that alcoholic consumption was on the rise.[33] The point is that because there was so little said about drinking prior to 1850 and because the subsequent remarks about it are so frequently described as *outrages à la pudeur,* it is difficult to avoid concluding that a new language had been adopted in response to what one supposes to be a new ethic, a Victorian ethic. The question of whether this was imposed from the top by a small group of administrators or whether this genuinely reflected a popular concern is really an impossible one to resolve. However, it is a fact that the change in language does correspond to a change in the trends of population and landed property. This is not, in my view, mere coincidence. By about 1860, the rural population had reached its subjectively determined optimum, and the solutions and images that had until recently provided an outlet from the pressures of intensification were no longer appropriate. The social "norm" had changed and what was regarded as "deviant" changed with it.

But I am oversimplifying things. Norms varied as much over space as they did over time. Thus the consequences of reaching a demographic optimum could differ according to the region. This is what I shall now attempt to show.

Regional contrasts in collective violence

The capital question is: Are we to consider the peasantry as pawns, political objects, manipulated by a few clever social engineers high in the ranks of power? or should we give them more credit and think of them as their own masters? The analysis of the preceding chapters speaks for the latter. Real choice, of course, must depend on real opportunities. Adequate proof has been given that there were fewer opportunities in the Orléanais than in the Nantais and that the reasons behind this were basically geographical. My argument has been that opportunity affects the psychology of the population (which is a long-handed way of describing the social norm). If we can consider violence as a valid indicator of that psychology, it is out of the conviction that man is not by nature violent but that he has a capacity for violence – he is violent by choice. Violence, I have further argued, becomes a plausible option when the level of intensification approaches its limits. This was surely the case of both our regions; I have just indicated what they had in common. Where they differed was in collective violence, that is, in violence that had widespread support in the rural community. Obviously, this was no longer deviant behavior. It conformed to the local norm, and inasmuch as one local norm differed from another, one local form of collective violence could be expected to differ from the other.

Both regions, then, pursued the same goal (the preservation of the peasant economy) but with different opportunities before them. Commercial stagnation had at least brought that fact to light: Nantais liberty was connected to the development of an independent economic sector in Nantes; Orléanais repression was tied up with the near total reliance of the regional capital on its hinterland. Its effect on local religious life was especially remarkable. Repression of the Orléanais had led to a more personal superstitious type of belief that obviously could not, as Durkheim would put it, serve as a principle of cohesion. Thus the motive for collective violence in the Orléanais was limited to immediate, material gain; it was directed against those who obstructed the supply of food. *Cuius regio, eius religio.* In the less-restrained atmosphere of the Nantais, inhabitants practiced their beliefs in the open. Collective violence was therefore of a more sacred parentage; its targets were the blasphemers and desecraters of the parish faith.[34]

But were the two types of violence, as some like to think, simply different ways of opposing the growing power of the French state? "Peasants against the state" – it is hardly the objective remark it first appears to be. The distinction between the Orléanais and the Nantais was not just political, between the Left and the Right, between Red and White. Each region was communicating a different message, with its own affirmations, its own contradictions. This "state" was a mythological beast whose shape and color changed with the region. In the Orléanais, it robbed the commonalty of the means to eat. In the Nantais, it was the idol and demon of one's religious beliefs.

That much is made clear if we look at the patterns of violence in the centers of settlement, the regional capitals. For both, the most serious troubles were in 1830. In Orléans, they took place in a poor suburb and were aimed at Loiret's tax bureau. On 10 August, a rabble of *bas peuple* gathered around the bureau's headquarters at Faubourg Bannier, screaming and smashing its windows. They were in even greater spirits when they returned on 2 September. More windows were broken, the building was entered, and the tax registers torn to pieces and burned. The crowd then went on a rampage through the streets of the suburb, smashing the windows of bakers and grain merchants until they arrived in front of a house belonging to sieur Chaufton's son. Sieur Chaufton was a "former plowman, now propertyholder" who had been accused of grain speculation. The house was burned to the ground.

Who were these *bas peuple* and why their violence? In the newspaper, they were "for the most part strangers to the suburban populations." The three leaders tried in Orléans that November consisted of a 30-year-old poulterer, an 18-year-old cabinetmaker, and the 32-year-old wife of a winegrower – not a very urban-looking team! As for the cause, the reports are consistent: "the high price of bread" and the general "high cost of living." The presence of the winegrower's wife thus has added significance; in the peasant economy, it was primarily the women who were directly responsible for getting food on the table. They were apparently women who led the crowd to sieur Chaufton's house.[35]

The closest parallel I have found in the Nantais was what occurred in Ancenis, the arrondissement capital, in 1846. Late that autumn, with food prices already high, the local government had the bright idea of raising a new tax on bread. Thereupon the bakers went on strike. Then, on 19 December, the authorities learned that "40 to 50 women (washerwomen and cooks) were planning a "riot" the following Sunday to get the price of bread reduced. The mayor's letter to the prefect showed special concern. There were going to be a lot of railway workers in town that Sunday because it was their payday and the "poor population" could expect their support. As it turned out, bitterly cold weather put a damper on the show. The crowd was small; there was no riot.[36]

Rioting out of material need was certainly not unknown in the Nantais. It took place in the poor quarters of the towns and was perpetrated by the poor with the possible support (and initiative?) of people in the country. But that was not what happened in Nantes in July 1830. Events there were directly tied to the dramatic political developments in Paris. News of Charles X's abusive Five Ordinances arrived in Nantes with the morning post on 28 July. The following evening, in the course of a meeting outside the city's theater, a scuffle broke out with the police. One policeman was killed and 18 demonstrators were taken prisoner. The next morning a crowd outside the post office heard the first news of fighting in Paris. Now a full-blown rebellion developed. Its participants had two clear demands: arms to free the prisoners and the creation of a national guard. At the Bourse, which had become the insurgents' general headquarters, it was decided that they should march on the old Château des Ducs in which the municipal authorities had barricaded themselves. Ten rebels died in the ensuing fight; the castle did not fall. But, without positive news from Paris, the authorities were forced to relinquish their powers to a five-member commission at the chamber of commerce (31 July). The prisoners were freed and the national guard set up.

Who were the rebels and why the violence? According to Guépin and Simon's account, workers played an important part. "Several workers and *chefs d'atelier*" were in the crowd that gathered at Place Graslin on 30 July; "five or six hundred youths accompanied by a larger number of workers" subsequently erected barricades and cut off the bridges over the Loire; and the actual combatants were "almost entirely composed of workers." But if they were workers, *they were fighting outside their quarters*: the center of the insurrection was in one of the richest parts of the city. One notes that this was neither the first nor the last time the theater at Place Graslin had been the scene of confrontation between youth and police.[37] And youth shared a large part of the responsibility for the violence. The demands for arms and the national guard were rejected in a meeting of senior merchants because, as their statement of 30 July read, "We don't need the youth here for our intention is not to revolt."

This does not explain the violence. My hunch is that the participants in the independent, commercial sector of Nantes' economy were dead scared, and just as rural youth were capable of translating fear into violence, so at Nantes it was the youth who took up the offensive. Guépin and Simon leave no doubt about the nature of their fear. They believed the authorities were playing for time. With the news of fighting in Paris, rumor spread that 200 cuirassiers in the Vendée were marching on Nantes. "Enemy at the gates!" was the watchword pronounced at the Bourse. Small wonder the rebels were so swift to seize the bridges leading south, to erect barricades prior to their attack on the castle. The Bourbon authorities had not only the castle canon to protect them but "two pieces of country aimed at their door."[38]

Politics, we have on the authority of one new philosopher, is nothing other, and never has been anything other, than a form of religion.[39] The very least we can say is that the conflict in Nantes was drawn along con-

spicuously *ideological* lines and that it arose out of reaction to the surrounding country's Catholicism. Some might find this paradoxical. After
all, it was the relative independence of Nantes' commercial and heavy industrial sectors that made Catholicism a viable rural practice, like
household industry and household agriculture. More, the source of
Nantes' own revival partly lay in the country. So shouldn't we expect har-
mony, not conflict? The answer, I think, is in the necessity of maintaining that degree of independence as a guarantee for the survival of either.
Under the tension created by increasing population pressure, each side
felt their independence threatened by the other, or, in the more
philosophical vein, felt the need to appropriate their own freedom from
the "other." Hence, the population in Nantes' fifth arrondissement
donned Phrygian bonnets whereas countrymen decorated their hats and
coats with the insignia of the Sacred Heart.[40]

Further, regional comparison shows how inadequate are the abstract
notions of "town versus country" or "the rural opposition to the state" in
explaining the violence. The troubles in Orléans on 2 September could
hardly be described as a clash between urban and rural forces – country
people might even have lent a hand. And it was not the whole of Nantes
that was up in arms in late July. Little is heard, for instance, from the artisanal districts in the east end of the city. Now there are those who might
explain that the whole of Orléans and the first, second, third, and fourth
arrondissements of Nantes were not really "urban" or that the fifth arrondissement was in some way the city's "spearhead." (Where was
Orléans?) I cannot see how this could add to the argument for a
rural–urban dichotomy.

The root of contention was neither the "city" nor the "state" but a
pressure of numbers, which had created, in a different manner in each
region, a fear of outsiders. This should become increasingly evident as
we move our attention out of the population centers and into the country.

Collective violence in the Orléanais: pillage, communal rights, and forest strikes

Collective violence in the rural Orléanais was not much more than a
glorified version of the criminal behavior already discussed. It was the
violence of marauding bands of *chauffeurs* (so-called because of their
habit of burning their victims' toes until they revealed the whereabouts of
the presumed hidden hoard). In 1800, 80 persons stood trial in Chartres
for robbery and murder committed in the Beauce, the Sologne, and the
Forêt d'Orléans. Twenty were acquitted and 21 were publicly hanged.
But that did not spell the end of this notorious Bande d'Orgères. In the
spring of 1803, after several murders had been committed on the borders

of Loiret and Seine-et-Oise, a very worried prefect wrote to the minister of justice that "many beggars and vagabonds" had congregated in the Bois de la Muette with plans – according to reports from one of his spies – to *chauffer* a few more farmers. Four to five hundred people are said to have belonged to this band prior to the Chartres hearings. It had its own "judicial code," its own "surgeon," and its own "curé" who married off willing members in elaborate mock ceremony (one more indication of how alien Catholicism was to these people). Beside them, Robin Hood's merry men seem children at play.[41]

Nor was forest outlawry at this scale confined to the first decade of the century. In March 1847, the inhabitants of 15 forest communes plundered the grain barges traveling the Canal d'Orléans. Police and troops were sent in and a number of arrests were made.[42]

These were not everyday events. They were, in fact, rather rare. But they do indicate that it was the poor and the landless in the Orléanais who resorted to collective violence; in other words, a group that was outside the mainstream of the peasant economy even though they owed their origin to pressures created within it. We have seen that the only way the number of properties could increase in the Orléanais was through the cultivation of the marginal territories, the Sologne and the Forêt d'Orléans. There was little or no room for further fragmentation within the more fertile subregions. But we have also noted that almost a generation passed between the surge in migration to the marginal lands in the 1830s and the growth in properties in the 1850s. Those 20 years, between 1830 and 1850, were among the most violent in the Orléanais of the nineteenth century.

The bitterest item of contention, though hardly new, was over communal rights, which, for all intents and purposes, meant the local residents' rights to pasture their beasts on designated land, often at designated times of the year, such as after the harvest. The character of these communal rights is betrayed by the fact that, in French, *terrains communaux* and *terres vaines et vagues* (literally "fruitless and empty lands") were virtually synonymous. Originally communal land had been land not worth contesting. Many would say that the subsequent attack on communal rights arose from a new "bourgeois" ethic of individuality. This might be so, but in itself it explains very little (we are back to the old characterization of peasants as political objects). Roger Dion noted that, in the Loire Country, individual encroachments onto these communal lands had been going on since the end of the eighteenth century and that the main offenders were *often small propertyholders*. The first areas affected were obviously the richest subregions, the Valley and the Beauce. In 1803, 20 cattle dealers sent a petition to the inspector of markets at Paris to protest the fact that the mayors of Loiret had "repealed an exclusive right" by preventing their animals from grazing on the side of the road leading to Paris. In this instance, the national government, in the persons of the inspector and the minister of the interior, came down against the opinion of the local government and of the mayors in particular. The population continued to grow. By the next generation, individual encroachments onto the forest and the less fertile subregions were beginning to have a serious effect.[43]

Most of the major forests in France, owing to a long history of royal appanages, came under the jurisdiction of the national government. It was therefore only natural that the regulations governing forest administration should come under the guise of national law. The Forest Code of 1827 was a response, a short-sighted administrative response, to population pressure. It was passed by the most reactionary ultra-conservative, royalist government of the century (how it could be viewed as a "bourgeois" law is quite beyond me). Nonetheless, it represents one of the most far-reaching legal attacks ever launched against the old communal privileges of the rural population. It involved tightening the restrictions on the gathering of wood and faggot and the pasturing out of animals. One faced imprisonment for the cutting or removal of newly planted trees and for grazing sheep and goats. A variety of offenses brought a heavy fine. One was not allowed to leave the road with cutting instruments, carts, or carriages; it was forbidden to light fires within the forest interior or within 200 meters of the forest limits; authorization was required to set up sawmills within 2 kilometers of the forest or to open lime ovens, brickfields or tileworks, perched houses, woodman's lodges, huts, or sheds within 1 kilometer, or build carpenters' workshops, timberyards, or wood stores within 500 meters. Communes that wanted to maintain their grazing rights had to show titles dating back further than 1676. What is more, each village had to keep its herd separate from the others and every year it had to send in a list of all the animals to the forest inspector. The place of pasture and the roads that could be used were determined by forest agents.[44]

Violence in the Orléanais didn't begin with the Forest Code, but its passage certainly created a pretext for the angry wave of the 1830s and 40s. The very same year that it went into law, 80 hectares of the Duke d'Orléans' woodland went up in flames. The police attributed it to "malevolence." Forest fires increased in scale and number. One of the worst was in April 1834 when 600 arpents, or roughly 300 hectares, were destroyed. Arsonists weren't very picky about their victims; they could be the state, the royal family, or simply private propertyholders, small and large alike.[45]

The immediate cause was, I would say, a combination of physical hardship and harassment. For a while, the administration was entirely opposed to the free removal of wood from the forest but, with the hard winters of the early 1830s, it was obliged to let the poor go in with their wheelbarrows to pick up dead wood, gorse, and heather. After 1835, only indigents registered at their mayor's office were permitted to gather wood, and even they could only take what they were able to carry on their backs. One letter from Bouzy's mayor is probably a fair enough reflection of what was going on in the forest during these two cheerless decades:

I have seen this [forest] administration, trampling underfoot the simplest rules of humanity, pitilessly condemn widows, orphans, the crippled, the old to carry *on their shoulders* from the forest to their cottages – distance, bad weather, poor roads notwithstanding – one miserable bundle of wood or litter. . . . I have seen M. de Wavrechin (a former inspector) demand in his conclusions a fine of 98 francs from sieur Blondeau (Victor) whose two cows had, last November, inadvertently wandered into an eight-year-old tree plantation. Yes, 98 francs! . . . I have seen in the court of petty sessions hundreds of villagers arraigned for forest offenses. The wretches appear covered with rags. On leaving they are resolved to defend themselves, to lay open their profound poverty. They want to say that the offense for which they are accused is insignificant, that the trial was unfair, that the guard bears a grudge against them. But they stutter, the word dies on their lips. . . . They are invariably condemned; the forest agents are always right.[46]

For woodcutters, particularly, the response to punishment was violence. Usually this took the form of intercommunal rivalry where the cutters of one village would attempt to stop those of another from felling their timbers. Exceptionally (as in 1847) it became a strike weapon in the effort to gain a better wage.[47]

Compared with the Nantais, collective violence in the Orléanais proved to be very limited. It occurred almost exclusively among the forest poor who, at this time, had little to do with the peasant economy as such. When the number of properties began to pick up, the violence subsided. But, like the repression that subsequently held down the number of properties in its richest subregions, this control of a violent option was not necessarily to the Orléanais' long-term advantage. To every advance made in population size, the Orléanais inhabitants could only respond with further repression. A strategy of the plebs,[48] one is tempted to say; there is always someone ready to work a willing horse.

Collective violence in the Nantais: Chouannerie

Most recent histories of the rural troubles that occurred in the West between 1793 and 1832[49] make a distinction between Chouannerie and the Vendée Wars. Chouannerie, it is said, was a dispersed kind of guerrilla activity, which recognized no guiding, centralized authority. It was chiefly found in the *bocage* country, north of the Loire. The Vendée Wars, on the other hand, were conducted by well-organized peasant armies. Their main theater was on the south side of the river. Like most such distinctions, what this one gives to simplicity it takes from reality. First, we can, at certain times, identify Chouannerie in the Nantais with the *bocages,* but with the *bocages* of the South (Retz–Vendée) almost as much as with those of the North (the Nantais Plateau). Second, the Vendée Wars were, in truth, only the most sensational aspect of violent activities repeated throughout the whole region and throughout the first 30 or 40 years of the nineteenth century. Because most of the violence was perpetrated by small bands, I prefer to think in terms of "Chouannerie," even though their violence did, in 1815 and again in 1832, take on the proportions of a full-scale Vendée War.

That is not to say that these two years were an exact repeat of Charette's, Lescure's, and Jacques Cathelineau's war. The armies were less organized in 1815 and 1832, and there was no march to the Norman coast in high hopes of meeting a foreign fleet (the hope of foreign intervention was, nonetheless, present). But there are a few parallels worth noting, all relevant to the timing of the revolts. In the first place, all three (1793, 1815, and 1832) occurred within the range of the most serious subsistence crises recorded during this period of intensification. In 1832, we must remember, there was one of the worst cholera epidemics of the century – and remember too that cholera spread fastest in areas with vast supplies of flowing water, areas like the West. In the second place, these revolts started in the spring, not the winter as was the case with most forest violence in the Orléanais. Winter was the season of greatest hardship; it was a likely time of troubles when the motivation was pure physical need. Spring was the season of Catholic festival and of military recruitment; it was a ripe moment to wage ideological battle. And in the third place, each revolt was intimately tied to some important national political development: the Revolution, the Hundred Days, and the Legitimists' offensive against Louis Philippe under the Duchess du Berry. The final objective of these rural rebels was not to rob grain, lower taxes, or add an extra portion to their daily bread; it was to tear down the tricolor from the church steeple.[50]

All this, however, needs to be seen in the context of the whole period. For the main issue really is how the material scarcity experienced at that time could be translated into a *regionwide* strategy designed along the lines of a religious myth (and not into the small local tussles we find in the Orléanais). Religion was more than a cause for soldiers of the Vendée armies. Rural bandits would call upon it. That was the message received in 1809 by one man who had denounced a band that had been robbing houses in the Nantais Plateau: "So it is here that you find the sellers of Christian flesh! You old bugger it's finished!" He escaped with his life, but it cost him dearly in meat and wine.[51]

Chouannerie was considered a threat to "public order" throughout the days of the Empire. And with reason. Troubles are reported in such diverse communes as Maisdon (Sèvre-et-Maine), Pont-Saint-Martin (Retz–Vendée), Les Sorinières (Sèvre-et-Maine), La Chevrolière (Retz–Vendée), La Boissière (Sèvre-et-Maine), Maumusson (the Plateau), Vallet (Sèvre-et-Maine), La Chapelle-Heulin (Sèvre-et-Maine). The southern half of the region does appear to have been the more agitated area, but quite clearly the agricultural type played no significant part whatsoever. Most of these troubles involved no more than wearing the white cockade in public or cries of *"Vive le Roy! A bas l'Empereur!"* But if the police were sent in – or worse still, troops of the line – they were likely to encounter a youth gang armed with sticks, and the mayor could expect a midnight visit. Troubles were commonest during fairs, church meetings – especially religious processions that were frequently cancelled by the mayor or even the prefect – and at recruitment. The events following the recruitment of 1813 read like a dress rehearsal for the Hundred Days. An armed band of roughly 90 peasants gathered in the arrondissement of Ancenis and attacked the garrison at Maumusson, wounding a couple of officers before retreating. An encampment at Vallet, Sèvre-et-Maine, likewise had a small posse to fend off.[52]

If this had been purely political, that is, if the disturbances arose from the conservative opposition to revolutionary government, they should have stopped with the Restoration. They didn't, at least not entirely. The rural population, wrote a mayor from one of the villages in the Vendée *bocages*, felt their king had abandoned them.[53] In point of fact, most of the shots fired from peasant guns during this period seem to have been limited to tax collectors, those of the Retz–Vendée being especially vulnerable (I have found no record of any fatalities). Violence was not an immediate response to the installation of the July Monarch either. The basis of widespread social tension was there all right. One can trace it back to the long-standing mutual fear – or, if one prefers, respect – between the independent commercial (not simply urban) economic sector and the rural (or household) sector – a fear already revealed during the July Days at Nantes. This was a *regional* phenomenon; it didn't exist in the Orléanais. It was a situation in part created, in part exacerbated by the intensification of population pressure. But it was brought to a head by political accident. Fear had led to the establishment of a national guard at Nantes. It resulted in the subsequent demand for the enforced disarmament of the countryside. Disarmament was conducted with the usual sensitivity of governments of that day. Instead of sending in local forces, regular troops were billeted in every corner of the country. Ten and sometimes 20 soldiers would be quartered in a single household. Houses were entered unannounced, arbitrary arrests were made, livestock slaughtered, robbery and even murder committed. Skirmishes had broken out well before the Duchess du Berry's arrival and the formal declaration of a state of siege in June 1832, and they continued long after her arrest in November. In the spring of 1833, the fighting actually intensified. Throughout that year, there were serious clashes between the inhabitants and the army, especially in the northern Plateau area. By 1834, however, this was confined to isolated incidents.[54]

Thereafter, the troubles in the Nantais were small by all accounts. Most of the communes of the region declared their adhesion to the provisional government in March 1848. And even though over the next months there were various reports of increases in "vagabondage," the Nantais faced nothing like the problems of other rural areas in France. A circular from the prefect to his underlings in August 1852 refers to the "four past years of trouble" that could only be expected to disappear slowly. He asked that cabarets be scrutinized for potentially subversive activities. Those were the last shows of violence in the region.[55]

Very little is said, in the documents I have studied, on the participants in collective violence (and this goes for both regions). There are a few references to youth gangs and particularly to youth liable to recruitment. We might contrast this with a list of 29 Chouans, Vendéens, and suspect individuals drawn up in An XII (1803–4).[56] These names look like not much more than a random cross section of the whole of rural society (men only). There are 3 artisans among them (a weaver/cultivator, a cooper, and a farrier's boy), 5 merchants (a cattle dealer and 4 small tradespeople), a cabaretier, one individual "living off his own work," a *fermier*, a well-to-do cultivator, and 17 names with no occupation given at all. Their average age was 35. Only 1 was under 25, 4 were over 45, and almost half of them were between 30 and 34. And bachelors made up more than their fair share. Over half were single; the rest, save 2, had children.

The most striking thing is, again, that there is no regional pattern. Some were residents of the Loire Valley; there were those from north of the river and those from the south, from intensively cultivated subregions as well as the *bocages*. The same kind of uniformity can be verified in other ways. The incidence of those failing to report to recruiting stations – of draft dodgers – is one of them. A list of 111 names sent to the prefect during the 1832 uprising includes 69 from the Nantais. A third of them were residents of Nantes, and about one-sixth came from each subregion (13 from the Plateau, 13 from Retz–Vendée, 11 from Sèvre-et-Maine, 12 from the Loire Valley). Then there are the data for the same period on arms seized by the army. These are not complete – we have only the nominal lists for June and July. The lists are divided into three parts: inhabitants from whom arms and munitions had been confiscated (1,812 names from the Nantais); ex-rebels who had returned to their homes and surrendered their arms (148); and inhabitants with provisional permits to keep their arms (630). A subregional breakdown is presented in Table 9.1, based on the 38 communes for which these lists are extant. The most significant facts are the high proportion of voluntary surrenders in Sèvre-et-Maine, though the absolute number is still small, and the slightly larger proportion of gun permits granted in the Loire Valley than in its neighboring subregions. The list of permits is the only one with the odd reference to the owner's occupation, the commonest of which are councillors, propertyholders, and *métayers*. The reasons given for the permits are that these were trustworhy citizens living in isolated farmsteads or next to a major road (we have noted the high incidence of robbery on the Nantes–Angers road). Finally, it is worth remarking that there were fewer arms seized in the northern *bocages*, the Plateau, than anywhere else![57]

We are now, I feel, in a position to identify intensification with two broad social facts, one economic, the other psychological. In economics, intensification means, quite obviously, an expansion of the areas under cultivation and the fragmentation of landholdings (the relative importance of either depending on the region). In psychology, it carries a sense of threat from the outside; the population develops a fear of the "other." Exactly how a population envisages the "other" depends, to a large extent, on the prevailing mythology because it seems from the evidence so certain that the distinguishing factor in regional collective violence was religion. The presence of the army in the Nantais, in 1831 at least, was the flashpoint of rebellion. Armies, as Richard Cobb shows at marvelous length, create fear.[58] But the rural population was not opposed to armies per se; the enemy lay in what that particular army represented: a band of *étrangers* bearing the devil's banner. In the Orléanais, there was no such uniting myth; there was no, or little, open religion. Where armed forces were present, there was violence, but it was comparatively restrained – and the neighboring subregions remained entirely indifferent.

2. Extension, ca. 1860–1914

When Ardouin-Dumazet visited the West in April 1895, he was struck by the inhabitants' detachment from the violent events of 60 years before.

The Vendée War seems to have been a storm whose memory has been blotted out. To listen to these people, their land was simply a field of action, their fathers were not in any way involved, and they even have the peculiar impression as if the Vendéens' appearance had been an invasion of people from afar.[59]

Time. Foreigners, who in the 1830's had been the immediate object – real or imagined – of fear and hostility, were identified by those living in the 1890s with their own fathers and grandfathers. The "other" had become

Table 9.1. *Approximate number of residents disarmed in the Nantais, June–July 1832*

Subregion	Number of communes disarmed	Number of residents with arms		
		Confiscated	Surrendered	Permitted
Plateau	8	257 (14.2)	0 (0.0)	173 (27.5)
Retz–Vendée	9	420 (23.2)	6 (4.1)	112 (17.8)
Sèvre-et-Maine	9	614 (33.9)	121 (81.8)	122 (19.4)
Loire Valley	12	512 (28.8)	21 (14.2)	223 (35.4)
Total	38	1,812 (100.1)	148 (100.1)	630 (100.1)

Note: Numbers in parentheses are percentages by subregion.
Source: AD Loire-Atlantique 1-M-510 Disarmament – *Etats nominatives.*

a part of the self. In the second half of the nineteenth century, we seem to encounter a novel mentality, where the chief means of defending the peasant economy is association, not violence, where the implicit intention of the population is a rejection of the father so as to place oneself in a better relationship with one's brother: a new means in pursuit of the same end. We cannot pinpoint the date. Attitudes are carried by generations and as long as those who fought the Republican armies remained the preponderant part of the population, their ideas would continue to dominate. The new attitude appears to belong to a generation born in the 1830s and 40s who came of age in the 1850s and 60s. We say this because the economic and social history of the subsequent period tells us there had been a definite change in demographic strategy.

The economy

We have seen that, after about 1870, the number of landed properties began to level off or decline. Population densities followed the same trend, one that had been preceded by a momentary increase in mortality during the Second Empire.[60] The rural economy, and the subjective labor–consumer balance upon which that economy was based, had to undergo some kind of adjustment.

Many characterize the latter years of the century as a time of "agricultural depression." The term is too strong, at least for the Loire Country. It was rather a period when agricultural production was brought into line with the novel demographic situation. True, several at the time spoke of "depression," but this came from the mouths of an earlier generation, from men like Jules Guyot who, in 1868, was still arguing that the primary goal of agriculture was "to produce the most possible, with the most possible men, in the smallest possible space."[61]

Peasants knew better. At bottom, the main development in their economy after 1860 was a growing preference for livestock, especially dairy farming, and the substitution of the older intensive crops with quicker-yielding crops, more adaptable to changing annual economic needs. There was an increasing preoccupation with commodities produced for immediate human consumption. This put wine in less favor, as it did the industrial crops like hemp and flax, whereas root crops and vegetables became more popular.

I have attempted, with a selected group of crops and livestock, to represent this development graphically (Figures 9.1–9.3). It has to be kept in mind that these graphs were drawn from very crude annual estimates, particularly, I would say, in the case of Loire-Inférieure, whose tables are dominated by neat round figures in the thousands and even millions. However, they are the official French governmental statistics, and these were probably the best existing in Europe at that time. They are, without an atom of doubt, a vast improvement over what we have available for the first half of the nineteenth century.[62]

The statistics do seem to indicate that a progressively larger part of the land was devoted to cereals, at least until about 1900 in the Nantais (or really Loire-Inférieure) or a little earlier in the Orléanais (Loiret). Examination of the figures from neighboring departments confirms the trend. There seems also to have been a general decline in the areas of intensive cultivation. Grasslands, on the other hand, became more and more extensive after around 1895. This last development was almost certainly tied to the growth in number of cattle, particularly cows, and horses owned or shared by some of the smallest cultivators. In the Nantais, horses replaced bullock as the foremost draft animals and this was, to a large extent, due to one of the few technological innovations adopted by the population during this period: a new, deep-cutting plow agile enough to be employed even in the vineyards (thus relieving cultivators of the annual time-consuming, back-breaking job of digging out the median between vine rows with spades and shovels).[63]

One question brought to mind is whether livestock and grain were, as some contemporaries thought, the symbols of speculation, rural exodus, and a decadent rural morality or whether, as the German Wilhelm Abel suggests, they were part of a new solution for a continent that had simply run out of cultivable space. I don't think it can be denied that the rural populations in both our regions were taking advantage of what we might call, for better or for worse, a national market. A more integrative spirit, a more cooperative mood, had begun to grip the countryside. A host of historical literature teaches us that this was due to the railway engineers. There must be some truth in this. But it was not just a technological problem. I have shown earlier the enormous delays – up to 20 years in the Nantais – in implementing plans for a railway network. The rail, it

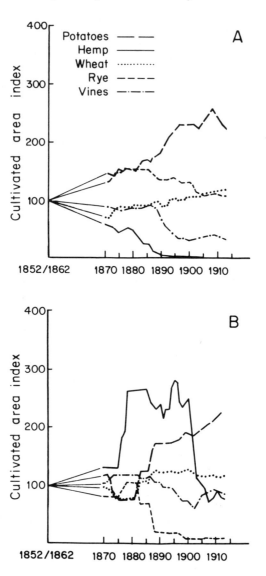

Figure 9.1. Change in cultivated area in (A) Loiret and (B) Loire-Inférieure, 1852–1913.

seems, was not well received by countrymen in the 1840s, whereas their sons in the 1860s probably looked upon it more favorably. (All the same, we have noted that in the less socially cohesive Orléanais local lines never were built.) The production of commodities that could be immediately marketed *needed* a sophisticated system of transportation. The ethical

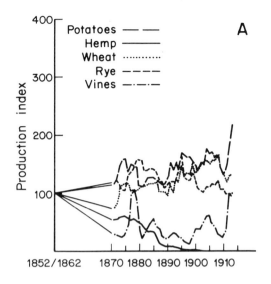

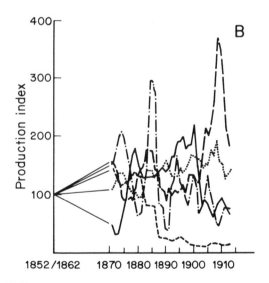

Figure 9.2. Change in agricultural production in (A) Loiret and (B) Loire-Inférieure, 1852–1913.

misgivings over the spread of *les bêtes et les blés,* which one frequently encounters at the beginning of this period (i.e., the 1860s and 70s), were an echo of a generation still convinced that the agricultural solution was further intensification. But the population in general was aware that an optimum had been reached.

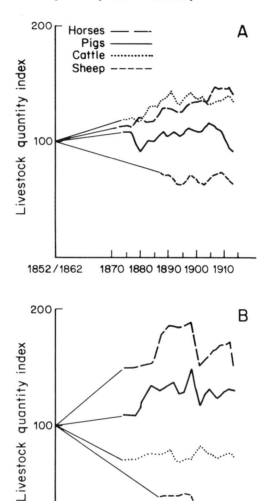

Figure 9.3. Change in quantity of livestock in (A) Loiret and (B) Loire-Inférieure, 1852–1913.

Numbers did not increase for every kind of livestock. Pigs and, from all one can gather, most farmyard animals remained fairly stable. There was a significant drop in the number of sheep because, in the first place, sheep are generally raised, not for their meat, but for their wool, and like hemp and flax, there was less interest in commodities that needed processing. Second, sheep are voracious eaters and a society that is *con-*

scious of land shortages is unlikely to show much forebearance for such beasts.

Let us return a moment to the crops. The contributors to the extension of cereals were wheat (though only to a limited degree), barley, and oats, the latter being primarily used as cattle feed. On the other hand, the cereals that are generally associated with the poorer subregions, such as rye, maslin (a mixture of wheat and rye), and buckwheat fell into decline; in fact, buckwheat did remain an important crop in the least fertile parts of the Nantais. It was not simply a matter of replacing the humble grains for the noble. Root crops made swift advances during the period. The graphs bear this out in the case of the potato. Beets also spread rapidly, especially in the Orléanais after their first appearance in the Beauce in the 1860s. I have already mentioned the retreat of the older intensive crops – hemp, flax, and, most important of all, the vine.

In addition to the change in the cultivator's attitude, one of the major causes of these developments was a plant ecology inherited from the period of intensification. Crowding increases the chances of disease in plants and animals as well as in people. Though one cannot say with any certainty, the contemporary agricultural and newspaper reports do lend credence to the impression that there was an evolution in plant diseases over the course of the nineteenth century. Thus, diseases of epidemic proportions broke out among the intensive crops in the 1830s and 40s. The most serious were fungi of one sort or another, which are, today, connected with cool, humid atmospheric conditions. Probably the best known is the "late blight," which ruined the potato harvests in western Europe in the 1840s and 50s. In 1845 and again in 1846, potatoes were wiped out in several parts of the Nantais. The July drought of 1847 seems to have saved the crop of that year, but in 1849, the harvest was again reduced by a third and, in some cases, a half. Half was lost in 1852 and right through to 1860 agricultural inspectors were referring to the presence of the disease, though by 1858 it was no longer considered serious.[64] Oidium, or "powdery mildew," was the blight's devilish partner working in the vines. Throughout most of the 1850s, the disease was ravaging vineyards. In one letter of September 1857 from the mayor of Couëron to Loire-Inférieure's prefect, it was reported that over half the vines of that commune had been grubbed out.[65]

Part of the cure for fungal infection was a series of hot dry summers in the 1860s. Rural historians like to persuade one another that this was a "golden age."[66] They didn't have to live through it. The years 1861, 1865, and 1869 were particularly rough. "For two months," went a dismal newspaper story at the end of August 1869,

not a drop of water has fallen in many a vineyard beyond the Loire, from its mouth to its source. Moreover, if one takes into consideration that the vine is touched throughout its course, to Lyon, to Marseille - no longer by oidium, but a disease below the soil, due to the presence of an insect which cuts radically into the roots thus killing the precious shrub – one will have some reason to be surprised at seeing rates to this very moment drop while the ailment has remained, to the present, without counterpart. The producing areas are not doing any business.[67]

Dry weather reduced the threat of oidium. It eradicated late blight. But it is difficult to convince oneself that these were the halcyon days later writers like to depict. The years of drought were every bit as grim as the years of rain. This must have been especially true for the small cultivator who relied on intensive crops. Also, by 1871, the accumulated effect of drought on harvests had left, according to reports from the Nantais, animals dying of starvation. Grain growers, perhaps, were at less of a disadvantage. But the blithe accounts so often made about this period are almost certainly an exaggeration.

Note in the preceding citation the reference to a new kind of enemy, insects. Better communications and the opening in the world of new areas of cultivation, principally the western United States, led to the spread of hitherto isolated pests. In the 1870s, potato harvests in the western parts of the Loire Country began to show the effect of the Colorado beetle. This was the small, striped bug that was largely responsible for keeping the level of potato production down in the 1880s and 90s (even though the area devoted to potatoes quite patently increased). We shall have a closer look, in a moment, at the insect – another American import – that chews vine roots for a living.[68]

A series of wet years in the late 1870s brought back some of the fungal diseases and reduced agricultural production in general. Eighteen seventy-nine was considered calamitous. From Nantes:

Very little grain, to the point that our peasants will have nothing to eat in six months; about half the potatoes and carrots are diseased; the vine in such a state that instead of 800 barrels, the average harvest, we will make 30 to 40 perhaps, if the frost sustained before the opening does not render the grape harvest entirely useless; livestock down in all our markets . . . ; in sum, misery or greater or lesser uneasiness everywhere.[69]

Calamitous, yes, but this was not 1812. Peasants did have something to eat after six months. The improved transportation and keen competition, both internal and foreign, that this provoked are generally recognized causes of the 20-odd year recession that followed. But the drop in population came first, by 10, if not 20, years. The recession merely accelerated a trend already in progress. In the Orléanais, the areas cultivated in vine and hemp rapidly diminished, whereas root crops spread. As we would expect, the Nantais proved more resistant. The reduction of vineyards is less apparent, and hemp, having appreciably grown in popularity in the 1870s, remained stable until 1900, when there was a general improvement in agricultural conditions.[70]

Grapes of wrath

In Chapter 6 we found vines occupying, in mid-century, somewhat less than a tenth of our two regions. But, judging from population distributions, one would guess that, at a minimum, one-quarter of the rural families (and several "urban" families as well, especially in Orléans) dedicated at least part of their land to the cultivation of grapes. Given the importance of vines in the French rural economy at large,[71] it is hardly surprising that the pest that destroyed so many of them has come to symbolize the late nineteenth-century agricultural recession. Our figures for the Orléanais indicate a reduction in vineyard surface prior to the spread of phylloxera. Loiret's director of agriculture said much the same in a letter to the minister of agriculture in 1878 when phylloxera still had no appreciable effect on wine production. He attributed the decline to late spring frosts. A tax administrator made a similar remark in a letter of 1892. Comparing the surface recorded in the first cadastre with the results of an 1879 survey, he found that vineyards had already been reduced in Loiret by a full third.[72] We see that in the Nantais, over the same period, the vineyard surface remained stable and even slightly increased. The explanation is simple: the Nantais still had the option of further intensification, the Orléanais did not. And that is what accounts for the very different regional responses to the phylloxera crisis.

Phylloxera is a small, greenish-yellow plant louse indigenous to the eastern United States. It survives by sucking sap from the roots of vines. The great problem in combating it is that, unless the winegrowers are in the habit of unearthing their own vines' roots (few do!), the insect's presence can go undetected from three to anywhere up to five or even six years. By then, it's too late. The vine will rot. This was also the basis of the nineteenth-century enologist's difficulty in tracing the origin and spread of the disease. Phylloxera was first discovered, in France, at the mouth of the Rhône in the departments of Hérault, Gard, and Vaucluse in 1869. Thus it must have been introduced into the country by 1865, at the latest. The general movement from there seems to have been northward to Paris and thence westward.[73]

In mid-September 1876, on the left bank of the Loire just opposite Orléans in a small vineyard, Les Maisons Rouges, a patch, 15 by 12 meters, of yellowing leaves was noticed by the owner, a certain M. Alleaume. The Société horticole was notified, which thereupon set up an investigatory commission. On 22 September, that commission formally declared the existence of phylloxera in the department of Loiret, adding that it had probably been present "for 3 or 4 years but that it has touched as yet no more than 4 or 5 ares of vineyard." A later report from the Académie des Sciences suggested the louse had not come from the Midi but had been carried in American vinestock introduced into the Orléanais by a couple of Prussian gentlemen, Haage and Schmidt, 15 years earlier! (Frenchmen, and especially Orléanais residents, had little love for Prussians in the 1870s.) At any rate, the local government acted swiftly. On 25 November, the prefect ordered a halt to the importation of all vinestock from America and from all areas proven to be infected in France. The village mayors and rural police were charged with the law's enforcement; inspections of agricultural commodities were made in every railway station in the department.[74]

The earliest direct references to phylloxera in the Nantais date from that same year, 1876, when a commission of defense against the pest was established. Seven years later, a report notes that a few vineyards in the departments of Deux-Sèvres and Vendée had been touched, but that Loire-Inférieure and Maine-et-Loire remained unscathed. Subsequent accounts indicate that phylloxera was first detected in the Nantais in 1884, but I have been unable to establish exactly where and when this happened.[75]

Phylloxera in the Orléanais thus had something like an eight-year lead over the Nantais. However, we should not make too much out of the fact. The greatest destruction of vines clearly occurred simultaneously in both regions, that is, after 1885. By 1879, only 5.5 hectares within the communes of Orléans and Saint-Jean-le-Blanc had been found infected, less than a hectare had been razed. In 1881, 44 hectares were reportedly infected and a total, since the discovery of 1876, of 37 hectares destroyed. Thereafter, the full extent of the scourge became evident: 1885, 795 hectares infected, 360 destroyed; 1886, 2,093 hectares infected, 719 destroyed ("this area has increased in considerable proportions" ran the report for that year); 949 hectares destroyed in 1887; 2,447 in 1888; 3,000 in 1889; 5,993 in 1890. By 1900, about 16,000 hectares of vineyard had been destroyed in the department of Loiret, 7,000 to 8,000 in the arrondissement of Orléans.[76] Reports from the Nantais are often conflicting, although they do confirm 1885–95 as the bleakest years. The disease does not appear to have been as destructive as in the Orléanais. The region lost, I would say, 2,000 to 3,000 hectares to phylloxera over these 10 years.[77] Between 1886 and 1889, a fresh outbreak of oidium did not improve matters. One even gets the impression that, in the Nantais, oidium was causing more of a problem for the winegrower than phylloxera.[78]

What solutions could the small winegrower consider? He could leave. Net rates of out-migration (see Figures 7.10–7.11) do not appear to correspond very closely with the decade of crisis. The highest rates of outward movement were after 1895 and occurred in subregions not noted for their viticulture – the Sologne, the Forêt d'Orléans, and the Nantais Plateau. In the detailed regional maps (Figure 7.12), Meung, on the right bank of the Loire west of Orléans, is one of the only winegrowing areas to have registered a significant net rate of emigration between 1881 and 1911. This surely bears out our earlier point: emigration is an option of the last resort. A second possibility was, of course, to find a substitute crop. This is what many Orléanais residents did. Asparagus, artichokes, and French beans were the favorites.

Then there was the option of trying to save the vine. All the possible forms of treatment were known from the time of the phylloxera's discovery. The most impractical remedy specialists were recommending in the 1870s was to flood the vineyards to a depth of 40 centimeters for a period of 40 to 50 days. It would have been impossible for the older vineyards on the hillsides, as terraces were not designed to be used as rice swamps. Even on the flatter lands, irrigation was far too primitive to permit such a technique. The common practice in the 1880s was to treat the vinestock with sulfur. The main problem here was cost; most experts agreed that it would require an outlay of about 150 francs/hectare in order to be effective. Of course, experts counted labor in terms of francs, as did the large vineyard owners of Bordeaux and the Midi. But in the Loire Country, where most vineyards were household enterprises, labor was not a marketable commodity; it had no price tag; it was a matter of personal survival. Chayanov's rule once more: work input in a peasant economy is relative to the internal needs of the family, not to the objective profits reaped from the market. This was one advantage the small winegrower had over the large.

In a recent study of the phylloxera crisis in the Beaujolais region, Gilbert Garrier has shown how the winegrowers' ability to absorb costs resulted in a more egalitarian relationship with the large propertyholders. (This has led him to christen phylloxera "le puceron bienfaisant," which is a little perverse.)[79] In our two regions, large landowners, with very few exceptions, were confined to the pasture- and cereal-type subregions and even there, for similar reasons, they were losing their influence (Chapter 8). Of greater interest is the regional contrast in the effort the winegrower was willing to expend to save his vineyard. This cannot be measured in absolute terms, but one cannot fail to note that the rate at which the vineyard area was reduced in the Nantais was significantly slower than in the Orléanais (Figure 9.1). Further, by 1910, almost as much land was planted in vines in the Nantais as at midcentury whereas the Orléanais was left with about one-third.[80]

Sulfur impeded the spread of phylloxera, it did not destroy it. Certain American vines, not all, native to the eastern seaboard and immune to the pest were what finally saved the French wine industry. The Noah and the Othello were the most important; the Riparia proved to be less effective. By the 1890s, phylloxera was so widespread that there was no longer any fear of importing these plants. In some vineyards – more so in the

Orléanais than the Nantais – American vines simply took the place of the older French stock. But in most cases, the older plants were grafted to American rootstalks. Again, this required an enormous investment in human labor. But more was needed than that. The individual winegrower was in no position, in the 1890s, to buy new vines. It had to be done through association. And this brings us to a social development that goes beyond the borders of the vineyard.

The growth of rural associations

An old anthropological premise is that it was a survival tactic that invented the group. We could certainly say as much for both the Chouans in the 1830s and the agricultural syndicates of the 1890s. (Fellowship and cooperation, the poets have been telling us for centuries, are not devoid of an aggressive impulse.) Only now it was the immediate past, an experience just beyond the pale of living memory, that the cultivator took as the "foreigner"; and, not surprisingly, he began to search among his contemporaries for the ally and friend who would help him achieve his ultimate purpose. The outsider was no longer necessarily an enemy; one was willing to recognize a community of interest. Thus, by the second half of the nineteenth century, popular attitudes had evolved in such a way as to make rural association a representation, or symbolization, of that interest. The tactic had changed, the goal had not.

Rural associations had, in fact, existed in France since at least the mid-eighteenth century.[81] For instance, a *société d'agriculture* was founded in Rennes in 1751 to serve the province of Brittany. According to the dictionary, the first mention of the term *comice agricole* dates from about the same period.[82] Though the idea might have been there, we find no evidence of any such *comice* in existence in our two regions prior to the July Monarchy. In 1836, two *comices agricoles* were founded for the arrondissement of Orléans to serve either side of the river Loire. They were later combined into one. In 1858, the prefect attempted to put through the department's general council a project that would have united the *comices* of Loiret's four arrondissements. The vigorous disapproval of Orléans' *comice* stopped that: "distances were an obstacle to the agriculturists' displacement" that a departmental *comice* would have required. In the Nantais, the *comice agricole* was not such a monolithic institution. The first one founded in the region, so it seems, was that of the canton of Saint-Mars-la-Jaille, in the Nantais Plateau, on 3 May 1836 (or roughly a month before the Orléanais' first two *comices*). By the late 1850s, around half of the cantons in the region had their own *comice*. In addition, a central *comice,* serving the whole department, was established in 1842, and a *comice* for the arrondissement of Ancenis started functioning in 1848.[83]

The membership of these *comices* was limited. Between their foundation and the early 1880s, there does not appear to have been much change in the absolute numbers enrolled. What growth there had been occurred at the beginning of their history, the 1840s and 50s. By 1880, the *comices* claimed a total of about 400 members in the Orléanais, and somewhere between 600 and 700 in the Nantais. The statutes invariably declared membership open to anyone owning or cultivating land within the *comice*'s jurisdiction, along with sons over the age of 21. Probably the annual subscription fees put a lot of the poorer people off: in the early 1880s, 5 francs for the arrondissement of Orléans, 6 francs if you owned property and 5 francs if you were a *fermier* for the arrondissement of Ancenis, 10 francs for the Comice agricole central of Loire-Inférieure. Most of those belonging to a *comice* were what the newspapers of the day – and the historians of our day – would call "notables." That essentially meant big landowners (see Chapter 5) – a poignant fact. For instance, the greater incidence of resident landownership that we have found in the Nantais helps explain why the *comices* were less centralized in this region. It also throws some light on the *comice*'s ruling passion, in the Orléanais, for the Sologne and the Beauce at the cost of ignoring the intensively farmed Loire Valley.

Of course, membership is not necessarily an accurate index of the extent and quality of the *comices'* influence. Many of those who wrote about the formation and growth of rural associations did so in order to place the affairs of farming into the more familiar perspective of the affairs of state, the French state. There is always the danger here of falling into the routine of academic box-building. We know the theme. First, the only political voice heard in the countryside is that of the "notable," the peasant's mediator and, explicitly or not, exploiter. Faced with a variety of challenges on the national political front, the notable is obliged to mobilize his rustic subordinates. The cat is now out of its bag; sooner or later the peasantry will organize their own associations and declare their political color, for the red or for the white. It is the tale of political integration. And it is biased, in that it starts with a historical pattern set by national legislators. And it is manifestly teleological. It has little to do with the social history of the rural Orléanais and Nantais. The small household cultivator had but shallow concern for the activities of deputies in Paris. (In fact, my own travels and conversations in these two regions suggest that, for most rural inhabitants, partisan politics in the mid-1970s – and I am thinking particularly of the 1974 presidential elections – remains subordinate to matters of local interest.) The reason I mention this is that the *comices agricoles* are frequently represented as a voice of reaction, of a selfish political elite. They most certainly were for Léon Gambetta. But for Jacques Bonhomme?

We have luckily been left a complete program of an agricultural show sponsored by the Comice agricole d'Orléans and held at Jargeau on 30 June and 1 July 1878.[84] At night fall, Saturday, 29 June, a peal of bells, a torchlight tattoo, and an artillery salute announced the opening of the festivities. Just in case anyone missed that, another salvo was fired at five o'clock the following morning to the accompaniment of the town band's chirpy reveille. At six, the firemen's company escorted *comice* members to the town hall to shake hands with local officials and then proceed together to church and celebrate high mass. This was followed by an exhibit of machines and instruments at the marketplace and an animal show at Place de la Porte-Neuve. Shortly after that, village bands – coming mainly from the canton or from the communes across the river – gathered at Place du Martroi to begin the music competition. In the meantime, an event that was always the center of attention in a *comice's* show had just started on a plot of land close by the town: the plowing contest. At the same spot, agriculturists and constructors were giving a demonstration of how to handle outside farm implements, and in a neighboring field, a special reaping contest got underway. At eleven, the town offered a lunch to the fireman's companies (again, mostly from the canton) who, after dessert, were given the responsibility of officially welcoming the prefect to town. At two, the formal distribution of prizes took place in a tent set up on, of all places for a festival *aux bords de la Loire,* the boulevard du Saumon. As usual, this began with a speech from the prefect. Betwen 1835 and 1880, the topics of the speech remained monotonously similar. As a matter of fact, anyone attending such a show in the Nantais would have heard, if he had wanted to, roughly the same thing: the *comices* have a very healthy effect on agriculture; immense wealth is derived from this industry; one can almost say that agriculture is the veritable and *unique* (always emphasized) source of wealth; and the government hasn't yet woken up to that fact. This would then be greeted by a hearty "*Vive la République!*" Half past four: a grand concert on the same boulevard given by all the village bands that had participated in the morning's competition. At five, the music awards were handed out, and later in the evening, there was another torchlight tattoo (with the village bands adding a rousing beat), fireworks, and a dance in the largest hall in Jargeau. Monday, beginning with a six o'clock reveille, was left to a series of odd sporting events: a frying-pan race, a masked sack race, a string contest, and, most symbolic of them all, the greasy pole (*mâts de cocagne*). The day ended with yet another tattoo.

Agricultural shows were the *comices'* major contribution to the growing sense of cohesion in the countryside. On paper, they were committed to several other functions, but my impression is that these were not very effective. The *comices* had been founded with the idea – very eighteenth-century, very physiocratic – of promoting a new science and technology in country quarters.

Allons donc, hommes éclairés de toutes les opinions, de toutes les conditions, propriétaires, cultivateurs, agriculteurs, industriels, savants, publicistes, à l'oeuvre! Confondez, dans un même but, dans une même intention, vos lumières, vos travaux et votre argent![85]

Their statutes ambitiously refer to libraries, standing committees on agricultural education, viticulture and forestry, the collective purchase of livestock, and the lending of farm instruments. The measures certainly had some influence. There is evidence, for instance, in both regions of a close working relationship between the *comices* and the departments' primary school inspectors; the *comices'* recommended reading materials were carefully considered in the school system (but this applied more to the university level). Orléans' *comice* played a prominent role in the reforestation of the Sologne. But the impact of all this on the day-by-day drudgery of the rural economy is far from clear. As for the attempts at improving equipment and livestock, *comice* administrators themselves admitted that they carried little weight. The Orléanais statutes explicitly laid out that whatever instruments it lent could be only used as a trial run, limited to three weeks. The Nantais *comices* were, in principle, more lenient. In their applications for government grants, the *comice* secretaries blamed the lack of success in providing equipment and livestock on insufficient funds. That was probably only part of the story. As the anonymous reporter from Ancenis' *comice* noted in 1883, *"fermiers* prefer to receive bounties in money."[86]

The *comices agricoles* were not the only rural associations in existence prior to 1880. The Orléanais *société horticole* was founded in 1839, that of the Nantais as early as 1828. These were highly specialized bodies whose primary purpose was research on plant treatment. We have seen the important part they played in identifying grape phylloxera. There was also the miscellany of local government groups dedicated to agriculture. Again, the Nantais seems to have had the lead here. A *société d'agriculture* was set up in Ancenis in 1820; I have found no counterpart in the Orléanais. To add to this, there were the odd insurance groups – their number, in fact, grew rather rapidly after the disastrous flood of 1856. But none of these organizations had a wide, popular base.[87]

Associations began to appeal with the realization that the old strategies connected with intensification had been absolutely exhausted. The first signal: a surge in migration toward the marginal territories in the 1830s and 40s. The second: the midcentury deceleration and, in the Orléanais, reversal of the secular trend of declining death rates. (Death, we noted in

Chapter 3, can initiate among the survivors a more positive awareness of the problems of intensification; the observed reversal was not very dramatic, but it perhaps exerted an effect.) The third: the lost momentum in the growing number of landed properties. We placed this at the point at which the death rate again started to drop and rural emigration pick up, that is, around 1870. By the 1880s, property growth had halted in all subregions save Retz–Vendée. The fourth: crop disease – the land was beginning to fail.

It was in this setting that the Orléanais and Nantais received news of the famous Association Law of 1884 (permitting the free formation of professional unions, vesting in them civic rights and responsibilities, and requiring no other formality than that their statutes be filed with the government). It is difficult to avoid speculating about the degree to which this law, like that of the Forest Code of 1827 or the various legislative acts concerning the Sologne, was a response to demographic pressures, though pressures of a different kind. To the extent that one is willing to accept that what happened in the Orléanais and the Nantais represented a national experience, we might willingly look upon the association law as the acknowledgement of a new generation's pacific strategy for survival. And I am thinking as much of the urban centers as of the rural hinterlands. For example, in 1886, a union of *compagnons* was organized in Nantes; *instituteurs* set up their own union in 1893; and in 1896, the railway workers formed one.[88] As in the case of collective violence, Orléans' citizens were evidently less inclined to organize themselves. There are, of course, several other factors that led to the passage of the 1884 law, most of which had nothing to do with these two regions. But is it correct to continue stressing "industrialization" (or, as it is now preferred, "modernization") when speaking of the union movement? National and world historians stand to lose touch with the most elementary temperament that pulls men into groups. Local history, less burdened by the need to prove purpose in process, comes closer to it. In the Orléanais and the Nantais, popular associations grew, not out of a "modern consciousness," but out of the mentality and strategy of a population *aware* that its subjectively determined optimum had been reached; the change in population and property trends demonstrates this. And if this is true, it could have happened before – whenever the population attained such a point (though the form of association could have differed).

At any rate, with the 1884 law, a new kind of association came into being, the agricultural syndicate. From the start, this was a popular, locally based organization. It won favor by confining its activities to the fulfillment of some very specific economic needs of the small cultivator. Naturally, once that need was satisfied, the syndicate no longer served a useful purpose, which is why so few attained anything like a permanent foothold in the country. In several instances, the statutes themselves imposed a time limit on the syndicate's existence. Incomplete records make it difficult to establish with any certainty how long the average syndicate functioned. The mean length of life of 6 syndicates in the Orléanais was 9 years; only 2 of them lasted more than 10. By contrast, among 13 syndicates in the Nantais, 6 founded in the late 1880s or early 1890s were still in existence at the outbreak of World War I, 2 others remained active for over 10 years, though 3 were dissolved within 5.[89]

From this meagre sample, we would estimate that, within the communes served by syndicates in the mid-1890s, approximately 1 household out of 10 participated in the Orléanais, 1 out of 6 in the Nantais. The conditions of admission were identical in both regions, with one important exception. In general, anybody who had anything to do with agriculture could become a member: propertyholders, *fermiers, métayers,* and even manufacturers and merchants involved in agricultural commerce. The annual membership fee was rarely more than 1 franc. Besides failure to pay this fee, you could lose your membership *"pour des motifs graves,"* which usually meant bankruptcy, "notorious insolvency," or "misdemeanor by deeds contrary to probity or blemishing honor." The one regional variation in the eligibility of members is closely tied to this issue of morality. Suzanne Berger has shown that the first syndicates in Lower Brittany were organized in meetings that immediately followed Sunday mass. She is speaking of the 1920s, but, given the high rates of church attendance and the proven role of religion in earlier collective movements, it would be reasonable to assume that the same had occurred in the Nantais in the 1880s and 90s. There is, in the Nantais, frequently an article in the statutes requiring members *"être de bonne vie et moeurs."* Some went further than that. Before an irate minister of justice had redrafted the statutes of the syndicate at Vritz, they asked that "members of the association make a point of observing and strive to make those who are under their tutelage observe the sabbath and the days of obligation." And its original title made known that this would be a syndicate serving the "parish" of Vritz, not the "commune."[90]

Thus, in the Nantais, a religious motive is confused with the economic. When we concentrate on the purely economic functions of the syndicates, we find little or no difference between the two regions. Those few who wrote on the subject affirm that the agricultural syndicates of this period were really only glorified boutiques.[91] Again, that was the basis of their success. Their essential purpose was to buy goods in bulk and redistribute them to members. The collective sale of agricultural products remained rare; the only organization I have found specializing in this was a milk cooperative at Fresnay (Retz–Vendée), modeled after the cooperatives of Vendée, Deux-Sèvres, and Charente-Inférieure.[92] At the least, this suggests that collective purchase, not sale, is the first need of a peasant society following a period of intensification. Several syndicates were set up to buy fertilizers that, with the increase in demand that intensification had fostered, had become a thriving business for the tricksters. (A good number of cultivators discovered that sawdust does little to enhance the potato.) In the Orléanais, a syndicate was established to buy and rent agricultural machines (the Syndicat d'industrie agricole d'Orléans). The Syndicat des agriculteurs de la Loire-Inférieure performed a similar task, among others, in the Nantais. But by far the most important undertaking of the agricultural syndicates was to help preserve the oldest of the intensive crops, the vine. They would buy new vine stock, they would buy the tools necessary for grafting, and they would set up demonstration vineyards within their constituencies. To describe the syndicate as a grass roots committee is too much of an anachronism. But it had a popular base. For example, the Syndicat viticole de Saint-Denis-en-Val (Loire Valley, Orléanais) divided their commune into five sections, which elected their own *chefs de section* responsible for delivering the commodities bought by the syndicate. In the 1890s, the French government started distributing funds to aid in the purchase of American vines. It was done in a pretty unsystematic manner. Most often, money was allocated by department and then redistributed to the syndicates that were actually responsible for the purchase. But, at times, it was granted directly to the syndicates (this led to splendid bureaucratic fuddles within the ministry of agriculture giving rise, among other things, to a new term, the *superficie syndiquée* – useful for a minister, meaningless in reality). What the documents do make clear is that it was the syndicates that acted first, through petitions, and not the government.[93]

So much for the regional similarity in the syndicates' economic function. I already suggested that the Nantais' Catholicism had a rallying effect on the syndical movement not to be found in the Orléanais. Greater participation is indicated directly by the documents on syndicates, indirectly by the fact that the area devoted to intensive crops, especially wine, did not decline nearly as much as in the Orléanais. Religion, I have said earlier, means politics. But, as in the case of collective violence, we should not fall into the trap of immediately trying to fit this into the national political grid. Local government officials were aware of that. Political commentary on the syndicates is commoner in the Nantais than the Orléanais, but it is couched in terms such as those used by Loire-Inférieure's procureur de la république when describing the Syndicat des agriculteurs de la Loire-Inférieure: "The syndicate passes for concerning itself strictly with politics in the department. This action is certainly pursued, but in an indirect way which is very difficult to apprehend." Or, the

Syndicate agricole de Carquefou: "This syndicate, though mainly composed of reactionary elements, does not seem to aim at busying itself with politics."[94]

Of the two regions, it was again in the Nantais that the most divisive political event of the second half of the century occurred. It revolved around the legal uncertainties regarding the proprietors' and *colons'* rights in the *vignes à complant*.[95] Both had been acting under differing assumptions that the vineyards were, de facto, their property: the proprietors because it was land rented out in kind, the *colons* because they worked the land *and* had the right to pass the object of their labor, the vines, on as an inheritance. In a society that understood property within a temporal framework, that stressed the lineal rather than the material dimension of family enterprise (Chapter 8), the *colons'* way of thinking made a lot of sense. Figure 9.1 shows that the area cultivated in vines began to decline around the middle of the 1880s. At that moment, the *colons* began asking for aid from the proprietors in reconstituting their vineyards as joint owners. Technically (at least from the point of view of an 1800 opinion of the counseil d'etat), the *colons'* "lease" expired with the vine. Or did it? A court had ruled in 1817 that the destruction of vines during the recent Vendée War could not be used as grounds for cancelling the contract *à complant*. There was thus a legal precedent in favor of the *colon* faced with the fortuitous destruction of his vines (though note: not legal protection within the strict context of French law).

Enter the politicians. In 1891, Charles Brunellière, a shipowner at Nantes and leader of the socialist (Guesdist) party in Loire-Inférieure, rented a house and a plot of land in the commune of Le Pallet (Sèvre-et-Maine) and immediately set about forming a syndicate for "*colons,* agricultural workers, [and] exceptionally proprietors of *vignes à complant* possessing no more than one hectare" to serve Le Pallet and two neighboring communes, Maisdon and La Haie-Fouassière. By the end of the year, the syndicate claimed 165 members, and two years later, almost 300. Brunellière in the meantime went trekking about the region to drum up more support. A *colon* syndicate was founded in Le Landreau in January 1892, and a year later another was set up at Vallet. In 1892, Brunellière had collected, purportedly, 2,000 signatures for a petition to the chamber of deputies demanding that, were the working partnership between proprietor and *colon* to break down, the land should be divided equally between the two. The chamber did nothing. Political lines were hardening.

A prefectorial report of 1894, though like any other subject to question, indicates that proprietors in the 1880s had been conciliatory, had, in certain instances, offered half the land, or had proposed various projects to reconstitute the vineyards. We do know that when the good sieur

Bonneau, in February 1889, ripped out all the vines from his 4-are plot his proprietor, De Cantrie, did nothing. When Bonneau harvested a crop of potatoes in 1890, De Cantrie again did nothing. Bonneau started replanting vines in January 1892. De Cantrie still did nothing. But with half the field replanted De Cantrie stepped in and forbade his *colon* the right to continue cultivating. The case went to court in 1895. Bonneau was not without legal defense, for down from Paris came the crack lawyer and newly elected socialist deputy of the Seine, Alexandre Millerand. The court, however, ruled that the *colon* had no rights to the soil and that the length of his lease was tied to the life of the vine; not even replantation could preserve the contract.

Brunellière drafted a second petition demanding that the chamber rescind the conseil d'état's decision of 1800, that it recognize the vineyards as transferable property of the *colon* as much as of the proprietor, and that it require the proprietor to negotiate with the *colon* any changes within the terms of contract (henceforth to be regarded as a concession in perpetuity). After much lobbying in Paris involving Millerand along with a few other well-placed deputies and finally with the intervention of the minister of agriculture a law was passed in November 1897 granting the *colons* the right to replant their vineyards without forfeiting the lease.

As I have already indicated, it was at about this point in time that the government began providing funds for the purchase of American vinestock. With the cultivators thus satisfied that their livelihood had been maintained, the syndicates returned to their role as boutiques. In the Orléanais, that is all they ever had been, the vast majority acting as distributors of vine plants. But syndicates in the Nantais had passed through a political phase in their development, that is, the population had shown, as it had in the first half of the century, a tendency to express its needs and interests in ideological terms. The fact that it happened is, in my view, more interesting than whether their ideology should be judged, today, as "progressive" or "backward," "democratic" or "reactionary," "modern" or "premodern." The Syndicat des propriétaires de la Loire-Inférieure, founded in 1895 by Yves Guitton, a notary at Nantes, to counter the *colon* syndicates of Sèvre-et-Maine, began losing members almost as soon as the 1897 law had been passed. It ceased to meet after 1905, and in 1908 it was officially dissolved. On the other hand, the *colon* syndicates combined in 1899 into the Union des syndicats de colons des vignes à complant et agriculteurs de la Loire-Inférieure, which would boast of a membership of 1,140. Again, its main business was to provide economic services. However, we find it sending delegates to the Congrès de la Fédération Socialiste de Bretagne at Lorient (Morbihan) in December 1903. In 1905, a republican Société des agriculteurs de la Loire-Inférieure was established "to compete with the reactionary Société d'agriculture de la Loire-Inférieure" (the former Comice central founded in 1842). It won a good following, as was demonstrated by its first agricultural show held in 1906. We could go on. Sometimes it is very difficult to tell what was the political color of a given syndicate. For instance, the Syndicat vinicole des propriétaires du Landreau et des communes voisines (a "society of small winegrowers") was an affiliate of the Société des agriculteurs, but its demands for greater import controls, the suspension of sugaring wines, and the provision in its statutes that all members "be in full possession of their civil rights" are more in line with the conservative Société d'agriculture. What matters is not the political side that these syndicates took but the presence of an ideological language well adapted to the singular religious mythology and high degree of social integration that had been the region's tradition throughout the nineteenth century[96]

The last three chapters have shown how, over the course of the nineteenth century, the rural populations of the Orléanais and the Nantais reacted to the pressures inherent in an economic strategy of intensified production in which the household continued to play a significant role. We have seen that, toward the end of the Second Empire, the trend began to reverse itself as the rate of increase in the number of smallholders leveled off and as more cultivators abandoned the older intensive type of crop for a quicker-yielding kind and for pasture farming. In this chapter, I have suggested that these two phases of economic development are reflected in the contrast in behavior between the first and second halves of the century. The contrast itself is rather easy to describe; no one could deny the violent character of the first half of the century or the growth of associations in the second. It is much more difficult to draw the possible links between those differences in behavior and the measurable structural changes that occurred in population and property. But the coincidence between violence and intensification and between association and what we have called extension is too great to be ignored. The regional distinction, observed in both periods, between the organized, ideological stance of the Nantais' population and the more immediate material demands of the Orléanais' population is also quite striking. Let me now attempt to bring these various factors together.

Conclusion: *Plus ça change . . .*

"The only advice I can give my successor," Napoleon is reputed to have told Ney in 1814, "is to change nothing in this country save the sheets of my bed."[1] Sheets were changed aplenty during the 100 years separating the abdication at Fontainebleau from the battle of the Marne. But, for all that, the young man of the Loire Country who went off to fight in Joffre's army left a village that would have been easily recognized by one of Napoleon's recruits. How much change had there been? And what exactly remained?

The essential development had been the midcentury shift in demographic strategy. Earlier I noted the difficulty in specifying a date; the new attitude was not adopted overnight, it was born in the minds of a generation that came of age during the Second Empire. We defined that new attitude as a change in the approach to resolving social tensions that originated within the peasant, or household, economy. Most of those tensions, we assume, never found dramatic enough expression to merit recording. The researcher works with fragments of information, the tip of an iceberg.

To help delineate the massive, complex structure that rests submerged, we made use of a theory derived from the work of anthropologists and economists who have been confronted with a similar problem. Classical market theory is not appropriate for the study of peasant economies because the principal motive for production is not economic profit but a subjective rationale that balances effort against need. In Chapter 3 we presented a reformulation of Alexander Chayanov's notions of a peasant economy that took into account intensive agricultures of the kind found in France. Beginning at the microeconomic level, we noted that the subjective decision making of the peasant household resulted in higher optimums of work intensity than in a market economy because the amount of effort that goes into production is relative to the internal needs of the family and not the absolute variables of the marketplace. A peasant agricultural crisis exists when that subjectively determined optimum level has been passed, when effort can no longer satisfy need. We noted four ways in which a household economy can break out of such a situation: (1) further intensification, which is possible to the degree that alternative means of supplementing the family income are available; (2) an increase in mortality; (3) the adoption of preventive checks on population growth such as emigration or contraception; and (4) cooperation between producers to limit costs.

280

Looking from a macroeconomic angle, we noted the importance of towns, though we showed that, although the economic initiative often comes from the countryside, the relationship between urban and rural sectors is not necessarily mutual. In fact, we questioned the utility of the concept of an urban sector. In the case of Nantes, we found a divided "urban" economy with one part directed toward external commerce, the other based on ties with the hinterland. Orléans had a more singular type of economy; it relied almost entirely on its hinterland.

The different sectors, in combination, define the economic environment or, if you will, the limitation on the choices that the rural household has available. To get an idea of what those limitations actually were in the Orléanais and the Nantais, we were obliged to consider all those sectors of the economy that were indispensable for the survival of the household as a producing unit. This led us to begin our analysis of the regions with a study of their principal cities. Nantes' dual orientation is reflected in the fact that its major industries included naval and machine construction, which brought about the formation of little cities within the city, and a chain of foodstuff enterprises that took advantage of both its links with the hinterland and overseas. The existence of a sector in Nantes that was essentially outside the rural economy was of enormous benefit to the inhabitants of the countryside because it left them the option of developing rural trades not taken over by the city. This encouraged a degree of exchange between communities in the Nantais that one does not seem to have witnessed in the Orléanais – the fact that the Nantais, by the beginning of this century, had over twice as much navigable waterway and one and a third as much railway as the Orléanais should not be forgotten. The household economy made the centralization of certain stages in the processing of food an unviable proposition for both cities; efforts to build central abattoirs and *halles au blé* in Nantes and Orléans met ultimate failure. But Orléans, being more dependent on its hinterland than Nantes, did manage to corner the major share of the region's textile and vinegar industries (though we saw that these were primarily artisanal enterprises, even within Orléans). The Orléanais rural household was therefore left with fewer options than the Nantais, which led, we argued, to a significantly greater sense of isolation.

This was first indicated to us by a study of some of the more articulate members of rural society, the large landowners, the *curés*, and the *instituteurs*. An analysis of landowner residence confirmed Orléans' dependence on its hinterland. Two out of every five large landowners in the Orléanais lived in Orléans at the time the first cadastre was drawn up (1822–37). At that time, only about one-third of the Orléanais' landowners lived on their holdings, which is to be contrasted to twice that proportion in the Nantais. The number of resident landowners did increase with the agricultural improvements in the Sologne after 1850. All the same, long leases and high rents indicated that Orléanais landowners were more interested in a fixed return from the land than in any direct involvement in its management, leaving that largely to local initiative. An analysis of the contrasting social situations of *curés* and *instituteurs* in the two regions brought to the fore the relative isolation of the Orléanais' countryside. In the Nantais, the intellectual chief was the *curé*, whereas in the Orléanais, it was, if anybody, the *instituteur*, though he never possessed anything like the prestige of the Nantais' *curé*. Neither *curé* nor *instituteur* could exert much influence in the Orléanais because the region failed to develop any common religious or political cause. Belief systems followed the whims of each relatively isolated community and were to a large degree independent of both church and school. We would agree with Gabriel Le Bras: the Orléanais was more pagan than enlightened.

In addition to such contrasts between the two regions, we considered the differences existing within them because these also affected the range of options available to any given community. By studying the spatial distribution of crops, livestock, and the like, we were able to get a rough idea of production possibilities within each of the geographic subregions. This enabled us to identify three agricultural "types," intensive, cereal, and pasture. However, we found no simple relationship between agricultural type and social structure. A case in point is the discovery that textile manufacture was relatively more important in the intensive-type subregions of Sèvre-et-Maine and the Nantais' Loire Valley than in the pasture-type subregions; in his study of the neighboring region of southern Anjou, Charles Tilly found the reverse.

That is not to underrate the important intraregional differences we detected in population and propertyholding patterns. Multiple households were somewhat more frequent in the pasture-type subregions of both the Orléanais and the Nantais than in the more intensively cultivated and more densely populated subregions, especially the valleys. Retz–Vendée, a pasture-type subregion of the Nantais, showed a pattern of growth in smallholdings that, although not nearly as dramatic, had some similarity with the form of property growth witnessed in the Sologne. Larger proportions of property were exchanged between relatives in subregions of high agricultural intensity than in subregions of low intensity. But, generally, social and economic patterns within subregions of a given agricultural type differed according to the region. There did not occur, for example, in Retz–Vendée and the Nantais Plateau, the same very high death rates of the first half of the century as were to be found in the Sologne and the Forêt d'Orléans. And although the fall in the death rate did ease off in the intensive-type subregions of the Nantais during the middle decades, this was nothing compared with the rise in mortality in the Orléanais Valley and, most especially, the Beauce. In the Orléanais, it was the pasture-type subregions that experienced the highest rates of net in-migration; in the Nantais, it was the intensive type. The greatest increase in the number of smallholdings took place, in the Orléanais, in the Sologne, a pasture-type subregion, whereas in the Nantais it occurred in Sèvre-et-Maine, an intensive-type subregion. Median property size actually increased in the Sologne and the Forêt; it declined in the Nantais Plateau and Retz–Vendée. And we saw that collective violence was limited, in the Orléanais, to the poorest inhabitants of the Forêt, whereas in the Nantais, it spread throughout the region.

All these facts confirmed a wider range of options open to rural households in the Nantais than in the Orléanais. It was, in other words, easier for the Nantais household to find that delicate equilibrium between, on the one hand, the self-imposed drudgery of work, production, and creation and, on the other, the satisfaction of its needs. Of the four major ways of breaking out of a crisis situation, the Nantais inhabitants had the possibility of choosing further intensification because alternative means of supplementing household income were available. Higher mortality rates and preventive checks on population growth were more an aspect of Orléanais society. And whereas rural cooperatives were to be found in both regions, they appeared to play a greater part in the lives of the Nantais inhabitants than of those of the Orléanais.

Through the dry statistics of nominal lists and civil registries, we can catch a glimpse of social ties within the rural household, the heart of the peasant economy: the mother–child bond, the sexual bond, the economic bond: need against work. Still dryer, still more voluminous statistics collected from the cadastre show us how that balance was maintained within the specific context of a peasant economy, the exploitation of the land – in this sense it is a unique source that deserves further study.

We suggested that bonding, at least inasmuch as it applied to the structuring of a peasant household economy, was weaker in the Orléanais than in the Nantais. A weaker mother–child bond, in this sense, is implied by a more extensive use of wet-nursing in the Orléanais and the earlier age at which children left the home. We also noted an apparent unwillingness, to be contrasted with the Nantais, to adopt children permanently – once the main drudgery of infant care had been completed, the child was returned to his mother's home. In the Nantais, on the rarer occasions that an infant was put out to another household, it was often permanently adopted into its new home. Weaker economic bonds are suggested by the shorter transitional periods in the Orléanais life cycle, particularly the period of adolescent apprenticeship in a separate family's household. This is important because these transitional occupants provided a kind of buffer around the family nucleus, permitting a flexibility in the economic operations of the household. In the Nantais, the transitional periods were significantly longer.

But property ties between kin may have actually been stronger in the

Orléanais. We estimated that about half the land exchanged in the Orléanais over the course of the century was between persons carrying the same name. In the Nantais, this accounted for approximately one-third. There is, then, a possible negative relationship between the biological bonds of the family and the property ties between kin. This would, in effect, be saying that agricultural intensity, as it approaches an optimum level, forces the adoption of controls that tend to weaken family bonds but, at the same time, strengthen the direct influence of families over the distribution of properties. That would help explain the more materialistic attitude of the Orléanais' inhabitants.

Another effect of demographic controls is a limitation on the amount of variation in the social and economic behavior of the populations. Measures of variance are often more significant than measures of central tendency. Our interest is less in how the average individual behaved than in the breadth of choices that the individual had before him. We have noted consistently lower variations in behavioral patterns in the Orléanais than in the Nantais. This came out most clearly in our regional comparisons of household structure, where the tendency for the Nantais was to fluctuate over time, whereas the Orléanais followed a more "disciplined" line of historical trends. Thus, the proportion of multiple households in the Orléanais, lower than the Nantais to begin with, showed indications of decline over the century, whereas in the Nantais, there appeared as many upward turns as downward. The mean household size in the Orléanais declined; in the Nantais, it simply varied until the last decades of the period when it, too, began to decline. The Orléanais, throughout the period, showed a significantly narrower distribution of children against the age of the household head than the Nantais. The number of household members outside the conjugal family unit was also generally lower in the Orléanais and showed less variation. Finally, there was the uninterrupted fall in the Orléanais' birth rate; in the Nantais, this trend was twice reversed, in the 1830s and the 70s.

We also saw that the controlled variation of household structure led, paradoxically, to a haphazard patterning of the life cycle when rural households were compared. The household maintained its rules of structure, which were pretty strict, especially in the Orléanais, but these rules did not yield predictable family cycles. The structure was, therefore, at once mightily constrained and at enormous liberty. The individual, at each stage of his life, had to follow certain rules of action that, when combined in group form, lent a suppleness to rural society at large giving it the means to absorb various changes in the environment. This was how rural society in the Orléanais and the Nantais – our imperfect peasant economy – managed to maintain its essential features over a period that most social historians would say was unstable at the very least. Preservation of the peasant household was the system's ultimate aim.

The first sign that the old strategy of intensification was failing to meet this goal was the increase of migration, in the 1830s and 40s, to the marginal territories. The population was at that time exerting a preventive check to avoid an agricultural crisis that would severely upset the household economy. More serious still was the reversal that occurred in the death rates of the 1850s and 60s. By the first and second decades of the Third Republic, the rural populations of the Orléanais and the Nantais had embarked on a new strategy of extension: the number of small-holdings declined and their size was extended (at least in the Nantais where fragmentation proper had occurred), new crops were adopted, dairy and pasture farming became more popular, rural emigration increased (though not as dramatically as some have suggested), and major strides were made in the cooperative movement. Put in more schematic, and hence simplistic, terms, by the last quarter of the century, the rural populations were following the third and fourth ways of preventing themselves from surpassing optimum levels of intensity (through the adoption of preventive demographic checks and cooperation) rather than the first two (through further intensification and an increase in mortality).

Many anthropologists and rural sociologists have observed the tendency of peasants to distinguish between outsiders and insiders, "them" and "us." I suggested in Chapter 9 that this sort of distinction was made in the minds of the residents of the Orléanais and the Nantais. But the object or, more correctly speaking, the "signified" in that distinction changed with time. During the period of intensification, the outsider was immediate and present in the form of brigands or in the form of armies; he was tinder for the flames of violence that so frequently flared in the first half of the century. In the period of extension, the outsider lay in the past. If I say the rural population developed a historical sense, I mean that it developed a feeling of mission; the population opened up and showed a willingness to court with those whose intentions would formerly have been held suspect. All populations have some historical sense. But here we are speaking of a particular kind, one that rejects the past or at least recognizes that one's daily habits are not identical with those of one's immediate ancestors. This, I believe, is part and parcel of the willingness to fraternize with a stranger. It is one aspect of the cooperative option that was finally pursued once intensification and the various tactics pertaining to it were deemed exhausted.

So, further intensification, higher rates of mortality, conscientious population control (contraception, migration), and cooperation were the options open to a peasant society when faced with an agricultural crisis of the type described in Chapter 3. The history of the Orléanais and the Nantais does indicate a similar chronological order as one option was chosen over another. But let's not be dogmatic. Suzanne Berger's interesting analysis of Breton associations in the twentieth century[2] suggests a very loose connection between the structure of local grouping and socioeconomic conditions. Berger, in looking at the various options open to group leaders, shows how the actual one chosen is more a matter of historical accident than of any deeper cause. But should we follow Berger in limiting that freedom to political elites? Obviously, I think not. The statistics show, the verbal accounts of land development, of violence, of association show the enormous role that chance played in the evolution of our two rural societies. The documents point to the existence of a freedom based on an opposition that I already referred to within the narrower context of family structure, *id est,* between the ordered vision that the individual has of his own experience of time and the disordered vision of the group in which he is to perform. Groups are the creation of necessity. In the same chapter I showed that the freedom exercised in group formation is the issue of repression. We are back to the Chayanovian labor–consumer balance, though now it has a broader meaning than it had at the outset of our work.

Association was not a discovery of the late nineteenth century, nor is it unique to peasant society. The distinctive aspect of that society, and the one we concentrated on in this study, is its basis in household agriculture. For further refinement of the term "peasant," we had to take a look at the socially acceptable range of alternatives that could be employed to maintain that form of agriculture. Peasant society needs a market, but even in the most intensively cultivated parts of the Loire Country, it was demographic pressure rather than the rules of the market that determined what would be planted, whether livestock should be preferred to cultivation, or vice versa. Cottage industry and wage labor supplemented household income, but in neither region did they ever become the predominant activity.

I have continually stressed the impossibility of mapping out all the alternatives considered, but our analysis has given an idea of the breadth of the range. Further, the examination of the cadastre showed how very well that household economy had been maintained (and, my own impression of agriculture in the Loire Country today, rural sociology notwithstanding, is that it still has a long way to go before it will pass for another "capitalist" – "modern"? – Middle West).

What factors determine the alternatives available? This study consistently showed space to be a more important variable than time: the dual base of Nantes' economy against Orléans' near total reliance on its hinterland; the greater homogeneity of Nantais society against the psychological isolation of Orléanais society; the greater variability in Nantais family structure and the longer transitional periods in the individual's life cycle than in the Orléanais. Social bonding appears to have been stronger in the Nantais, but it was also a region of youth, of extended youth, and a region that turned tension and conflict outward into ideology.

I am not denying that there was change. But I do feel historians, particularly specialists of the last two centuries, have spent too much of an effort trying to prove change, at the cost of ignoring what has been constant, what remains of our past – of blinding themselves from evidence that this is not a world we have lost, obliterated. I am not, either, advocating nostalgia. Their lives were no more, no less poetic than our own; they were hardly more noble, but I cannot vouch that they were more dishonorable. Nor were they more miserable. There is evidence of a freedom derived from that constant, a freedom of action and thought far greater than many of the more stalwart proponents of change would ever be willing to admit.

If we must designate a first cause, it is not economic, it is not political, but that enigmatic fact of identity or similarity once known as "culture."

Notes

Chapter 1. Aims and scope

1. For good summaries on this question see Tom Kemp, *Economic Forces in French History* (London, 1971), pp. 155–213; Claude Fohlen, "The Industrial Revolution in France, 1700–1914," in *The Fontana Economic History of Europe: The Emergence of Industrial Societies, Part I,* ed. Carlo M. Cipolla (London, 1973), pp. 7–75; and François Caron, *An Economic History of Modern France* (New York, 1979). One ought to note that, since I began this study, it has become increasingly evident to economic historians, on both sides of the Channel, that France was not "backward." See, for example, Patrick O'Brien and Caglar Keyder, *Economic Growth in Britain and France, 1780–1914* (London, 1978).

2. Such is the case of Maurice Agulhon's comprehensive works on the department of Var, *La Vie sociale en Provence intérieure au lendemain de la révolution* (Paris, 1970b), and *La République au village* (Paris, 1970a); Philippe Vigier's *La Seconde République dans la région alpine* (Paris, 1963b), 2 vols; and the still earlier work of Paul Leuilliot, *L'Alsace au début du XIXe siècle, 1815–1830* (Paris, 1959–60), 3 vols. Ted Margadant's *French Peasants in Revolt: The Insurrection of 1851* (Princeton, 1979), though primarily concerned with politics, is the best recent publication I know in English on rural France prior to the Second Empire.

3. For example, Placide Rambaud and Monique Vincienne, *Les Transformations d'une société rurale: la Maurienne (1961–1962)* (Paris 1964); Michèle Dion-Salitot and Michel Dion, *La Crise d'une société villageoise: "les survivanciers," les paysans du Jura français (1800–1970)* (Paris, 1972); Patrice Higonnet, *Pont-de-Montvert: Social Structure and Politics in a French Village, 1700–1914* (Cambridge, Mass., 1971), which is a jewel. Two regions of the Massif Central have been scrutinized in Jean Merley, *Histoire de la Haute-Loire de la fin de l'Ancien Régime au début de la Troisième République* (Le Puy, 1974), 2 vols; and Alain Corbin, *Archaisme et modernité en Limousin au XIXe Siècle* (Paris, 1966). Even Eugen Weber's survey, *Peasants into Frenchmen: The Modernization of Rural France, 1870–1914* (Stanford, 1976), devotes an undue amount of attention to the backcountry, which, though useful for his thesis, does lead to some distortion; see Maurice Agulhon's review, "Frenchification of France," *Times (London) Literary Supplement,* 6 May 1977. A more statistical approach is taken in William H. Newell, *Population Change and Agricultural Development in Nineteenth Century France* (New York, 1977).

4. For a recent affirmation, on a cross-national basis, of the tenacity of cultural values in the face of "industrialization," see Frederick C. Fliegel, "A Comparative Analysis of the Impact of Industrialism on Traditional Values," *Rural Sociology,* XLI (1976), pp. 431–51.

288

5. Teodor Shanin, *The Awkward Class* (Oxford, 1972).
6. For an overtly anti-Marxist commentary, published during the Cold War, see David Mitrany, *Marx against the Peasant: A Study in Social Dogmatism* (Chapel Hill, N.C., 1951). Michael Dugget, "Marx on Peasants," *Journal of Peasant Studies,* II (1975), pp. 159–82, goes out of his way to paint a more sympathetic picture of Marx's attitude but arrives at more or less the same conclusion.
7. Two recent examples of a Marxist approach to the peasant question are those by Robert Brenner, "Agrarian Class Structure and Economic Development in Pre-Industrial Europe," *Past and Present,* LXX (1976), pp. 30–75; and William Roseberry, "Rent, Differentiation and the Development of Capitalism among Peasants," *American Anthropologist,* VII (1976), pp. 45–58.
8. H. H. Gerth and C. Wright Mills, eds. and trans., *From Max Weber* (Oxford, 1958), p. 192.
9. Karl Polanyi, "The Economy as Instituted Process," in *Trade and Market in the Early Empires,* eds. K. Polanyi, C. M. Arensberg, and H. W. Pearson, (Glencoe, Ill., 1957), chap XIII.
10. For Weber's views on social stratification and class structure, also see *The Theory of Social and Economic Organization* (New York, 1947), chap. IV.
11. Ralf Dahrendorff, *Class and Class Conflict in Industrial Society* (Boston, 1959).
12. Gerth and Mills, eds. and trans., *From Max Weber, p. 180.*

Chapter 2. The Loire Country

1. F. Lebrun's anthology on the Loire Country includes within the area all the old provinces of Maine, Anjou, the Touraine, and Orléanais (François Lebrun, ed., *Histoire des Pays de la Loire* [Toulouse, 1972]). We would add the Breton Comté de Nantes (the present department of Loire-Atlantique) for reasons that should become clear in the text.
2. Hilda, Ormsby, *France: A Regional Geography* (London, 1950), p. 6.
3. The following paragraphs are largely drawn from Edouard Bruley, *Géographie des pays de la Loire* (Paris, 1937); Roger Dion, *Le Val de Loire* (Tours, 1934); L. Gallouédec, *La Loire: étude de fleuve* (Paris, 1910); and Jacques Gras, *Le Bassin méridional: étude morphologique* (Rennes, 1963).
4. The avoidance of needless mention of minor towns and villages has meant that the boundaries described in the text are not very precise. The geological map (Figure 2.1) gives much better detail.
5. Bruley, *Pays de la Loire,* pp. 118–19.
6. The two geological regions provide a basis for Tilly's contrast in southern Anjou: the Mauges, centering on Cholet, is part of the Massif Armoricain and the 'Saumurois" is still in the Paris Basin; Charles Tilly, *The Vendée* (Cambridge, Mass., 1964).
7. In 1957 the name of the department was changed to "Loire-Atlantique." However, because this is a nineteenth-century history, it will be less confusing to continue to refer to the department as "Loire-Inférieure."
8. A. Bachelier and A. Vince, *Histoire et géographie de la Loire-Atlantique* (Rennes, 1961), p. 8.

9.   Geological descriptions of Loire-Inférieure can be found in Bachelier and Vince, *Loire-Atlantique,* pp. 7-22; and André Ferré, *Les Marges méridionales du Massif de l'Ouest: Poitou, Pays Vendéens, Basse Loire* (Paris, 1929).

10. Dion, *Val de Loire,* p. 454; Michel Gruet, "Avant l'histoire," in *Pays de la Loire,* ed. Lebrun, p. 53.

11. The present motorway connecting Paris to the South, the *Autoroute du Sud* (A6), follows this old trade route very closely. It passes within 75 km of Orléans.

12. For a good review of the development of the Loire Country as a religious, political, and commercial center during the Middle Ages and the Early Modern Period, see Lebrun, ed., *Pays de la Loire,* chaps. 4-9; and Jean Delumeau, ed., *Histoire de la Bretagne* (Toulouse, 1969), chaps. 4-9.

13. Thus, in the thirteenth century, a powerful company of merchants was formed with the aim of keeping the Loire clear for shipping and providing a sort of insurance for its members. The Compagnie des Marchants Fréquentant la rivière de Loire et autres fleuves descendant en icelle, with its headquarters at Orléans, raised its own taxes and tolls and took on some of the most powerful lords of the area, forcing them to provide unobstructed passage for the company's shipping through river sections that still came under feudal ownership. Time and money were no drawback to the legal battles that ensued. L. Gallouédec cites one case that kept the lawyers busy for 227 years. (Trial of Clisson d'Angers, 1430-1657, in Gallouédec, *La Loire,* p. 6). The company was finally divested of its essential powers in 1680, though it survived as a rather awkward, inefficient organization up to 1772, in Gallouédec, *La Loire,* pp. 2-8; see also M. Le Mené, "La Fin du Moyen-Age" and F. Lebrun, "Les XVIIe and XVIIIe siècles, les hommes, les travaux et les jours," in *Pays de la Loire,* ed. Lebrun, pp. 194, 257.

14. This was despite the ambitions of policymakers in Paris who continued to focus their attention on the East Indies. Colbert, for example, tried to develop commercial links between the Loire Country and the Spice Islands. Shortly after founding the French East Indies Company (1664), he set up a governing body in Nantes. According to the nineteenth-century historian Guilbert, this met little local response; see "Nantes" in Aristide Guilbert, ed., *Histoire des villes de la France* (Paris, 1845), vol. I, p. 279.

15. Georges Lefebvre, *Etudes Orléanaises* (Paris, 1962), vol. I, p. 151.

16. J. Meyer, "Le Siècle de l'intendance," in *Bretagne,* ed. Delumeau, p. 316.

17. Chartres, Blois, Saumur, and Laval stood somewhere between ten and fifteen thousand; Montargis, Chateaudun, Vendôme, Romorantin, Chinon, La Flèche, and Mayenne were between five and ten thousand; F. Lebrun, "Les XVIIe et XVIIIe siècles," in *Pays de la Loire,* ed. Lebrun, pp. 244-5.

18. Dion, *Val de Loire,* pp. 49-57.

19. Lefebvre, *Etudes Orléanaises,* vol. I, pp. 111-13; E. Fournier, "Orléans," in *Villes de la France,* ed. Guilbert, vol. II, p. 602.

20. Armel de Wismes, *La Vie quotidienne dans les ports bretons aux XVIIe and XVIIIe siècles: Nantes, Brest, St. Mâlo, Lorient* (Paris, 1973), pp. 160-202.

21. Dion, *Val de Loire.*
22. Paul Bois, *Paysans de l'Ouest* (Paris, 1960), pp. 571–4. For Bois' general view on the whole Loire Country, see "Révolution et contre-révolution," in *Pays de la Loire,* ed. Lebrun, pp. 311–61.
23. Marc Bloch, *Les Caractères originaux de l'histoire rurale française* (Paris, 1952), vol. I, pp. 35–57.
24. This is the basis of the distinction between *terres chaudes* and *terres froides.* The *terres chaudes* are the enclosed land under permanent cultivation; the *terres froides* are unenclosed territories that were only occasionally cultivated; see Bloch, *Caractères originaux,* vol. I, pp. 62–3.
25. Thus, limestone is the ideal base for cereals because it is, in chemical terms, alkaline (a prerequisite for such crops), and, physically, it is permeable (thus ensuring a dry topsoil). On the other hand, clays, chiefly because of their holding properties on water, tend to be acidic, a quality that is generally associated with woodland, as found in the West. In the South, much of the topsoil was so acidic that, left untended, it would result in a natural rankness of even wooded vegetation. For specific comments on regional soil conditions, see Bruley, *Pays de la Loire,* pp. 81–2, 102, 108; Ormsby, *France,* pp. 81, 124; Bachelier and Vince, *Loire-Atlantique,* p. 11; and a general summary on the relationship between soil conditions and vegetation in A. N. Strahler, *Introduction to Physical Geography* (New York, 1965), chaps. 11 and 12.
26. Statistics from France, Ministre du Commerce, *Documents statistiques sur la France* (Paris, 1835). Note that our term "the Orléanais" is not to be confused with the old province, the Orléanais, which spread over approximately four modern departments.
27. Bibliothèque Municipale Orléans, ms. 586, of 201, *Mémoires* (1700–10) of Christophe Sauvageon, prior of Sennely, quoted in Gérard Bouchard, *Le Village immobile: Sennely-en-Sologne au XVIIIe siècle* (Paris, 1972), p. 47.
28. Bouchard reports that over one-third of those born in the parish of Sennely in the eighteenth century died before their first birthday, compared with a national average of 23%; two-thirds did not reach the age of 20. Bouchard, *Le Village immobile,* p. 47.
29. See Fournier, "Orléans," in *Villes de la France,* ed. Guilbert, vol. II, p. 586; E. Robert, *Histoire du Loiret* (Orléans, 1947), pp. 23, 37.
30. Lefebvre, *Etudes Orléanaises,* vol. I, pp. 35–40.
31. AD Loire-Atlantique 1-M-2022, *Aperçu de l'état des animaux et de la manière dont on les gouverne dans le département de la Loire-Inférieure,* April 1807.
32. France, Statistique générale de la France, *Annuaire statistique de la France* (Paris, 1903), vol. XXV.

Chapter 3. "The theory of peasant economy"

1. I am not suggesting that the creature described in *Politics* had material views identical to those of Smith's or Ricardo's archetypes. (In fact, there are elements of the kind of subjective economy discussed in this chapter.) I merely mean to say that we can trace the pedigree back to Aristotle.
2. It would seem that researchers in areas outside of Europe have shown a

greater interest than Europeanists, most notably Polly Hill, *Studies in Rural Capitalism in West Africa* (Cambridge, 1970); and Sidney Mintz, *Caribbean Transformations* (Chicago, 1974); though in the case of Spain, there is Davydd Greenwood's *Unrewarding Wealth: The Commercialization and Collapse of Agriculture in a Spanish Basque Town* (Cambridge, 1976).

3. Marcel Mauss, *Manuel d'ethnographie* (Paris, 1947), p.102.

4. Marcel Mauss, "Essai sur le Don," *Année sociologique,* I (1923-24), pp. 30-186.

5. Karl Polanyi, "The Economy as Instituted Process," in *Trade and Market in the Early Empires,* eds. K. Polanyi, C. M. Arensberg, and H. W. Pearson (Glencoe, Ill., 1957), chap. XIII.

6. Among many, see D. Thorner, "Peasant Economy as a Category in Economic History," in *Peasants and Peasant Societies,* ed. T. Shanin (New York, 1971), pp. 201-18; Eric R. Wolf, *Peasants* (Englewood Cliffs, N.J., 1966); the important collection of essays in George Dalton, ed., *Economic Development and Social Change: The Modernization of Village Communities* (New York, 1971); and two earlier classics, Robert Redfield, *Peasant Society and Culture* (Chicago, 1956); and Raymond Firth, *Malay Fishermen: Their Peasant Economy* (London, 1946).

7. The question has been raised whether this should be attributed to Marx or whether it is the invention of later "deviationists." The debate centers around differing interpretations of the *German Ideology* and, more important still, the posthumously published *Grundrisse.* But, whether said by Marx or not, this schema of development by stages (or a schema similar to it) can be taken as the imprint of most Marxist historians writing today.

8. Wolf, *Peasants,* p. vii. The idea is also implied in Thorner's essay in *Peasants and Peasant Society,* ed. Shanin.

9. For example, G. M. Foster, "Peasant Society and the Image of Limited Good," in *Peasant Society: A Reader,* eds. J. M. Potter, M. N. Diaz, and G. M. Foster (Boston, 1967), pp. 300-23.

10. A. V. Chayanov, *The Theory of Peasant Economy,* eds. D. D. Thorner, B. Kerblay, and R. E. F. Smith (Homewood, Ill., 1966).

11. Classical market economists do not study decision-making strategies. Polly Hill shows that they assume that the market's participants, driven by competition, will behave in predictably uniform ways. Hill's own "indigenous economics" represent a major challenge to this assumption, though I find that the notion of uneven capital distribution, which she derives from entrepreneurial processes of discovery, better fits her twentieth-century West African migrant farmers than nineteenth-century French peasants; see Hill, *Rural Capitalism.* Samuel L. Popkin's *The Rational Peasant: The Political Economy of Rural Society in Vietnam* (Berkeley, 1979) is a very good recent example of a study of decision-making strategies in yet another totally different environment.

12. Strictly speaking, drudgery is not the equivalent of labor input because the level of drudgery depends on worker productivity as well as hours of work. As E. Paul Durrenberger and Nicola Tannenbaum note, "It is not the labor-consumer balance which determines the level of production. Instead it is the intersection of the drudgery and utility curves. The utility curve varies with the consumer-worker ratio, cost of equipment, capital investment, cost of rented land, etc." ("A Reassessment of Chay-

anov and His Recent Critics," *Peasant Studies,* VIII [1979], p. 59).
However, Chayanov does use the term "labor–consumer balance," as
shorthand for describing the intersection of the two curves, and I shall
do the same here.

13. Honoré de Balzac, *Les Paysans* (Paris, 1968), p. 65.

14. Julian Pitt-Rivers, ed., *Mediterranean Countrymen: Essays in the Social
     Anthropology of the Mediterranean* (Paris, 1963), especially pp. 21–2;
     and E. Friedl, "Dowry and Inheritance in Modern Greece," in *Peasant
     Society,* eds. Potter et al., pp. 57–62.

15. See John W. Mellor, *The Economics of Agricultural Development*
     (Ithaca, N.Y., 1966). One might describe this as a mixed commer-
     cial–subsistence system or, to borrow from Polly Hill once more, as a
     combination of "cash activities" with "own consumption" (Hill, *Rural
     Capitalism,* p. 3). But the subsistence side of the system has to be put in
     proper perspective. All it really refers to is that aspect of economic ra-
     tionality that takes shape beyond the parameters of the marketplace,
     not a vestige of some earlier system. Indeed, this might be a hidden
     aspect of our own economies today; see, for instance, Dennis R. Mills's
     comments about the do-it-yourself element of the contemporary British
     economy, which is made up almost entirely of family labor and which
     constitutes, in the form of "moonlighting," perhaps as much as 7.5% of
     the entire economy, in *Lord and Peasant in Nineteenth Century Britain*
     (London, 1980), p. 226.

16. A description of this can be found in Charles P. Kindleberger, *Eco-
     nomic Growth in France and Britain, 1851–1950* (Cambridge, Mass.,
     1964).

17. The classics are Wilhelm Abel, *Crises agraires en Europe XIIIe–XXe
     siècle* (Paris, 1973); Bernard H. Slicher van Bath, *The Agrarian History
     of Western Europe, A.D. 500–1850* (London, 1963); and C. E. La-
     brousse, *Esquisse du mouvement des prix et des revenus en France au
     XVIIIe siècle* (Paris, 1933).

18. "Community" is taken to mean a collection of inhabitants who are in
     regular personal contact on a daily or weekly basis – often defined in an-
     thropology as a "face-to-face" group.

19. A. L. Kroeber, *Anthropology* (New York, 1948), p. 284.

20. We join with Samuel Popkin in criticizing anthropologists for their use
     of the metaphor "penetration" to describe the processes of innovation in
     rural societies. This places too much emphasis on outside initiatives
     (Popkin, *Rational Peasant,* pp. 34, 63–72).

21. Edward Fox, *History in Geographic Perspective: The Other France*
     (New York, 1971), p. 37. Rather than distinguishing "town types," we
     would prefer to confine the comments to particular urban sectors. Fox,
     in fact, focuses his work on a fairly specific commercial class and not an
     entire urban population. See our own comments on "town types" later.

22. Ibid.

23. See, especially, Janet Abu-Lughood, "Migrant Adjustment to City Life:
     The Egyptian Case," in *Peasant Society,* eds. Potter et al., pp. 384–98;
     Emilio Willems gives some insight into this problem by using the exam-
     ple of nineteenth-century Cologne, in "Peasantry and City: Cultural
     Persistence and Change in Historical Perspective, A European Case,"
     American Anthropologist, LXXII (1970), pp. 528–44. Jean Vidalenc
     writes that "the fortifications of Paris in 1840 . . . included within their

walls whole villages or fragments such as Belleville, Montmartre or Montrouge whose inhabitants dedicated themselves to the production of vegetables and dairy products" (*La Société française de 1815 à 1848: le peuple des campagnes* [Paris, 1970], p. 36).

24. Thomas Malthus, *First Essay on Population* (New York, 1965) pp. 118–19.

25. This has been suggested by E. A. Wrigley, *Population and History* (New York, 1969), p. 68.

26. Emmanuel Le Roy Ladurie, "Pour un modèle de l'économie rurale française au XVIIIe siècle," *Cahiers d'histoire*, XIX (1974), pp. 5–27.

Chapter 4. Relative space: town and country

1. See Traian Stoianovich, *French Historical Method: The Annales Paradigm* (Ithaca, N.Y., 1976), chap. 3.

2. Eugène Hatin, *La Loire et ses bords, guide pittoresque du voyageur d'Orléans à Nantes et d'Orléans à Nevers par les bateaux à vapeur* (Orléans, 1843), p. 11.

3. The boats were almost as efficient traveling upstream. The *Inexplosibles* would leave Tours at 5:00 A.M. to arrive at Orléans at 5:15 P.M. (*Journal du Loiret,* 21 June 1843). By river, Tours is about 130 km from Orléans, so boats taking the trip downstream averaged 18–20 kph (11–12 mph) and upstream, about 11 kph (7 mph). This evidently impressed early nineteenth-century travelers.

4. Ange Guépin and Eugène Bonamy, *Nantes au XIXe siècle* (Nantes, 1835), pp. 383–427.

5. *Journal du Loiret,* 4 November 1837.

6. Hatin, *La Loire et ses bords,* pp. 118–28.

7. *Le Phare de la Loire,* 21 July 1875.

8. Adolphe Joanne, writing in 1874, puts Nantes in fourth place in merchant tonnage and third in customs dues, but he gives no statistics and does not cite his source (*Géographie de la Loire-Inférieure* [Paris, 1874b], p. 36).

9. Saint Nazaire was never understood in Nantes as a rival but rather as a partner, a port accessible to heavy ocean-going vessels, which would bring more business to Nantes, especially after the opening of the Nantes–Saint Nazaire rail link in 1857. Both the chambre de commerce and the conseil municipal had invested heavily in the development of Saint Nazaire; see AM Nantes, *Délibérations du Conseil municipal,* 12 November 1850. It is interesting to note that this development coincided with an increased interest that France was showing in American cotton, a trade that Nantes, apparently, was hoping to catch; see *L'Union Bretonne,* 17 September 1851.

10. This was an obsession in the 1890s and 1900s that was marked with some degree of success. Between 1891 and 1894, total tonnage traded in the Port of Nantes increased 22% as a result of the opening of a new maritime canal. But it was only after 1917, with the American employment of Nantes for the disembarkment of troops and the later major modifications made on the flow of the river, that the port's depressed economic state changed; see AD Loire-Atlantique 1-M-520, *Tonnage de la navigation avant et depuis l'ouverture du Canal . . . ,* n.d.; and M. Gibert, *La Loire maritime et le Port de Nantes* (Nantes, 1947).

11. Statistics are from a table entitled "Mouvement des entrepôts en 1913

(quantités entrées en quintaux métriques)." I have converted these figures to metric tons by dividing by 10; see France, Statistique générale de la France, *Annuaire statistique de la France*. Ministère du Travail et de la Prévoyance sociale (Paris, 1917), vol. XXXIV.

12. AM Nantes, *Délibérations du Conseil municipal*, 15 January 1853.

13. Ibid.

14. Ibid., 3 August 1845.

15. Ibid., 7 July 1847.

16. The ships, of course, set sail from Saint Nazaire, but Nantes continued to be the spokesman, indicating again how closely the two ports cooperated. The belligerency toward Le Havre became particularly bitter in the 1880s when the Compagnie Transatlantique, which monopolized all the lines, wanted to concentrate its business in one port, Le Havre. For a very lengthy debate, see ibid., 23 December 1882.

17. Guépin and Bonamy, *Nantes au XIXe siècle*, p. 336.

18. One individual called up to speak for French Guinea claimed, "la traite a entièrement cessé;" AN C 808 (No. 55), *Commission chargée d'examiner la proposition de M. de Tracy, relative à l'abolition de l'esclavage*. Slavery was finally abolished in 1848.

19. For detailed commodity listings, see Guépin and Bonamy, *Nantes au XIXe siècle*, pp. 343–58, for the 1830s; Joanne, *Géographie de la Loire-Inférieure, pp. 36–7* for the 1870s; and E. Orieux and J. Vincent, *Histoire et géographie de la Loire-Inférieure*, (Nantes, 1895), pp. 430–9, for the 1890s. One notices little change in the type of commodities traded when comparing the three lists.

20. Hatin, *La Loire et ses bords*, p. 119.

21. AN C 3020, *Enquête sur la situation des classes ouvrières*, Loire-Inférieure, 1873.

22. AD Loire-Atlantique 1-M-520, Direction du Personnel et du Secrétariat, *Situation ouvrière*, 20 October 1894.

23. As in other parts of France, the *compagnons* of Nantes were responsible for a certain amount of street violence, which resulted in some particularly repressive local laws in the first half of the nineteenth century. For example, in 1845, the prefecture forbade workers:
"1, to meet and march in groups on the public way;
2, to decorate themselves in public with the insignia of the *compagnonnage*, whatever the pretext;
3, to carry canes or . . . any other symbols of gathering *[ralliement]*"
[*Le Colibri*, 1 June 1845].

24. AN F^7 12360, folder entitled "Retraite de l'Union des Compagnons du devoir . . ., Nantes, 1831–1906."

25. E. Larue's Grand Bazar and Nouvelles Galeries were founded in 1877; the Docks de l'Ouest, specializing in food distribution, was founded in 1887. See the responses of these three establishments in AN C 7464, *Enquête du commerce*, Loire-Inférieure, 1912.

26. A municipal councillor had this to say in 1899: "Messieurs, for several years we have seen stores shut and remain unoccupied for extended periods of time in our streets and squares of the town center"; see AM Nantes, *Délibérations du Conseil municipal*, 6 October 1899.

27. AN C 7464, Response of the Chambre syndicale de la nouveauté.

28. Guépin and Bonamy, *Nantes au XIXe siècle*, pp. 396–8.

29. Orieux and Vincent, *La Loire-Inférieure*, p. 302.

30.   AD Loire-Atlantique 1-M-520, Le Commissariat spécial de police, *Rapport . . . sur la situation générale de la circonscription,* La Basse-Indre, 20 March 1872.

31.   The iron industry was somewhat of an exception. Though a great deal of the metal was supplied by French fields, such as in the Nivernais or Berry, it was also imported from England and Sweden; see Joanne, *Géographie de la Loire-Inférieure,* p. 33.

32.   Ibid., p. 32.

33.   Orieux and Vincent, *La Loire-Inférieure,* p. 302.

34.   On several occasions, the refineries' preference for overseas sugar came up against government policy. A period of especially bitter recrimination followed the abolition of subsidies for colonial sugar in 1831; see Georges Lerat, *Etude sur les origines, le développement et l'avenir des raffineries nantaises* (Paris, 1911), pp. 83–131.

35.   AD Loire-Atlantique 1-M-1953, *Tableau du Mouvement Commercial des Engrais du 27 août 1852 au 7 août 1853.*

36.   Guépin and Bonamy, *La Loire et ses bords,* pp. 398–402.

37.   Ibid., p. 402.

38.   Orieux and Vincent, *La Loire-Inférieure,* p. 304.

39.   It is well worth noting here Theodore Zeldin's observation that, at a national level, tinned foodstuffs did not become as widespread in France, despite the technological lead, as they were to become in nineteenth-century Britain and America. He suggests that this might have been because "food producers preferred to stick to traditional methods of adulteration, which were well developed, in order to reduce the cost of food, rather than embark upon the expensive investment that canning required, or else that retail profits in the retail grocery trade were so high that the preserving of food by the housewife in the home was an established alternative." If the food industry at Nantes can be taken as a typical case – it was, after all, one of the leading producers of preserved foods – then one might add the degree to which canning was integrated into a rural, household-type economy; see Theodore Zeldin, *France 1848–1945,* (Oxford, 1977), vol. II, pp. 738–9.

40.   Sevin-Mareau, *Mémoires sur les causes de la décadence de l'industrie manufacturière et commerciale à Orléans . . .* (Orléans, 1828), pp. 14–17.

41.   AM Orléans, *Délibérations du Conseil municipal,* 22 and 29 February, and 6 August 1832.

42.   Sevin-Mareau, *Mémoires sur les causes,* pp. 20–6.˙

43.   *Journal du Loiret,* 6 June 1838.

44.   Ibid., 25 June 1857.

45.   It ought to be pointed out that Table 4.4 has been found to correspond very closely to information given in an 1848 parliamentary enquiry. One suspects they were based on the same source: AN C 957, Assemblée Constituante, *Enquête sur le travail agricole et industriel . . . ,* 25 mai 1848, Canton d'Orléans.

46.   *Journal du Loiret,* 25 June 1857.

47.   Fête des fabricants et marchands de vinaigre de la ville et des environs d'Orléans, 20 août 1888, (Orléans, 1889).

48.   Courtin-Rossignol, *Origine et historique de la fabrication des vinaigres dans l'Orléanais* (Orléans, 1891), p. 8.

49. Edouard Fournier, "Orléans," in *Histoire des villes de la France* ed., Aristide Guilbert (Paris, 1845), vol. II, p. 602.
50. *Journal du Loiret,* 25 June 1857.
51. Ardouin-Dumazet, *Voyage en France, 1ère série: le Morvan, le Val de Loire, le Perche* (Paris, 1902), p. 158.
52. This *fête* is mentioned in R. Gilbert, *Une Famille ouvrière d'Orléans* (Paris, 1894), p. 8.
53. Sevin-Mareau, *Mémoires sur les causes,* p. 6.
54. Adolphe Joanne, *Géographie du département du Loiret* (Paris, 1874a), pp. 31–5.
55. *Journal du Loiret,* 16 January 1869.
56. Once a week a rabbit was served as the "plate of honor" on the family's table. The father was a woolcarder; see Gilbert, *Une Famille ouvrière,* pp. 5–7.
57. AN C 3020, *Enquête sur la situation des classes ouvrières,* 1872–1875.
58. AM Orléans, *Délibérations du Conseil municipal,* 29 December 1849.
59. See, for example, France, Statistique générale de la France, *Annuaire statistique de la France* (Paris, 1879–1917), 34 vols.
60. For the year 1903, the *Annuaire statistique* gives 15,161 metric tons transported by 336 boats.
61. *Le Pays de Retz,* 12 April 1903.
62. *Journal du Loiret,* 21 and 25 May 1836.
63. L. Gallouédec, *La Loire: étude de fleuve* (Paris, 1910), p. 213.
64. *Journal du Loiret,* 24 December 1835.
65. Ibid., 1 March 1832.
66. AN C 957, Assemblée Constituante, *Enquête sur le Travail agricole et industriel . . . , 1848,* Canton de Cléry-Saint-André.
67. AD Loire-Atlantique 1-M-1953, Inspection d'Agriculture, *Rapport général sur les opérations des Comices agricoles . . . ,* 21 June 1843.
68. Guépin and Bonamy, *Nantes au XIXe siècle,* pp. 376–7.
69. The rural violence of this period will be discussed in Chapter 9.
70. The same gentleman supervised the construction of Orléans' warehouse; see AM Orléans, *Délibérations du Conseil municipal,* 29 February 1832.
71. *Journal du Loiret,* 27 July 1828 and 30 April 1829.
72. The terms are cited in AM Nantes, *Délibérations du Conseil municipal,* 8 November 1837.
73. Ibid.
74. *Journal du Loiret,* 31 July 1834.
75. Ibid., 1 November 1829.
76. Ibid., 18 April 1830.
77. Ibid., 4 May 1844, 24 July 1862, and 3 April 1886.
78. AM Orléans, *Délibérations du Conseil municipal,* 23 December 1837.
79. *Journal du Loiret,* 6 June 1838.
80. Ibid., 24 June 1843.
81. AM Nantes, *Délibérations du Conseil municipal,* 1 August 1831.
82. Ibid., 8 November 1837. The Rouen line was opened, significantly enough, one day after the inauguration at Orléans (2 May 1843).
83. The junction between the Paris–Orléans line and the western line was 4 km north of Orléans, at Fleury-les-Aubrais. In the 1850s, an effort was made to construct a station at this point, but it failed as a consequence of Orléans' objections. In the 1880s, the same attempt was made and

met with the same results. It was not until the twentieth century that the station was built. Now a traveler going directly to Tours does not even necessarily have to see Orléans. See *Journal du Loiret,* several issues between 8 June 1852 and 14 December 1854; AM Orléans, *Délibérations du Conseil municipal,* 3 November 1887.

84.   AN C 957, Assemblée Constituante, *Enquête sur le travail agricole et industriel . . .* , 1848, Canton de Cléry-Saint-André.

85.   *Journal du Loiret,* 9 January 1841.

86.   The city council was divided on the question of the possible advantages of the Vierzon line but finally voted in favor of it because it felt this might lead to the construction of a Paris–Marseille line through Orléans (which never actually happened); see AM Orléans, *Délibérations du Conseil municipal,* 25 February 1842.

87.   *Journal du Loiret,* 21 February 1866.

88.   *La Sologne,* 3 June 1858. A veritable revolution was, in fact, taking place in the Sologne, in part due to the opening of agricultural canals; see Chapter 8.

89.   Joanne, *Loiret,* p. 37; Joanne, *Loire-Inférieure,* p. 38.

90.   *Courrier de la Campagne,* 7 February 1876.

91.   These deliberations are our main source. Although undoubtedly frustrating for many at the time, these regulations give today's historian an opportunity to build a rough picture of the distribution and regularity of nineteenth-century markets by consulting the deliberations of the city councils at Nantes and Orléans, along with contemporary local newspapers, which invariably announced the most important gatherings. The sources are extremely bulky – the city council deliberations of Nantes and Orléans, alone, account for about 150 hefty, hand-written volumes – and even then they do not give the complete picture, as some of the very brief entries clearly indicate.

92.   In 1821, the city council authorized the construction of three covered shelters for the markets that had grown up in the city center, thus giving them an air of permanence as well as affording them protection from bad weather.

93.   The most important were the Foire Saint Aignan, that took place every November, and the Foire du Mail, that took place every June, both lasting usually for about two weeks. There was, in addition, one regular market for calves, established in 1828, which was held every Monday and Wednesday.

94.   Ibid., 19 January 1873.

95.   Orieux and Vincent, *La Loire-Inférieure,* p. 434.

96.   Yves-Marie Bercé, *Fête et révolte: des mentalités populaires du XVIe au XVIIIe siècle* (Paris, 1976), pp. 183–7.

97.   In 1823 there were 69 butchers at Nantes; 20 of them had their own slaughterhouses, 32 had to share facilities, and the remainder relied on others. Industries based on animal products had to depend on the butchers not only for the raw product itself but also in many cases for the processing. The manufacture of tallow, for example, was forbidden outside the premises of the slaughterhouse, though, in actual fact, many candle makers did do this (AM Nantes, *Délibérations du Conseil municipal,* 30 December 1823).

98.   Ibid., 29 January 1894.

99.   AM Orléans, *Délibérations du Conseil municipal,* 17 December 1821.

100.   There is also, of course, the possibility that the demands were often
        never even presented to the council, whose main topics of deliberation
        clearly revolved around commerce.
101.   Ibid., 25 July 1856.
102.   *Journal du Loiret,* 8 March 1829. One could be held up for 4 hours by
        tax inspectors just to get one liter of wine across Orléans (Ibid., 15
        March 1829). Petitions from various groups poured into city hall.
        Among the most disgruntled were the livestock producers of the
        Sologne who complained that for their bullock they were being charged,
        on average, 21% of their value and those of Limousin and Berry were
        paying only 6 and 7%. This evident disparity moved the city council to
        consider taxation by weight, but it finally ruled this out as impractical
        (AM Orléans, *Délibérations du Conseil municipal,* 29 June 1827). In the
        Nantais, the widely cultivated Gros Plant wines had to pay in taxes often
        more than 100% of their value if they were carried into Nantes (AD
        Loire-Atlantique, *Statistique des vignobles,* 26 November 1829).

Chapter 5. The connectors

1.   Jean Duvignaud, *Fêtes et civilisations* (Paris, 1973), p. 106.
2.   Robert Redfield, *Peasant Society and Culture: An Anthropological Ap-
        proach to Civilization* (Chicago, 1956).
3.   *Courrier de la Campagne,* 11 July 1875.
4.   The "cadastre" is a French property survey made for the purposes of
        taxation. The *matrices cadastrales,* containing details on properties,
        listed by propertyholder in alphabetical order, to be found in every com-
        mune of the department are deposited at *AD Loiret.* The Pinson prop-
        erties are to be found in the *matrices* of the communes of Cercottes,
        Chevilly, Creuzy, Gidy, and Huêtre, all completed in 1822. The family
        is not to be found in any of the second *matrices cadastrales* (1913),
        which are deposited at the *Service du Cadastre* in Orléans.
5.   I am referring to the Colas des Francs, whose properties are to be found
        in the second *matrices* for the communes of Ardon, Bricy, Chaingy,
        Coinces, Férolles, Mezières, Saint Cyr-en-Val, Sennely, Tigy, and
        Vienne, *Service du Cadastre, Orléans;* the Colas family owned only 221
        hectares at the time of the first cadastre; see the *matrices* for the com-
        munes of Cravant, Saint Denis-en-Val, and Vitry, which were com-
        pleted in 1829, 1828, and 1825, respectively (*AD Loiret*).
6.   The methods employed for studying the cadastre will be discussed in
        detail in Chapter 8. The information presented here is based on a list of
        names drawn from all propertyholders possessing over 50 hectares of
        land; see the brief remarks made later.
7.   In Chapter 9 I shall indicate how these agricultural shows and their
        parent *comices* might be related to the demographic structure of par-
        ticular historical moments.
8.   The letter is so unusual we might well doubt its authenticity (*Journal du
        Loiret* 12 June 1844).
9.   Bernard H. Slicher van Bath, *The Agrarian History of Western Europe,
        A.D. 500-1850* (London, 1963), p. 7.
10.   Arthur Young, *Travels in France, 1787, 1788, 1789* (London, 1924),
        p. 19.
11.   See, notably, François-P. Gay, *La Champagne du Berry* (Bourges,

1967), pp. 152–4; and Abel Poitrineau, *La Vie rurale en Basse Auvergne au XVIIIe siècle* (1726–1789) & Paris, 1965), vol. I, pp. 141–69.

12.   About the same percentage area is recorded for state properties in the second cadastre. The actual transfer of the Crown lands to the state took place in 1850. For details on the history of the domain, see Paul Domet, *Histoire de la Forêt d'Orléans* (Orléans, 1892).

13.   This is against 45% in the Nantais. The confiscation of the Crown lands had little or no effect on these figures because they were transferred directly to the state (see earlier comment).

14.   Emile Zola, *La Terre* (Paris, 1972), p. 146.

15.   The occupation is given for about one-third of all the landowners recorded.

16.   Guépin and Bonamy reported that the wealthiest individuals at Nantes spent only the winter months in the city; in the summer they lived "in a cheerful country house on the edge of one of the numerous rivers which cross our department" (Ange Guépin and Eugène Bonamy, *Nantes au XIXe siècle* [Nantes, 1835], p. 458).

17.   Ardouin-Dumazet, *Voyage en France, 1ère série: Le Morvan, le Val de Loire, le Perche* (Paris, 1902), p. 107. For further comments on the "agricultural revolution" in the Sologne, see Chapter 8, section 2.

18.   John McManners' *Church and State in France, 1870–1914* (New York, 1973) provides an excellent introduction to the national rivalries born out of this issue during the latter part of the nineteenth century.

19.   Charles Tilly, *The Vendée* (Cambridge, Mass., 1964), p. 104.

20.   AN F[19] 5692 Etienne, Evêque d'Orléans to Conseiller d'Etat, Paris, 14 Brumaire An XI (5 November 1802).

21.   AN F[19] 5836 Félix, Evêque d'Orléans to Ministre des Cultes, Orléans, 22 July 1956.

22.   *Courrier de la Campagne,* 14 December 1873.

23.   This list of functions was drawn up by Charles Tilly, who was describing southern Anjou at the end of the eighteenth century, but numerous references in the press and other contemporary records suggest that the list is just as pertinent to the Orléanais and the Nantais in the nineteenth century, though, as we shall see shortly, in differing degrees; see Tilly, *Vendée,* p. 101. These mundane functions were almost universal in eighteenth-century France. For the diocese of Gap, see Timothy Tackett, *Priest and Parish in Eighteenth-Century France* (Princeton, 1977), pp. 151–69.

24.   For a general background, see Georges Duveau, *Les Instituteurs* (Paris, 1957); and Félix Ponteil, *Histoire de l'enseignement en France, 1789–1965* (Paris, 1966).

25.   Peter V. Meyers provides valuable information on the evolving duties and roles of the *instituteur* in "The French Instituteur, 1830–1914" (Rutgers, 1972), which is reproduced, in summary, in "Professionalization and Societal Change: Rural Teachers in Nineteenth-Century France," *Journal of Social History,* IX (1976), pp. 542–58. I have also made use of Barnett Singer's "The Teacher as Notable in Brittany, 1880–1914," *French Historical Studies,* IX (1976), pp. 635–659, and "From Patriots to Pacifists: The French Primary School Teachers, 1880–1940," *Journal of Contemporary History,* XII (1977), pp. 413–34.

26.   Singer, "The Teacher as Notable," p. 646.

27. This was at least true in the Orléanais and the Nantais, where non-Catholics made up a negligible part of the population.
28. I am thinking, in particular, of Michel Vovelle's *Piété baroque et déchristianisation* . . . (Paris, 1973). See the comments on this work and others in Emmanuel Le Roy Ladurie, "Chaunu, Lebrun, Vovelle: la nouvelle histoire de la mort," in *Le Territoire de l'historien* (Paris, 1973), pp. 393–403; and Régine Robin, *Histoire et linguistique* (Paris, 1973), pp. 89–94.
29. Christiane Marcilhacy, *Le Diocèse d'Orléans au milieu du XIXe siècle* (Paris, 1964); Marius Faugeras, *Le Diocèce de Nantes sous la Monarchie Censitaire (1813–1822–1849)* . . .(Fontenay-le-Comte, Vendée, 1964), 2 vols., which should be compared with the more recent work of Fernand Boulard, "Matériaux pour l'histoire religieuse du peuple français: aspects de la pratique religieuse en France, 1802–1939: l'exemple des Pays de Loire," *Annales ESC,* XXXI (1976), pp. 761–801.
30. Le Bras writes, "By religious life we mean the adhesion of spirit, the submission of conduct and the public hommage to a divine Being. For a Catholic: belief in the dogmas, exercise of the virtues, sacramental and cultural practice. Faith, morality, observance are then the essence: without this trilogy, no true Catholicism. Neither pure orthodoxy, nor pure honesty, nor especially strict attendance would be recognized to suffice" (Gabriel Le Bras, *Etudes de sociologie religieuse* [Paris, 1955-6], vol. II, pp. 615-6).
31. Ibid., vol. II, p. 403.
32. Ibid., vol. I, p. 165
33. Ibid., vol. I, pp. 161-2.
34. Ibid., vol. I, p. 71.
35. These results are, however, appreciably higher than Dupanloup's previously cited estimates (6–7%).
36. Marcilhacy, *Le Diocèse d'Orléans.*
37. See comments by Tilly, *Vendée,* pp. 100-3, for the neighboring southern Anjou.
38. Boulard, "Matériaux pour l'histoire religieuse," pp. 782-8; Faugeras, Le Diocèse de Nantes, vol. II, pp. 245-8.
39. AD Loire-Atlantique 1-M-1953, *Inspection d'agriculture,* 26 July 1853.
40. AN F¹⁹ 5832 Alexandre, Evêque de Nantes to Ministre des Cultes, Nantes, 11 January 1854.
41. AN F¹⁹ 441 Garnier, Ancien vicaire-général de Nantes to Conseiller d'Etat, Administration des Cultes, Nantes, 1 October 1815. This letter was a plea to the newly installed royal government to grant him his full pension after he had been dismissed for supporting Napoleon during the Hundred Days. He finally received a little over half of that pension; Administration générale des Cultes, Paris, 9 November 1815.
42. Primary school inspections for Loire-Inférieure, AN F¹⁷ 118 (for 1833), AN F¹⁷ 9338 (for 1857–8).
43. AN F¹⁷* 118, *Enquête sur la situation des écoles primaires,* arrondissement d'Ancenis, 1833.
44. AN F¹⁹ 5832, J. Leblais, instituteur, to Inspecteur primaire de l'arrondissement, Ligné, 30 January 1867.
45. AN F¹⁷ 9338.
46. Orléans was the most devout part of this un-Catholic country. Michael

Phayer ascribes this to the presence of foundling hospitals (Michael Phayer, "Politics and Popular Religion: The Cult of the Cross in France, 1815-1840," *Journal of Social History,* XI [1978], pp. 346-63). Professor Phayer has also kindly made available to me unpublished parts of this study, which contain details on the Orléanais during the July Monarchy. See also Michael Phayer, *Sexual Liberation and Religion in Nineteenth-Century Europe* (London, 1977).

47.   Le Bras, *Etudes,* vol. II, p. 404.

48.   Judith Silver confirms the presence of a popular anticlericalism in the neighboring Vendômois and cites some vivid examples of this. Unlike her, however, I would not interpret this as a logical phase of political apprenticeship: if the Vendômois was anything like the Orléanais, one must conclude that the *curé* had never, in the nineteenth century at any rate, commanded much prestige (Judith Silver, "French Peasant Demands for Popular Leadership in the Vendômois (Loir-et-Cher), 1852-1890," *Journal of Social History,* XIV [1980], pp. 278-85). Evidence of anticlericalism in the region in the late eighteenth century is given in J. Gallerand, *Les Cultes sous la Terreur en Loire-et-Cher* (Blois, 1928).

49.   Cléry-Saint-André is the burial site of Saint Louis. His actual remains were destroyed during the Wars of Religion in the sixteenth century.

50.   *Journal du Loiret,* 4 May 1836. The troubles are also described in AN F⁷ 4056, *Rapport annuel de la gendarmerie,* Orléans, 6 January 1837.

51.   It was a superstition that struck Zola's imagination; see Emile Zola, *La Terre* (Paris, 1972), p. 69.

52.   See quotation cited earlier.

53.   *Journal du Loiret,* 10 January 1830.

54.   *Courrier de la Campagne,* 31 July 1881.

55.   Emmanuel Le Roy Ladurie and Paul Dumont, *Anthropologie du conscrit français* (Paris, 1972); Singer, "The Teacher as Notable," p. 655; François Furet and Jacques Ozouf, *Lire et écrire: l'alphabétisation des Français de Calvin à Jules Ferry* (Paris, 1977).

56.   The growth in the number of schools was gradual in both regions and appears to have been independent of the major legislative innovations of the century. However, one does note two waves of sharp increase: the 1850s and 60s, and the early 1880s (i.e., prior to the Ferry law). My information used in this paragraph on the 1830s and 50s is drawn from AN F¹⁷* 118 and 119 and F¹⁷ 9338.

57.   Claude Lévi-Strauss, "Le Sorcier et sa magie," in *Anthropologie structurale* (Paris, 1959), pp. 196-203.

Chapter 6. The rural economy in toto

1.   See, for example, Edward Fox, *History in Geographic Perspective: The Other France* (New York, 1971), which has been briefly analyzed previously, Chapter 3, Section 1; Henri Mendras, *Sociétés paysannes* (Paris, 1976).

2.   P. Vidal de la Blache, *Principes de géographie humaine* (Paris, 1922), p. 133.

3.   AN F¹⁰ 2705, *Enquêtes agricoles décennales: questionnaires, 1862,* Loire-Inférieure and Loiret.

4.   Georges Lefebvre, *Etudes Orléanaises* (Paris, 1962), vol. I, p. 15, de-

scribing the region in the eighteenth century, notes that the triennial rotation existed in the Beauce and was in the process of being adopted in the Valley; the Forêt d'Orléans and the Sologne were apparently still dominated by a biennial rotation. Lefebvre's comments appear to lean heavily on Roger Dion, *Le Val de Loire* (Tours, 1934), whose own statements seem to have been strongly influenced by Marc Bloch, *Les Caractères originaux de l'histoire rurale française* (Paris, 1952), vol. I, pp. 35–57.

5.   This distinction between the interior of the Sologne and a transitional zone adjoining the Valley persists into the twentieth century; see Jean Arvengas, *Histoire d'un village de Sologne: Marcilly-en-Villette des origines à nos jours* (Beaugency, Loiret, 1952), p. 48.

6.   According to the instructions given in the inquiry, one was supposed to record as fallow only those lands left in a *permanently* uncultivated state. However, the large figures recorded for such fertile subregions as the Beauce and the Valley suggest that the local commissioners included under this category all uncultivated territory found within their cantons at the moment of the enquiry.

7.   Jules Guyot, *Etude des vignobles de France* (Paris, 1868), vol. III, pp. 205–32.

8.   AN F[10] 435, *Tableau des terres cultivées en vignes,* Nantes, 10 November 1807.

9.   See, for instance, AN F[10] 305, Prefect of Loire-Inférieure to Ministre de l'Intérieur, Nantes, 4 September 1824.

10.   Guyot, *Etude des vignobles,* vol. II, p. 605.

11.   Ibid.

12.   The Beauce of the Orléanais was not the only part of this vast open plain to possess wines. One specialist of the region wrote, "The presence of vines in the Beauce might seem to the reader to be a geographic paradox. . . . It is nonetheless true that for centuries those vines have been spread around valley edges such as the hillsides of the Aigre [Eure-et-Loir], where poorly informed critics have reproached Zola for having 'introduced' them *(sic),* or the hillsides of the Loire, or of the Eure where a few stunted vines still linger on. . . . But yes, vines in the Beauce, in the Beauce Chartraine and the Beauce Dunoise, but also – to confound the paradox – in the *Plain,* the *Flatlands* and the *Highlands;* these vines are said in our country to have been planted by the monks" (Charles Marcel-Robillard, *Le Folklore de la Beauce* [Paris, 1966], vol. II, p. 7).

13.   See Ardouin-Dumazet's comments, *Voyage en France, 16ème série, De Vendée en Beauce* (Paris, 1898), pp. 219–21.

14.   Ardouin-Dumazet, *Voyage en France, 1ère série, Le Morvan, le Val de Loire, le Perche* (Paris, 1902), pp. 164–5.

15.   Variables on culture are expressed in terms of the percentage of area of each canton; variables on livestock are in numbers per household. A second correlation matrix has been drawn up in which livestock are expressed in numbers per square kilometer. Twelve pairs were found to be significantly different from those presented in Table 6.3, although only 2 of them, both concerning vines, implied a difference in the actual direction of the relationship. The 12 pairs were: sheep with cereals ($r = +.63 \neq +.36$), poultry with potatoes ($r = -.12 \neq -.41$), poultry with grass ($r = +.71 \neq +.42$), horses with vines ($r = +.31 \neq -.31$), cattle with vines ($r = -.28 \neq -.53$), sheep with vines ($r = +.34 \neq -.37$),

horses with sheep ($r = +.22 \neq +.80$), horses with pigs ($r = +.46 \neq +.20$), horses with poultry ($r = -.03 \neq +.40$), sheep with cattle ($r = +.60 \neq +.00$), sheep with poultry($r = +.03 \neq +.50$). None of these differences notably alter the general conclusions presented in the text.

16. I am using a .05 significance level.

17. Because one does not count pairs between the same variable, there is obviously a larger absolute number of pairs between cultures and livestock than the rest (25 to 20). Nevertheless, the statement still holds: whereas 44% of the total possible pairs between culture and livestock are statistically significant, this is true for only 30% of all other pairs.

18. The strong coefficient between horses and sheep tells us that a strong relationship existed between the two and that the relationship was positive, but it gives us *no* idea of how the number of sheep changed against horses. That would require another statistic, which, it was decided, would probably be misleading, given the likelihood of inaccuracies in the original data. When livestock are calculated in numbers per square kilometer, the coefficient falls to $+.22$.

19. AD Loire-Atlantique 2-M-64 to 100.

20. The Archives Communales (AC) from five of these communes have recently been transferred to the departmental archives: AD Loiret, Série 0 Supplément, Tournoisis, Saint-Péravy, Bouzy, Trainou, and Ardou. The lists from Baule, Dry, and Darvoy were still in the possession of the village *mairies* at the time this research was undertaken.

21. This theme is found, for instance, in Anton Blok's otherwise remarkable study, *The Mafia of a Sicilian Village 1860–1960* (New York, 1975).

22. The French term "domestique" was used more frequently in the countryside in reference to full-time farmworkers. The 1851 census is one of the few sources actually to make the distinction between household and farm *domestiques;* see Theresa McBride, *The Domestic Revolution: The Modernization of Household Service in England and France, 1820–1920* (New York, 1976), pp. 11 and 139, n. 8. I shall discuss this important aspect of rural society in greater detail in Chapter 7.

23. France, Ministre de l'Agriculture de du Commerce, Statistique de la France, *Industrie* (Paris, 1850), vol. III. This is the same source as employed in the compiling of Tables 4.3 and 4.4.

24. Exact locations of establishments are only rarely given for the Nantais.

25. AD Loire-Atlantique 1-M-488, Sub-prefect to Prefect, Ancenis, 26 Floréal An VIII (15 May 1800); 1-M-518, *Rapport sur la situation politique, morale et matérielle . . .* , Ancenis, 18 December 1860; *Progrès de la Loire-Inférieure,* 30 January 1881; and E. Orieux and J. Vincent, *Histoire et géographie de la Loire-Inférieure* (Nantes, 1895), p. 305.

26. AN C 957, Assemblée Constituante, *Enquête sur le travail . . .* , Canton de Chateauneuf, 1848.

27. Statistique de la France, *Industrie.*

28. They should, however, be considered more skilled as workers than the coal miners because they received two years of apprenticeship starting between 13 and 15 years of age. No children were hired in either the quarries or the stonemasons' yards (AN C 3353, *Enquête sur la situation ouvrière de la France, Loiret,* Response of the Société de Secours Mutuels de Fay-aux-Loges, 1884).

29. Practically all the responses from the cantons of both regions to the 1848 parliamentary enquiry begin with a statement along the lines,

"There is only one industry in this canton, agriculture" (AN C 956–957, Assemblée constituante, *Enquête sur le travail* . . . , 1848).

30. Together, these 13 establishments employed a total of 480 persons.

31. There are a number of works that deal with the textile industry of the West prior to the Revolution. Of special note are: R. H. Andrews, *Les Paysans des Mauges au XVIIIe siècle* (Tours, 1935); Paul Bois, *Paysans de l'Ouest* (Le Mans, 1960); François Dornic, *l'Industrie textile dans le Maine et ses débouchés internationaux 1650–1815* (Le Mans, 1955); and Charles Tilly, *The Vendée* (Cambridge, Mass., 1964).

32. However, police reports for the first half of the century do make frequent reference to the existence of "several cotton spinners" in the Orléanais. They would have presumably been found largely in the Beauce and the Valley; see, especially, AN F^7 36818, *Statistique personnelle et morale, 1790–1830*.

33. France, Ministre de l'Agriculture, du Commerce et des Travaux, Statistique de la France, *Territoire et population* (Paris, 1855). Georges Dupeux confirms the prevalence of owner–cultivators in the middle Loire in his *Aspects de l'histoire sociale et politique du Loir-et-Cher, 1848–1914* (Paris, 1962), pp. 110–20.

34. Paul Bois, "Révolution et Contre-révolution," in *Histoire des Pays de la Loire,* ed. François Lebrun (Toulouse, 1972), pp. 311–61. Bois' idea of homogeneity has been developed much further in *Paysans de l'Ouest.*

35. The 1851 census has been checked in two communes of the Beauce belonging to the arrondissement of Pithiviers, Teillay-le-Gaudin, and Boisseaux. In both cases, propertyholders accounted for less than 15% of the total population active in agriculture.

36. AN C 957, Assemblée Constituante, *Enquête sur le travail* . . . , Canton d'Artenay, 1848.

37. He was describing a village in the Beauce Chartrain, but the situation there was not very different from the Orléanais; see Ephraim Grenadou and Alain Prévost, *Grenadou, paysan français* (Paris, 1966), p. 10. Practically the only source emphasizing the existence of a large proportion of local labor is Noel Parfait's memoir of the Beauce written in the 1880s. Parfait, an old 48er, was at that time parliamentary deputy for Eure-et-Loir. A portion of this memoir is reproduced in Henri Lizier, *Chartres et la Beauce au temps de Louis-Philippe, 1830–1848,* (Chartres, 1972), pp. 215–20.

38. AN C 3353, *Enquête sur la situation ouvrière de la France* (1884).

39. Ibid.

40. The actual character of these properties will be discussed in Chapter 8.

41. Bois, *Paysans de l'Ouest,* p. 431.

42. "1. *Fermier, fermière* who gives half the crop as rent . . . 2. Abusively. *Fermier* in general," E. Littré, *Dictionnaire de la langue française* (Paris, 1863).

43. F.-J. Pinson, *Dictionnaire des lieux habités du département de la Loire-Inférieure* (Nantes, 1857), p. v.

44. "Direct exploitation" is taken to mean land that is put to the immediate use of the cultivator whether or not rent is owed to another. It should not be confused with the French *faire-valoir direct,* which refers solely to owner–cultivators.

45. AD Loire-Atlantique 1-M-1953, *Des divers modes d'exploitation des terres dans la Loire-Inférieure,* 9 April 1855.

46.   This point is made by Charles Delacommune, *L'Exode rural et l'associa-tion en Vendée* (Paris, 1914), pp. 113–22, who also describes some of the contracts of the *métayage* system.

47.   Henri Millet, *Histoire de la Sologne depuis 1850* (Paris, 1911), p. 24.

48.   The terms "tenanciers" and "complanteurs" were also sometimes used; see AD Loire-Atlantique 1-M-520, unsigned, undated manuscript prob-ably written in response to a circular from the ministry of the interior, 4 October 1894.

49.   AD Loire-Atlantique 1-M-2012, Département de la Loire-Inférieure, *Statistique des vignobles,* 26 November 1829; 1-M-1953, *Des divers modes d'exploitation . . .* , April 1855; 1-M-520, *Notes sur la viticulture dans la Loire-Inférieure en 1894;* 1-M-2023, Augustin-Delalande, *Rap-port fait au nom de la commission nommée par arrêté préfectoral en date du 24 avril 1895 . . .* ; Jean Meyeı, *La Noblesse bretonne au XVIIIe siècle* (Paris, 1966), vol. II, pp. 755–77.

50.   Belgian labor is mentioned in France, Ministre de l'Agriculture, *La petite propriété rurale en France: enquêtes monographiques (1908–9)* (Paris, 1909), p. 131.

51.   One reads in the *Courrier de la Campagne,* 13 July 1879: "Notice to cultivators. This year the military authority requires new formalities from cultivators soliciting soldiers for work in harvest. The applicants must: address their application to the prefecture on stamped paper in-dicating the area and the exact place of their exploitation, have the mayor of their commune send a certificate in support of their applica-tion, and finally *make known the precise date at which they desire the soldiers to be put at their disposition.* Omission of just one of these for-malities will result in the return of the application to the mayor of the applicant's commune and will thus cause a prejudicial delay for the cultivator."

52.   AN C 957, Assemblée constituante, *Enquête sur le travail . . .* , Canton d'Artenay, 1848, cited earlier.

53.   AN F^{10} 2705, *Enquêtes agricoles décennales: questionnaires, 1862, Loire-Inférieure.*

54.   References to this form of hiring are found in the responses to the 1848 parliamentary enquiry from the cantons of Artenay, Chateauneuf, and Cléry. See also Noël Parfait's memoir in Lizier, *Chartres et la Beauce,* p. 218 and Marcel-Robillard, *Le Folklore de la Beauce,* vol. V, pp. 21, 40.

Chapter 7. Peasant family and peasant population

1.   Henry Mendras, *La Fin des paysans: innovations et changement dans l'agriculture française* (Paris, 1967), pp. 77–8.

2.   The words are actually those of Eugène Minkowski, *Le Temps vécu, études phénoménologiques et psychopathologiques* (Paris, 1933), p. 16, cited in Anna-Teresa Tymieniecka, *Phenomenology and Science in Contemporary European Thought* (New York, 1962), p. 141.

3.   We are actually referring to the *matrices cadastrales.*

4.   "Microdemography" and "macrodemography" might be unpalatable, but what other terms are possible? To continue making the distinction between "micro-" and "macroeconomics" would, in this context, be an unwarranted distortion of the generally accepted definition of the terms. E. A. Hammel ("The Zadruga as Process," in *Household and Family in Past Time,* eds. Peter Laslett and Richard Wall [Cambridge,

1972], p. 337) employs the terms "micro-" and "macrovariation," but the distinction seems, to me, too general. Tamara Hareven ("The Family as Process: The Historical Study of the Family Cycle," *Journal of Social History,* VII [1974], p. 325) suggests "family time" and "social time," but this is too specific for our purposes – we are not only interested in the family at the individual level. That leaves us, alas, with "micro-" and "macrodemography." See also the theoretical comments of Tamara Hareven, "The Historical Study of the Life Course," and of Glen Elder, "Family History of the Life Course," in *Transition: The Family and the Life Course in Historical Perspective,* ed. Tamara Hareven (New York, 1978), pp. 1–64.

5.   A. V. Chayanov, *The Theory of Peasant Economy,* eds. D. D. Thorner, B. Kerblay, and R. E. F. Smith (Homewood, Ill., 1966), pp. 53–69.

6.   Chayanov, *Theory,* p. 68.

7.   Lutz Berkner, "The Stem Family and the Developmental Cycle of the Peasant Household: An Eighteenth-Century Austrian Example," *American Historical Review,* LXXVII (1972), pp. 398–418. The data are more convincing in Berkner's "Inheritance, Land Tenure and Peasant Family Structure: A German Regional Comparison," in *Family and Inheritance,* eds. Jack Goody, Joan Thirsk, and E. P. Thompson (Cambridge, 1976), pp. 71–95.

8.   AN C 956-957, Assemblée Constituante, *Enquête sur le travail . . . ,* 1848.

9.   AN C 3353, *Enquête sur la situation ouvrière . . . ,* 1884.

10.   Most discussions of demographic methodology are, in fact, not published in book form but in articles that unfortunately are often buried in some of the most inaccessible journals in the world. Nevertheless, there are still a large number of books that can serve as useful starters, among which the following deserve mention: Louis Henry's two introductory texts, *Manuel de démographie historique* (Geneva, 1967) and *Démographie: analyse et modèles* (Paris, 1972); Peter Laslett and Richard Wall, eds., *Household and Family in Past Time* (Cambridge, 1972); A. H. Pollard, Farhat Yusuf, and G. N. Pollard, *Demographic Techniques* (Elmsford, N.Y., 1974) – one of the best, briefest, and least expensive introductions; Mortimer Spiegelman, *Introduction to Demography* (Cambridge, Mass., 1968); and two collections of essays edited by E. A. Wrigley, *An Introduction to English Historical Demography from the Sixteenth to the Nineteenth Century* (London, 1966) and *Nineteenth-Century Society: Essays in the Use of Quantitative Methods for the Study of Social Data* (Cambridge, 1972). Most of the techniques employed in this study, both regarding the analysis of the nominal lists and the other demographic materials, can be found in these books.

11.   See Laslett and Wall, eds., *Household and Family,* pp. 86–9.

12.   For the Nantais, AD Loire-Atlantique 2-M-2 to 347, the communes of Joué-sur-Erdre (1836 missing) and Pannecé – the Plateau; La Marne and Saint Aignan – Retz-Vendée; Chateauthébaud and Mouzillon – Sèvre-et-Maine; La Chapelle-Bassse-Mer, Montrelais and Thouaré – Valley. For the Orléanais, the communes of Saint Péravy and Tournoisis (1836, 1841 missing) – Beauce; Ardon – Sologne; Bouzy-la-Forêt (1841 missing) and Trainou (1836 missing) – Forêt; Baule* (1911 missing), Darvoy* (1911 missing), and Dry* (1866, 1896, 1901, 1906, 1911 missing) – Valley, where the asterisks indicate that the lists were still at

the *mairies* at the time this research was undertaken; otherwise at AD Loiret, Série O Supplément. For a description of the actual layout of the nominal lists, see L. Henry, *Manuel,* chap. II.

13.   Theoretically it would have been better to weight each case according to the number of housefuls rather than the number of individuals within each subregion, but there is no such information available. For populations in the subregions of the Nantais, we have relied on the communal totals given in INSEE, Direction régionale de Nantes, *Populations par communes de 1801 à 1962* (Nantes, 1966). The equivalent INSEE publication for the Orléanais provides data only from 1851 onward. For totals earlier than this date, we have relied on the *Annuaire du Loiret* (Orléans, 1838–52).

14.   Guy Thuillier, *Aspects de l'économie nivernaise au XIXe siècle* (Paris, 1966), pp. 33–45; Roger Dion, *Le Val de Loire* (Tours, 1934), p. 485; Lutz Berkner and John Shaffer, "The Joint Family in the Nivernais," *Journal of Family History,* IV (1979), pp. 150–62.

15.   Jacques Dupâquier, "Habitat rural et démographie: l'exemple de l'Ile-de-France," *Annales de démographie historique, 1975,* pp. 65–6. Jean-Louis Flandrin explains the existence of *communautés* in terms of agricultural type. Like Thuillier, he notes that they are found primarily in isolated stock-raising regions where there is a continual, long-term demand for labor, in mountainous regions such as the Cévennes, the Velay, the highland areas of Périgord and Quercy, Limousin, Upper Provence, and Dauphiné, in addition, of course, to the well-documented region of stem families, the Pyrennees. He argues that *communautés* were not to be found in the Sologne because, in the eighteenth century, landowners made wage-labor profitable by converting arable land into pasture "comme beaucoup de grands propriétaires anglais l'avaient fait dès le XVIe siècle." Perhaps, but our own research has indicated few signs of this sort of commercialization *à l'anglaise* in the Sologne of the first half of the nineteenth century (Jean-Louis Flandrin, *Familles: parenté, maison, sexualité dans l'ancienne société* [Paris, 1976], pp. 75–91).

16.   The actual figures are as follows:

	Households per houseful (%)			
	1	2	over 2	*N* (weighted)
Orléanais				
1846–1866	95.1	4.4	0.5	451
1872–1886	88.8	9.7	1.5	366
1891–1911	92.4	6.4	1.2	423
1846–1911	92.3	6.6	1.1	1,240
Nantais				
1846–1866	94.2	5.1	0.7	709
1872–1886	95.0	4.6	0.4	589
1891–1911	90.9	8.4	0.7	727
1846–1911	93.3	6.1	0.6	2,024

The first two censuses, 1836 and 1841, have been omitted because they record individuals only by household, not houseful.

17. W. A. Armstrong, "Social Structure from Early Census Returns," in *An Introduction,* ed. Wrigley; W. A. Armstrong, "A Note on the Household Structure of Mid-Nineteenth Century York in Comparative Perspective", in *Household and Family,* eds. Laslett and Wall, pp. 205–14; Michael Anderson, *Family Structure in Nineteenth-Century Lancashire* (Cambridge, 1971).

18. $t = 5.919$ with 3669 df. The difference of means is therefore significant at the .001 level. Tests of significance have been done for all computations on comparative data and, unless otherwise indicated in the text or tables, differences in the cited means and proportions are significant at the .05 level.

19. Laslett notes that the mean household size in France had fallen below 4.0 by 1880 (Peter Laslett, "Mean Household Size in England Since the Sixteenth Century," in *Household and Family,* eds. Laslett and Wall, p. 139).

20. Chayanov, *Theory,* p. 54.

21. Robin Fox, *Kinship and Marriage* (New York, 1967), pp. 37–8.

22. Thus, in the case of members outside the conjugal family unit, a comparison of the seven censuses taken prior to 1870 with the five taken after 1890 indicates a rise in the Orléanais of households without outside members from 72.1 to 82.0%, and in the Nantais, the situation appears to remain stable (66.2–67.8%). From the contingency tables from which those statistics were calculated (the tables have the 16 census years as one dimension, the number of outside members as another), we have derived γ (gamma, a measure of assocation) $= -0.05$ for the Orléanais and $+0.02$ for the Nantais. Projecting the region as a third dimension and then controlling for that variable, $\gamma = 0.00$, where $\chi^2 = 123.39$ with 150 df for the Orléanais and 250.63 with 180 df for the Nantais. Thus variation between the cells is not significant at the .001 level for the Nantais. Tables comparing the number of children with the census year produce a similar result.

23. The percentage of households with no member outside the conjugal family unit was distributed as follows:

	Households (%)	N_w		Households (%)	N_w
Beauce	81.4	265	Plateau	56.6	402
Sologne	63.9	134	R–V	68.3	543
Forêt	67.6	205	S-et-M	72.1	490
Valley	78.9	699	Valley	67.1	692

The mother–child bond is discussed further within the context of the developmental cycle. For a breakdown of children by subregion, see Table 7.8.

24. See Edward Shorter, *The Making of the Modern Family* (New York, 1975), pp. 79–80. General methodological problems are also discussed in Peter Laslett's collection of essays, *Family Life and Illicit Love in Earlier Generations* (Cambridge, 1977). See also the special edition,

"Family and Sexuality in France," *Journal of Family History* II, no. 3 (Fall 1977).

25.   Shorter's main source on premarital sexual activity is illegitimacy rates, which could be calculated for our two regions from the vital registries. The published statistics are only broken down by department, thus confusing urban rates with rural rates, one subregion's rates with another's. For the clergymen's comments, see Christiane Marcilhacy, *Le Diocèse d'Orléans au milieu du XIXe siècle* (Paris, 1964), chap. 6.

26.   See earlier comments on bonding; some of the legal issues are discussed in Chapter 8, Section 3.

27.   Female singulate mean ages at marriage from the departmental figures (Loire-Inférieure, Loiret) are given in Etienne Van De Walle, *The Female Population of France in the Nineteenth Century: A Reconstruction of 82 Departements* (Princeton, 1974), pp. 351, 354.

28.   Van De Walle estimates a drop from 24.8 to 23.5 for Loiret and a mean age of 26.7 in 1831 and 26.8 in 1901 for Loire-Inférieure. In Loire-Inférieure, there was, in fact, a slight increase in the mean age during the first decade or so of the Third Republic, with a high of 27.1 estimated for 1881 (ibid.). The lack of a distinct trend in the Nantais confirms a pattern that we already noted in the proportion of multiple households, the mean household size, and the number of members outside the conjugal family unit.

29.   Ibid., pp. 79–92.

30.   We also ought to note that the censuses are assumed to have taken place on 1 January of each census year (except for 1872 where we assume 1871), thus assuring a five-year intercensal period.

31.   The TFR is sometimes called the "completed family size," which is rather misleading in the context of household analysis.

32.   Etienne Gautier and Louis Henry, *La Population de Crulai, paroisse normande* (Paris, 1958); T. F. Sheppard, *Lourmarin in the Eighteenth Century: A Study of a French Village* (Baltimore, 1971). E. A. Wrigley, "Family Limitation in Preindustrial England," *Economic History Review,* XXIX (1966a), pp. 82–109; Gérard Bouchard, *Le Village immobile: Sennely-en-Sologne au XVIIIe siècle* (Paris, 1972); not to forget those record-breaking Hutterites of twentieth-century America:

Age	Age specific fertility rate	Age	Age specific fertility rate
15–19	.300	35–39	.406
20–24	.550	40–44	.222
25–29	.502	45–49	.061
30–34	.447	TFR	12.44

Ansley Coale, "Factors Associated with the Development of Low Fertility: An Historic Summary," in *United Nations Economic and Social Council World Population Conference, 1965* (New York, 1967), vol. II, p. 205.

33.   Philippe Ariès, *Centuries of Childhood: A Social History of Family Life* (New York, 1962), p. 40. The theme of growing "affectivity" between mother and child is today widespread. To cite the best known: Shorter,

Modern Family; Flandrin, *Families;* Lawrence Stone, *The Family, Sex and Marriage in England, 1500–1800* (New York, 1977).

34. Flandrin, *Familles,* pp. 192–5.
35. *Courrier de la Campagne,* 2 November 1879.
36. See Van De Walle, *Female Population,* pp. 15–25.
37. Here I define "infant" as a child under three years of age.
38. Arnold van Gennep, *The Rites of Passage* (Chicago, 1960), pp. 50, 53.
39. René Berthieu, "Les Nourrissons à Cormeilles-en-Parisis (1640-1759)," *Annales de démographie historique, 1975,* pp. 259–89; Olwen H. Hufton, "Women and the Family Economy in Eighteenth-Century France," *French Historical Studies,* IX (1975), pp. 12–13; George Sussman, "The Wet-Nursing Business in Nineteenth-Century France," *French Historical Studies,* IX (1975), pp. 306–7; Abel Chatelain, "Migrations et domesticité féminine urbaine en France, XVIIIe siècle-XXe siècle," *Revue d'histoire économique et sociale,* XLVII (1969), p. 522.
40. Shorter, *Modern Family,* p. 182.
41. Etienne Van De Walle and Samuel Preston, "Mortalité de l'enfance au XIXe siècle à Paris et dans le département de la Seine," *Population,* XXIX (1974), pp. 96–7; Sussman notes that "instead of sending their newborn infants away to the wet nurses' homes in the country, in the nineteenth century these families [the wealthy] brought the nurses into their homes (the *nourrice sur lieu*). But the major development after the Revolution was the increase in the demand for rural wet nurses by sections of the working class and lower middle class" (Sussman, "Wet-Nursing Business," pp. 307–8).
42. Ange Guépin and Eugène Bonamy, *Nantes au XIXe siècle* (Nantes, 1835), pp. 513–14.
43. I am defining "nursling" as a child under two years of age not related to the head of household. The lists sometimes state, but not always, whether a child was a nursling or not.
44. The methods adopted by Berthieu ("Les Nourrissons," pp. 260–2) would probably work just as well for the nineteenth-century *état civil;* Yves Blayo and Louis Henry found that 81.2% of the nurslings whose deaths had been recorded in the parish and civil registries of Brittany–Anjou between 1740 and 1829 came from towns with ten to fifty thousand inhabitants and only 9.8% came from rural communes (Yves Blayo and Louis Henry, "Données démographiques sur la Bretagne et l'Anjou de 1740 à 1829," *Annales de démographie historique, 1967,* p. 156).
45. Not realizing their importance, we unfortunately did not include these distinctions in our own sample data. This is partly due to the fact that, in many cases, kinship was not mentioned and that all we had to go on was the surname: common surnames (husband's or wife's side – maiden names were practically always given) were assumed to indicate blood kin. However, in retrospect, a more detailed method of recording kinship could have been more revealing than originally believed.
46. The proverb is cited by Henri Noilhan, *Histoire de l'agriculture à l'ère industrielle* (Paris, 1965), p. 406.
47. This is not meant to sound glib. Freud described introversion as "the deflection of the libido away from the possibilities of real satisfaction and its excessive accumulation upon phantasies previously tolerated as harmless. An introverted person is not yet neurotic, but he is in an unstable condition; the next disturbance of the shifting forces will cause

symptoms to develop, unless he can yet find other outlets for his pent-up libido. The unreal character of neurotic satisfaction and the disregard of the difference between phantasy and reality are already determined by the arrest at this stage of introversion" (Sigmund Freud, *A General Introduction to Psycho-analysis* [New York, 1935], p. 326).

48. The Parsonian blend of psychoanalysis and sociology presents withdrawal and a sense of autonomy as a sort of precondition for the organization of a rational, differentiated society. The idea is derived from the German sociological notions of historical process developed at the turn of the century and bears an especially close resemblance to the dichotomous thought of Ferdinand Tönnies. The process, according to this interpretation, is an irreversible one from a traditional associational society to a modern contractual society with each member assigned his special role. Two of the weaknesses of the argument lie in its overly idealized conception of the "modern Western family" – with father playing an external, instrumental role and mother playing an internal, emotional role – and the assumption that emotional withdrawal necessarily leads to social inclusion and rational differentiation. This leaves little room for cultural diversity and makes any explanation of behavioral varieties of the kind found in our two regions extremely difficult. Talcott Parsons and R. F. Bales, *Family, Socialization and Interaction Process* (Glencoe, Ill., 1955); Talcott Parsons, *Structure and Process in Modern Societies: A Collection of Essays* (Glencoe, Ill., 1960); Fred Weinstein and Gerald Platt, *The Wish to Be Free: Society, Psyche and Value Change* (Berkeley, 1969).

49. Van Ginneps *Rites;* p. 29.

50. Given the fact that a census is a static, photographic image of a constantly developing population, the larger number of members outside the conjugal family unit that was found in the Nantais could itself be owing to the more prolonged transitional periods.

51. Within the category of "cultivator," as employed in Figure 7.4, we have also included individuals recorded as being owner–cultivators, winegrowers, *fermiers,* and *métayers.* The winegrowers accounted for a little over half the category in the Orléanais. In the Nantais, if all those professions were excluded, the number in this category would have been reduced by less than 2%.

52. It should be remembered that the census enumerators, with reason, made very loose use of their terminology.

53. Again, the terminology was loosely employed, but less loosely, it would appear, than in the Nantais.

54. One may note that the age distributions of relatives peak for men and women in their 20s or early 30s, i.e., at the age of marriage. This largely represents couples moving into their parents' household, presumably because they had no land of their own to exploit. But this phenomenon has to be kept in proper perspective: the total number of related outside members aged 25 to 34 is 141, or under 0.01% of entire population sampled.

55. Pearson's *r* between the year of birth of the head of household and his age is − .42, a spurious relationship because the older household heads of the first censuses were born in the eighteenth century and the younger household heads of the last lists were born in the 1880s and even 1890s.

This effect has to be controlled if the head's year of birth is to be used as a measurement of historical time.

56.   Occupational scores are given in Table 7.8. Obviously the assumption that occupation can be measured on an interval scale is a bit extreme; in part of the analysis, the various occupational categories will be treated as nominal.

57.   It should be remembered that the weight factors, when multiplied out for the entire sample, equal unity. Thus, the number of weighted cases is not very different from the number of unweighted cases in each occupational category. The number of weighted cases has been rounded to the nearest whole number, which sometimes leads to curious results when the N_w is low. An example of this is seen in the occupational category of "rentier," where the real N_w is somewhere between 0 and 0.5. There are about the same number of unweighted cases for each subregional category. Ideally, the unweighted N should have been included in the table. However, that would have been not only time consuming but also expensive.

58.   This was calculated by adding the square of the independent variable to the regression equation, giving $Y = a + b_1X + b_2X^2$, where Y is the dependent variable (in this case, the total number of children), X the independent variable (the head's age), a a constant, and b_1 and b_2 the slope of the curve.

59.   For a discussion of some of the problems involved in the sociological applications of path analysis, see Otis Dudley Duncan, "Path Analysis: Sociological Examples," *American Journal of Sociology* LXXII (1966), pp. 1–16; Richard P. Boyle, "Path Analysis and Ordinal Data," *American Journal of Sociology,* LXXV (1970), pp. 461–80, calms the nerves of those who hesitate to include variables based on anything less than an interval scale.

60.   An interesting study of the probabilities of transition from one household type to another, which comes to conclusions very similar to my own, though rather different in its methodology, is by Etienne Van De Walle, "Household Dynamics in a Belgian Village, 1847–1866," *Journal of Family History,* I (1976), pp. 80–94.

61.   Marshall Sahlins, *Stone Age Economics* (Chicago, 1972), p. 95.

62.   Ibid.

63.   One might want to adopt Malthus's terminology and describe these two demographic alternatives as "positive" and "preventive checks." From the point of view of the outside observer, Malthus's argument and my own are virtually identical. However, from the point of view of our subjective decision makers, they are not. Thus, for Malthus, preventive checks are the products of foresight and positive checks (which will result in higher mortality rates) arise in societies "guided either by a stronger passion, or a weaker judgement." But "foresight" varies according to who is doing the foreseeing. Malthus's preventive checks could be viewed in some societies as lacking in foresight; it really depends on how the society's members choose to define the optimum level of population. See Thomas Malthus, *First Essay on Population* (New York, 1965), pp. 61–70.

64.   AD Loire-Atlantique 1-M-1936-1961, 3-M-86-87.

65.   For the decennial lists of the Nantais (1802-1912), see AD Loire-

Atlantique, *Série E.* For the Orléanais (1802-62), see AD Loiret 30500-30547. The decennial lists of the Orléanais dated later than 1862 are deposited in the Archives of the Tribunal de Première Instance, Palais de Justice, rue de la Bretonnerie, Orléans. I would like to take the opportunity here of thanking the substitut du procureur for authorizing my consultation of these documents. The decennial lists for the city of Nantes from 1852 onward are deposited in the Archives municipales, Nantes.

66. France, Direction régionale de Nantes, *Populations par commune;* France, Direction régionale d'Orléans, *Populations par commune;* France, *Annuaire du Loiret* (occasionally *Almanach*) (Orléans, An XI-1912).

67. Let me note another problem here: Prior to 1831, the population totals given in the local publications are clearly no more than rough estimates. This is evident from the unusually large number of round rates that turn up in our calculations for this period, even when nine-year running means are used. For this reason, migration rates are plotted only after 1820. However, none of the rates prior to 1830 should be taken too seriously. For a discussion of the inaccuracies of these early censuses from the point of view of France as a whole, see Van De Walle, *Female Population,* pp. 15-20.

68. E. A. Wrigley, *Population and History* (New York, 1969), pp. 62-80, 164-80.

69. For example, the last plague epidemic in France spread from the Port of Marseille in 1721. Smallpox ceased to attack populations at epidemic levels after the 1830s (Frederick F. Cartwright, *Disease and History* [New York, 1972], pp. 120-9). For a good general history of disease, see William H. McNeill, *Plagues and Peoples* (New York, 1976).

70. For a discussion of one of the last of such crises, that of 1815-16, see John D. Post, "Famine, Mortality, and Epidemic Disease in the Process of Modernization," *Economic History Review,* XXIX (1976), pp. 14-37.

71. It should, however, be noted that 1870 was a year of exceptionally high mortality, probably partly the result of the German occupation. Out of a total of 3,580 deaths, the 10 most fatal diseases (together with the number of deaths) were as follows: smallpox (547), tuberculosis (351), pneumonia (339), enteritis (276), bronchitis (194), dysentery (179), typhus (134), meningitis (131), cerebral apoplexy (122), vaguely determined circulatory ailments (100) (*Le Phare de la Loire,* 16 October 1871).

72. *Journal du Loiret,* 22 March 1849.
73. Ibid., 29 March 1849.
74. Ibid., 31 March 1849.
75. Ibid., 2 June 1849.
76. Ibid., 5 June 1849.
77. Ibid., 20 September 1849.
78. *Le Colibri,* 29 October 1848.
79. Ibid., 5 November 1848.
80. *L'Union Bretonne,* 9 July 1849.
81. Ibid.
82. Ibid.
83. Ibid., 23 August 1849.

84.   Ibid., 21 and 29 September 1849.
85.   Ibid., 23 April 1850.
86.   "It is to be noted that the affected arrondissements are, as almost everywhere else, those whose territory is crossed by our river" (Ibid., 9 July 1849). In a study of the cholera epidemic of 1832 in the department of Seine-et-Oise, Catherine Rollet and Agnès Souriac have made the same observation, (Catherine Rollet and Agnès Souriac, "Le Choléra de 1832 en Seine-et-Oise," *Annales ESC,* XXIX [1974], pp. 938–42).
87.   One possible cause was a warming trend in the climate, which set in at the middle of the century. But such reasoning remains highly speculative; see Emmanuel Le Roy Ladurie, *Times of Feast, Times of Famine: A History of Climate Since the Year 1000* (New York, 1971), pp. 7–22, 61, 94–5, 227.
88.   The decennial tables after 1882 for 23 communes of the Nantais were not to be found in the departmental archives and so are presumably still deposited in the archives of the Palais de Justice, Nantes, into which I was unable to gain access.
89.   The cultivator's wife was an object of special attention probably because (although it was rarely said) there was an awareness that women played an important role in rural migrations; the geographical mobility of women, we have established, was greater than that of men. See *L'Echo Nantais,* 10 October and 7 November, 1865; *Courrier de la Campagne,* 21 November 1875; and for a comment on the woman's role in more recent times, Mendras, *La Fin,* pp. 225–6.
90.   It would be wrong to imagine that these sorts of commentary only began with the Third Republic. The 1848 parliamentary enquiry is filled with them, e.g., AN C 956 Canton of Legé, or AN 957 Chateauneuf. There were fewer newspaper articles of this genre before 1860 because the kind of paper that used to print them simply did not exist.
91.   "Nantes is one of the towns of France where one lives the longest" (*L'Indépendance de l'Ouest,* weekly ed., 17 May 1873).
92.   Beggars were the most surveyed migrants. As an example of the high proportion of outsiders frequently found among them, one could cite the records for 1845: out of a total of 525 beggars arrested, only 25 were from the Nantais region. "Among these 525 beggars one must still count a large number of children from Lower Brittany. . . . Savoy and the Two Sardinias also supply a large number of beggars . . . " (*Le Breton,* 1 September 1847). Police reports of the Third Republic continue to note that most beggars were from outside the department, e.g., AD Loire-Atlantique 1-M-578, *Nantes ville, Situation . . .* , June 1880.
93.   Georges Dupeux, "La Croissance urbaine en France au XIXe siècle," *Revue d'histoire économique et sociale,* LII (1974), pp. 183–4.
94.   Urban historians do frequently point out that migrations to the major city centers were usually made in short hops rather than in one single move – a theme that can be traced back at least as far as Adna Ferrin Weber, *The Growth of Cities in the Nineteenth Century* (Ithaca, N.Y., 1899).
95.   I am, of course, only referring to the Orléanais and the Nantais. A study by Paul Hohenberg indicates that many of our conclusions could be generalized to a national level. However, Hohenberg's work is based on departmental statistics; little is known about migratory movements within the smaller agricultural regions (Paul Hohenberg, "Migrations et

fluctuations démographiques dans la France rurale, 1836–1901," *Annales ESC,* XXIX [1974], pp. 461–97).

96.   Actually the "principle" upon which these rates were calculated is not the total population of each commune in 1881 but an estimate derived from averaging the communal totals of 1881 and 1886. This was necessary in order to be absolutely sure that an inaccurate statistic in the census could not affect the results.

97.   For the identity of these and other communes mentioned in the text, see Figures 2.2 and 2.3.

Chapter 8. Peasant properties

1.   *Journal du Loiret,* 8 February 1860.
2.   *L'Echo du Loiret, de la Beauce, et de la Sologne,* 15 September 1867.
3.   Honoré de Balzac, *Le Curé de village* (Paris, 1972) p. 258.
4.   Honoré de Balzac, *Les Paysans,* (Paris, 1968), p. 439.
5.   Frédéric Le Play, *La Réforme sociale en France* (Paris, 1901), 3 vols.
6.   Edmond Demolins, *Anglo-Saxon Superiority: To What It Is Due* ("A quoi tient la supériorité des Anglo-Saxons") (New York, 1898), pp. 135–59.
7.   See comments by Placide Rambaud and Monique Vincienne, *Les Transformations d'une société rurale: la Maurienne (1561–1962)* (Paris, 1964), p. 108.
8.   Michèle Dion-Salitot and Michel Dion, *La Crise d'une société villageoise: les "survivanciers," les paysans du Jura français (1800–1970)* (Paris, 1972) pp. 23–68 might be the exception (esp. pp. 49–66), although their actual analysis of property life cycles is based on only a few case families. The most comprehensive study of the cadastre yet published is Philippe Vigier's *Essai sur la répartition de la propriété foncière dans la région alpine: son évolution des origines du cadastre à la fin du Second Empire* (Paris, 1963a), covering five departments. André Siegfried's employment of the cadastre in *Tableau politique de la France de l'Ouest sous la Troisième République* (Paris, 1913) has been shown to be somewhat superficial. Some regional monographs have made use of the cadastre, notably Paul Bois, *Paysans de l'Ouest* (Paris, 1971) pp. 18–23, 42–60; and Georges Dupeux, *Aspects de l'histoire sociale et politique du Loir-et-Cher, (1848–1914),* (Paris, 1962), pp. 97–110; see also J. Harvey Smith, "Work Routine and Social Structure in a French Village: Cruzy in the Nineteenth Century," *Journal of Interdisciplinary History,* V (1975), pp. 359–60. From the point of view of methodology, some studies of earlier forms of the French cadastre have been proven useful, particularly Emmanuel Le Roy Ladurie's work on the *compoix* in *Les Paysans de Languedoc* (Paris, 1969); and Gérard Béaur, "Le Centième Denier et les mouvements de propriété: deux exemples beaucerons (1761–1790)," *Annales ESC,* XXXI (1976), pp. 1010–33. See also the unpublished Mémoires de Maîtrise of two of Vigier's students on two cantons in the Orléanais: Michel Leray, *Evolution de la répartition de la propriété foncière dans le canton d'Artenay (Loiret) de 1813 à 1913* (Tours, 1971); and Ramon Poivet, *Evolution de la répartition de la propriété foncière et de l'exploitation agricole dans le canton de Jargeau (Loiret) de 1834 à 1913* (Tours, 1970).

9.   Matrices of the first cadastre of the Orléanais were deposited at AD

Loiret; second cadastre at the Service du cadastre, Orléans. With the exception of a few consulted in AD Loire-Atlantique, all the matrices of the Nantais were at the Service du cadastre, Nantes, at the time this study was undertaken.

10.   A "parcel" was defined as a portion of land distinguished from the surrounding land either by its ownership or by the use to which it was put. Land belonging to one propertyholder and differing in its cultivation only by its particular stage in a given crop rotation was considered to form a single parcel (France, Ministre de l'Agriculture, du Commerce et des Travaux, Statistique de la France. *Territoire et population* [Paris, 1855], vol. II, p. xii).

11.   Strictly speaking, the basic cadastral unit is a *cote* rather than a property. A property might stretch over more than one commune, in which case it would have fragments appearing in more than one matrix. The only way of getting a truly accurate picture of property structure would be through a reconstruction of the kind presented in Chapter 5 on the properties of over 50 hectares. De Foville calculated that for the whole of France there were 63 properties for every 100 *cotes* in 1851, 59.4 for every 100 in 1879. He attributed the decline to an increase in geographic mobility (Albert de Foville, *Le Morcellement: études économiques et statistiques sur la propriété foncière* [Paris, 1895], p. 67). Ramon Poivet indicates 78 properties per 100 *cotes* in the canton of Jargeau in 1835, 67 per 100 in 1913 (Poivet, *Canton de Jargeau,* p. 13).

12.   We have been able to identify the places of residence for all but 5% of the sample with the aid of F. J. Pinson, *Dictionnaire des lieux habités du département de la Loire-Inférieure* (Nantes, 1857).

13.   *Propriété bâtie* was included in the matrices until 1882 when it was separated into a different register. The actual area of land occupied by constructions continued to be recorded, but without the estimated value and other details on the constructions themselves.

14.   France, Ministre de l'Agriculture, du Commerce et des Travaux, Statistique de la France. *Territoire et population* (Paris, 1855), Vol. I, p. xii.

15.   The communes selected from the Nantais (with date of cadastre's origin) are: Joué-sur-Erdre (1839) and Pannecé (1839) – the Plateau; La Marne (1838) and Saint Aignan (1828) – Retz–Vendée; Chateauthébaud (1832) and Mouzillon (1821) – Sèvre-et-Maine; La Chapelle-Basse-Mer (1822), Montrelais (1824), and Thouaré (1834) – Valley. From the Orléanais: Saint Péravy (1827) and Tournoisis (1827) – Beauce; Ligny-le-Ribault (1825) and Marcilly-en-Villette (1825) – Sologne; Bouzy-la-Forêt (1825) and Trainou (1837) – Forêt; Baule (1829), Bou (1836), Darvoy (1834), and Dry (1828) – Valley. It is perhaps regrettable that a larger sample could not be made but this was not possible; a single property spread over several folios could take as much as a day to code!

16.   The full code of relationship is as follows: 0, no information available on buyer (seller); 1, area existing at date of cadastre's origin; 2, land accorded to one of the coparceners (only found in the few cases of shared property); 3, buyer has same surname as seller; 4, buyer has a different surname from seller; 5, buyer (seller) is the commune; 6, buyer (seller) is a road company (usually government); 7, buyer (seller) is a rail company; 8, reclaimed land or land destroyed (e.g., river action).

17.   AD Loire-Atlantique 1-M-1953, Inspecteur d'Agriculture, *Des divers*

modes d'exploitation des terres dans la Loire-Inférieure, Nantes, 9 April 1855.

18. France, Ministre de l'Agriculture, *La petite propriété rurale en France: enquêtes monographiques (1908–9)* (Paris, 1909).

19. AD Loire-Atlantique 1-M-2012, Prefect, Département de la Loire-Inférieure, *Statistique des vignobles: questions adressées par Son Excellence, le Ministre des Finances,* Nantes, 25 November 1829.

20. De Foville, for instance, calculated that the average size of property in 1881 in Loire-Inférieure was 3.25 hectares; in Loiret it was 3.94 (de Foville, *Morcellement,* p. 82). These figures, which concur with our own, are well below the averages that Paul Bois indicates for the west of France at about the same date (Bois, *Paysans,* p. 19).

21. "Total surface" actually means the sampled surface, or about 8,000 hectares from either cadastre.

22. Le Play, *La Réforme sociale,* vol. II, pp. 44–106, esp. pp. 72–3.

23. This is derived by recoding the total areas of a property for each year of its existence into the percentile score as computed in the first sample (see p. 206)

24. See E. P. Thompson, "The Grid of Inheritance: A Comment," in *Family and Inheritance: Rural Society in Western Europe, 1200–1800,* eds. Jack Goody, Joan Thirsk, and E. P. Thompson, (Cambridge, 1976), pp. 328–360.

25. Ardouin-Dumazet, *Voyage en France, 1ère série: Le Morvan, le Val de Loire, le Perche* (Paris, 1902), pp. 167–9.

26. This has also been noted in Gérard Béaur's article on the eighteenth-century property movements in the area administered by the bureau of Maintenon on the banks of the Eure, as contrasted with the bureau of Janville in the center of the Beauce, which includes a part of the Orléanais Beauce (Béaur, "Centième Denier," pp. 1015–6).

27. See André Ferré, *Les Marges méridionales du Massif de l'Ouest: Poitou, Pays Vendéens, Basse Loire* (Paris, 1929), pp. 119–20.

28. (1) The division of property as a consequence of increasing population; (2) the parceling of land as a consequence of the multiplication of enclosures or the growing variety in the modes of exploitation; (3) the dispersion of properties into disseminated plots (of the kind described by Le Play in his *village à banlieue*). See de Foville, *Morcellement.*

29. Henri Baudrillart, *Les Populations agricoles de la France* (Paris, 1885), vol. I, p. 551.

30. AD Loiret M-241, *Déposition de M. Rabourdin, cultivateur, ex-maire de Férolles,* 1866, cited in Roger Dion, *Le Val de Loire* (Tours, 1934), p. 663.

31. For England, G. E. Mingay, "The Agricultural Depression, 1730–50," *Economic History Review,* VIII (1956), pp. 323–38; for France, Michel Morineau, *Les Faux-semblants d'un démarrage économique: agriculture et démographie en France au XVIIIe siècle* (Paris, 1971).

32. E. Robert, *Histoire du Loiret* (Orléans, 1947), p. 57.

33. A brief history of early canal schemes was given in *La Sologne,* 8 May 1858. One of the first was that proposed by Leonardo da Vinci in the sixteenth century; see Keith Sutton, "A French Agricultural Canal – The Canal de la Sauldre and the Nineteenth-Century Improvement of the Sologne," *Agricultural History Review,* XXI (1973), p. 51.

34. *Journal du Loiret,* 15 June 1848.
35. Ibid., 12 August 1848.
36. Ibid.
37. *La Sologne,* 3 June 1858.
38. Henri Millet, *Histoire de la Sologne depuis 1850* (Paris, 1911), pp. 62 –7, 76.
39. First cadastre: heath and marsh, 16,534 hectares; wood, 12,182 hectares; arable, 23,724 hectares. Second cadastre: heath and marsh, 4,417 hectares; wood, 20,714 hectares; arable, 30,823 hectares.
40. *Journal du Loiret,* 1 February 1853 and 8 September 1880; Millet, *Sologne depuis 1850,* pp. 83–110.
41. See Ester Boserup, *The Conditions of Agricultural Growth: The Economics of Agrarian Change under Population Pressure* (Chicago, 1965).
42. See *Journal du Loiret,* 26 August 1840.
43. See Robert Besnier, *Cours d'histoire du droit français* (Paris, 1955), p. 289.
44. AN F^{10} 2353, *Curage du Cosson, 1856.*
45. Gérard Bouchard found only one "peasant proprietor" and one "artisan proprietor" in the eighteenth-century parish of Sennely (Gérard Bouchard, *Le Village immobile: Sennely-en-Sologne au XVIIIe siècle* [Paris, 1972], pp. 134–5). Ownership of the land, we have insisted, is one of the conditions of peasant economy.
46. Pierre Catala, "Les successions," in *Le Droit français: principes et tendances du droit français,* ed. René David (Paris, 1960), pp. 60–7; Jean-Philippe Lévy, *Cours d'histoire du droit privé (la famille)* (Paris, 1966), pp. 190–8; René David, *French Law: The Structure, Sources and Methodology* (Bâton Rouge, 1972), pp. 11–16, 162–7.
47. For a striking example of a contrast between formal legal principle and practice found in the Pyrenees, see Pierre Bourdieu, "Les Stratégies matrimoniales dans les systèmes de reproduction," *Annales ESC,* XXVII (1972), pp. 1105–27.
48. Jean Yver, *Essai de géographie coutumière: égalité entre héritiers et exclusion des enfants dotés* (Paris, 1966). Emmanuel Le Roy Ladurie places Yver's distinctions within a more rustic framework in "Système de la coutume: structures familiales et coutume d'héritage en France au XVIe siècle," *Annales ESC,* XXVII (1972), pp. 825–46, an English translation of which appears in Goody, et al., eds., *Family and Inheritance,* pp. 37–70.
49. Yver, *Essai,* p. 106.
50. There was, in fact, a whole body of French customary law that defined a legal "thing" according to its temporal and not its physical aspect; see Ralph Giesey, "Rules of Inheritance and Strategies of Mobility in Prerevolutionary France," *American Historical Review,* LXXXII (1977), pp. 271–89.
51. Lévy, *Cours d'histoire,* pp. 16, 19–21.
52. Ansley Coale and Paul Demeny, *Regional Model Life Tables and Stable Populations* (Princeton, 1966). Mortality levels have been established by taking the female life expectancies at birth for Loire-Inférieure and Loiret as calculated by Etienne Van De Walle, *The Female Population of France in the Nineteenth Century: A Reconstruction of 82 Depart-*

ments (Princeton, 1974), Table 8.1. In imitation of Van De Walle, we have used the "North" tables for Loiret and the "West" tables for Loire-Inférieure.

53.   Jean Bonhomme inherits 1.00 hectares from his father Jacques in 1850; in 1860 he sells 0.50 hectares to his neighbor Gérard Bidon; and in 1870 the remaining 0.50 hectares are passed on to his son Jules. Up to and including 1859 (0 through 45 PCUs, or 5 PCUs per annum), a total of 1.00 hectares has been transacted, all with a person of the same surname, so the kin area index would equal 1.00. From 1860 to 1869 (46 through 95 PCUs), 1.50 hectares have been transacted; the kin area index would now be 1.00/1.50, or .667. In 1870 (95 through 100 PCUs), the index would be 1.50/2.00, or .750.

54.   Bonhomme's land once more: The average area would be $[10(1.00) + 10(0.50)]/20 = 0.75$ hectares. Given the formula $100x_i/\bar{x}$, where x_i is the total area at a given moment and $\bar{x}$ the average, the property area index for 0 through 45 PCUs would be 133, for 46 through 95 PCUs would be 67, and for 96 through 100 it would be 0.

Chapter 9. Crisis and stability

1.   See Emmanuel Le Roy Ladurie's contribution to *Histoire économique et sociale de la France,* Tome I: *De 1450 à 1660,* eds. Fernand Braudel and C. E. Labrousse (Paris, 1977), vol. II, pp. 481–865.

2.   This was also the case of the majority of shopkeepers in the towns at the beginning of this century. See AN C 7464-5, *Enquête du commerce,* Loire-Inférieure and Loiret, 1912.

3.   "Extensification" is unpoetic and "consolidation" is a word that must be used advisedly, as the last chapter should have already demonstrated.

4.   *Journal du Loiret,* 1 and 8 October 1836.

5.   Roger Dion, *Le Val de Loire* (Tours, 1934); Georges Dupeux, *Aspects de l'histoire sociale et politique du Loir-et-Cher,* 1848-1914 (Paris, 1962), p. 78.

6.   The civil war of 1815, discussed later, was probably another contributing factor. A letter dated 1 December 1807 from a *juge de paix* to the minister of the interior (AN F^{10} 435) points out how the vineyards of his canton, La Chapelle-sur-Erdre, had fallen into a state of neglect following the destruction wrought in the 1790s. Shouldn't we expect the same after 1815?

7.   Though it might surprise those who like to trace the ubiquitous spud back to the days of Sir Walter Raleigh, the potato was not commonly seen on European tables before the nineteenth century. See Wilhelm Abel, *Crises agraires en Europe (XIIIe–XXe siècle)* (Paris, 1973), pp. 286, 334, 354.

8.   AD Loire-Atlantique 1-M-1953, *Situation agricole du département - Rapports annuels;* Dupeux, *Aspects de l'histoire,* p. 202.

9.   Henri Sée, *Histoire économique de la France: les temps modernes (1789-1914)* (Paris, 1942), pp. 137-40; Jean Chombert de Lauwe, *Bretagne et pays de Garonne* (Paris, 1946), pp. 59-61; AD Loire-Atlantique, 1-14-1953, *Situation agricole du département -* Rapports annuels. On the innovative small French farmer, see Peter Simoni, "Agricultural Change and Landlord–Tenant Relations in Nineteenth-

Century France," *Journal of Social History* XIII (1979) pp. 122, 133, n. 39.

10. David Landes, "The Statistical Study of French Crises," *Journal of Economic History,* X (1950), pp. 195–211; AN F^{19} 5692, Borros de Garnanson to Minister of interior, Orléans, 25 February 1812; Gérard Walter, *Histoire des paysans de France* (Paris, 1963), pp. 402–4; E. Robert, *Histoire du Loiret* (Orléans, 1947), p. 50; AD Loire-Atlantique 1-14-1953, *Situation agricole,* 10 August 1847.

11. See my earlier comments on Malthus's distinction between "positive" and "preventive checks" (n. 63 of Chapter 7).

12. How much of a contrast does this make with the seventeenth and fourteenth centuries? A systematic comparison of these three peasant agricultural crises could be very instructive. See Le Roy Ladurie, in *Histoire économique et sociale,* eds. Braudel and Labrousse, vol. II, pp. 481–865.

13. *Emile Durkheim on the Division of Labor in Society* (New York, 1933), pp. 98–9.

14. Howard S. Becker, *Outsiders: Studies in the Sociology of Deviance* (Glencoe, Ill., 1963).

15. Georges Lefebvre, *The Great Fear of 1789* (New York, 1973), p. 172.

16. AN F^7 3681^8, Trimesterly report, Orléans, 6 Floréal An X (25 April 1802). For the sources on the Nantais, see the references in my later discussion on insurrection.

17. AD Loire-Atlantique 1-14-495, 496, 509. Police correspondence of 1815 and 1832. AN F^7 36818, Monthly report, Orléans, 4 July 1820; and Prefect to Directeur général, Police du Roy, Orléans, 26 July 1814. AN F^7 4052, Monthly report, Nantes, 9 September 1832. On *l'esprit public,* see Richard Cobb, *The Police and the People* (London, 1970), pp. 49–81.

18. See Mona Ozouf, *La Fête révolutionnaire, 1789–1799* (Paris, 1976), p. 114.

19. I get the impression that Eugen Weber's "archaic stage" in peasant politics (local and personal as opposed to national) is just that. It bespeaks less of archaism than of novelty and an excited imagination (Eugen Weber, *Peasants into Frenchmen: The Modernization of Rural France, 1870–1913* [Stanford, 1976], p. 241).

20. Ibid., pp. 50–66; Charles Tilly, "France," in Charles Tilly, Louise Tilly, and Richard Tilly, *The Rebellious Country, 1830–1930* (Cambridge, Mass., 1975), pp. 78–80.

21. Howard Zehr, *Crime and the Development of Modern Society: Patterns of Criminality in Nineteenth-Century Germany and France* (London, 1976).

22. Tilly, "France," p. 79.

23. Zehr, *Crime,* p. 39.

24. Tilly, "France," p. 79.

25. Zehr, *Crime,* p. 115. Charles Tilly's figures are based on serious crimes tried in the assize courts. "The error here is serious," notes Zehr, "and provides a perfect example of the potential for misinterpretation inherent in crime statistics. Besides the increasing number of property crimes which were simply dropped, more and more cases were sent to lower courts . . . in order to speed up the process of justice and to increase the probability of convictions" (Zehr, *Crime,* p. 146 n.11).

26.   I am struck by the similarity in style – and especially the use of poison (perverse symbol of a society still obsessed with its nutrition?) – with the accounts of rural murder I found and Mary Hartman's account of 13 "middle-class" murderesses in nineteenth-century Britain and France. The implication, of course, is that there was nothing very specific about the *style* of French rural murder; the same thing was going on in the West End of London. See Mary Hartman, *Victorian Murderesses* (New York, 1977).

27.   This newspaper article also appeared in the *Journal de Chartres.* It resembles, in several ways, Zola's fictional account of old Fouan's murder by his son and daughter-in-law *(La Terre),* and it is quite possible, given the time and place of the event, that Zola's inspiration came from the article. For an assessment of Zola's use and interpretation of his sources, see Gregor Dallas and Micheline Herz, "Zola, Darwin et les paysans," *Bulletin 2: Société des Professeurs Français en Amérique* (1978–9), pp. 83–115.

28.   Michel Foucault ed., *Moi, Pierre Rivière, ayant égorgé ma mère, ma soeur, et mon frère . . . : un cas de parricide au XIXe siècle* (Paris, 1973).

29.   *Journal du Loiret,* 24 August 1834.

30.   *L'Echo Nantais,* 21 November 1868.

31.   AD Loire-Atlantique 1-M-490, Prefect to Ministre de l'intérieur, Nantes, 19 September 1846.

32.   This is not to deny complaints about drinking in earlier times. There are, for instance, records of clergy expressing dismay at heavy drinking in the eighteenth century. See Olwen H. Hufton, *The Poor of Eighteenth-Century France,* (Oxford, 1974), p. 363. It is also worth noting that Madame de Wolmar forbade wine drinking among her domestics in Jean-Jacques Rousseau's *La Nouvelle Héloise,* in *Oeuvres complètes* (Paris, 1839), vol. II, p. 407.

33.   National figures on the consumption of wine are provided by Zehr who also analyzes their relationship to crime (Zehr, *Crime,* pp. 45–6, 90, 98–9, 118–19, 133, 175–6).

34.   Natalie Zemon Davis makes some interesting points of comparison between the "religious riot" and the better known "food riot" in *Society and Culture in Early Modern France* (Stamford, 1975), chap. 6.

35.   *Journal du Loiret,* 5 September, 12 September, 7 October, and 4 November 1830; AN F 4055, Police reports for 1830.

36.   AD Loire-Atlantique 1-M-515, Letters between the commissaire de police, the mayor, the sub-prefect, the procureur du tribunal de première instance, and the prefect, Ancenis, 10–13 December 1846.

37.   See especially AN F⁷ 4051, Annual report for 1817, Nantes, 10 January 1818; AD Loire-Atlantique 1-M-51, Mayor of Nantes to Prefect, Nantes, 19 October 1840.

38.   Ange Guépin and Gabriel Simon, *Evénements de Nantes pendant les journées des 25, 29, 30 et 31 juillet 1830 par plusieurs témoins oculaires* (Nantes, n.d. [1830–?]).

39.   Bernard-Henri Lévy, *La Barbarie à visage humain* (Paris, 1977), pp. 159–65. See also André Glucksmann, *Les Maîtres penseurs* (Paris, 1977), pp. 14–15, 204–23; not forgetting Sigmund Freud, *Civilization and Its Discontents* (New York, 1962).

40.   An interesting sequel to these July Days in Nantes took place at the birth

of the Third Republic (or shortly before or shortly after, depending on the way one likes to date these things). Three trainloads of pilgrims ("mostly countrywomen") arriving in Nantes from Lourdes were attacked by a crowd ("of many youths") gathered at the station on 26 September 1872. The violence, though far less serious than in 1830, indicates how persistent the mutual suspicions just described were. AD Loire-Atlantique 1-M-520 and 522 Nantes, ville, *Situation politique, morale . . .* , 29 September 1872; Le Commissaire de police, *Rapport sur des événements . . .* , 29 September 1872; Commissaire central, *Rapport à Monsieur le Préfet sur les événements . . .* , 27 September 1872.

41. P. Leclair, *Histoire des brigands, chauffeurs et assassins d'Orgères* (Chartres, An VIII); A. F. Coudray-Maunier, *Histoire de la Bande d'Orgères* (Chartres, 1858), which is lifted word for word from Leclair, who participated in the trial; AN F⁷ 36818, Correspondence between the prefect, the inspecteur général de la gendarmerie, and the minister of justice, Germinal–Thermidor An XI (April–July 1803).

42. AN F⁷ 4058, Monthly report for March, Orléans, 4 April 1847. For a report on the trial, see *Journal du Loiret,* 23 September 1848.

43. Dion, *Val de Loire,* pp. 456–9; AN F⁷ 35818, Petition dated 15 Messidor An XI (3 July 1803) and correspondence between the Inspecteur des marchés des subsistences, le grand juge (minister of the interior), and the prefect, 17 Messidor-14 Thermidor An XI (5 July–1 August 1803); Maurice Agulhon, *La République au Village* (Paris, 1970a), 80–92; Paul Domet, *Histoire de la Forêt d'Orléans* (Orléans, 1892).

44. Most of these regulations were not actually new; many dated back to the seventeenth century. The novelty was that they were enforced. See Domet, *Forêt d'Orléans,* pp. 166–225.

45. AN F⁷ 4055–4058, Police reports; *Journal du Loiret,* 27 April 1834.

46. *Journal du Loiret,* 27 March 1849.

47. AN F⁷ 4056 and 4058, Reports, for example, of 1833 and 1847.

48. On "plebs," see Michel Foucault, *Recherches logiques,* no. 4, 1977, which is cited by Glucksmann in his own discussion of the problem (Glucksmann, *Maîtres penseurs,* pp. 168–70). Foucault's analysis of power as a tactic that is exercised rather than an object that is possessed is particularly interesting within this context. See, for example, Michel Foucault, *Surveiller et punir: naissance de la prison* (Paris, 1975), pp. 27–35, 194–6; or Michel Foucault, *The History of Sexuality* (New York, 1980), vol. I, pp. 8–13, 44–9, 77–102.

49. Paul Bois, *Paysans de l'Ouest* (Paris, 1960); Georges Bordonove, *La Vie quotidienne en Vendée pendant la Révolution* (Paris, 1974); Emile Gabory, *Les Bourbons et la Vendée* (Paris, 1947) and *Les grandes heures de la Vendée* (Paris, 1961); Charles Tilly, *The Vendée* (Cambridge, Mass. 1964).

50. AD Loire-Atlantique 1-M-495, Correspondence between *Lieutenant de la gendarmerie* and the prefect, April–May 1815; AD Loire-Atlantique 1-14-509-511, Police correspondence, 1832. The seizure of religious buildings is one of the characteristic acts of the religious riot as described by Davis, *Society and Culture,* p. 163.

51. AD Loire-Atlantique 1-M-490, Police report, 16 August 1809; Yves-Marie Bercé, *Fête et révolte: des mentalités populaires du XVIe au XVIIIe siècle* (Paris, 1976), p. 23.

52. Police reports and correspondence, AD Loire-Atlantique 1-M-486-491; AN F⁷ 3681⁷.

53. AN F⁷ 3681⁷, Mayor of Palluan to Mayor of Nantes, 29 August 1818.

54. AD Loire-Atlantique 1-M-509-512, Police reports and correspondence; AN F⁷ 4052, Monthly and annual police reports; AN F¹⁹ 5741, Correspondence of the prefect, ministre de l'instruction publique et des cultes, and the bishop of Nantes. For the military excesses of 1831, see the twenty-five-thousand-word report submitted to the council of ministers in 1833 and reproduced in *La Gazette de la France (Editions des provinces),* 22 June 1833, conserved in AD Loire-Atlantique 1-M-511.

55. AD Loire-Atlantique 1-M-515-516.

56. AN F⁷ 3027, *Etat nominatif des ex-Chefs Chouans et Vendéens des Départements de la Loire-Inférieure et de Maine et Loire dont la résidence dans ces Contrées est nuisible au bon ordre et à la tranquilité [sic] publique,* 21 Pluviose An XII (9 February 1804).

57. AD Loire-Atlantique 1-M-510, Le Capitaine de recrutement, *Recrutement de la Loire-Inférieure,* Nantes, 14 July 1832; *Disarmement – Etats nominatifs,* June and July 1832.

58. Richard Cobb, *Les Armées révolutionnaires* (Paris, 1961).

59. Ardouin-Dumazet, *Voyage en France, 16ème série: De Vendée en Beauce* (Paris, 1898), pp. 79–80.

60. Urban growth rates also slowed during this period, at the national as well as local level. See Georges Dupeux, "La Croissance urbaine en France au XIXe siècle," *Revue d'histoire économique et sociale,* LII (1974), pp. 173–89.

61. Jules Guyot, *Etudes des vignobles de France* (Paris, 1868), vol. II, p. 438.

62. France, Ministre de l'Agriculture, du Commerce et des Travaux Publics, Statistique de la France, *Statistique agricole* (Paris, 1858–60), 2 vols.; Ministre de l'agriculture, Statistique de la France, *Agriculture: Résultats généraux de l'enquête décennale de 1862* (Strasbourg, 1870); Ministre de l'Agriculture, Statistique agricole de la France, *Résultats généraux de l'enquête décennale de 1882* (Nancy, 1887); Ministre de l'Agriculture, Statistique agricole de la France, *Résultats généraux de l'enquête décennale de 1892* (Paris, 1897); Statistique de la France, *Statistique annuelle, 1871–98* (Paris, 1874–1900), 28 vols.; Statistique générale de la France, *Annuaire statistique de la France, 1878–1915* (Paris, 1879–1917), 34 vols.; Ministère de l'Agriculture, *Statistique agricole annuelle, 1885–1914* (Paris, 1886–1916), 30 vols.

63. Georges Dupeux found, in Loir-et-Cher, after 1850 an increase in the demand and use of farm tools but most of these were of traditional design (Dupeux, *Aspects de l'histoire,* p. 212). Henri Mendras pointed out that one of the reasons new technology was so slow to spread was because, in contrast to a factory where resources are brought to machines, on the land, machines have to be brought to the resources (Henri Mendras, *Sociologie de la campagne française* [Paris, 1959], pp. 15–16).

64. AD Loire-Atlantique 1-M-1953, Agricultural reports; *L'Union Bretonne,* 23 August 1849.

65. AD Loire-Atlantique 1-M-1953 and 2012, Agricultural reports and correspondence.

66. Most is in imitation of Michel Augé-Laribé's classic *La Révolution*

agricole (Paris, 1955). For a recent example, see the third volume of Georges Duby and Armand Wallon, eds., *Histoire de la France rurale* (Paris, 1976), which is not to misprize the thoroughness and sheer elegance of the series in general.

67. *Journal du Loiret*, 30–31 August 1869.

68. On beetles, see *Courrier de la Campagne*, 25 August 1878.

69. Ibid., 5 October 1879.

70. For a general account of the French agricultural recession, see Jean Lhomme "La Crise agricole à la fin du XIXe siècle en France: essai d'interprétation économique et sociale," *Revue économique* XXII (1970), pp. 522–53; and Charles P. Kindleberger, *Economic Growth in France and Britain, 1851–1950* (Cambridge, Mass., 1964). For the Loire Country, see Dion, *Val de Loire,* and Dupeux, *Aspects de l'histoire.*

71. In the mid-1870s, wine was France's first export, and taxes on wine formed 15% of the national budget (Charles K. Warner, *The Wine-growers of France and the Government since 1875* [New York, 1960], p. 1).

72. AD Loiret 12-M-9, Directeur de l'agriculture to Ministre de l'agriculture, 31 August 1878; Directeur des contributions directes to Prefect, 7 September 1892.

73. The best contemporary account I have found of the history, symptoms, and recommended treatments of phylloxera is Prosper de Lafitte, *Quatre ans de luttes pour nos vignes et nos vins de France: mémoires, opuscules et articles* (Bordeaux, 1883). The *Journal du Loiret,* 19 August 1869, notes that phylloxera first appeared outside Nîmes (Gard) in 1868.

74. *Journal du Loiret* and *Courrier de la Campagne,* issues of September 1876–January 1877.

75. AD Loire-Atlantique 1-M-2012, Correspondence; *Le Progrès de la Loire-Inférieure,* 29 July 1883.

76. AD Loiret 12-M-9, Annual reports; Directeur de l'agriculture to Ministre de l'agriculture.

77. AD Loire-Atlantique 1-M-520, Correspondence and reports.

78. AN F[10] 1609, Prefect to Ministre de l'agriculture, Nantes, 4 April 1887.

79. Gilbert Garrier, "Aspects et limites de la crise phylloxérique en Beaujolais ou le puceron bienfaisant (1875–1895)," *Revue d'histoire économique et sociale,* LII (1974), pp. 190–208.

80. Enquiries made in 1903, 1906, 1909, and 1912 show the Orléanais to have had a net loss of one-third of its vineyard area since the onset of phylloxera. Another third, as I have already indicated, was lost between 1850 and 1880. AD Loiret 12-M-56, *Enquêtes sur la situation du vignoble,* 1903–12.

81. Historians have been sparing in their comments about the early days of rural associations. I know no good secondary source on the subject (though the number of studies on twentieth-century associations is expanding). The following titles are useful. The relevant contributions of Georges Duby and Armand Wallon, eds., *Histoire de la France rurale* (Paris, 1976), vol. IV; Marcel Fauré, *Les Paysans dans la société française* (Paris, 1966); Henri Noilhan, *Histoire de l'agriculture à l'ère industrielle* (Paris, 1965); Paul Houée, "Mouvement coopérative agricole et développement rural," *Revue des études coopératives,* L (1971), pp. 145–64.

82. *Petit Robert* (Paris, 1967): (1760) *Comices agricoles:* réunion, assemblée

des cultivateurs d'une région qui se proposent de travailler au perfectionnement, au développement de l'agriculture. . . . The French word "comice" is derived from the Latin "comitium," a voting assembly or an assembly of the people.

83.   AN F^{10} 1585, *Comptes rendus* of the *comices agricoles*, Loiret; F^{10} 1592, Same for Loire-Inférieure; articles appearing in *Journal du Loiret*, 25 June and 27 July 1836 and 20 March 1858.

84.   *Journal du Loiret*, 29 June 1878.

85.   Ibid., 25 June 1836.

86.   AN F^{10} 1585 and 1592.

87.   Ibid.; AD Loire-Atlantique 1-M-1916 and 1978.

88.   AN F^7 12360.

89.   AN F^{12} 4697, Statutes and histories of the *syndicats agricoles;* AD Loire-Atlantique 1-M-1958, Same. This file also contains a pamphlet, Ministère de l'agriculture, *Syndicats Professionnels Agricoles* (Paris, 1899), listing syndicates by department. Ten local and 1 central syndicates are listed for the Orléanais; 15 local and 3 central syndicates are listed for the Nantais. Comparison with other sources within the same files makes it clear that these lists are incomplete. They do, however, add to the impression that syndicates were more widespread and participation was greater in the Nantais than in the Orléanais.

90.   AN F^{12} 4697; AD Loire-Atlantique 1-M-1917 and 1955; Suzanne Berger, *Peasants against Politics: Rural Organization in Brittany, 1911– 1967* (Cambridge, Mass., 1972), pp. 80–2.

91.   I have cited the new important studies earlier (n. 81).

92.   *Le Pays de Retz*, 14 June 1903. For the development of milk cooperatives in this part of the country, see Charles Delacommune, *L'Exode rural et l'association en Vendée* (Paris, 1914).

93.   AN F^{12} 4697; AD Loire-Atlantique 1-M-1958; AD Loiret 12-M-9, *Secours alloués au Département du Loiret . . .* (1911); AN F^{10} 1609, *Conseil général, extrait du procès-verbal de la séance du 19 avril 1887* (a policy report on how to combat vine mildew, delivered by M. Chevalier d'Escot); AD Loire-Atlantique 1-M-2012, *Distribution gratuite de plants américains* (1904).

94.   AD Loire-Atlantique 1-M-1958; AN F^{12} 4697.

95.   See Chapter 6, Section 2; AN F^{12} 4697; AD Loire-Atlantique 1-M-1958; 1-M-520, Response to circular of ministre de l'intérieur, 4 October 1894; 1-M-2023 Augustin Delalande, *Rapport . . .* (Nantes, 1895); Philippe Gratton. *La Lutte des classes dans les campagnes* (Paris, 1971), pp. 224–7.

96.   AD Loiret 12-M-9; AN F^{12} 4697; AN C 7392, *Enquête viticole,* 1907; AD Loire-Atlantique 1-M-1917 and 1958.

Conclusion

1.   Cited by Josette Alia and Bernard Guetta, *Le Nouvel Observateur,* 4–10 March 1978.

2.   Suzanne Berger, *Peasants against Politics: Rural Organization in Brittany, 1911–1967* (Cambridge, Mass., 1972).

Bibliography

Documents

Archives nationales (AN)
C	Procés verbaux – Assemblées nationales
F 7	Police générale
F 10	Agriculture
F 11	Subsistance
F 12	Commerce et industrie
F 17	Instruction publique
F 19	Cultes

Archives départementales (AD) de Loire-Atlantique
1-M-	486–623	Police générale
1-M-	1636–1707	Dénombrements de la population
1-M-	1917–2750	Agriculture
2-M-	1–348	Listes nominatives
7-P-	1*–775	Matrices cadastrales (first and second cadastres – incomplete)

Archives départementales (AD) du Loiret
Note: Most materials deposited in AD Loiret were destroyed in 1940.

12 M	Agriculture
O	Archives communales – those deposited at AD Loiret
19556–19983	Matrices cadastrales (first cadastre)

Archives municipales (AM), Nantes
Délibérations du conseil municipal
Etat civil

Archives municipales (AM), Orléans
Délibérations du conseil municipal
Etat civil

Archives communales (AC)
Délibérations des conseils municipaux
Listes nominatives (for Orléanais only)

Service du cadastre, Nantes
Matrices cadastrales (first and second cadastres)

Service du cadastre, Orléans
Matrices cadastrales (second cadastre)

327

Newspapers

Nantais

Le Bourgmestre
Le Breton
Le Colibri
Courrier de Nantes
L'Echo Nantais
Feuille Commerciale et Maritime de Nantes
L'Indépendence de l'Ouest
Journal de Nantes et de la Loire-Inférieure
Le Pays de Retz
Le Phare de la Loire
Le Progrès de la Loire-Inférieure
L'Union Bretonne

Orléanais

Courrier de la Campagne
L'Echo du Loiret, de la Beauce, et de la Sologne
Journal du Loiret
La Sologne

Books, Articles, and Theses

Abel, Wilhelm. *Crises agraires en Europe, XIIIe–XXe siècle*. Paris: Flammarion, 1973.

Ackerman, Evelyn Bernette. *Village on the Seine: Tradition and Change in Bonnières, 1815–1914*. Ithaca, N.Y.: Cornell University Press, 1978.

Agulhon, Maurice. *La République au village*. Paris: Plon, 1970a.

Agulhon, Maurice. *La Vie sociale en Provence intérieure au lendemain de la Révolution*. Paris: Etudes Robespierristes, 1970b.

Agulhon, Maurice. "Frenchification of France." *Times* (London) *Literary Supplement*, 6 May 1977.

Anderson, Michael. *Family Structure in Nineteenth-Century Lancashire*. Cambridge University Press, 1971.

Andrews, R.H. *Les Paysans des Mauges au XVIIIe siécle*. Tours: Arrault, 1935.

Ardouin-Dumazet. *Voyage en France, 16ème série: De Vendée en Beauce*. Paris: Berger-Levrault, 1898.

Ardouin-Dumazet. *Voyage en France, 1ère série: Le Morvan, le Val de Loire, le Perche*. Paris: Berger-Levrault, 1902.

Ariès, Philippe. *Centuries of Childhood: A Social History of Family Life*, trans. Robert Baldick. New York: Random House, 1962.

Arvengas, Jean. *Histoire d'un village de Sologne: Marcilly-en-Villette des origines à nos jours*. Beaugency, Loiret: Imp. Notariale, 1952.

Augé-Laribé, Michel. *La Révolution agricole*. Paris: Michel, 1955.

Babonaux, Yves. *Villes et régions de la Loire moyenne: Touraine, Blésois, Orléans*. N. place: SABRI, 1966.

Bachelier, A. and Vince, A. *Histoire et géographie de la Loire-Atlantique*. Rennes: Oberthur, 1961.

Baker, Allan R. H. "Ideological Change and Settlement Continuity in the French Countryside: The Development of Agricultural Syndicalism in Loir-et-

Cher During the Late-Nineteenth Century." *Journal of Historical Geography,* VI (1980), pp. 163–77.

Balzac, Honoré de. *Le Médecin de campagne.* Paris: Poche, 1966.

Balzac, Honoré de. *Le Curé de village.* Paris: Poche, 1972.

Balzac, Honoré de. *Les Paysans.* Paris: Poche, 1968.

Baudrillart, Henri. *Les Populations agricoles de la France.* 3 vols. Paris: Hachette, 1885.

Béaur, Gérard. "Le centième denier et les mouvements de propriété: deux exemples beaucerons (1761–1790). *Annales ESC,* XXXI (1976), pp. 1010–33.

Becker, Howard S. *Outsiders: Studies in the Sociology of Deviance.* Glencoe, Ill.: Free Press, 1963.

Bell, Rudolph. *Fate and Honor, Family and Village: Demographic and Cultural Change in Rural Italy Since 1800.* University of Chicago Press, 1979.

Bell, Rudolph. "The Transformation of a Rural Village: Istria, 1870–1972." *Journal of Social History,* VII (1974), pp. 243–70.

Bercé, Yves-Marie. *Croquants et Nu-pieds: les soulèvements paysans en France du XVIe au XIXe siècle.* Paris: Gallimard, 1974.

Bercé, Yves-Marie. *Fête et révolte: des mentalités populaires du XVIe au XVIIIe siècle.* Paris: Hachette, 1976.

Berger, Suzanne. *Peasants against Politics: Rural Organization in Brittany, 1911–1967.* Cambridge, Mass.: Harvard University Press, 1972.

Berkner, Lutz. "The Stem Family and the Developmental Cycle of the Peasant Household: An Eighteenth-Century Austrian Example." *American Historical Review,* LXXVII (1972), pp. 398–418.

Berkner, Lutz and Shaffer, John. "The Joint Family in the Nivernais. *Journal of Family History,* IV (1979), pp. 150–62.

Berthieu, René. "Les Nourrissons à Corneilles-en-Parisis (1640–1759)." *Annales de démographie historique, 1975,* pp. 259–89.

Besnier, Robert. *Cours d'histoire du Droit français.* Paris: Les Cours de Droit, 1955.

Blayo, Yves and Henry, Louis. "Données démographiques sur la Bretagne et l'Anjou de 1740 à 1829." *Annales de démographie historique, 1967,* pp. 91–171.

Bloch, Camille. *Etudes sur l'histoire économique de la France (1760–1789): Le commerce des grains dans la généralité d'Orléans. . . .* Paris: Picard, 1900.

Bloch, Marc. *Les Caractères originaux de l'histoire rurale française.* 2 vols. Paris: Colin, 1952–6.

Blok, Anton. *The Mafia of a Sicilian Village, 1860–1960.* New York: Harper & Row, 1975.

Bois, Paul. *Paysans de l'Ouest.* Paris: Mouton, 1960 (2nd ed. Paris: Flammarion, 1971).

Bois, Paul, ed. *Histoire de Nantes.* Toulouse: Privat, 1977.

Bordonove, Georges. *La Vie quotidienne en Vendée pendant la Révolution.* Paris: Hachette, 1974.

Boserup, Ester. *The Conditions of Agricultural Growth: The Economics of Agrarian Change under Population Pressure.* Chicago: Aldine, 1965.

Bouchard, Gérard. *Le Village immobile: Sennely-en-Sologne au XVIIIe siècle.* Paris: Plon, 1972.

Boulard, Fernand. "Matériaux pour l'histoire religieuse du peuple français: aspects de la pratique religieuse en France, 1802–1939: l'exemple des Pays de Loire." *Annales ESC,* XXXI (1976), pp. 761–801.

Bourdieu, Pierre. "Les Stratégies matrimoniales dans les systèmes de reproduction." *Annales ESC,* XXVII (1972), pp. 1105–27.

Boyle, Richard P. "Path Analysis and Ordinal Data." *American Journal of Sociology,* LXXV (1970), pp. 461–80.

Braudel, Fernand and Labrousse, C. E., eds. *Histoire économique et sociale de la France.* Tome 1: *De 1450 à 1660.* 2 vols. Tome 3: *L'Avènement de l'ère industrielle* (1789–1880). 2 vols. Paris: PUF, 1976–7.

Brekilien, Yann. *La Vie quotidienne des paysans en Bretagne au XIXe siècle.* Paris: Hachette, 1966.

Brenner, Robert. "Agrarian Class Structure and Economic Development in Pre-Industrial Europe." *Past and Present,* LXX (1976), pp. 30–75.

Bruley, Edouard. *Géographie des pays de la Loire.* Paris: Rieder, 1937.

Burguière, André. *Bretons de Plozévet.* Paris: Flammarion, 1975.

Caron, François. *An Economic History of Modern France.* New York: Columbia University Press, 1979.

Cartwright, Frederick F. *Disease and History.* New York: Random House, 1972.

Chartier. *Rapport sur l'épidémie de choléra à Nantes en 1884.* Nantes: Mellinet, 1885.

Chatelain, Abel. "Migrations et domesticité féminine urbaine en France, XVIIIe siècle–XXe siècle." *Revue d'histoire économique et sociale,* XLVII (1969), pp. 506–28.

Chayanov, A. V. *The Theory of Peasant Economy,* eds. D. D. Thorner, B. Kerblay, and R. E. F. Smith. Homewood, Ill.: Irwin, 1966.

Chombart de Lauwe, Jean. *Bretagne et pays de Garonne.* Paris: Centre National d'Information Economique, 1946.

Chorley, G. P. H. "The Agricultural Revolution in Northern Europe, 1750–1880: A Demographic Contribution to the Standard of Living Debate." *Economic History Review,* XXXIV (1981), pp. 71–93.

Clout, Hugh. *Agriculture in France on the Eve of the Railway Age.* London: Croom Helm, 1980.

Coale, Ansley. "Factors Associated with the Development of Low Fertility: An Historic Summary." In *United Nations Economic and Social Council World Population Conference,* 1965, vol. II, pp. 205–9. New York: United Nations, 1967.

Coale, Ansley and Demeny, Paul. *Regional Model Life Tables and Stable Populations.* Princeton University Press, 1966.

Cobb, Richard. *Les Armées révolutionnaires.* Paris: Mouton, 1961.

Cobb, Richard. *The Police and the People: French Popular Protest, 1789–1820.* Oxford University Press, 1970.

Corbin, Alain. *Archaïsme et modernité en Limousin au XIXe siècle, 1845–1880.* 2 vols. Paris: Rivière, 1975.

Coudray-Maunier, A. F. *Histoire de la Bande d'Orgères.* Chartres: Pétrot-Garnier, 1858.

Courtin-Rossignol. *Origine et historique de la fabrication des vinaigres dans l'Orléanais.* Orléans: Syndicat du commerce des vins, spiritueux & vinaigres en gros de l'arrondissement d'Orléans, 1891.

Dahrendorff, Ralf. *Class and Class Conflict in Industrial Society.* Boston: Routledge & Kegan Paul, 1959.

Dallas, Gregor and Herz, Micheline. "Zola, Darwin et les paysans." *Bulletin 2: Société des Professeurs Français en Amérique* (1978–9), pp. 83–115.

Dalton, George, ed. *Economic Development and Social Change: The Modernization of Village Communities.* New York: Natural History Press, 1971.

David, René, ed. *Le Droit français: principes et tendances du droit français.* Paris: Librairie Générale de Droit et de Jurisprudence, 1960.

David, René. *French Law: The Structure, Sources and Methodology,* trans. Michael Kindred. Bâton Rouge: Louisiana State University Press, 1972.

Davis, Natalie Zemon. *Society and Culture in Early Modern France.* Stanford University Press, 1975.

Delacommune, Charles. *L'Exode rural et l'association en Vendée.* Paris. Giard & Brière, 1914.

Delorme, B. *Souvenirs d'un vieux Nantais, 1808-1888.* Nantes: Schwob, 1888.

Delumeau, Jean, ed. *Histoire de la Bretagne.* Toulouse: Privat, 1969.

Demolins, Edmond. *Anglo-Saxon Superiority: To What It Is due ("A quoi tient la supériorité des Anglo-Saxons").* trans. Louis B. Lavigne. New York: Fenno, 1898.

Denizet, H. *La Sologne.* Orléans: Herluison, 1900.

Dion, Roger. *Le Val de Loire.* Tours: Arrault, 1934.

Dion-Salitot, Michèle and Dion, Michel. *La Crise d'une société villageoise: les "survivanciers," les paysans du Jura français (1800-1970).* Paris: Anthropos, 1972.

Domet, Paul. *Histoire de la Forêt d'Orléans.* Orléans: Jacob, 1892.

Dornic, François. *L'Industrie textile dans le Maine et ses débouchés internationaux, 1650-1815.* Le Mans: Belon, 1955.

Duby, Georges and Wallon, Armand, eds. *Histoire de la France rurale.* 4 vols. Paris: Seuil, 1975-6.

Dugget, Michael. "Marx on Peasants." *Journal of Peasant Studies,* II (1975), pp. 159-82.

Duncan, Otis Dudley. "Path Analysis: Sociological Examples." *American Journal of Sociology,* LXXII (1966), pp. 1-16.

Dupâquier, Jacques. "Habitat rural et démographie: l'exemple de l'Ile-de-France." *Annales de démographie historique, 1975,* pp. 65-8.

Dupeux, Georges. *Aspects de l'histoire sociale et politique du Loir-et-Cher, 1848-1914.* Paris: Mouton, 1962.

Dupeux, Georges. "La Croissance urbaine en France au XIXe siècle." *Revue d'histoire économique et sociale,* LII (1974), pp. 173-89.

Durand, Georges. *Vin, vigne, et vignerons en Lyonnais et Beaujolais.* Paris: Ecole des Hautes Etudes en Sciences Sociales, 1979.

Durkheim, Emile on the Division of Labor in Society, trans. George Simpson. New York: Macmillan, 1933.

Durrenberger, E. Paul, and Tannenbaum, Nicola. "A Reassessment of Chayanov and His Recent Critics." *Peasant Studies,* VIII (1979), pp. 48-63.

Duveau, Georges. *Les Instituteurs.* Paris: Seuil, 1957.

Duvignaud, Jean. *Fêtes et civilisations.* Paris: Weber, 1973.

"Family and Sexuality in France." *Journal of Family History,* II, no. 3 (Fall 1977), spec. ed.

Faucher, Daniel. *La Vie rurale vue par un géographe.* Toulouse: Institut de Géographie, 1962.

Faucher, Daniel. *Le Paysan et la machine.* Paris: Minuit, 1954.

Faugeras, Marius. *Le Diocèse de Nantes sous la Monarchie Censitaire (1813-1822-1849): la reconstitution catholique dans l'Ouest après la Révolution.* 2 vols. Fontenay-le-Comte, Vendée: Lussaud, 1964.

Fauré, Marcel. *Les Paysans dans la société française.* Paris: Colin, 1966.

Ferré, André. *Les Marges méridionales du Massif de l'Ouest: Poitou, Pays Vendéens, Basse Loire.* Paris: PUF, 1929.

Fête des fabricants et marchands de vinaigre de la ville et des environs d'Orléans, 20 août 1888. Orléans: Girardot, 1889.

Firth, Raymond. *Malay Fishermen: Their Peasant Economy.* London: Paul, Trench, Trubner, 1946.

Flandrin, Jean-Louis. *Familles: parenté, maison, sexualité dans l'ancienne société.* Paris: Hachette, 1976.

Flandrin, Jean-Louis. *Les Amours paysannes, XVIe–XIXe siècle.* Paris: Gallimard, 1975.

Fliegel, Frederick C. "A Comparative Analysis of the Impact of Industrialism on Traditional Values." *Rural Sociology,* XLI (1976), pp. 431–51.

Fohlen, Claude. "The Industrial Revolution in France, 1700–1914," *The Fontana Economic History of Europe: The Emergence of Industrial Societies, Part I,* ed. Carlo M. Cipolla, pp. 7–75. London: Fontana, 1973.

"Foires et marchés ruraux en France." *Etudes rurales,* LXXVIII–LXXX (1980), specs. eds.

Foucault, Michel, ed. *Moi, Pierre Rivière, ayant égorgé ma mère, ma soeur, et mon frère. . . : un cas de parricide au XIXe siècle.* Paris: Gallimard, 1973.

Foucault, Michel. *Surveiller et punir: naissance de la prison.* Paris: Gallimard, 1975.

Foucault, Michel. *The History of Sexuality.* Vol. I: *An Introduction.* New York: Random House, 1980.

Foville, Albert de. *Le Morcellement: études économiques et statistiques sur la propriété foncière.* Paris: Guillaumin, 1895.

Fox, Edward. *History in Geographic Perspective: The Other France.* New York: Norton, 1971.

Fox, Robin. *Kinship and Marriage.* New York: Penguin Books, 1967.

France. Ministre de l'Instruction Publique et des Beaux-Arts, Comité des Travaux historiques et scientifiques. *La Statistique agricole de 1814.* Paris: Rieder, 1914.

France. Ministre des Travaux Publics, de l'Agriculture et du Commerce. Statistique de la France. *Territoire et population.* Paris: Imp. Royale, 1837.

France. Ministère des Travaux Publics, de l'Agriculture et du Commerce. *Archives statistiques.* Paris: Imp. Royale, 1837.

France. Ministre du Commerce. *Documents statistiques sur la France.* Paris: Imp. Royale, 1835.

France. Ministre de l'Agriculture et du Commerce. Statistique de la France. *Agriculture.* 4 vols. Paris: Imp. Royale, 1840–1.

France. Ministre de l'Agriculture et du Commerce. Statistique de la France. *Industrie.* 4 vols. Paris: Imp. Royale & Nationale, 1847–52.

France. Ministre de l'Agriculture, du Commerce et de Travaux Publics. Statistique de la France. *Statistique agricole.* 2 vols. Paris: Imp. Impériale, 1858–60.

France. Ministre de l'Agriculture. Statistique de la France. *Agriculture: Résultats généraux de l'enquête décennale de 1862.* Strasbourg: Berger-Levrault, 1870.

France. Ministre de l'Agriculture, du Commerce et des Travaux. Statistique de la France. *Territoire et population.* Paris: Imp. Impériale, 1855.

France. Ministre de l'Agriculture. Statistique agricole de la France. *Résultats généraux de l'enquête décennale de 1882.* Nancy: Berger-Levrault, 1887.

France. Ministre de l'Agriculture. Statistique agricole de la France. *Résultats généraux de l'enquête décennale de 1892.* Paris: Imp. Nationale, 1897.

France. Statistique de la France. *Statistique annuelle, 1871–98.* 28 vols. Paris: Imp. Nationale, 1874–1900.

France. Statistique générale de la France. *Annuaire statistique de la France, 1878–1915.* 34 vols. Paris: Imp. Nationale, 1879–1917.

France. Ministère de l'Agriculture. *Statistique agricole annuelle, 1885–1914.* 30 vols. Paris: Imp. Nationale, 1886–1916.

France. Ministère du Travail et de la Prévoyance sociale. Statistique générale de la France. *Statistique des familles en 1906.* Paris: Imp. Nationale, 1912.

France. Ministère du Travail et de la Prévoyance sociale. Statistique générale de la France. *Statistique des familles et des habitations en 1911.* Paris: Imp. Nationale, 1913.

France. Ministre de l'Agriculture. *La petite propriété rurale en France: enquêtes monographiques (1908–9).* Paris: Imp. Nationale, 1909.

France. *Annuaire de Loiret* (occasionally *Almanach).* Orléans: An XI–1912.

France. Direction régionale de Nantes. *Populations par commune de 1801 à 1962.* Nantes: INSEE, 1966.

France. Direction régionale d'Orléans. *Populations par commune de 1851 à 1961.* Orléans: INSEE, 1966.

Freud, Sigmund. *Civilization and Its Discontents,* trans. James Strachey. New York: Norton, 1962.

Freud, Sigmund. *A General Introduction to Psycho-analysis,* trans. Joan Rivière. New York: Simon and Schuster, 1935.

Furet, François and Ozouf, Jacques. *Lire et écrire: l'alphabétisation des Français de Calvin à Jules Ferry.* 2 vols. Paris: Minuit, 1977.

Gabory, Emile. *Les Bourbons et la Vendée.* Paris: Hachette, 1947.

Gabory, Emile. *Les grandes heures de la Vendée.* Paris: Club du Meilleur Livre, 1961.

Gallerand, J. *Les Cultes sous la Terreur en Loir-et-Cher.* Blois: Grande Imprimarie, 1928.

Gallouédec, L. *La Loire: étude de fleuve.* Paris: Hachette, 1910.

Garrier, Gilbert. "Aspects et limites de la crise phylloxérique en Beaujolais ou le puceron bienfaisant (1875–1895)." *Revue d'histoire économique et sociale,* LII (1974), pp. 190–208.

Gaston-Martin. *Nantes au XVIIIe siècle: l'ère des négriers (1715–1774).* Paris: Alcan, 1931.

Gautier, Etienne and Henry, Louis. *La population de Crulai, paroisse normande.* Paris: PUF, 1958.

Gay, François-P. *La Champagne du Berry.* Bourges: Tardy, 1967.

Gerth, H. H. and Mills, C. Wright, eds. and trans. *From Max Weber.* Oxford University Press, 1958.

Gibert, M. *La Loire maritime et le port de Nantes.* Nantes: Chambre de Commerce, 1947.

Giesey, Ralph. "Rules of Inheritance and Strategies of Mobility in Prerevolutionary France." *American Historical Review,* LXXXII (1977), pp. 271–89.

Gilbert, R. *Une Famille ouvrière d'Orléans.* Paris: Réforme sociale, 1894.

Glucksmann, André. *Les Maîtres penseurs.* Paris: Grasset, 1977.

Goody, Jack, Thirsk, Joan, and Thompson, E. P., eds. *Family and Inheritance: Rural Society in Western Europe, 1200–1800.* Cambridge University Press, 1976.

Gras, Jacques. *Le Bassin méridional: étude morphologique.* Rennes: n. pub., 1963.

Gratton, Philippe. *La Lutte des classes dans les campagnes.* Paris: Anthropos, 1971.

Greenwood, Davydd. *Unrewarding Wealth: The Commercialization and Collapse of Agriculture in a Spanish Basque Town.* Cambridge University Press, 1976.

Grenadou, Ephraim and Prévost, Alain. *Grenadou, paysan français.* Paris: Seuil, 1966.

Guépin, Ange and Bonamy, Eugène. *Nantes au XIXe siècle.* Nantes: Sebire, 1835.

Guépin, Ange and Simon, Gabriel. *Evénements de Nantes pendant les journées des 25, 29, 30 et 31 juillet 1830 par plusieurs témoins oculaires.* Nantes: Sebire, n.d. [1830–1?].

Guilbert, Aristide, ed. *Histoire des villes de la France.* 6 vols. Paris: Perrotin & Fournier, 1845.

Guyot, Jules. *Etudes des vignobles de France.* 3 vols. Paris: Masson, 1868.

Halpern, Joel M. *A Serbian Village: Social and Cultural Change in a Yugoslav Community.* New York: Harper & Row, 1967.

Hareven, Tamara. "The Family as Process: The Historical Study of the Family Cycle." *Journal of Social History,* VII (1974), pp. 322–9.

Hareven, Tamara, ed. *Transition: The Family and the Life Course in Historical Perspective.* New York: Academic Press, 1978.

Hartman, Mary. *Victorian Murderesses.* New York: Schocken, 1977.

Hatin, Eugène. *La Loire et ses bords, guide pittoresque du voyageur d'Orléans à Nantes et d'Orléans à Nevers par les bateaux à vapeur.* Orléans: Gatineau, 1843.

Henry, Louis. *Manuel de démographie historique.* Geneva: Droz, 1967.

Henry, Louis. *Démographie: analyse et modèles.* Paris: Larousse, 1972.

Higonnet, Patrice. *Pont-de-Montvert: Social Structure and Politics in a French Village, 1700–1914.* Cambridge, Mass.: Harvard University Press, 1971.

Hill, Polly. *Studies in Rural Capitalism in West Africa.* Cambridge University Press, 1970.

Hobsbawm, E. J. *Primitive Rebels: Studies in Archaic Forms of Social Movement in the 19th and 20th Centuries.* New York: Norton, 1965.

Hohenberg, Paul. "Migrations et fluctuations démographiques dans la France rurale, 1836–1901." *Annales ESC,* XXIX (1974), pp. 461–97.

Houée, Paul. "Mouvement coopérative agricole et dévoloppement rural." *Revue des études coopératives,* L (1971), pp. 45–64.

Hubscher, Ronald H. *L'Agriculture et la société rurale dans le Pas-de-Calais du milieu du XIXe siècle à 1914.* 2 vols. Arras: Commission Départementale des Mouvements Historiques du Pas-de-Calais, 1980.

Hufton, Olwen H. *The Poor of Eighteenth-Century France.* Oxford University Press (Clarendon Press), 1974.

Hufton, Olwen H. "Women and the Family Economy in Eighteenth-Century France." *French Historical Studies,* IX (1975), pp. 1–22.

Joanne, Adolphe. *Géographie du département du Loiret.* Paris: Hachette, 1874a.

Joanne, Adolphe. *Géographie de la Loire-Inférieure.* Paris: Hachette, 1874b.

Jones, E. L., and Parker, W. N., eds. *European Peasants and Their Markets.* Princeton University Press, 1975.

Kemp, Tom. *Economic Forces in French History.* London: Dobson, 1971.

Kindleberger, Charles P. *Economic Growth in France and Britain, 1851–1950.* Cambridge, Mass.: Harvard University Press, 1964.

Kroeber, A. L. *Anthropology.* New York: Harcourt, Brace, Jovanovich, 1948.

Labrousse, C. E. *Esquisse du mouvement des prix et des revenus en France au XVIIIe siècle.* Paris: Dalloz, 1933.

Lafitte, Prosper de. *Quatre ans de luttes pour nos vignes et nos vins de France: mémoires, opuscules et articles.* Bordeaux: Féret, 1883.

Landes, Davis. "The Statistical Study of French Crises." *Journal of Economic History,* X (1950), pp. 195–211.

Laslett, Peter. *Family Life and Illicit Love in Earlier Generations: Essays in Historical Sociology.* Cambridge University Press, 1977.

Laslett, Peter and Wall, Richard, eds. *Household and Family in Past Time.* Cambridge University Press, 1972.

Lavergne, Léonce de. *Economie rurale de la France depuis 1789.* Paris: Guillaumin, 1860.

Le Bras, Gabriel. *Etudes de sociologie religieuse.* 2 vols. Paris: PUF, 1955-6.

Lebrun, François, ed. *Histoire des Pays de la Loire.* Toulouse: Privat, 1972.

Leclair, P. *Histoire des brigands, chauffeurs et assassins d'Orgères.* Chartres: Lacombe, An VIII.

Lefebvre, Georges. *Etudes Orléanaises.* 2 vols. Paris: CNRS, 1962-3.

Lefebvre, Georges. *The Great Fear of 1789,* trans. Joan White. New York: Harper & Row, 1973.

Le Goff, T. J. A. *Vannes and Its Region: A Study of Town and Country in Eighteenth-Century France.* Oxford University Press (Clarendon Press), 1981.

Le Play, Frédéric. *La Réforme sociale en France.* 3 vols. Paris: Dentu, 1901.

Lerat, Georges. *Etude sur les origines, le développement et l'avenir des raffineries nantaises.* Paris: Rousseau, 1911.

Leray, Michel. "Evolution de la répartition de la propriété foncière dans le canton d'Artenay (Loiret) de 1813 à 1913." Mémoire de Maîtrise, University of Tours, 1971.

Le Roy Ladurie, Emmanuel. *Les Paysans de Languedoc.* Paris: Flammarion, 1969.

Le Roy Ladurie, Emmanuel. *Times of Feast, Times of Famine: A History of Climate Since the Year 1000,* trans. Barbara Bray. New York: Doubleday, 1971.

Le Roy Ladurie, Emmanuel. "Système de la coutume: structures familiales et coutume d'héritage en France au XVIe siècle." *Annales ESC,* XXVII (1972), pp. 825-46.

Le Roy Ladurie, Emmanuel. *Le Territoire de l'historien.* Paris: Gallimard, 1973.

Le Roy Ladurie, Emmanuel. "Pour un modèle de l'économie rurale française au XVIIIe siècle." *Cahiers d'histoire,* XIX (1974), pp. 5-27.

Le Roy Ladurie, Emmanuel and Dumont, Paul. *Anthropologie du conscrit français.* Paris: Mouton, 1972.

Leuilliot, Paul. *L'Alsace au début du XIXe siècle, 1815-1830.* 3 vols. Paris: SEVPEN, 1959-60.

Lévi-Strauss, Claude. *Anthropologie structurale.* Paris: Plon, 1959.

Lévy, Bernard-Henri. *La Barbarie à visage humain.* Paris: Grasset, 1977.

Lévy, Jean-Philippe. *Cours d'histoire du Droit privé (la famille).* Paris: Les Cours de Droit, 1966.

Lhomme, Jean. "La Crise agricole à la fin du XIXe siècle en France: essai d'interprétation économique et sociale." *Revue économique,* XXII (1970), pp. 522-53.

Lizier, Henri. *Chartres et la Beauce au temps de Louis-Philippe, 1830-1848.* Chartres: Legné, 1972.

Loubére, Leo A. *The Red and the White: A History of Wine in France and Italy in the Nineteenth Century.* Albany: SUNY Press, 1978.

McBride, Theresa. *The Domestic Revolution: The Modernization of Household Service in England and France, 1820–1920.* New York: Holmes & Meier, 1976.

McManners, John. *Church and State in France, 1870–1914.* New York: Harper & Row, 1973.

McNeill, William H. *Plagues and Peoples.* New York: Doubleday (Anchor Press), 1976.

Malthus, Thomas. *First Essay on Population.* New York: Kelley, 1965.

Marcel-Robillard, Charles. *Le Folklore de la Beauce.* 8 vols. Paris: Maisonneuve & Larose, 1965–72.

Marcilhacy, Christiane. *Le Diocèse d'Orléans au milieu du XIXe siècle.* Paris: Sirey, 1964.

Margadant, Ted W. *French Peasants in Revolt: The Insurrection of 1851.* Princeton University Press, 1979.

Martin, Alexis. *Une visite à Orléans.* Paris: Hennuyer, 1895.

Martin, Louis. *Au Temps de la marine de Loire: les souvenirs d'un vieux batelier.* Orléans: Houze, 1943.

Mauss, Marcel. "Essai sur le Don." *Année sociologique,* I (1923–4), pp. 30–186.

Mauss, Marcel. *Manuel d'ethnographie.* Paris: Payot, 1947.

Mellor, John W. *The Economics of Agricultural Development.* Ithaca, N.Y.: Cornell University Press, 1966.

Mendras, Henri. *Sociologie de la campagne française.* Paris: PUF, 1959.

Mendras, Henri. *La Fin des paysans: innovations et changement dans l'agriculture française.* Paris: SEDEIS, 1967.

Mendras, Henri. *Sociétés paysannes.* Paris: Colin, 1976.

Merley, Jean. *Histoire de la Haute-Loire de la fin de l'Ancien Régime au début de la Troisième République.* 2 vols. Le Puy: Archives Départementales, 1974.

Meyer, Jean. *La Noblesse bretonne au XVIIIe siècle.* 2 vols. Paris: SEVPEN, 1966.

Meyers, Peter V. "The French Instituteur, 1830–1914." Ph.D. dissertation, Rutgers, 1972.

Meyers, Peter V. "Professionalization and Societal Change: Rural Teachers in Nineteenth-Century France." *Journal of Social History,* IX (1976), pp. 542–58.

Millet, Henri. *Histoire de la Sologne depuis 1850.* Paris: Giard & Brière, 1911.

Mills, Dennis R. *Lord and Peasant in Nineteenth Century Britain.* London: Croom Helm, 1980.

Mingay, G. E. "The Agricultural Depression, 1730–50." *Economic History Review,* VIII (1956), pp. 323–38.

Mintz, Sidney. *Caribbean Transformations.* Chicago: Aldine, 1974.

Mitrany, David. *Marx against the Peasant: A Study in Social Dogmatism.* Chapel Hill: North Carolina University Press, 1951.

Morin, Edgar. *Commune en France: la métamorphose de Plodémet.* Paris: Fayard, 1967.

Morineau, Michel. *Les Faux-semblants d'un démarrage économique: agriculture et démographie en France au XVIIIe siècle.* Paris: Colin, 1971.

Newell, William H. *Population Change and Agricultural Development in Nineteenth Century France.* New York: Arno, 1977.

Noilhan, Henri. *Histoire de l'agriculture à l'ère industrielle.* Paris: de Boccard, 1965.

O'Brien, Patrick and Keyder, Caglar. *Economic Growth in Britain and France, 1780–1914.* London: George Allen & Unwin, 1978.

Orieux, E. and Vincent, J. *Histoire et géographie de la Loire-Inférieure.* Nantes: Grimaud, 1895.

Ormsby, Hilda. *France: A Regional Geography.* London: Methuen, 1950.

Ozouf, Mona. *La Fête révolutionnaire, 1789–1799.* Paris: Gallimard, 1976.

Parsons, Talcott. *Structure and Process in Modern Societies: A Collection of Essays.* Glencoe, Ill.: Free Press, 1960.

Parsons, Talcott and Bales, R. F. *Family, Socialization and Interaction Process.* Glencoe, Ill.: Free Press, 1955.

Phayer, Michael. *Sexual Liberation and Religion in Nineteenth-Century Europe.* London: Croom Helm, 1977.

Phayer, Michael. "Politics and Popular Religion: The Cult of the Cross in France, 1815–1840." *Journal of Social History,* XI (1978), pp. 346–63.

Pinson, F.-J. *Dictionnaire des lieux habités du département de la Loire-Inférieure.* Nantes: Guéraud, 1857.

Pitt-Rivers, Julian, ed. *Mediterranean Countrymen: Essays in the Social Anthropology of the Mediterranean.* Paris: Mouton, 1963.

Poitrineau, Abel. *La Vie rurale en Basse Auvergne au XVIIIe siècle (1726–1789).* 2 vols. Paris: PUF, 1965.

Poivet, Ramon. "Evolution de la répartition de la propriété foncière et de l'exploitation agricole dans le canton de Jargeau (Loiret) de 1834 à 1913." Mémoire de Maîtrise, University of Tours, 1970.

Polanyi, Karl. "The Economy as Instituted Process," in *Trade and Market in the Early Empires,* eds. K. Polanyi, C. M. Arensberg, and H. W. Pearson. Glencoe, Ill.: Free Press, 1957.

Pollard, A. H., Yusuf, Farhat, and Pollard, G. N. *Demographic Techniques.* Elmsford, N.Y.: Pergamon, 1974.

Ponteil, Félix. *Histoire de l'enseignement en France, 1789–1965.* Paris: Sirey, 1966.

Popkin, Samuel L. *The Rational Peasant: The Political Economy of Rural Society in Vietnam.* Berkeley: University of California Press, 1979.

Post, John D. "Famine, Mortality, and Epidemic Disease in the Process of Modernization." *Economic History Review,* XXIX (1976), pp. 14–37.

Potter, J. M., Diaz, M. N., and Foster, G. M., eds. *Peasant Society: A Reader.* Boston: Little, Brown, 1967.

Price, Roger. *An Economic History of Modern France.* New York: St. Martin's Press, 1981.

Rambaud, Placide and Vincienne, Monique. *Les Transformations d'une société rurale: la Maurienne (1561–1962).* Paris: Colin, 1964.

Redfield, Robert. *Peasant Society and Culture: An Anthropological Approach to Civilization.* University of Chicago Press, 1956.

Robert, E. *Histoire du Loiret.* Orléans: Luzeray, 1947.

Robin, Régine. *Histoire et linguistique.* Paris: Colin, 1973.

Rollet, Catherine and Souriac, Agnès. "Le Choléra de 1832 en Seine-et-Oise." *Annales ESC,* XXIX (1974), pp. 938–42.

Roseberry, William. "Rent, Differentiation and the Development of Capitalism among Peasants." *American Anthropologist,* VII (1976), pp. 45–58.

Rousseau, Jean-Jacques. *La Nouvelle Héloise,* in *Oeuvres complètes.* Vol. II. Paris: Lefèvre, 1839.

Sahlins, Marshall. *Stone Age Economics.* Chicago: Aldine, 1972.

Sée, Henri. *Histoire économique de la France: les temps modernes (1789–1914).* Paris: Colin, 1942.

Sevin-Mareau. *Mémoires sur les causes de la décadence de l'industrie manufacturière et commerciale à Orléans. . . .* Orléans: Jacob, 1828.

Shanin, Teodor, ed. *Peasants and Peasant Societies.* New York: Penguin Books, 1971.

Shanin, Teodor. *The Awkward Class.* Oxford University Press, 1972.

Sheppard, T. F. *Lourmarin in the Eighteenth Century: A Study of a French Village.* Baltimore: Johns Hopkins University Press, 1971.

Shorter, Edward. *The Making of the Modern Family.* New York: Basic Books, 1975.

Siegfried, André. *Tableau politique de la France de l'Ouest sous la Troisième République.* Paris: Armand Colin, 1913.

Silver, Judith. "French Peasant Demands for Popular Leadership in the Vendômois (Loir-et-Cher), 1852–1890." *Journal of Social History,* XIV (1980), pp. 277–94.

Simoni, Peter. "Agricultural Change and Landlord–Tenant Relations in Nineteenth-Century France." *Journal of Social History,* XIII (1979), pp. 115–35.

Singer, Barnett. "The Teacher as Notable in Brittany, 1880–1914." *French Historical Studies,* IX (1976), pp. 635–59.

Singer, Barnett. "From Patriots to Pacifists: The French Primary School Teachers, 1880–1940." *Journal of Contemporary History,* XII (1977), pp. 413–34.

Slicher van Bath, Bernard H. *The Agrarian History of Western Europe,* A.D. 500–1850, trans. O. Ordish. London: Arnold, 1963.

Smith, J. Harvey. "Work Routine and Social Structure in a French Village: Cruzy in the Nineteenth Century." *Journal of Interdisciplinary History,* V (1975), pp. 357–82.

Spagnoli, Paul G. "Population History from Parish Monographs: The Problem of Local Demographic Variations." *Journal of Interdisciplinary History,* VII (1977), pp. 424–52.

Spiegelman, Mortimer. *Introduction to Demography.* Cambridge, Mass.: Harvard University Press, 1968.

Stearns, Peter N. *Old Age in European Society: The Case of France.* New York: Holmes & Meier, 1976.

Stoianovich, Traian. *French Historical Method: The Annales Paradigm.* Ithaca, N.Y.: Cornell University Press, 1976.

Stone, Lawrence. *The Family, Sex and Marriage in England, 1500–1800.* New York: Harper & Row, 1977.

Strahler, A. N. *Introduction to Physical Geography.* New York: Wiley, 1965.

Sussman, George. "The Wet-Nursing Business in Nineteenth-Century France." *French Historical Studies,* IX (1975), pp. 304–28.

Sutton, Keith. "A French Agricultural Canal – The Canal de la Sauldre and the Nineteenth-Century Improvement of the Sologne." *Agricultural History Review,* XXI (1973), pp. 51–6.

Tackett, Timothy. *Priest and Parish in Eighteenth-Century France.* Princeton University Press, 1977.

Thabault, Roger. *Mon village: ses hommes, ses routes, son école.* Paris: Delagrave, 1944.

Thuillier, Guy. *Aspects de l'économie nivernaise au XIXe siècle.* Paris: Colin, 1966.

Tilly, Charles. *The Vendée.* Cambridge, Mass.: Harvard University Press, 1964.

Tilly, Charles, Tilly, Louise, and Tilly, Richard. *The Rebellious Century, 1830–1930.* Cambridge, Mass.: Harvard University Press, 1975.

Tymieniecka, Anna-Teresa. *Phenomenology and Science in Contemporary European Thought.* New York: Farrar, Straus & Giroux (Noonday), 1962.

Van De Walle, Etienne. *The Female Population of France in the Nineteenth Century: A Reconstruction of 82 Departments.* Princeton University Press, 1974.

Van De Walle, Etienne. "Household Dynamics in a Belgian Village, 1847–1866," *Journal of Family History,* I (1976), pp. 80–94.

Van De Walle, Etienne and Preston, Samuel. "Mortalité de l'enfance au XIXe siècle à Paris et dans le département de la Seine." *Population,* XXIX (1974) pp. 89–107.

Van Gennep, Arnold. *The Rites of Passage,* trans. Monika B. Vizedon and Gabrielle L. Caffee. University of Chicago Press, 1960.

Viallon, Jean-Baptiste. *La Croissance agricole en France et en Bourgogne de 1850 à nos jours.* New York: Arno, 1977.

Vidal de la Blache, P. *Principes de géographie humaine.* Paris: Colin, 1922.

Vidalenc, Jean. *La Société française de 1815 à 1848: le peuple des campagnes.* Paris: Rivière, 1970.

Vigier, Philippe. *Essai sur la répartition de la propriété foncière dans la région alpine: son évolution des origines du cadastre à la fin du Second Empire.* Paris: SEVPEN, 1963a.

Vigier, Philippe. *La Seconde République dans la région alpine.* 2 vols. Paris: PUF, 1963b.

Vovelle, Michel. *Piété baroque et déchristianisation en Provence au XVIIIe siècle: les attitudes devant la mort d'après les clauses des testaments.* Paris: Plon, 1973.

Vovelle, Michel. *Ville et campagne au XVIIIe siècle: Chartres et la Beauce.* Paris: Editions Sociales, 1980.

Walter, Gérard. *Histoire des paysans de France.* Paris: Flammarion, 1963.

Warner, Charles K. *The Winegrowers of France and the Government since 1875.* New York: Columbia University Press, 1960.

Weber, Adna Ferrin. *The Growth of Cities in the Nineteenth Century.* Ithaca, N.Y.: Cornell University Press, 1899.

Weber, Eugen. *Peasants into Frenchmen: The Modernization of Rural France, 1870–1914.* Stanford University Press, 1976.

Weber, Max. *The Theory of Social and Economic Organization.* Oxford University Press, 1947.

Weinstein, Fred and Platt, Gerald. *The Wish to Be Free: Society, Psyche and Value Change.* Berkeley: University of California Press, 1969.

Willems, Emilio. "Peasantry and City: Cultural Persistence and Change in Historical Perspective, A European Case." *American Anthropologist,* LXXII (1970), pp. 528–44.

Wismes, Armel de. *La Vie quotidienne dans les ports bretons aux XVIIe et XVIIIe siècles: Nantes, Brest, St. Mâlo, Lorient.* Paris: Hachette, 1973.

Wolf, Eric R. *Peasants.* Englewood Cliffs, N.J.: Prentice-Hall, 1966.

Wolf, Eric R. *Peasant Wars of the Twentieth Century.* New York: Harper & Row, 1969.

Wright, Gordon. *Rural Revolution in France: The Peasantry in the Twentieth Century.* Stanford University Press, 1964.

Wrigley, E. A. "Family Limitation in Preindustrial England." *Economic History Review,* XXIX (1966a), pp. 82–109.

Wrigley, E. A., ed. *An Introduction to English Historical Demography from the Sixteenth to the Nineteenth Century.* London: Weidenfeld & Nicolson, 1966b.

Wrigley, E. A. *Population and History.* New York: McGraw-Hill, 1969.

Wrigley, E. A., ed. *Nineteenth-Century Society: Essays in the Use of Quantitative Methods for the Study of Social Data.* Cambridge University Press, 1972.

Wylie, Laurence, ed. *Chanzeaux: A Village in Anjou.* Cambridge, Mass.: Harvard University Press, 1966.

Young, Arthur. *Travels in France, 1787, 1788, 1789.* London: Bell, 1924.

Yver, Jean. *Essai de géographie coutumière: égalité entre héritiers et exclusion des enfants dotés.* Paris: Sirey, 1966.

Zehr, Howard. *Crime and the Development of Modern Society: Patterns of Criminality in Nineteenth-Century Germany and France.* London: Croom Helm, 1976.

Zeldin, Theodore. *France, 1848–1945.* 2 vols. Oxford University Press (Clarendon Press), 1973–7.

Zola, Emile. *La Terre.* Paris: Poche, 1972.

Index

abattoir, 69, 281, 298n97
Abel, Wilhelm, 261
Achenau, river, 60
adaptation in peasant economy, xiii, 23,
 147–9, 153–6, 164–6, 167, 179, 187–9,
 190, 193, 194–6, 232, 239, 240,
 259–61, 266, 267, 268–70, 283–4,
 285–7
administrative units, French, 17–18
adoption, child, 160–1, 162, 283
Aegean, the, 33
Africa, 49
agricultural crisis, *see* peasant agricultural
 crisis
agricultural depression, *see* peasant agricultural crisis
agricultural regions, 17, 18–22, 95–6,
 109–10, 113; *see also* agricultural
 types; soil conditions
agricultural shows, 74–6, 272, 279; see
 also *comices agricoles*
agricultural types, 110, 131, 153, 204, 257,
 282; defined, 113, 148; *see also* cereal-
 type agriculture; intensive-type
 agriculture; pasture-type agriculture
Agriculture de l'Ouest de la France, 242
Aigre, river, 303n12
Aigrefeuille, 128
Alençon, 86
Alleaume, Monsieur, 267
Alps, the, 14
America, 15, 49, 266, 267, 168, 269, 276,
 278, 286, 294n9,10, 296n39
Ancenis (arrondissement), 18, 92, 108,
 109, 125, 141, 187, 242, 257
Ancenis (town), 22, 70, 82, 186–7, 194,
 203, 250
Anderson, Michael, 143
Anetz, 187
Angers, 12, 54, 63, 247, 259
Anjou, 10, 20, 106, 118, 226, 282,
 300n23, 311n44
anthropological theory, 24, 25, 27, 32,
 73–4, 114–16, 120, 137–9, 145–7,
 178–80, 280, 285; *see also* economic
 theory
apples, 109
arboriculture, 109, 222–3, 254, 257
Ardon, 141, 299n5

Ardouin-Dumazet, 58, 59, 82, 109,
 211–12, 261
Aristotle, 24, 291n1
armies and army recruitment, 128, 251,
 255–7, 272, 285, 306n51
Armstrong, W.A., 143
arson, 246, 250, 254
Artenay, 18, 61, 70, 76, 105, 107, 122,
 141, 194
artificial grasses, 108, 112–13, 242; *see
 also* fodder crops
artisans, 15, 50, 53, 56–8, 118–19, 122,
 129, 140–1, 144, 251, 258, 281, 304n28
Artois, 15
Association Bretonne, 242
Association law (1884), 274–5
Atlantic Ocean, the, 14, 15, 31
Austria, 57, 140
Authon, river, 12
Aydes, Les, 59

Baguenault, 224
Balzac, Honoré de, 28, 197, 202
ban de vendanges, 59
Bande d'Orgères, 252–3
Bannier, faubourg, 59, 68, 250
Barbechat, 22
Bardon, Le, 18
barley, 58, 105, 134, 265
Basse-Indre, *see* Indre
Baule, 205
Beauce, the, 14, 17, 18, 22, 61, 66, 70,
 80; defined, 18, 20, 113; dependent
 labor in, 122, 128, 129, 305n37; disturbances in, 246, 247, 248, 252–3; landed property in, 75, 80, 121, 122, 123,
 201, 205, 209, 211–13, 224, 234–5,
 236, 318n26; physical geography, 10,
 60–1; population and family structure,
 43, 153, 174, 186, 189, 193, 194, 282;
 produce of, 58, 69, 105, 107, 109, 112,
 113, 119, 211–12, 265, 303n4, 303n12,
 305n32; religion and beliefs in, 87,
 90–1, 211–12, 229; rural associations
 in, 271
Beaugency, 20, 63, 70, 82, 97, 109, 113,
 194, 197, 216
Beaujolais, 269
Béaur, Gérard, 318n26

341

DATE DUE
